Pigot & Co.'s Metropolitan Guide & Book Of Reference To Every Street ... And Public Building In The Cities Of London & Westminster [&c.]

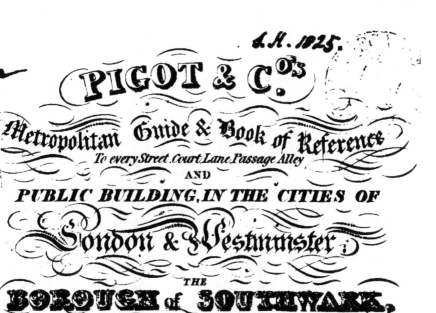

L.H. 1825.

PIGOT & C°s

Metropolitan Guide & Book of Reference

To every Street, Court, Lane, Passage, Alley

AND

PUBLIC BUILDING, IN THE CITIES OF

London & Westminster

THE

BOROUGH of SOUTHWARK,

and their Respective Suburbs:

Compiled & Arranged from Actual Survey & accompanied with a New Plan of London divided into Seventy districts, which are referred to by figures in the Street &c List.—The whole made so easy of Comprehension, as to be essentially valuable to Strangers. & of the greatest use to the Resident Nobility, Gentry. Merchants, Tradesmen, &c.

Pigot & Son Eng^rs Manch^r

LONDON.

Published at the Directory Office, 24, Basing Lane & 16, Fountain St Manchester & sold by Simpkin & Marshall Stationers Court, Sherwood, Jones, & C°. Longman, Hurst, & C°. Paternoster Row, E.C. & J. Rivington, St Pauls Church Y^d &c. Jarvis Newg^t S^t. Chappell & Son, Royal Exchange, Hatchard & Son, Piccadilly & by all other Booksellers in Town & Country

PREFACE.

WHEN the unequalled and daily increasing extent of the British Metropolis is considered, it will be superfluous to extol the utility of a work, which will enable a stranger, in a short time, to make himself familiarly acquainted with all its intricate intersections. It cannot have escaped general observation, that the London Street Lists, hitherto published, although many of them are accompanied with tolerably accurate Maps or Plans, are, as Tables of Reference, of comparatively little use. The reason is obvious: the connection between the Maps and the Street Lists is, in all of them, too remote, and too difficult of comprehension for any one, who consults them with a view of being directed to any particular street, court, or alley.

In the work now offered to the public this objection has, it is hoped, been completely removed. The References from the Street List to any particular place, or places on the Map, are intelligible and plain; the marginal numbers, prefixed to the Streets, under the heads Reference to Plan, direct, with perfect accuracy, to the corresponding place in each appropriate circle or section of the Map; and although the name of every court, lane, passage, or alley should not be found inserted in the Map, (for, on the present scale, it is impossible that it should be) yet few, if any, have been omitted in the printed list, and the figure directs as nearly as possible to the place in the Map, where it would have been mentioned, if room could have been afforded for its insertion. To obviate all difficulty in every possible case, the meanest or most obscure court, in this vast and increasing capital, is pointed out by a reference to the number of the house, in the more conspicuous street, court, &c. to which the inquirer must turn, in order to find the exact place he wants. More than this cannot possibly be done; and the proprietors can confidently and honestly affirm, that this has not been accomplished without a long, expensive, and laborious actual survey. Whatever may be said of the originality of the idea, the work itself has been the result of personal inquiry and investigation. The Historical and Descriptive Account of the Metropolis, although concise, contains much useful and interesting information, the compilers having been anxious to present to the public a work of compendious utility, and of a conveniently portable size. With respect to the List of the Public Buildings, the proprietors risk nothing, when they assert, that the one, which is given in the present publication, is infinitely more perfect than any which has preceded it, because it is, beyond controversy, the most copious ever offered to the public, and the References to them are, like those to the streets, rendered plain and easy to all.

Of the Map itself the publishers need scarcely speak; let it be compared with any other plan of the British Metropolis on the same scale, and the comparison will infallibly be in favour of that which is now published.

CONTENTS.

INDEX

TO THE HISTORICAL AND DESCRIPTIVE ACCOUNT
OF LONDON.

A BRIEF

HISTORICAL AND DESCRIPTIVE ACCOUNT

OF

LONDON.

ANCIENT HISTORY.

LONDON, for population, wealth, and commerce, as the seat of the arts and sciences, and the capital of the British empire, may justly be considered the queen of cities. It is sufficiently distant from the sea to be secure against any sudden attack by a descent of an enemy on the coast, yet the noble river which passes through it makes it a port into which ships of the largest mercantile class can enter securely at all periods of the year, as the severest frosts seldom close it. The produce of all nations flows into it with a never-failing stream, making it the grand depot and centre of the commerce of the world. As the seat of government the immense resources of the British empire are wielded from it, influencing, in a less, or greater degree, all the nations of the globe, ruling the fate of the numerous millions of Hindostan, and, by its superior energies, giving direction to the mightiest powers of Europe. For numbers, opulence, and refinement, London stands unequalled—Rome alone, when mistress of the world, could form a parallel.

The origin of this wonderful city recedes beyond the earliest dawning of our history, its position will best enable us to trace its rise. Situated on a lake, (as all the marshy ground to the south of the river once was,) and near a ford, the first occurring from the sea, it must have been a station of some consequence among a rude people. According to Dr. Stukely, the river *Fleta*, which now passes under Fleet-market, and *Walbrook*, once flowing where the present Walbrook stands, were the natural

boundaries and defences of the original city: a line passing
from one to the other, along Lad-lane and Cateaton-street,
points out the third side—the Thames forming the limit on
the fourth.   Its situation gives countenance to the etymo-
logy of its present name, from the British words *Llyn
Din*, the " town on the lake," from whence our *London*
may be derived.

The earliest notice of the district about London that
can be relied upon is to be found in the commentaries of
Cæsar, who speaks of *Civitas Trinobantum*. Ammianus
Marcellinus calls the town *Augusta Trinobantum;* he notices
it being an ancient town named formerly *Londinium*.
In Tacitus is an account of the revolt of *Boadicea;* he
also says, that in 61 *Londinium*, or *Colonia Augusta*, was
a great mart of trade, though not dignified by the name
of colony.   The retreat of Seutonius, and the occupation
of London by Boadicea, indicate that it was not then a
walled Roman station; yet, in the reign of the Emperor
Severus, it was considered a wealthy city.   In the year
359, eight hundred ships were said to be employed in the
port of London for the exportation of corn alone. Although
the precise time is not known at which walls were erected
to enclose the city, no doubt is entertained that they were
the work of the Romans.   They commenced from where
the present Tower stands, and by the Minories they proceeded to Aldgate, and along Camomile-street, by Cripplegate, to Aldersgate, and turning to the south passed on
to Ludgate, whence, inclining west to new Bridge-street,
they went along Fleet-ditch to another fort at the river,
measuring, according to Stow, two miles and a furlong,
defended by towers and bastions at different distances.
The walls were 22 feet and the towers 40 feet high.   One
of the towers was standing until lately in Shoemakers'-
row, Aldgate.   Remains of the wall are yet to be seen
in Cripplegate Church-yard, and in some courts near
Ludgate-hill.   Whittaker traces remains of the labours of
the Romans on the south of the Thames, and more
palpably in the sea wall constructed to protect the fens of
Essex.   A part of the old London wall was very lately
discovered, in a state of very good preservation, by pulling
down the houses in Hand and Pen-court, in Trinity-square.
It is built with a rough flinty sort of stone, is about fifty

feet long, twenty feet high, and eight feet thick ; and is now left standing for the inspection of the curious, to whom a piece of masonry of such great antiquity must be highly interesting.

In 597, Augustine, a monk, introduced christianity into England. London was made a bishop's see in 604, and shortly after a cathedral church was erected on the site of St. Paul's. In 664 it was visited by the plague, and in 798, a fire almost consumed it. When Egbert united the Heptarchy a *Wittena-gemot,* or parliament, was held here in 833, in consequence of Danish irruptions. These marauders plundered the city twice, massacring the inhabitants. But the great Alfred gaining possession of London in 884, strengthened and repaired it, and planned the municipal government, which, after undergoing many changes, finally settled into its present shape. About the year 1000 a wooden bridge was erected, and in 16 years afterwards Canute, the Dane, attempted to plunder the city from his fleet, but being unable to pass the bridge, he cut a canal for his ships through the marshes on the south side ; he was repulsed, but a peace finally gave him possession of the city.

An impost of £83,000 Saxon was levied at this time upon the English, out of which London paid £11,000, a strong indication of its wealth and consequence. On the death of Harold, William Duke of Normandy advanced towards London, when, upon the clergy declaring in his favour, he was admitted, and on Christmas day, 1066, was crowned. A charter, granted in the first year of the reign of William, written in the Saxon language, is yet preserved in the city archives. In 1078 the white tower was built, to awe and controul the inhabitants In 1100 Henry I. for the services rendered him by the citizens, rewarded them with an important charter, by which, on payment of a quit rent of £300 per annum, they acquired the sheriff-wick of Middlesex and the right of appointing a justiciary. About this time we find the privileges of the city reduced to writing. London assisted Stephen to obtain the crown, and in 1139 purchased of him the right of chusing its own sheriffs for a hundred marks of silver. Henry II. extorted large sums of money from the citizens. It was in the reign of this monarch that Fitzstephen, a monk, wrote his description of London, from which it appears to have been at the time a wealthy and populous city. The brutal fanaticism of the populace was shewn on the coronation of Richard I. in the massacre of the unhappy and persecuted Jews residing in London.

Shortly afterwards the chief magistrate was stiled mayor instead of bailiff ; and in two successive charters the former privileges of the citizens were confirmed, and new ones granted as usual, on payment of certain sums, by which they claim the conservatorship of the river Thames, the right of removing wears, &c. In the reign of John, we find the " Barons of the city of London" authorized to choose a mayor annually, or to continue the same in office at their own discretion: the citizens took part with the barons in their contest with this monarch.

In 1211 commenced the cutting of a ditch without the walls 200 feet wide, and the forest of Middlesex being about the same time dis-forested, the suburbs were greatly enlarged. In the time of Edward I. the city was without a mayor for 12 years, during which time it was governed by a *Custos* appointed by the king, but afterwards the ancient privileges were confirmed. The city was divided into 24 wards, governed by aldermen, each ward choosing common council men from among the citizens, who were to advise and direct the aldermen in their management of the city's affairs. A proclamation was issued by Edward II. forbidding the use of sea coal, on account of its smoke and being injurious to the health of the citizens. Successive charters ordained that the mayor should be one of the judges for the trial of criminals in Newgate, that Southwark should be granted for the benefit of the citizens, and that the mayor might have gold or silver maces carried before him. The dreadful pestilence, which at this time ravaged the greater part of the world, is said to have destroyed in London 100,000 persons ; a piece of waste land near where the Charter-house now stands was supposed to have received no less than 50,000 dead bodies ; it terminated in 1357. The entry of Edward, the celebrated Black Prince, into London, was in the preceding year celebrated with extraordinary splendour. The formidable insurrection of Wat Tyler, in 1380, was extinguished by the decisive conduct of Sir William Walworth,

mayor of London, in consequence of which the dagger
was added to the city arms. Wickliffe, the celebrated
reformer, flourished about this period. The oppressions
and excessive exactions of Richard induced the citizens
to hail the elevation to the throne of Henry IV. : the privileges of the city were by him extended, and some
obnoxious statutes repealed. The return of Henry V.
after the victory of Agincourt, was celebrated in London
in the most magnificent style.

The lighting of the city at night by lanterns at this
time, marks the career of improvement. The reign of
Henry the VI. saw Jack Cade and his associates enter the
city triumphantly. Lord Say and others were executed by
them, but upon a general pardon being offered, Cade was
deserted, and, resisting apprehension, was killed. Bricks
were at this time made in Moorfields, and the rents of
houses in the city were from 6s. 8d. to £3. per annum.
Various articles manufactured in London were, by parliament, prohibited importation for a period to be limited by
the king, at the time that William Caxton, citizen and
mercer, introduced the valuable art of printing. In four
successive periods the plague, and what was called the
sweating sickness, made dreadful ravages ; at one time
30,000 and at another 20,000 persons were destroyed by
these terrible visitations, yet improvement continued.
Houndsditch was arched over, the river Fleet made navi-
gable to Holborn-bridge, and the beautiful structure called
Henry the Seventh's chapel at Westminster erected.
Empson and Dudley, rapacious ministers of Henry, op-
pressed the citizens greatly by their exactions ; yet, when
Henry VIII. attempted to raise money without the sanction
of parliament, they had the spirit to resist, and principally
through their opposition the project was abandoned, and
all those who opposed it pardoned.

The suppression of monasteries in this reign made an
important alteration in London, which was crowded with
religious houses. Many persons at the same time suffered
for their religious opinions ; yet the progress of the reformation continued, until, in the reign of Edward VI. it
obtained for a short time the ascendency. The suppression
of the monasteries was followed by the erection of Christ,
Bridewell, and St. Thomas's Hospitals; the two latter

for the relief of the sick and maimed poor, and the former
for education. Taverns and public houses were limited to
forty in the city and its liberties and to three in Westminster. A charter in 1551, granted to the lord mayor,
aldermen, and citizens lands and tenements in Southwark,
with the manor and its appurtenances, the assize of bread,
wine, beer, and ale, a fair for three days, and the offices
of coroner, escheator, and clerk of the market. The
triumph of catholicism under Mary, caused many of those
scenes to be acted which have so often disgraced the bigots
of different sects.

A map, yet extant, published in the reign of Elizabeth,
(which commenced in 1558,) gives us a plan of London as
it then was; by this it appears that the crowded part of
the city was between the river and Cornhill, Cheapside,
and Newgate-street. Building had not extended much
east of the Tower, Goodman's-fields were pasture grounds;
Whitechapel had only a few houses; Houndsditch but a
single row; Spital-fields, from the back of the church,
were quite open, a tolerably regular street, with occa-
sional intervening spaces, extended to Shoreditch church;
but from the Tower to Bishopsgate, and on to Lothbury,
was generally garden ground; about Coleman-street were
the greatest number of buildings; from Bishopsgate to
Moor-fields and Finsbury was unbuilt on. In these fields
were several windmills, extending to the east side of
Whitecross-street; St. John's-street passed by the priory
of St. John to the monastery of Clerkenwell, beyond which
were fields. Goswell-street was called the road to St.
Alban's. From Clerkenwell to Gray's Inn-lane were pasture or garden grounds. The village of Holborn joined
London; and from Holborn-bridge to Gray's Inn houses
extended, the backs opening into the fields. An open road
continued to the village of St. Giles, which was a small
cluster of houses on the right, called to the present day
St. Giles'-in-the-fields. The Strand had houses on both
sides, among which were mansions of the nobility and
prelates, having on the south gardens extending to the
river; the present names of the streets indicate the situation of many of them, as Arundel-street, Villiers-street,
Northumberland-street, &c. The garden of the convent
of Westminster, since called Covent-garden, extended

to St. Martin's-lane, where there were a few houses, and reached to St. Giles's. Hedge-lane, now called Whitcomb-street, was literally a lane between two edges, as its name imported. The Hay-market was a space hedged on each side. Spring-gardens were real gardens extending to the Cock-pit and Tilt-yard, now the Treasury. The space between Piccadilly and Pall-mall was unbuilt. From King-street to the abbey, and from Whitehall to Palace-yard, the land was built upon; yet Westminster was but a small town on the south-west and south sides of St. James's Park. Lambeth was a little village, a considerable distance from Southwark, on the south side of the river. A row of houses commenced opposite White-friars, and extended along the river, with gardens and fields behind them, to opposite the Steel-yard, where were several streets. From London-bridge the borough penetrated to the south a considerable way, and to the east the buildings continued to opposite the Tower. A theatre, with gardens, occupied the site of the present Christ-church. Elizabeth is stated to have often partook of the diversion of bear beating, at a building opposite Queen-hithe. London-bridge itself was crowded with houses.

From the foregoing account it will be seen how small London was then compared with what it is at present, yet its size so alarmed the ministers of Elizabeth, that, to prevent the fatal consequences of the plague to such numerous assemblages, strange to tell, a proclamation was issued forbidding the erection of buildings on new foundations. The persecutions on the continent for religious opinions, about this time, drove immense numbers of valuable artizans to London, which continued to increase in population and extent in spite of restriction. The exertions made by the citizens against the Spanish armada evince the prosperity that had been experienced; 10,000 men were raised and paid, and sixteen well equipped ships supplied. On the accession of James, that dreadful scourge the plague, which had before so often ravaged London, broke out and raged with greater violence than at any former period since the time of Edward III. This was followed by the gunpowder-plot. The colonization of London-derry and Coleraine, the bringing of the New River to

London by Sir Hugh Myddleton, and the commencement of paving with flag stones took place in this reign.

No sooner had the plague subsided, which had broke out again at the commencement of the reign of Charles, and carried of 35,000 persons, than the struggle commenced between the king and the people, and London, having suffered severely by lawless exaction, was naturally driven to take the side of the people. Under the Commonwealth building advanced with rapidity, and another proclamation was issued to impede it. Subsequently the citizens declared for a free parliament in opposition to the *Rump Parliament* of Richard Cromwell, and concurred with General Monk in the restoration of Charles II. Shortly after acts were passed for paving and lighting the streets, and widening the avenues. Often had London been visited by the plague, but in the year 1665 commenced that which has been distinguished by the name of the "great plague." It began in 1665, and continued until January, 1666, the deaths went on increasing from 500 to 8000 weekly; the digging of graves soon ceased, and large pits were excavated, in which the bodies were laid with decent regularity; but at length the number of the dead became so great that all regard to form was abandoned; deeper and more extensive excavations were made, into which the bodies of all ranks and both sexes were thrown promiscuously. The inhabitants of whole districts were swept away together. All law proceedings were suspended, the inns of courts were shut up. No business was done, and so completely was the town deserted that grass grew in the principal streets of the city. One hundred thousand persons were supposed to have been the victims of this dreadful scourge.

In a few months after the termination of the plague, that terrible conflagration took place, known by the name of the "great fire," which broke out September 2, 1666; and the city being built principally of wood, it raged for four successive days and nights, destroying within the walls nearly five-sixths of the city; and without the walls ravaging a space equal to the remaining sixth. From the report of surveyors (as appears by an inscription on the monument) we find that the ruins extended over 436 acres; that the fire consumed 400 streets, 13,200 dwelling houses, 89 churches, besides chapels, four of the city-gates, hospitals, libraries, schools, and a great many public and private splendid buildings. The total loss was estimated at ten millions sterling. These successive calamities did not destroy the spirit of the people. An act of parliament passed for rebuilding the city, which was done in little more than four years, in a more commodious and healthful style.

In 1684 the THAMES was frozen over, and streets of shops were erected on it. Three years after a religious persecution raging in France, several thousand protestants were driven from their homes, a great proportion of whom settled in the suburbs of London, particularly about Soho and Spitalfields, where many of their descendants now reside. To this may be ascribed the origin of so much silk business being done in that part of the town, as they worked principally in jewellery and silk weaving. The latter has been brought to an unrivalled state of perfection by the Spitalfields weavers. When the attempts of James threatened the introduction of arbitrary power, the city of London warmly concurred in the invitation to the Prince of Orange, and the flight of James facilitated the glorious revolution, so important in its example and effects to England, if not to the world. In the first year of William and Mary the rights and privileges of the city were fully confirmed; and shortly afterwards the numerous sanctuaries, which had become great nuisances, were suppressed, except that of the mint, which existed to a later period. A dreadful storm of wind, in 1703, did damage to the estimated amount of two millions sterling to the city alone. After a long dry season, in 1716, a south west wind blew the water so completely out of the Thames, that thousands passed it on foot both above and below the bridge. About this time fifty new churches were erected, the expences being defrayed by a duty on coal.

PROGRESSIVE IMPROVEMENT OF LONDON.

The town went on increasing in size, particularly to the west, including St. Giles's and St. Martin's-in-the-fields, but the village of Mary-le-bone was still distant; Buckingham-house and many other large buildings were erected, and the general structure of St. Paul's Cathedral was completed. Party walls of stone or brick were ordered, and parish engines directed to be kept to check the spreading of conflagrations. Shortly after the accession of George I. a fire destroyed 120 houses in Thames-street, and merchandize to a great amount. This was succeeded by the rebellion of 1715, which greatly agitated the metropolis. The Septennial Act passed at this period; and in 1720 London was the scene of the fraud denominated the *South Sea bubble.* In 1733 the city distinguished itself by its opposition to the excise scheme of Sir R. Walpole. In the early part of George II.'s reign, great complaints were made of the daring robberies committed in the streets in open day.

The town continued enlarging to the north of Oxford-road as far as Mary-le-bone-lane; several new parishes were added to it. Fleet-ditch was arched over, and a general lighting, by parish assessment, took place. Westminster-bridge was erected, and new roads made across George's-fields. Grosvenor-square was built, and a new road formed from Paddington to Islington. A short time prior to the accession of George III. an act was passed enabling the corporation to improve the avenues leading to the city as it might think necessary, which led to judicious alterations during his reign. Blackfriars-bridge was constructed; and instead of that offensive nuisance Fleet-ditch, the elegant streets called Bridge-street and Chatham-place arose : building and improvement proceeded also rapidly on the south side. About 1673 the present mode of paving the foot paths was generally adopted, and, in pursuance of an act, the projecting signs were taken down, names of streets, &c. were placed at their corners, and tolls established for the better paving cleansing, and lighting of the town. In 1780 riots were suffered to attain such a height that Newgate, the King's Bench and the Fleet were burnt; by tardy military interference they were at last suppressed, and upwards of twenty of the rioters executed. The year 1784 was remarkable for the ascent of Lunardi in a balloon from the artillery ground, it was the first ærial voyage witnessed in England.

When the French revolution produced a war between this country and France, the city of London " thanked his majesty, and assured him of its readiness to support the honour of his crown." In 1794 the doctrine of constructive treason was attempted to be established in the trials of Hardy, Horne Tooke and others, but it failed, and they were acquitted. On the 23d. of July, in the same year, the dreadful fire in Ratcliffe-highway broke out, which destroyed nearly 700 houses ; tents from the tower were afforded to the sufferers, and the sum of £20,000. was raised for their relief. The suspension of cash payments by the Bank of England will long distinguish the year 1797, the order of council was dated February 26. The bankers and merchants of London powerfully aided Government at this period. When the war terminated in 1801, the metropolis was brilliantly illuminated on October 1st. and the succeeding day. The peace, however, was of short duration. War was declared May 16th, 1803, and, upon alarm of invasion, the city of London took the lead in enrolling volunteers to defend the country ; London and Westminster alone counted 27,077. In 1814 the metropolis once more rejoiced in the return of peace, and although all the benefits that were anticipated from it have not immediately resulted, yet a well founded belief may be entertained that a city, which has experienced, for so long a time, almost uninterrupted prosperity, will continue in the same career. The causes of its greatness yet exist. The skill, probity, wealth, and enterprise, which have distinguished the citizens, exist in as great a degree at present as at any former period, and will no doubt bear them triumphantly through the difficulties they may have to encounter,

PRESENT STATE OF LONDON.

London at present is divided by the river into two parts, but lying principally on the northern bank, it is frequently divided into five parts, according to the popular mode of distinguishing them. The city, Westminster, the west end of the town, the east end of the town and Southwark ;

of these the west end is distinguished for its elegant streets and squares, being the residence of the nobility and opulent classes. The city is the seat of commerce, and includes the ancient part of the town. The east end contains the docks, and is devoted to shipping concerns. Southwark abounds in manufactories of iron, glass, soap, hats, &c. and is the residence of numbers connected with the navigation of the river. Westminster contains many government offices, the courts of justice, and the two houses of parliament. Besides these the outer border of London touches upon Paddington, Somerstown, Pentonville, Islington, and Hoxton to the north; Bethnal-green and Mile-end to the east; Rotherhithe, Newington, Lambeth, and Vauxhall to the south; and Knightsbridge and Chelsea to the west, including spaces now covered with buildings, not distinguished by any district name, as that between Bloomsbury-square and Somerstown, where a great number of elegant streets and some handsome squares have lately arisen.

London extends from west to east, or from Knightsbridge to Poplar, nearly eight miles; and from south to north, or from Newington Butts to Islington, nearly five miles; the circumference of the whole will not be much less than thirty miles. Excluding the Thames it may be fairly estimated that the buildings of London cover the enormous extent of sixteen square miles. The Thames averages about a quarter of a mile in breadth, and about twelve feet in depth; the tide extends fifteen miles above the town, materially assisting in the navigation of the river. It is computed that London contains at present upwards of 8000 streets, lanes, &c. &c. and 176,000 houses; and according to the returns of the population made in 1821 contained the following inhabitants viz:

In the City of London within the walls	56,174
City of London without the walls	69,260
City and Liberties of Westminster	182,085
Out Parishes within the Bills of Mortality	702,530
Parishes not within the Bills of Mortality	215,642

Making a grand total in the Metropolis of - 1,225,691

The principal streets, like the river, run from west to east. There are two lines of them that form main channels of communication, the more southern of which is, on an average, about a quarter of a mile from the Thames, commencing at Westminster Abbey, and by the Strand, Ludgate-hill, Watling-street, &c. leads to Tower-hill, beyond which is Ratcliffe-highway, conducting to Poplar; this line keeps to the bending of the river. The northern line may be traced through Oxford-street, by Holborn, Cheapside, Leadenhall-street, and Whitechapel, to Mile-end, six miles in length, and nearly straight; these are connected by streets that cross them.

The following are the lengths of some of the streets— Oxford-street 2304 yards; Upper Thames-street 1331, Tottenham-court-road 1177, Holborn (High) 1045, Bishopsgate-street 1045, Piccadilly 1694, Whitechapel 1281, and the New Commercial-road 5280. The great entrances to London are by spacious roads, well lighted, and adorned with rows of handsome houses. The streets are well paved, and path-ways raised and paved with flags, generally in very good order; and within a few years they have been brilliantly illuminated with gas, that very superior method of lighting streets having been first adopted in London. The shops are unrivalled for splendour, as well as for their immense stocks of rich and elegant articles. The crowds of people that constantly throng the streets, and the immense number of coaches and other vehicles that are continually passing, give animation to the scene, and remind the stranger that he is in the first city of the world.

The PUBLIC BUILDINGS of London are numerous, and many of them worthy of the metropolis, but they are not so conspicuous as those of some other cities on the continent, utility rather than appearance having been consulted at their erection. For its size and venerable antiquity the TOWER claims our first notice. The commencement of it has been attributed to the Romans, but we cannot rely upon any account respecting it before the time of William I. He built what is now called the White Tower, a large square structure, with four watch towers, and situated near the middle of the present fortress Other erections and fortifications have been added at different periods. The whole, within the walls, comprises an extent of a little more than twelve acres; a ditch encircles it, which measures round the exterior 3156 feet; it is broad towards Tower-hill, but narrower next the river, from

B

which it is divided by a handsome wharf, where is a platform, formerly mounted with sixty-one pieces of cannon. Many guns are also placed on different parts of the walls; a stone bridge, over the ditch at the west end, forms the chief entrance; there are gates on this bridge which are opened and shut morning and night with particular formalities. This was a palace as well as a fortress until the time of Elizabeth, but has been since used chiefly as a state prison and a place of security for arms and valuable crown property.

The MINT, which is situated on Tower-hill, is an elegant and substantial structure, with a long stone front, consisting of three stories, surmounted by a handsome balustrade; the wings are decorated with pilasters, the centre with six demi-columns and a pediment, ornamented with the arms of the United Kingdom, very finely executed; over the porch is a gallery, balustrades, &c. of the Doric order. The building was designed by Mr. Smirke, and contains every department necessary for the different operations of coining. A fire, which took place here in the summer of 1815, did considerable damage to the interior, but fortunately it did not injure the appearance of this beautiful edifice, which has every appearance of a nobleman's mansion. A large reservoir of water is now constructed opposite the building, enclosed by iron railing.

Since Whitehall was burnt in 1695, St. JAMES'S PALACE has been the general town residence of the sovereigns of England. It is situated at the south-west end of Pall Mall, and possesses many appartments, well calculated for state purposes, that are convenient and handsome, but it is a very ordinary brick building; towards the Park are the state appartments, this is the best part of the palace, external as well as internal: some of the appartments of this palace, at the east end were destroyed by a fire a few years ago and have not since been rebuilt.

At the distance of a few hundred yards stands BUCKINGHAM-HOUSE, the residence of the late Queen; It was made a royal residence in 1761, and in 1775 was settled on the Queen in case she survived her consort. His late Majesty frequently resided here with the Queen. The front is of red brick, with white stone pilasters, &c. In

the interior the staircase is much admired, where may be
seen some fine specimens of the labours of the celebrated
Canaletti, when he was in England. In the gardens behind this palace is now erecting a MEWS for his Majesty,
instead of that in Charing-cross : the building is of brick,
ornamented with stone from the base to the top of the first
window : it will be a very extensive and handsome pile of
building, forming a square, and will soon be completed.
—Mr. Nash is the architect.

CARLTON PALACE, the town residence of the present
monarch, his Majesty George IV. has not an imposing
appearance, in consequence of the front being so low.
The facade has a centre and two wings rusticated, without
pilasters, an entablature and balustrade. The portico has
six composite columns, and a pediment, with a frieze and
tympan, crowned with the arms of the Prince of Wales.
On the centre of the entablature of a handsome colonnade
in front is a neat military trophy. At the back are beautiful gardens, quite retired. The appartments in the interior
are much admired; on approaching the grand staircase
the effect produced by the management of the light excites
admiration. Four rooms contain a collection of armour,
supposed to be the finest in the world. Here also is the
golden throne of the late King of Candy, with a sun at the
back, having diamond eyes. The throne-room, the coun-
cil-chamber, and the dining-room are splendidly furnished.
The plate-room is unequalled in the world; the plate is
chiefly gilt and generally modern, occupying three sides of
a large room; some of it belonged to King Charles; it
presents a most splended sight; squares of plate glass,
worth 35l. each, inclose the whole. The new conservatory,
built under the direction of Mr. Hopper, is 72 feet long,
23 broad, and 20 high. It is in the style of the chapel of
Henry VII. in Westminster Abbey, and by the management of the light, it is thought to shew the ornaments
in a superior manner to that unrivalled piece of architecture,
for such a rich specimen of the florid Gothic style, an admirable simplicity pervades the whole. There are some
fine busts of Fox, the Marquis of Hastings, &c. and many
admirable paintings, ancient as well as modern. The
front is brilliantly illuminated with gas ; it was the first
open place lighted with that valuable modern discovery.

KENSINGTON PALACE, at present the residence of the Duke of Sussex, is situated in the middle of those fine gardens, which are open to the public, and frequented for their charming walks, known by the name of "Kensington Gardens."

St. JAMES'S PARK is a very pleasing promenade; Henry VIII. first collected the waters, and from a marsh formed a park. The canal, the work of Charles II. is 100 feet broad, and 2800 feet long. The park, with the adjoining green park, which extends to and along Piccadilly, while it adds to the beauty of the district must increase the healthfulness of the metropolis, not only by affording pleasant walks for exercise, but by admitting a more free circulation of air. These fine and extensive walks have lately been very greatly improved at night, by numerous gas lamps, which are supported by elegant iron pillars, on each of which is a crown and the letters G. R. These brilliant lights add much to the comfort and convenience of those who go through St. James's-park late in the evening, as it is now a finely illuminated walk.

HYDE PARK, situated further to the west, before the time of Henry VIII. belonged to the monastery of St. Peter, Westminster, but in that monarch's reign it became crown property. It contained 620 acres in 1652, but was ascertained in 1790 to be no more than 394 acres, in consequence of Kensington gardens and other spaces being detached from it. This park has been often used for military exhibitions, but is capable of being made very beautiful; plantations of trees have lately improved its appearance. The sheet of water at the south-west end, called the Serpentine River, is supplied by a small stream wich rises near Bayswater, and, passing through Kensington-gardens, expands in the park, adding greatly to its beauty. Near this water is the celebrated Rotten-row, the fashionable resort of equestrians; and at certain seasons, the display of carriages, for their number, their varied and tasteful decorations, and the beauty of the horses, is not to be parallelled in the world. The principal entrance to this delightful park is through the gate at Hyde-park-corner, at a short distance from which, within the park, is erected the famed and noble figure of ACHILLES. It stands upon a basement and plinth of Dartmouth grey granite, with a simple pedestal of Aberdeen red granite. The height of the statue is rather more than eighteen feet ; the whole, with the artificial mound, from the line of the road, being thirty-six feet in height. The head of this commanding figure turns almost towards the residence of the hero whose glories it commemorates in the following inscription in bronze :—

To Arthur, Duke of Wellington,
And his brave companions in arms,
This statue of Achilles,
Cast from cannon taken in the battles of
Salamanca, Vittoria, Toulouse
And Waterloo,
Is inscribed by
Their Countrywomen,
And placed on this spot the 18th day of June, 1822,
By command of his Majesty
George IV.

The weight of the statue cannot be estimated at less than 33 or 34 tons. In its composition 12 twenty-four pounders were melted, but the metal of cannon being by itself unfit it was necessary to add about one-third of more fusible and pliant metal ; the whole is thus equal to the above immense weight. The extremities were separated from the trunk in casting, but in order to unite them the artist adopted the new process of fusion, which avoids all risk of separation, and renders the junction of the parts invisible. The surface of the body, the limbs, and the head are all as exquisitely finished as if the production were a copy of only as many inches as it is feet. It is truly a work bold in design and admirable in execution, and is a lasting monument of the skill and ingenuity of Mr. Richard Westmacot, the artist by whom it was constructed.

The newly laid out park to the north, called the REGENT'S PARK, as it exceeds the others in extent, (should the course of improvement continue in the same direction) will shortly surpass them in attraction. The rides and walks are very tastefully designed, and they present on Sundays very lively and pleasing scenes of gaiety and fashion. This park begins to be a very favourite resort and is occasionally full of company.

B 2

After the residences and domains of royalty, the pile of building known by the general name of WESTMINSTER HALL claims our attention. Here assemble the peers and commons of the United Kingdom, to exercise their legislative functions, and here are also the principal courts of justice. The old hall was erected by William Rufus, but rebuilt by Richard II. On the coronation of Queen Eleanor, Henry III. in the hall and rooms adjacent, feasted 6000 poor men, women, and children, on the day of his public entrance into London with his Queen.   Richard II. when he kept his Christmas here, is said to have entertained, each day, 10,000 guests, employing 2000 cooks. Westminster-hall itself exceeds in dimensions any other room in Europe that is not supported by pillars, being 270 feet in length, 74 in breadth, and 94 in height. This noble room is the scene of the coronation feasts of the kings of England. The most august courts of justice are also held here, for the trials of peers accused of treason, or other high crimes and misdemeanors. The trial of the late Lord Melville took place in the hall. It was also the scene of the trial of Charles I. In adjoining parts of the same pile of building are the Courts of Chancery, Exchequer, King's Bench, and Common Pleas. The exterior of this ancient pile has lately been under repairs, and now looks extremely handsome. In the interior of the hall a large wooden partition and roof extends from one end to the other, which is built for the purpose of containing the records of the Common Pleas. Without the western wall of the hall are built four additional courts, viz: for the Lord Chancellor, the Vice-Chancellor, the King's Bench Judges, and for the Justification of Bail; the whole are in a line with the present Courts of Pleas and Exchequer, having entrances from the hall; they are not yet finished to admit of business being transacted in them. There will also be entrances from the open street, when these courts are complete.

The HOUSE of LORDS is fitted up in a room lately called the Court of Requests; it is ornamented with the fine old tapestry designed and executed by the two Vrooms, representing the defeat of the Spanish Armada in 1588. At the upper end of the room is the throne where the King, on certain important occasions, is seated, crowned and adorned with the various insignia of royalty. The cellar known by the name of Guy Faux's cellar, is near Old Palace Yard; it is yet examined at the commencement of every session, in presence of the usher of the black rod. A new and elegant entrance is just completed at the south end for his majesty, when he attends the House of Lords; it is built in a semi-circular form, with gothic windows. and stained glass; it forms an elegant sort of hall, leading to the grand staircase of the House, and no doubt but it will prove a great convenience to our Monarch, when he honours the Lords with his presence.

The celebrated St. STEPHEN'S CHAPEL, where assemble the representatives of the Commons of England, was built by King Stephen, and rebuilt by Edward III. It is small and plain; there are galleries at each side for the use of the members, and a very small one at the end for strangers, who are by the members never presumed to be present; here reports of the speeches for publication in the newspapers are taken under every disadvantage, but as the reputations of the orators depend so much on the fidelity of the reports, it is to be presumed that at no distant period additional facilities will be given to the reporters. The speaker's chair, highly ornamented, is at a distance from the wall; in front of it is a table, at which clerks sit. The seats of the members occupy each side and both ends of the room, except the passages; five rows of seats rise in gradation above each other; that on the floor to the right of the speaker is called the treasury bench, opposite to it the leading oppositionists usually take their seats.

Near Waterloo-bridge, on the Strand side, a handsome structure is just completed for the DUCHY of LANCASTER, where will be established the offices for the receipts of the revenues attached to that Duchy. This building is erected on immense arches, rising immediately from the Thames, which the front faces. The entrance is from a terrace which overlooks the water. It is altogether a handsome and substantial looking edifice, of fine stone, and is highly effective when viewed from the bridge. Adjoining, and running in a straight line towards the Strand, is just finished a row of very elegant private houses, which are very ornamental to the approach to the river. Towards the east of the metropolis there have been also lately erected some very fine piles of building.

The LONDON INSTITUTION, in Moorfields, is a su-perb stone edifice, and is a distinguished monument of our national improvement in science. The front is of considerable extent, looking to the south, decorated with Corinthian pilasters, surmounted with a balustrade. This elegant building is 108 feet in length, exclusive of the wings, which are 16 feet. A short distance from this is just built the Opthalmic Infirmary, the interior of which for convenience, does the designer the highest credit: the exterior is very neat, and adds greatly to the beauty of that part of the city. The houses round the iron railing, in this ancient part, now only known by the name of Moor-fields, are getting very forward, and it will soon be as elegant a place of residence as any about London.

CATHEDRALS.

The structures appropriated to religious worship are so numerous, that a slight sketch only can be given of the principal, at the head stands that truly noble edifice ST. PAUL'S. It is considered inferior only to St. Peter's, at Rome. The ancient Gothic cathedral, consumed by the great fire in 1666, stood on the site of the present church, which occupies the whole space of Ludgate-hill. The first stone was laid on the 21st. June, 1675, and the last in the year 1710, so that the whole was completed in 35 years. Sir C. Wren was the architect, and he lived to see it finished. Shortly afterwards the Queen and both Houses of Parliament attended divine service in it. The west front, towards Ludgate-street, has a noble aspect; at the north-west and south-west corners two beautiful turrets are erected, the south containing the clock, and the north the belfry. In front of the great north entrance is a semi-circular portico. The southern door is nearly similar. The east end is semicircular, and ornamented with fine sculpture. The sublime dome rises from the intersecting lines of the great cross, in most beautiful proportion and awful grandeur. On the summit of it is a handsome lantern, adorned with Corinthian columns, and surrounded at its base by a balcony ; on the lantern rests a gilded ball and cross, of immense size and weight, which was put up a short time since in lieu of the old one ; it is considered the finest piece of gilt copper work in the kingdom, and has a very grand effect. The ball is six feet diameter, and will contain 12 persons ; the copper of the whole weighs 4 tons, 12 cwt and measures 27 feet from the bottom of the gilding to the top. The ball is in two parts only, and rests upon ornamented gilded brackets ; the iron work necessary for its support in the interior, weighs above three tons, making the entire weight near eight tons. The whole of this ponderous ornament was begun, executed, and placed in its present situation, in the short space of 14 weeks, by Messrs. R. and E. Kepp, of Chandos-street, Covent-garden. Within the south-west pier a circular staircase leads to the whispering gallery, from whence the view is strikingly impressive. The whispering gallery is itself a great curiosity, as the slightest breathed whisper is distinctly heard across the dome, the diameter of which at this part is 100 feet. The bell is greatly admired, its tone is readily distinguished from that of all the other bells in the metropolis ; it is tolled only on the death of one of the royal family, the Lord Mayor, the Bishop of London, or the Dean of the Cathedral. Monumental decorations give additional interest to the interior, among which is one to the memory of Howard, the celebrated prison reformer and philanthropist, and others in honor of Sir W. Jones, Sir J. Reynolds, and Dr. Johnson ; there are also monuments commemorative of Abercrombie, Sir J Moore, and others who distinguished themselves during the late war. In a vault, under the centre of the dome, the perishable remains of Lord Nelson are interred ; here strangers, when visiting the cryptæ, are shewn a sarcophagus of black and white marble, resting on a pedesdal, with " HORATIO VISC. NELSON," inscribed on it. The sarcophagus and pedestal were prepared by Cardinal Wolsey, and brought from his tomb-house, at Windsor. There is also a monument of the great Nelson, by Flaxman. The ground plot of the cathedral is 2 acres, 16 perches, and 70 feet. The various dimensions are, length, from east to west within the walls, 500 feet ; from north to south, through the transept, 285 feet ; the circuit 2292 feet; the height, exclusive of the dome, 160 feet; height, to the top of the cross, 404 feet. The entire of the interior of this magnificent cathedral has very lately been thoroughly repaired, painted and beautified, and was again opened for public worship a short time ago, after being for some time closed.

From traditional stories WESTMINSTER ABBEY claims a high antiquity; it was said to have been erected on the remains of a Roman temple, but Sir C. Wren could find no Roman remains, yet accounts concur in representing it as nearly coeval with the introduction of Christianity into the island. In the reign of Edward the Confessor it was rebuilt in a very magnificent style, in the form of a cross. Henry II. pulled it down, enlarged the plan of the abbey, and added a chapel; and Henry VII. erected that part called Henry VII.'s chapel, which is considered one of the finest specimens existing of that style of architecture. The ancient church was greatly neglected until parliament voted a sum of money for its repairs; and so completely did Sir C. Wren perform the work, that it is in fine condition at the present day. The marble altar piece was given by Queen Anne. The chair, with the mosaic pavement, is altogether a most admirable piece of workmanship. At this altar, and in the centre of the four great pillars under the lantern, are performed the offices of crowning and enthroning the kings of England. On the outside, the new towers and the magnificent portico, styled Solomon's gate, are the most admired. Henry VII.'s chapel is to the east of the abbey, and so joined as to make them appear one building. It is adorned with 16 Gothic towers, projecting in different angles, and beautifully ornamented. The light, which is admitted from a double range of windows, is so happily disposed as to charm the sight and fill the mind with reverential awe. Entering from the east of the abbey, by steps of black marble, which lead to the body of the chapel, the nave and side aisles have a noble cathedral-like appearance. The gates are of brass and curiously worked. The lofty ceiling is adorned with a great variety of figures. The east view, from the entrance, exhibits the brass chapel and tomb of the founder. There are fourteen windows in the upper and nineteen in the lower range. The roof is supported on arches, between the nave and side aisles, which turn upon 12 Gothic pillars. The length of the chapel within is 99 feet, the breadth 66, and the height 54. This chapel was designed as a sepulchre for those of the royal blood only, and the intention of the founder has been generally adhered to. The outside has lately undergone a complete repair, and is finished in so fine a style as to be the admiration of a l who view it. In a vault under the chapel is the place of interment of the present royal family. The monuments in various parts of the abbey are extremely numerous, even to name them all would occupy much space; that of the great Shakespeare, in poet's corner, is elegant and expressive. A black marble slab informs us that it was left to Mr. P. Moore to erect, even that to point out where lie the remains of Sheridan, the brightest genius of our days.

CHURCHES.

St. Margaret's Church, to the north of the abbey, has the beautiful window representing the whole of the history of the crucifiction of our Saviour, the figures are much and deservedly admired. This church contains also the remains of Sir W. Raleigh In the city, behind the Mansion-house, stands St. Stephens, Wallbrook, the master piece of Sir C. Wren. In elegance and proportion it is said to surpass every other modern structure; it is original, simple, chaste, and beautiful. Bow Church, in Cheapside, underwent considerable repairs about two years and a half ago. The tower and spire were rebuilt, precisely after the original design, which was also Sir C. Wren's, and stands unrivalled for elegance in the kingdom: it contains a fine set of bells, but after the re-building of the tower, the ringing of them was suspended till within a few months ago, from a fear that so much agitation would injure, if not bring down the tower; but a meeting having been held in the vestry-room, the ringers were asked if they would brave the danger, and ring a merry peal, to which they consented, and executed some fine changes; until that period they were chimed only, but they are now rung upon every joyful occasion. The interior of this church has also just undergone a complete repair, painting, &c. and a new and elegant clock, with new dials, is put up in place of the old one; it strikes the quarters on four bells, and it is in contemplation to light it with gas.

The church of St. Paul's, Covent-garden, stood long a monument of the genius of Inigo Jones; it was, however, unfortunately burnt about 26 years ago, but has been rebuilt after the original design.

St. Martin's-in-the-fields is an elegant stone edifice, with a portico, which is considered to be the greatest architectural beauty of its kind in the metropolis; and it is expected that this fine piece of masonry will be soon seen to greater advantage, as a noble street is opening in front, which will run from Pall-mall east to St. Martin's church. The tower and spire are particularly handsome; the tower contains a fine set of bells, and the ringers still receive money that was left them by the famous Nell Gwyn.

St. George's, Bloomsbury, is singular in its position, standing north and south. Besides these there are many other churches distinguished for particular architectural beauties, as St. Bride's, Fleet-street, and St. Dunstan's-in-the-East, for their towers and spires; St. Michael's, Corn-hill, for its tower, and St. Clement Danes for its steeple; in St. Giles's, Cripplegate, our great epic poet, Milton was buried, Pancras church has an interest with many on account of the number of celebrated foreigners interred in its cemetary; here may be seen the monument of the unfortunate Paoli. Sir T. Picton, slain in the memorable battle of Waterloo, was buried here; but the new church of St. Pancras must please all who view that singularly elegant structure, which is now completed; it is calculated to hold 4000 persons, and for real beauty it surpasses every other church in London, St. Paul's excepted. The portico, which fronts the west, is a fac-simile of the Erectheum, or Temple of Neptune, Erectheus, at Athens. The tower resembles that of the Temple of the Winds; and at the entrance to the vaults, instead of

pillars, are Grecian statues, after the manner of another
Greek temple. The first stone of this superb edifice was
laid by his royal highness the Duke of York, on the 1st.
day of July, 1819 ; and on the stone is an inscription, in
ancient Greek, which reads in English—" May the light
of the blessed Gospel, thus ever illuminate the dark
temples of the Heathen ;" this is copied from one of the
before-mentioned temples. The architect was Mr. Inwood,
and the whole building was completed under the direction of
Mr. I. Seabrooke. There are an immense number of other
churches spread over the metropolis, amounting to 252 ; besides which there are about 200 chapels, or meeting-houses,
of protestant dissenters, 15 Roman Catholic chapels, 40
foreign churches and chapels, and six Jews' synagogues.
A Roman catholic chapel, on a very extensive scale, has
lately been erected in Moorfields ; the building is of brick,
but we understand it is to be cased with composition,
when it will have a handsome appearance ; the interior is
very handsome and finely decorated.

The new churches in progress in the metropolis and
environs are, viz :—one in Regent-street, in the parish of
St. George, is in a great state of forwardness, and it is
expected will be finished in December 1824 ; the style of
architecture is Ionic, of the temple of *Minerva Polias, at
Pricui*, it will have an elegant portico and cupola, and
will accommodate a congregation of 1580. It was begun
in April, 1823, and the government grant for its erection was 5,555*l.*

In Langham-place, Mary'bone, an elegant church was
begun to be built the 18th of November, 1822, and should
be completed in March, 1824 ; the style of which is Grecian, with Corinthian portico and spire ; it is calculated
to accommodate 1761 persons, and is estimated to cost
19,514*l.*

In Wyndam-place, Mary'bone, is nearly finished a very
handsome church of Ionic architecture, with a portico
and tower ; it was begun in the autumn of 1821 ; the
foundations were laid at different times, as possession
of the ground was obtained ; this church, when finished, will accommodate 1828 persons, and the estimate
is 28,000*l.*

In Stafford-street, Mary'bone, a beautiful church was

c

begun in July, 1822, which is intended to be finished in September, 1824; the style of which is Roman, of the Ionic order, it is estimated at 19,743, and to hold a congregation of 1844; this church will be completed with an elegant portico and cupola.

In the Waterloo-road, in the parish of Lambeth, a new church, of the Doric style of architecture is in a very forward state towards completion; it was begun on the 30th of June, 1823, and is to be finished about July, 1824. This church will have a portico and steeple, and the situation where it is erecting is excellent to display the beauty of the building, the estimate for which is 18,119*l.* It will accommodate 2032 persons.

At Chelsea, St. Luke's church is just completed; its style is Gothic; with a tower and porches. The first stone was laid on the 12th of October, 1820, and the grant towards the erection of it was 8,333*l.* 6*s.* 8*d.* It is built to accommodate 2005 persons.

At Camberwell, the first stone of a new church was laid on the 23d of April, 1822, intended to accommodate a congregation of 1734; the government grant is 5000*l.* for this church, the style of which is Doric, with a portico and steeple; it is very nearly finished, and both the exterior and interior are correspondingly handsome.

A church at Greenwich, the style of which is Grecian, of the Ionian Ionic order, with a portico and tower, was begun to be built in June, 1823, to accommodate 1713 persons, and it is intended to be finished in October, 1824. The grant for this church was 11,000*l.*

At Hackney, a church was begun the 17th of Nov. 1821, which is now completed; the estimate for which was 16,500*l.* It is a handsome structure in the Doric style of architecture, with a portico and cupola, and will accommodate a congregation of 1820.

A church of Grecian style of architecture, of the Corinthian order, with a steeple and portico, was begun on the 14th of April, 1823, at Norwood, in the parish of Lambeth, it will be a very handsome building, and will hold about 1412 persons; the estimate was 12,387*l.* 8*s.* 3*d.* This church is expected to be finished about June, 1824.

At Brixton, in the parish of Lambeth, a church was begun to be built on July 1st, 1822, which is to be completed next December; its style is Doric, with a portico, tower and steeple. This church will accommodate a congregation of 1926; the estimate for the erection of it was 15,340*l.*

At Kennington, in the parish of Lambeth, a large, handsome church is erecting, which was begun the 1st of July, 1822; style, Grecian Doric, with a portico, tower and cupola. It will accommodate 2016 persons, the estimate for building it was 15,248*l.* This church is in a great state of forwardness.

A church was begun to be built on the 2nd of June, 1823, in Beckford-place, Newington, the style of which is Grecian, estimated at 18,468*l.* This church, when built will accommodate a congregation of 2000; it will be a spacious structure, and is intended to be finished in December, 1824.

In Suffolk-street, Newington, another large and handsome church was begun on the 2nd of June, 1823, of the Corinthian style of architecture, with a portico and tower, for the accommodation of 2048 persons. This church will be completed in the summer of 1824, and is estimated at 15,775*l.*

A church of Roman style, with Ionic steeple and portico, is just completed, in Old-street, St. Luke's, it was begun to be built on the 22nd of January, 1822, and will contain a congregation of 1608. It is estimated to cost 15,065*l.*

In Regent-square, St. Pancras, a church of Grecian Ionic style, with portico and tower, was begun on the 26th of August, 1822, estimated at 16,528*l.* and to hold 1832 persons.

In Somers-town, St. Pancras, another church was begun on the 26th of August, 1822, the style of which is entirely Gothic, with a tower, and pinnacles; it is calculated to hold a congregation of 1985, it was estimated at 14,291*l.* This church is in a forward state towards its completion.

It is also in contemplation to build several more churches and chapels, the plan for one is already approved to be built in Hanover-square, Pimlico, in the Grecian style, and many others are under consideration.

SCHOOLS PUBLIC.

The establishments for education are numerous; at the
head of them may be placed CHRIST'S HOSPITAL, commonly known by the name of the Blue Coat School; it is
situated near Newgate-street.   In the time of Edward the
VI. its founder, it consisted of only a grammar school for
boys, and a school for girls; but mathematics are now
taught, particularly those branches which relate to navigation.   From 1000 to 1200 boys and girls receive their
education, and are also boarded and clothed; they are
afterwards apprenticed out.   It is said that greater impar-
tiality is observed now in conducting it than was formerly
the case.   Westminster School, situated in the abbey, was
founded by Elizabeth in 1560; there are 40 queen's scholars, besides many others belonging to eminent families;
they are here prepared for the universities.   Westminster
emulates Eton.   The Charter-house was founded by Thomas
Sutton, in the reign of James I.; besides expending
£20,000 upon the establishment, he left to it estates to
the value of £4,500 per year; the scholars are instructed
in classical and other branches of learning, are boarded
and lodged, and when at the university each student is
allowed £20 per year, for eight years; if put out appren-
tices £40 each is given with them.   St. Paul's school was
instituted by Dr. Colet, for the education of 153 boys,
particularly in Latin, Greek, Hebrew, and various oriental
languages, who are qualified for the universities.   The
school house and the masters' houses and apartments used
to be situated in St. Paul's Church-yard, but they have
lately been taken down, and a new and handsome building
for the purpose is now in a state of forwardness, on the same
site.   It will be an extensive and elegant stone structure and
highly ornamental to that part of the city.   Merchant Tailors'
school educates 300 boys, many of them are afterwards sent
to St. John's, Oxford.   The free school at Harrow also enjoys
a high reputation.   It is estimated that there are not less than
4000 private schools in and about the metropolis.

Besides the parish schools there are also many other charity schools, such as those formed by the benevolent society of St. Patrick, for the education of children born of poor Irish parents, residing in the metropolis. A handsome building for this praiseworthy institution, has recently been erected in Stamford-street, Blackfriars-road, under the patronage of his majesty, whose subscriptions to it have been very munificent. This structure has a neat centre and entrance, over which are the king's arms, well executed; the building has two wings, that on the right is the school-room : behind is a large enclosed yard or play-ground. There is also a school for the support and instruction of poor Welch children. An asylum has been established with success to teach the deaf and dumb, it is situated in the Old Kent road; and within the last 30 years great exertions have been made to extend the benefit of education to the bulk of the labouring people. Among those who have laboured in that good cause Joseph Lancaster stands conspicuous. The new system introduced by him and Dr. Bell is now acted upon extensively ; some idea may be formed of its success from the number of schools united to the national society in 1812 compared with the number in 1818; in the former year there were only 52, containing 8000 children, but in 1818 they had increased to 1239, containing 180,000 children. Sunday schools have also been established so generally, that it is said 50,000 children attend them in the metropolis alone : the teachers give their assistance gratuitously.

LONDON abounds also in institutions to instruct and assist the unfortunate. The school for the indigent blind is to instruct those without sight to work at making threads, lines, mats, baskets, &c; it is situated near the Obelisk, St. George's-fields, and has been very successful. The Magdalen, formed in 1758, has been the means of reclaiming great numbers of those unhappy females who had been driven into the paths of prostitution. The Asylum, in Lambeth, for deserted female orphan children, has been eminently useful in saving poor girls from that state from which it is the object of the former charity to rescue them. The same liberal and charitable feeling for the unfortunate is equally conspicuous with the Jews, they have a very large school-house, near the Hackney-road,

c 2

and an extensive hospital in Mile End-road. Their mode
of providing for their poor is by teaching them to make
shoes, chairs, &c. and their charitable institutions are well
conducted and liberally supported by the more opulent of their persuasion.

HOSPITALS.

The hospitals form a conspicuous feature of the metropolis, they are numerous, splendid, and many of them well
endowed.   At their   head   stands GREENWICH HOS-
PITAL.—It is situated on the south bank of the Thames,
and has a noble aspect.   There are four large stone buildings, which form a grand whole.   The terrace is nearly
1000 feet in length ; in the   square is a statue of
George II. : the building altogether has a most magnificent appearance.   It is a retreat for seamen, disabled from
service by wounds, age, or other infirmities, and for the
widows and children of such as died fighting the battles of
their country.   Every seaman in the royal navy pays six-
pence a month out of his wages, towards the support of
this hospital.   The pensioners are clothed in blue, and
allowed a shilling a week, besides shoes, linen and stock-
ings.   The navy asylum is an excellent structure, lately
erected, for the purpose of educating 3,000 seamen's
children.

CHELSEA HOSPITAL is for soldiers what Greenwich
is for seamen ; it was originally intended for a college of
divinity, hence it is frequently called Chelsea College.
The building is spacious, standing upon about 40 acres of
ground, the front contains a chapel and hall ; the other
two lines are four stories high, and divided into wards and
galleries, two in a story, each containing 26 apartments
for the soldiers.   This royal building is a handsome erection of brick, ornamented with stone.   The front next to
the Thames is more decorated, and has a very elegant and
pleasing effect ; the principal parts form three sides of a
square, the centre building having a noble portico, with a
piazza on each side ; the other two parts have fine and co.-

responding porticos. The area formed by the buildings on this side the hospital terminates with a balustrade; beyond which are spacious gardens, and two pieces of water, with trees and walks on each side, reaching to the Thames, from which is a communication with the gardens by stairs. This fine national institution was begun by Charles II. (whose statue is erected on a pedestal in the centre of the area, facing the river) continued by James II. and finished by William III. The plan of the edifice was the design of Sir C. Wren. A new building was lately erected at the south end for the surgeon of this establishment, the style of the architecture corresponds with the other parts of the structure. The in-pensioners are generally about 400, exclusively of the officers and servants; there are also a great many out-pensioners, who occasionally do duty in garrisons. The expence of this hospital is defrayed out of the poundage of the army, and by one day's pay from each officer and private soldier every year. The royal military asylum at Chelsea is a handsome building. It admits 700 boys and 300 girls, children of soldiers.

The GENERAL HOSPITALS, to be found in every district of the metropolis, are so numerous that we can do little more than enumerate them. St. Thomas's, in the Borough, is an extensive range of buildings, consisting of four spacious quadrangular courts, that have the appearance of a palace. In the middle of the second is a statue of brass of Edward VI. There are hot and cold baths, and an excellent circular theatre, where courses of lectures are delivered to great numbers of students, who come from all parts of the country, to learn the London practice. The hospital is for the poor who are sick, or who have been maimed by accident, and is of great utility, relieving, on an average of ten years, 9,000 persons, at an expence of £10,000 annually. Near to St. Thomas's is Guy's Hospital, named from its founder Mr. Guy, and by him so munificently endowed, that it is said to have an income of £20,000 per annum. It was established for the reception of 400 diseased persons and 20 incurable lunatics, for whom a separate building is provided; but the yearly in-patients, on an average of 10 years, are now 2,250, the out-patients about 2,000. This hospital has also a theatre for lectures, and one evening in the week there is a debate in medical subjects.

ST. BARTHOLOMEW'S HOSPITAL is an extensive
pile of building : the exterior, towards Giltspur-street, is
a fine piece of Doric architecture, with a large arched
gate, and foot-way on each side. A good figure of Henry
VIII. stands on a pedestal, over the key-stone, in a niche ;
underneath this statue is the following inscription :—" St.
Bartholomew's Hospital, founded by Rahere, Anno 1122,
refounded by Henry VIII. 1546." Above is a severed circular pediment, on the segment of this recline two emble-
matic human figures, one representing lameness, the other
sickness. The grand pile next to Smithfield is well worthy
of notice. In the centre of the great quadrangle is (lately
put up) a curious cylindrical pump, enclosed within a
handsome iron railing, which is ornamental as well as
very useful to the hospital. The staircase in this building
was painted by Hogarth gratuitously. This institution
affords relief to as many of the afflicted as St. Thomas's.
Middlesex, London, and Westminster Hospitals are also
eminently useful in the same way. Besides these there
are the Small-pox Hospital at Battlebridge, the Queen's,
London, Westminster, and British Lying-in Hospitals, for
poor pregnant women, and institutions for affording assistance to lying-in women at their own houses. Bethlem
Hospital and the Hospital of St. Luke are for the reception
of lunatics ; the former is an immense structure, lately
erected in St. George's fields, extending in front 300 feet—
it cost £100,000. There are also other hospitals amounting in all to 18, and 25 dispensaries, in different parts of
the town, affording assistance to the afflicted, and reflecting
the highest honour on the enlightened benevolence of the
inhabitants of the British metropolis.

We cannot pass unnoticed the numerous societies established for benevolent purposes, among which are the
Philanthropic Society in St. George's-fields, for the prevention of crime and the reform of the criminal poor, on
the principle of employment and separation into classes ;
the Royal Humane Society, for the recovery of apparently
drowned persons; the society for the relief of those confined for small debts ; the National Benevolent Institution ;
the Marine Society ; the Westminster Benevolent Society ;
the African Institution, &c. &c. There are also 107 almshouses for the support of aged persons. The liveries of

London alone distribute upwards of £75,000 in charities annually.

In enumerating other public buildings of the metropolis, the BANK OF ENGLAND, from the importance of its concerns, claims early attention. It is erected on a part of the bed of the ancient rivulet called "Wallbrook." The buildings are irregular in form, comprising eight courts, many large public offices and committee-rooms, the rotunda, &c.; beneath there are more buildings than above, but the principal range of rooms is on the ground floor. In the rotunda stockholders commonly assemble to buy and sell their stock, it is also a resting place for persons coming to receive their dividends. This pile of building is so extensive, and the architecture so various, that it is useless for us to attempt a description of it. Its general appearance is that of a handsome, but solid and durable, range of buildings. The Stock Exchange, lately erected at the end of Capel-court, has taken from the rotunda of the bank most of the stock brokers who formerly assembled in it. A new room has been added contiguous to the Stock-Exchange, where all business in the foreign funds is transacted.

The ROYAL EXCHANGE is one of the finest structures for the purpose in Europe. It stands upon a plot of ground 203 feet in length, and 171 in breadth. The area in the middle is 61 perches, in which mercantile men meet daily for purposes of business. It was founded and built at the sole expence of Sir Thomas Gresham, who was an opulent merchant in London, and who, with several of the aldermen, laid the first stone of this extensive pile, on the 7th. June, 1667, the whole was completed in a comparatively short time, and opened on the 28th. September, 1669. Lately, very extensive repairs have been done to the exterior of this building, the old tower was taken down some time ago, by order of the Gresham Committee, and a new one of the most elegant design is just finished: it consists of a square story, in the centre of which is a niche, occupied by a whole length figure of Sir Thomas Gresham; on each side, on pedestals supported by the cornice, are two large and finely executed figures—the four representing Europe, Asia, Africa, and America; above is raised an octagon, which contains the clock, having four faces to the cardinal points, the whole is surmounted by a dome, with a pedestal and vane, crowned by a grasshopper, the founder's crest. Numerous emblematical ornaments decorate the front, and at each corner of the tower is placed a large dragon rampant, supporting the shield-part of the city arms. This noble structure has a most magnificent appearance from Cornhill. The whole interior has lately undergone a complete repair.

On the south side of Leadenhall-street is the EAST INDIA HOUSE, it has a very fine front; here all the important business of this company is transacted. In the interior the sale room is much admired; the building is very extensive.

Near where Cornhill and Lombard-street unite, stands that magnificent structure the MANSION HOUSE, the residence of the Lord Mayor of London. It is a lofty building, with numerous architectural decorations. In the interior, the Egyptian hall commands the highest admiration. On the east side of Fish-street-hill is that fine specimen of modern architecture, designed by the great Sir C. Wren, known by the name of " the Monument," erected in remembrance of the destructive fire of London. It is the finest of all modern columns, being 24 feet higher than the pillar of Trajan, at Rome. From the pavement it is 202 feet in height, the staircase within contains 345 steps.

A little below London-bridge, on the north side of the river, may be seen the immense and magnificent new CUSTOM-HOUSE; it is worthy of the city of London, and calculated to give a stranger an exalted idea of its extensive commercial transactions. The first stone was laid October 25, 1813, and it was opened for public business May 12, 1817. In the interior the rooms are well arranged to facilitate the despatch of business, and the great throngs continually pouring in and issuing from it, in business hours, indicate the extent of its transactions. The long room is surpassed by Westminster-hall alone, we believe, being 190 feet in length, 66 feet wide, and 55 feet high, without pillars to support the roof. There is a new wharf in front, from which, or from the river, the building is seen to advantage.

Passing now to the west, the POST-OFFICE, in Lombard-street, as a building, scarcely attracts attention ;

but it is intended to build a new one, and a large space
of ground was cleared (at an enormous expence) some
time ago, where St. Martin's-le-grand stood, the right
hand side of which was taken down. It now lays open ;
but it is expected it will be immediately begun of, as
the Lords of the treasury have taken it out of the hands of
the city, and are (we understand) going to prosecute the
design forthwith, with great metropolitan splendour.

We proceed on to GUILDHALL, where the principal
corporation business of the city is transacted. The front
is Gothic, but has a striking appearance. The large hall
is 153 feet long, 48 broad, and 55 high ; here the elections
for members of parliament and for the lord mayor take
place; public meetings are also held here, and city feasts
given. The Emperor Alexander, of Russia, was entertained in the hall at a great expence. The old Blackwell
Hall, which formerly stood near to Guildhall, and which
was a depot for woollen cloths, was taken down a short
time since, and on its site is erected a large handsome
brick building, for the commissioners of bankrupts to
hold their sittings for the meeting of creditors : this building has greatly improved the appearance of that part of
the city.

At the end of Fleet-street is TEMPLE-BAR, the only remaining boundary gate of the city ; and further to the
west, in the Strand, is that fine collection of buildings
called SOMERSET HOUSE, used for government offices,
the meetings of the royal society, and society of antiqua-
rians. There is also here an annual exhibition of paintings and sculptures. On the south side is a terrace along
the Thames, the view from which challenges admiration,
equalling any other in the interior of the metropolis. It
is seen to advantage from Waterloo-bridge. This extensive pile of building never was completed; viewing it from
this bridge, the spectator will see that part of the western
wing is incomplete.

Continuing west we come to NORTHUMBERLAND
HOUSE, one of the fine mansions which were formerly
so numerous between the Strand and the river. This
grand edifice contains upwards of 140 rooms; the gardens,
extending to the river, form an enchanting retreat in the
very heart of the capital. This palace, as it may now

justly be styled, has lately undergone a most complete repair; and the centre part of the structure, which is not seen from the street, has been entirely rebuilt of fine Portland stone. The interior is new furnished, and decorated in the most magnificent manner. The grand staircase consists of steps of the most beautiful polished marble; in front of the first flight is an orchestra, the top of which is supported by two superb scagliola pillars: the sides of the walls, from the ground to the first grand landing, is composed of the same ingenious composition, and has every appearance of the finest polished yellow marble. Over this costly staircase is a large sort of sky-light and ceiling, which is ornamented with paintings by the first-rate artists We can only give a faint idea of this superb flight of stairs, the cost of which alone has been upwards of £25,000; and the furniture and decorations of four of the principal rooms amount to 40,000*l.* There have been upwards of two hundred thousand pounds laid out on this mansion, to make it fit for the town residence of his grace the Duke of Northumberland, who has not (since he came to the title) resided in it till within these few months. The exterior next to the Strand is now very ornamental, and adds greatly to the beauty of that part of London.

The ADMIRALTY-OFFICE, HORSE-GUARDS, TREASURY, and WHITEHALL are contiguous to each other, and form perhaps the best assemblage of handsome buildings in the metropolis; they are all used for public offices. The new Court-house, near Westminster-hall, deserves attention from the admirer of architecture.

The public buildings connected with the study of the law are called the INNS of COURT. The principal are the Middle and Inner Temple, so named from having been erected by the Knights Templars. The gardens belonging to these buildings are a favourite resort in the summer, the principal one, having a fine gravel walk along the Thames, is a delightful promenade: a small basin, with a fountain spouting up water, has a pleasing effect, in another part of the Temple. Thaives' Inn; Clifford's Inn; Barnard's Inn; Staple Inn; Sargeant's Inn; Clement's Inn; Lyon's Inn; New Inn; and Furnival's Inn, the last has lately been rebuilt in a very handsome style, is now an ornament to that part of Holborn where it is situated ; and, although a brick building, it is a noble pile, and the front, over the entrance, is decorated with handsome stone pillars, supporting a pediment, and altogether it has an elegant appearance. Gray's Inn deserves particular notice for its fine garden, which is a most agreeable promenade, and is open to the public in summer. Gray's Inn is situated on the north side of Holborn, and derives its name from the Lord Grays, who had a house there. Lincoln's Inn, the garden of which is considered one of the finest promenades within the capital, formerly belonged to the Earl of Lincoln. These Inns are generally occupied by gentlemen of the legal profession. Other splendid buildings (which by Italians would be called palaces,) belonging to the nobility are so numerous, that even a list of them would exceed the limits we have prescribed to ourselves.

BRIDGES.

In no one respect does London more surpass other capitals than in the number of its magnificent bridges. There are in all six of them, connecting the southern with the northern part of the metropolis. The following are their dimensions : London-bridge, 900 feet, Southwark-bridge (cast iron) 708, Blackfriars-bridge 940, Waterloo-bridge, within the abutments, 1242, Westminster-bridge 1223, and Vauxhall-bridge (iron) 860. LONDON-BRIDGE being an ancient structure, is inferior to the more modern erections; it consists of 19 arches of unequal dimensions: formerly there was a draw-bridge upon it, which made it an important military post for the times. It was then covered with wooden houses, when, upon a fire breaking out at the south end, crowds came from the city to assist in extinguishing it, but while thousands were on the bridge it took fire at the north end, placing immense numbers between the two fires, which rapidly approached each other. On this occasion it is said 3,000 persons perished ; perhaps a still greater number of lives have been lost since the first erecting of the bridge by the fall of water when the tide recedes, the space for the passage of the water being too small. When houses were on the bridge the road was only 23 feet wide, but now the space is 45 feet

D

between the balustrades. It is now finally settled that this ancient bridge is to be taken down, and another more convenient and elegant one erected in its stead. The wheels that used to be on each side, belonging to the London Water-works Company, are already demolished, and the space were they were erected is cleared. The design of the new bridge is determined upon, and it is expected that this great undertaking will commence immediately; it will be situated very near the old bridge, on the side towards Blackfriars.

London had for a long period known the convenience of only one bridge, but in the year 1739 was commenced that elegant structure designated WESTMINSTER-BRIDGE, which was completed in eleven years, and esteemed at the time the finest in the world. Monsieur Labelye had the honour of being the architect. Under the water it was computed that there were £40,000 value in stone and other materials. The entire expence was £389,000, which was defrayed by parliament. It was built entirely of stone, and is 44 feet wide, having on each side a fine balustrade of stone. In 1760 was begun the beautiful bridge called BLACKFRIARS-BRIDGE, designed by Mr. R. Mylne; it was finished in 1768, at an expence of £152,840. There are nine arches, the centre one being 100 feet wide. The breadth of the foot-way is seven feet each side, the carriage-way 27 feet. The elliptical arches have a very fine effect. The fourth stone bridge is now called WATER-LOO-BRIDGE; it crosses the river from the Strand to Lambeth-marsh. For simplicity of architecture, solidity of structure, and great extent, this is undoubtedly the finest stone bridge in the world. Together with the adjoining roads, it is said to have cost the enormous sum of £1,100,000. Mr. G. Dodd was the engineer, who commenced the building, but it was constructed principally under the direction of Mr. Rennie. The arches are elliptical, nine in number, of equal size, and the road over it quite level, it is entirely of granite, and was finished in little more than six years. Besides the stone bridges there are two constructed of cast iron. That near to Vauxhall, and called VAUXHALL-BRIDGE, is light and elegant. It was erected by Mr. Walker, for £150,000. There are nine arches, and the breadth of the road is 36 feet.

SOUTHWARK-BRIDGE is, however, that which is likely the most to astonish the stranger. This stupendously grand iron bridge extends across the Thames with only three arches!! Rennie, the celebrated engineer, has the merit of the design, and he also superintended the erection; the whole was completed for £800,000, including the avenues. The two piers in the river are 60 feet high, from the bed of the river to the top of the parapet, and from low to high water mark 24 feet in breadth, the two side arches are 210 feet each in span, and the centre arch 240 feet, exceeding Sunderland arch four feet in span. The scientific manner in which the centerings of this and Waterloo-bridge were constructed excited high admiration so accurately was every thing calculated, and so excellent the workmanship, that the centre arch of Southwark-bridge settled to an eighth of an inch of what was anticipated. Below London-bridge the river is generally crowded with shipping to the distance of four miles, averaging in the width nearly 500 yards; the greater part of this extent is commonly distinguished by the names of the upper, middle and lower pools.

DOCKS.

Formerly vessels had to load and unload at the quays between London-bridge and the Tower, but since 1802 capacious docks have been constructed in Wapping and the Isle of Dogs. The LONDON-DOCKS were commenced in 1802, and contain 20 acres. There are extensive warehouses on the north quay, and also a large tobacco warehouse, covering 14 acres of ground. The capital of the present company is £2,200,000. Another dock of 14 acres is proposed to be made in Shadwell, communicating with the present London docks. The West India Docks are formed in the narrowest part of the Isle of Dogs, one dock for loading and the other for unloading; the two, containing 54 acres, are capable of accommodating all shipping engaged in the West India trade. The canal to the south is designed to render unnecessary the circuitous navigation round the Isle of Dogs. Capacious docks were shortly afterwards constructed for the East India shipping,

which include the Brunswick dock at Blackwall. The
works were completed in 1806. All East India ships must
be unloaded in these docks. The formation of so many
docks was the cause of the fine commercial road being
made, which is 70 feet wide, with a pavement of 20 feet
in the middle. The distance from the Royal Exchange to
the East India docks is three miles and a half by this road.
The Regent's canal connects the grand junction canal at
Paddington with the river Thames at Limehouse, uniting
the interior navigation of the country north of the town
with the port. London, as a port has been greatly
improved by these superior conveniences for shipping,
and the whole routine of business has undergone an entire
alteration since the construction of the docks. It has been
computed, that the total amount of property shipped and
unshipped in the port of London, in one year, amounts to
nearly seventy millions, and there are employed in the ex-
ports and imports about 4000 ships and not less than 15,000
cargoes annually enter the port. On an average there are
2000 ships in the river and docks, together with 3000
barges and other small craft employed in lading and unlading them; there are also about 2300 barges engaged in
the inland trade, and 3000 wherries and small boats for
passengers; in navigating the wherries and craft 8000 watermen gain a livelihood by it, and 4000 labourers are employed in assisting in the lading and unlading the ships,
besides the crews of the several vessels, and 1200 revenue
officers are constantly doing duty in the port of London.

BRITISH MUSEUM.

Collections of rare productions of nature and art are
numerous in London; and although the buildings in which
they are exhibited are not always striking in their architectural display, they cannot be omitted in a description of
it. At their head stands the BRITISH MUSEUM, in
Russel-street, Bloomsbury-square. This is the grand national depository of whatever is rare and valuable in manuscripts and books, exquisite productions of art, natural
and artificial curiosities, antiquities, &c. It is uncom-
monly rich in manuscripts; the Harlean library alone

contained 7000. The collection of D'Eves is considered very rare. Here is also the Cottonian library, and that collected by the late Dr. Burney, which is particularly rich in Greek works. The King's libraries were the collection of centuries; and a most princely addition has just been made to the museum by a gift from his present Majesty; we cannot convey to the public an idea of the value of this rich present better than by inserting the King's letter to Lord Liverpool, which we are proud in having the opportunity of doing.

(COPY) 15th Jan. 1823

DEAR LORD LIVERPOOL—The King, my late revered and excellent father, having formed, during a long series of years, a most valuable and extensive library, consisting of about 120,000 volumes, I have resolved to present this collection to she British nation; whilst I have the satisfaction, by this means, of advancing the literature of my country, I also feel that I am paying a just tribute to the memory of a parent whose life was adorned with every public and private virtue.

GEORGE.

On the 3rd. of February, 1823, a meeting of the trustees of the British Museum was held, to consider the best mode of disposing of this princely gift, at which the question was adjourned for further consideration; so that it is yet undecided whether it shall be incorporated with the national library, or a separate establishment shall be formed for it under the same direction. The purchase of the curiosities of Sir Hans Sloane led to the establishment of this museum, which was appointed for their reception. It now contains an immense collection, among which, not the least valuable, are the celebrated Elgin marbles, brought by the nobleman of that name from Greece, and the Hamilton marbles, the Portland vase, a collection of fossil remains, particularly the human skeleton in limestone, from Gaudaloupe, the skull and horns of the Irish elk, and an interesting assemblage of curiosities from the South Sea, collected principally by our great countryman, Captain Cook. Also, lately has been added, the statue of Memnon, sent from Egypt by Belzoni; likewise the sarcophagus of Alexander the Great, which is the most perfect of any that enrich this invaluable collection; and nume-

D 2

rous other rare and ancient relics have been sent from
Egypt within these two years. It is intended to make a
considerable addition to the size of the present building,
as great numbers of the most valuable subjects of the museum are now kept out of sight from the want of room to
display them; and we doubt not but this circumstance, in
conjunction with his Majesty's late present, will induce
the directors to erect, immediately, a building worthy of
containing subjects of such inestimable value. The museum is open to public inspection on Mondays, Wednesdays,
and Fridays, between the hours of ten and four:—no money
is permitted to be given to the attendants.

The SOCIETY of ARTS have an establishment in the
Adelphi, where is an extensive collection of models and
machines, considered the finest in the world; admission
may be obtained by applying at the office of the society.

The ROYAL ACADEMY, in Somerset-house, has an
annual exhibition; lectures have also been delivered here
on architecture, perspective, anatomy, sculpture, and
painting. There are also many collections of paintings,
&c. exhibited at the British Institution, Pall Mall;
the Panorama, Leicester-square; Linwood's gallery of
needle-work; and Du Bourg's cork models, in Grosvenor-
street.

The collection of rare living animals, at EXETER-
CHANGE, Strand, is worthy of inspection. The Tower
has some fine animals, and many curious and valuable
articles, which cause it to be generally visited by the en-
quiring stranger; as is Woolwich also, on account of its
fine dock-yards for building ships of war and its being the
royal arsenal; immense magazines of military stores are
to be seen here. There are also numerous societies instituted for the advancement of the arts and sciences, some
of which have valuable collections; among which may
be named the Royal Society, the Linnean Society, the
British Mineralogical Society, the Geological Society, the
Russell Institution, &c.

LITERATURE is much cultivated in London; the number of works constantly issuing from the press is astonish-
ing. The publication of books is very extensive, but
cannot be easily estimated; some account may however
be given of periodical publications: there are 12 reviews

and journals published quarterly, 40 and upwards of reviews, journals, and magazines published monthly, besides, a great many weekly literary publications, in which
we find treated with ability theology, mathematics, chemis-
try, medicine, mechanics, natural history, agriculture,
manufactures, the belles lettres, fashion, &c. &c.   The ac-
tivity and intelligence of London is no where better exhibited than in the newspaper press : with the regularity of
the sun, thousands of newspapers are distributed, morning
and evening, conveying amusement and important information, not only to the metropolis, but, by the agency of
the post-office, to every part of the British dominions.
The result of an investigation, which took place in 1814
and 1815, shewed that the morning papers published daily
about 20,000, and the evening papers about 15,000; in
addition to these there were 90,000 published per week, of
two-days, three-days, and weekly papers.   From this
statement it may be conceived what powerful means London
possesses of influencing the public mind throughout the
empire.

THEATRES.

In so populous a city, it is to be presumed that theatres
will be found corresponding to its numbers and magnitude ;
compared, however, with continental capitals, the Theatres of London are few for its immense population: but
there are some which, for design, convenience, and embel-
lishment, will bear a comparison with the most celebrated
in Europe.

The ITALIAN OPERA-HOUSE, or KING'S THEA-
TRE, is near to Carlton-palace.   Besides Italian operas,
which are performed generally by natives of Italy, there
is a corps de ballet, whose performance is commonly in
the Parisian style.   This house has a beautiful interior.
There are five tiers of boxes, nearly all private property,
which hold about 900 persons, and are mostly filled by those
of the first rank and fashion—curtains draw in the front
of the boxes in the Italian manner; the pit and gallery
hold 800 persons each.   The stage is 60 feet from the wall
to the orchestra, 46 feet across from box to box, and 80

feet from wall to wall; from the floor of the pit to the dome is 55 feet. Performances commence in December and usually continue to August, on Tuesday and Saturday each week. Admission to the pit is 10s. 6d. and gallery 5s. The exterior of this extensive structure has recently been rebuilt in the most splendid style, and corresponds with the magnificent buildings that are adjacent. A noble piazza extends round the entire of the theatre, and underneath are respectable and well furnished shops, which give a fashionable interest to the whole. In the centre of this immense edifice, fronting the Haymarket, and considerably elevated above the piazza, are two long tablets, each containing groups of emblematical figures, nearly as large as life, very finely executed in basso relievo.

COVENT-GARDEN THEATRE is calculated to hold 3000 persons, and to produce, when full, £700. It is built after a design of Mr. Smirke, jun. who combined in his plan that fine specimen of Doric architecture, the temple of Minerva, at Athens, and though not equal to the original, the principal front in Bow-street is magnificent. The interior of the house is tastefully ornamented; there are three ranges of boxes, two galleries, and a spacious pit. The stage is well proportioned; the form of the body of the house approaches to the circular. The use of gas for lighting has greatly improved the interior of of the London theatres. The grand chandelier which hangs from the centre, itself a conspicuous ornament, sheds a brilliancy and cheerfulness over the whole of the house, making the coup d'œil strikingly grand when it is full. This theatre has been newly decorated and the interior altogether much improved this season, by some very judicious alterations in the audience part of the house.

DRURY-LANE THEATRE, or as it was frequently called "Old Drury" is more ancient than Covent-garden, but is not at present so large. This theatre has had to struggle with embarrassments for a long time; it is now under the management of Mr. Elliston, who rents it at 10,560l per annum. It has, lately undergone a complete repair; the interior of the house has, with the exception of the internal walls and lobbies, been entirely reconstructed. The grand points which give most satisfaction, are the contraction of the audience part and the extention of the stage ; the roof is also lowered six or seven feet, and, by a very admirable plan, the whole circle is obvious to the audience. The roof is adorned with a radii of gold from the central lustre, and studded with rich gilded ornaments to a fine cornice of the same dazzling character. The upper gallery is diminished by a wide passage all round the back and a similar passage opened between the slips. The ornament of the front of the third circle is a rich gold wreath on a white ground ; the circle below has one of the most classical and elegant patterns, most eminently chaste and magnificent ; the dress circle is adorned with thirteen painted designs from Shakespear's plays, which are superbly framed with pannels, cornices, &c. The boxes throughout are thrown forward nearly their own depth, and in the dress circle the space thus gained has been converted into 12 close boxes, resembling those in the English Opera-house. Below the dress circle are the private boxes, as before, plain arched openings in the pannel which surrounds. The pit is in every way comfortable, and every alternate bench is fitted up with a back. The general form of the audience division is not now the form of a horse shoe as before ; the sides run contracted a little into the proscenium, and the stage or orchestra boxes continue the line ; these latter are superbly adorned with two fluted and elegantly gilded pillars on each side, which have longitudinal interstices quite open, so that persons in the boxes can see the stage through them. The proscenium itself is equally splendid, being surrounded by rich scrolls of dead and bright gold. To match the rest of this gorgeous theatre, the new drop scene is a curtain of scarlet and gold, richly adorned, and produces a most grand effect by its brilliancy and vast surface. There are no stage doors, but there is an opening in the curtain in the centre, through which the performers come to give out the play, speak prologues, &c. A new green-room and dressing-rooms have been built towards Vinegar-yard. The old palings and other nuisances are to be removed, and a set of neat shops, a-la-palais royale, erected in their stead. With these splendid improvements Drury-lane is now the most magnificent and convenient theatre that ever was opened to the public ; the rapidity in designing and executing these changes is of itself a sufficient subject for astonishment: the expence is estimated at from 15 to £20,000. The performances at this grand national theatre are now most judiciously arranged; the performers are numerous and of the first rate talent, and we hope, and do not doubt, where so much industrious exertion has been used, united to the individual merits of Mr. Elliston as an actor, but he will realize his most sanguine expectations. The prices of both houses are the same, 7s. boxes, 3s. 6d. pit 2s. gallery, 1s. upper gallery. They are closed for a short time in the summer. These two are the grand theatres for the display of British dramatic talent, and are probably not to be equalled, in all their varied excellencies, in any other part of the world.

The HAYMARKET THEATRE is open only during the summer season. It has been lately rebuilt, near its old site in the Haymarket, exactly opposite to Charles-street. The erection of this handsome structure commenced in February, 1821, was finished in four months, and in the July following was opened to the public. A chaste simplicity distinguishes the building, which consists of an elegant portico, above which, at a considerable elevation, are nine circular windows, and the sashes being connected, they form an elegant frontlet. The theatre is lofty, and the whole exterior is covered with a handsome and durable stucco, reflecting altogether great credit on the architect. The interior of this theatre has been altered since it was rebuilt, and it differs from all the rest in London in point of shape. The audience part forms three sides of a square, and each box has a projection similar to a balcony. The decorations are simple and neat, and it has a pleasing and quite a novel effect. The prices are boxes 5s. pit 3s. gallery 2s. upper gallery 1s.

Within a few years an attempt has been made, with some success, to establish a theatre for the production of English operatic dramas. The new theatre in the Strand, formerly the Lyceum, was opened January 15, 1816, for the performance of English operas, but it has had to encounter formidable opposition from the winter houses. The interior of this theatre is distinguished by its novel and tasteful decorations, particularly in what is called the body of the house; the management of the gas light produces also a new and pleasing effect. The pit is elevated more than in any other theatre in town, improving that part of the house materially. The principal entrance is from the Strand, and contiguous to the boxes are a handsome lobby and saloon. In this theatre Mr. Matthews has amused the town with his whimsical performances; his success reflects great credit on his attractive powers. The prices of admission are the same as at the Haymarket.

There are also the SURRY THEATRE, in St. George's-fields, the interior of which has undergone a complete metamorphose this season, and it is now fitted up in a very modern and elegant manner, and the audience part is much improved. ASTLEY's AMPHITHEATRE, near Westminster-bridge, celebrated for its equestrian performances; and SADLER's WELLS, near Islington, which introduced the novelty of aquatic exhibitions. But foremost among these stands the COBOURG THEATRE, situated at the end of the road from Waterloo-bridge to Lambeth-marsh; its admirable adaption to dramatic representation is universally acknowledged. In the saloon are likenesses of the late lamented Princess Charlotte and the Prince of Cobourg. A novelty of a very singular nature was lately introduced at this theatre in a splendid glass curtain. This magnificent mirror, on the rising of the curtain, which is before it, reflects the whole interior of the house and audience in a distinct manner— the effect is magical and surprising. It is composed of many large glasses, so put together as to make it appear one entire plate, in a carved frame, richly gilded in burnished gold. The glass and frame measure 36 feet in height and 32 in width. It is altogether 5 tons in weight, and reaches to the proscenium, latterly this splendid appendage has not been exhibited. The OLYMPIC PAVILION, at the end of Drury-lane, is small, but neat, and often takes the overflow from the large houses. The ADELPHI THEATRE, in the Strand, has been lately purchased by Mess. Rodwell and Jones. The ROYALTY THEATRE, in Well-street, Goodman's-fields, is under the management of Mr. Dunn, and has lately undergone a complete repair, and is now a very superb little theatre: the decorations in the interior are very splendid and tasteful. The performances are generally melo-dramas, ballets, and lively afterpieces, which are got up in a style that would not disgrace a larger theatre. The WEST LONDON is a neat little theatre in Tottenham-court road, where the performances are similar to the Royalty. This house generally opens in the spring and fall of the year, for a few months each time. These minor theatres have licences under the 25th of George II.

In enumerating the public amusements of London VAUXHALL GARDENS must not be omitted; these have long been celebrated for their brilliant illumination, diversified by lamps of various colours. The orchestra is splendid, and has a striking appearance from the front of it; there is occasionally some good singing. The extraordinary performances on the rope have lately given eclat to this place. There are few scenes more calculated to astonish those unaccustomed to such sights than Vauxhall-gardens on a gala night, when full of company and splendidly illuminated,—it reminds of the impression made by fairy tales in early life. This delightful place of evening amusement was lately advertised for sale by auction, and it was supposed would have been sold for building ground, but two spirited gentlemen, Messrs. Bish and Gye, of the London wine and tea company, purchased the gardens on a lease, and opened them in 1822 in a most magnificent and novel manner, which gave the greatest pleasure and satisfaction to many thousands who visited them.

For some persons the Fives-court, in St. Martin's-lane, has attractions; here *sparring* is to be occasionally seen, by the most eminent prize-fighters of the day. The sporting world assemble at Tattersall's, near Hyde-park; and there are subscription-rooms and clubs for the fashionable world at the Argyle-rooms, Almack's, at Brookes's and Boadle's clubs, St. James'-street, and at the United Service club, Waterloo-place, besides others of equal fashion and note.

The sources from whence supplies are obtained to support the immense population of London will, of course, be extremely various; but we may trace, with tolerable distinctness, five separate streams of wealth, that are flowing into it. 1. The rent of the land of the united kingdom is largely expended in London by the nobility and gentry. —2. The interest of the national debt is the principal revenue of great numbers resident in town.—3. The numerous government offices and courts of law, existing in the metropolis, afford handsome incomes to a very numerous class.—4. The mercantile business of London supports and enriches a large portion of its inhabitants, and—5. The manufactures of the metropolis,—which are more numerous and extensive than a superficial observer would readily believe. In an opulent and luxurious nation there is always a great demand for elegant and valuable articles. London may be considered the seat of manufacture of all such of a superior quality, and from it not only is the country extensively supplied, but large quantities are continually exported to the colonies. Considerable quantities of raw silk are worked up, but a good deal of that trade is removing to Manchester. The porter of London is highly celebrated.

The CIVIL GOVERNMENT of the metropolis is various; that of the city of London has, by charter, been given to the lord mayor, aldermen, common council, and freeholders of London. The city is divided into 26 wards, each ward elects annually common council men. The aldermen are chosen for life, one from each ward, by the free householders, excepting in the ward of Bridge-without. The election in that ward is in the court of aldermen, who choose from among those who have passed the chair. The lord mayor is chosen annually, on the 29th September, in the following manner: the livery, assembled in Guildhall, choose two aldermen, one of which is selected (generally the senior) by the court of aldermen, and he is declared the lord mayor elect. The livery have, however, lately exercised their right of re-electing the same lord mayor, Mr. Alderman Wood, two years in succession. The lord mayor, aldermen who have passed the chair, the recorder, and the common sergeant are judges of oyer and terminer, for the city of London and county of Middlesex. The lord mayor is conservator of the rivers Thames and Medway, and perpetual commissioner in affairs relating to the river Lea. His authority is requisite in all corporation business. The lord mayor elect enters on his office on the 9th November, on which day there is a grand procession of the lord mayor, the lord mayor elect, the aldermen, recorder, and sheriffs, from Guildhall to the Thames; they proceed by barges to Westminster in great state, where the prescribed oaths are taken; a magnificent enter-

E

tainment at Guildhall generally terminates the business
of the day. The sheriffs were formerly selected in various
modes, but now they are chosen yearly by the livery, and
are sheriffs of the city of London, and form, jointly, one
sheriff for the county of Middlesex. The recorder is appointed for life by the lord mayor and aldermen, salary
£2,500. Common halls are to be convened on the requisition of the livery to the lord mayor, who presides at them.
The city, from an early period, possessed peculiar privileges in its military government, but they were materially
altered in the year 1794, by an act of parliament. The
quarter sessions for Middlesex are held in the county hall,
on Clerkenwell-green. The city of London sends four
members to the house of commons.

The city of WESTMINSTER is comprised in the united
parishes of St. John and St. Margaret and their liberties, and
contains seven parishes. Before the reformation Westminster was under the government of the abbot and monks,
but at present the high steward is the principal magistrate;
he is chosen by the dean and chapter. The high bailiff
purchases his place, and holds it for life. The civil
government of Westminster is less popular than that of
the city of London; yet as each inhabitant householder
has the right of voting for two members of parliament,
it has often been the scene of very severe popular struggles.
Southwark is governed by a steward and bailiff, under the
lord mayor of London, and returns two members to
parliament.

The other parts of the METROPOLIS have 27 stipen-
diary magistrates, appointed to superintend the police and
take cognizance of offences in their districts; offices for
them are established in Bow-street, Great Marlborough-
street, Hatton-garden, Worship-street, Shoreditch, Lam-
beth-street, Whitechapel High-street, Shadwell, Queen-
square, and Union-street, Southwark. There is also the
Thames police office, Wapping. Each office has attached
to it a number of police officers; in addition to these
there are constables and watchmen. The city of London
maintains 765 watchmen and 38 patroles; and it is said
that the watchmen, patroles, and constables, every night
on duty in and about the metropolis, amount to more than
3,000, yet depredations are committed to such an extent

as to make it doubtful that something must be wrong in
the system of police. Undoubtedly it will be found difficult to prevent robberies in a town containing such immense
numbers, and so great a variety of characters, yet it is
hoped that means may yet be devised of greatly checking
that enormous extent of plundering, so much and so justly
complained of for many years past.

The POPULATION in 1801 was 900,000, including a
25th part for the shipping; in 1811 it rose to 1,050,000;
and, according to the census taken in 1821, was 570,236
males and 655,458 females, making a total of 1,225,694.
In the year 1700 it was estimated at 674,350. It appears
that from the widening of the streets and the conversion
of the houses into warehouses, &c. the population of the
ancient city has, as might be expected, considerably diminished; three-fifths is the computed extent since the
beginning of the last century.

The PRISONS of LONDON are Newgate, the city and
county jail for felons, and till very lately debtors were also
confined in it; but a large prison was built in Whitecross-
street, much to the credit of the city, for debtors alone,
and where those are now sent who otherwise would have
been obliged to go to Newgate. This building is a large
mass of solid stone, with every appearance of strength and
security for its unfortunate inhabitants; the Session-house,
where the trials take place, is adjoining—Clerkenwell
Prison, Clerkenwell-green—the Borough Compter—the
House of Correction, Coldbath-fields, (here a sort of trial
has been given to a superior mode of managing prisoners,
which is supposed to have failed)—Tothill-fields, Bridewell
—Giltspur-street, Compter, which is very near to Newgate
—King's Bench Prison—Fleet Prison—the Milbank Penitentiary, where a new system of management is now in a
course of trial; and, in addition to these, about as many
more in different parts of the town. A tread-mill has
lately been established in Coldbath-fields Prison, and it
has been attended with the most salutary effects. The
diminution of crime in the metropolis was very considerable
the last year, and, by the prison discipline that is now
generally adopted, it is hoped that it will still decrease.

MARKETS.

A city containing so immense a population must, of course, require an enormous supply of provisions, to facilitate which there are numerous Markets established in various parts; that in Smithfield is the greatest for live cattle, the numbers sold on Mondays and Fridays are immense; Leadenhall and Newgate-markets supply country killed meat, poultry, pigs, eggs, butter, &c. &c. to the whole of the metropolis. Billingsgate was first established and opened on the 10th May, 1693, by virtue of an act of parliament, as a free market, for the sale of fish, six days in a week, with permission to sell mackarel on Sundays, before and after divine service. It is considered the worst supplied market in London, owing principally to the irregularity of the arrivals of the boats which bring up the fish. In Mark-lane is the corn market, this important article is generally sold by sample, the grain often being at the time on board vessels in the river; the Haymarket, Smithfield, Whitechapel, and recently Paddington and Southwark, supply the bulky articles hay and straw. Milk is very regularly distributed; great numbers of cows are kept in the vicinity of the metropolis for furnishing a supply of this beverage; one person alone, in the neighbourhood of Islington, generally keeps a thousand cows for this purpose. Fruits and vegetables are vended in many of the markets; but the quantities to be seen at Covent-garden and Spitalfields markets, early in the mornings of the summer market-days, are astonishingly great. The distilleries in the vicinity, and the numerous porter breweries in London, keep up a copious supply of their respective articles. Coal is the only fuel used; it pays a small duty; numerous vessels are employed in conveying it from Newcastle: there is a market for it in Thames-street, resorted to principally by the great dealers.

That important article WATER is now well supplied; for a long time the New River and the London-bridge water-works were the only sources; these latter are now given up, and the interest in them is joined to the new river company. At present there are, in addition, the East London water-works, the West Middlesex water-works, the South London and the Kent water-works, all these contribute materially to the health, cleanliness, and comforts of the town.

For rapid and certain means of communication the two-penny post is of singular utility; and should business or pleasure require personal attendance hackney coaches ply in the streets at all hours: the fares are fixed, and various precautions taken to prevent extortion. Coaches are hourly passing to and returning from the towns and villages adjacent, in every direction. Steam vessels depart at stated periods, proceeding both up and down the river. Great attention is paid to the cleansing of the streets; and the new mode of lighting with gas makes it less disagreeable to pass through them at night. In short, human ingenuity seems to be ever on the alert to devise superior modes of contributing to the public accommodation; and it may be truly said that London combines a greater number of conveniences than any other city in the world. To all these we may add the liberality and superior intelligence of the inhabitants, and we shall then cease to feel surprised that it is considered so desirable a place of residence.

RECENT IMPROVEMENTS.

Numerous alterations and improvements have been recently made in the streets and buildings of the metropolis; the entrances to the bridges have opened new lines; the interruption of the great northern line at Snow-hill has been removed by the formation of Skinner-street, and great improvements have been made near Temple-bar. A new road has been very recently formed from Bishopsgate-street through Hoxton and Holloway, which is shorter by a mile, for mails and coaches going to the north, than the old way by the city-road. Another fine road, two miles in length, from Vauxhall-bridge to Camberwell-green, is just completed; it is lighted with lamps the whole way, and forms one of the most handsome roads about the metropolis. A new road has also been opened from Southwark-bridge to the turnpike at Newington-causeway, which is of great utility, as it shortens the distance above half a mile, and renders it unnecessary to pass through the borough.

In no other part of London has improvement proceeded at so rapid a rate, within a few years, as in the line between Carlton-palace and the Regent's-park. St. Alban's-street, which formerly faced the palace, with the houses which intervened between the north end of that street and Piccadilly, have been taken down, and a magnificent street formed, equal in width to Pall-mall; it crosses Piccadilly, and is terminated by a beautiful structure called the County Fire-office. To the left is a most superb colonade named the Quadrant. To the north, and at the end of this noble crescent, on the site of the ancient Swallow-street, is another beautiful street extending to Oxford-street, where is an elegant circus of the most fashionable and brilliant shops ; it then passes on to and unites itself with Portland-place. Throughout this line the tiers of houses, all cased with a durable composition which resembles fine white stone, are in various styles of architecture, blending variety with regularity and simplicity with ornament, and, upon the whole, present a magnificence not to be surpassed in the world. Adjoining Jermyn-street is opened at each end ; and Charles-street now leads into the Haymarket, where the new Theatre forms a handsome terminating object. Suffolk-street and the north side of Cockspur-street have been taken down, and splendid quadrangles of new buildings are in a course of erection, which will form a street, continuing the line of Pall-mall, called Pall-mall east, and will finish by throwing open that splendid portico of St. Martin's church. The King's mews will be taken down as soon as the building which is now erecting is finished behind Buckingham-house. The whole of these improvements are under the immediate patronage of his Majesty, and they reflect the highest credit on his taste. A very attractive alteration has been lately made in Piccadilly, called BURLINGTON ARCADE, which consists of a long enclosed promenade, forming a communication between Piccadilly and Burlington gardens : it is fitted up on each side with a great number of fashionable shops in elegant variety. The light is admitted through sky-lights, which reach over the whole length of this novel building. The entrance at each end is very handsome, and a porter in livery stands at each gate throughout the day, to keep out improper persons. The brilliancy of the shops and the great number of elegantly dressed people who are constantly walking in this arcade, have made it one of the most fashionable lounges in the metropolis. Connected with this pleasing resort is the Western-Exchange, the principal entrance of which is in Bond-street. It is a grand depot of fashion and warehouse for luxurious and expensive articles. There are also other similar places at the west end of the town called bazaars, the most extensive and elegant of which is in Soho square : it contains an almost endless variety of ornamental and useful articles displayed in the most tasteful style that fancy can suggest. The ground floor of this bazaar is a very large space, and when filled with visitors, as it generally is before dinner, it presents a scene of brilliancy that is not to be equalled in London. A row of eight very elegant houses is erected in Privy gardens, nearly opposite the Treasury, the fronts facing Charing-cross; each house is a mansion of itself, and the whole are highly ornamental to that fashionable part of the town. In all parts of the town improvements and additions are proceeding with as much spirit as at any former period; warranting a belief that, in a few years, the British metropolis will exceed all others in its various embellishments as much as it surpasses in opulence, extent, and population.

The Villages in the vicinity of London, which form a cordon around it, extending to a distance of five or ten miles, have increased in size with the metropolis itself, and are many of them now in reality populous towns, inhabited by great numbers who almost daily visit town in their carriages. The country also abounds in fine buildings, with surrounding embellishments, where the native beauty of the scenery is heightened by art, under the direction of that superior taste which England is acknowledged to possess in gardening and pleasure grounds; indeed in whatever direction London is approached, numerous elegant villas and tasteful erections, with appropriate de-

corations, announce to the traveller that he is in the vicinity of the metropolis.　Near the great roads to Ports-
mouth and Dover, as well as to the great northern and
western roads, the country, for many miles from the town
is studded with splendid mansions and parks, that give an
exalted idea of the opulence of the possessors.　The valley
of the Thames, for soft scenic beauty, is justly considered
unequalled in the world; every bend of the river opens to
the view new charms; but Richmond-hill, the celebrated
Richmond-hill, combines in its prospect every thing in-
cluded in the term beautiful—it is the admiration of all who
view it.　This district may be truly called classic ground;
it was long the favourite seat of genius.　Here Thompson
wrote his "Seasons," and Pope's residence at Twickenham
is yet visited with lively interest.　Proceeding up the
river we arrive at the palace of Hampton-court, presented
by Cardinal Wolsey to Henry VIII. and long the residence
of royalty; the interior has much to gratify the most refined taste, among which may be named the celebrated
cartoons of Raphael ; here is also the great vine, said to
surpass all others in Europe.

At the distance of 21 miles from London stands WIND-
SOR CASTLE, the favourite residence of our late monarch ; to the situation of this extensive range of buildings
it is impossible to do justice.　From the noble terrace,
faced with free stone, the ground rises with a gentle slope,
and on the top of the hill stands the castle; the whole has
the most commanding and beautiful views.　From one
part the eye can distinguish twelve different counties.
William I. selected the situation and built the castle.　The
state appartments of this noble palace that were occupied
by his late Majesty, are now fitted up in the most splendid
style for his present Majesty, where he occasionally
resides.

Among other beautiful places in this direction are Oat-
lands, Claremont House, once the residence of the
late lamented Princess Charlotte, and Kew-palace and
gardens, the residence of her late Majesty Queen Charlotte; these contain numerous works of art of the most
exquisite kind; in short, in this earthly paradise nature
has lavished her beauties in the most profuse abundance,
and opulence and taste have laboured for centuries to ac-

cumulate the finest productions of human genius. After the river passes London, though its banks are not embellished equal to those above, yet Greenwich, Blackheath, and Shooter's-hill, offer fine and extensive views; the Thames, now of more Majestic breadth, rolling beneath, while the county of Essex is seen stretched out beyond it. Wimbleton, with its fine park, and even the neighbourhood of Hampstead and Highgate, in other parts, would be esteemed beautiful situations, but here they are all eclipsed by the superior beauties of the immediate valley of the river.

With all its attractions London is, in a considerabe degree, forsaken in the autumn of the year, when the noble and the opulent seek the retirement of the country, or the more fashionably attended bathing places on the sea coast. At such times the town is said to be empty, although a stranger, would be surprized at hearing it so characterized, when he witnesses its still thronged streets, and crowded public places. But with winter returns all its gaiety and fashion, and by the time of the meeting of parliament, which generally takes place in the beginning of Feb. it is said to be full. London is then in its most brilliant state; those who provide decorations, whether for houses or persons, are all in requisition; numerous balls, routs, assemblies, &c. put in motion the whole fashionable world; rich equipages dash along the streets, or crowd to the scene of attraction for the night. The theatres are filled, and at the termination of the performances a scene nightly occurs that baffles all description, the streets blocked up with numerous carriages, all wanted at the same moment; the struggles of the drivers to disentangle themselves; the bawling for particular carriages by link boys, with flaming torches in their hands, the eager running of servants with their showy liveries, all intermixed with ladies and gentlemen in their gayest dresses, anxiously seeking their carriages amidst the confusion, while the centinels, stationed at the theatre doors, view it all with silent apathy; the noise of voices shouting, whips cracking, and coachmen swearing; the chaotic mixture of the dirty link boy, the livered lackey, and the starred noble, with splended jewels, waving plumes, and glittering bayonets, all form a scene that must be witnessed to be conceived.

At this period London is more particularly the grand arena upon which talent is exhibited, whether we look at the political struggles in St. Stephen's, or the emulative display of rival fashionables. A morning's drive shows off at once the tasteful equipage and the driver's skill; and lectures and exhibitions put forth their most attractive powers. The nightly efforts of political orators are furnished by those active purveyors to public gratification the newspapers; at the breakfast table, on the following morning, the same vehicles gratify vanity by accounts of splendid entertainments past, and announce others to come. The regular arrival of fresh fashionables is announced to join the gay throng. London is indeed a world within itself, and has a character perfectly distinct from all other places. An immense mass of talent and genius is retained, by its rewards or its homage, to labour for its gratifiacation. The poet, the dramatist, the essayist, and the novelist, furnish a succession of mental treats; the traveller toils, and the philosopher studies, and London receives the earliest tribute of their labours. In short, here are found assembled the statesman and the philosopher, as well as the votary of fashion and dissipation; the artist and the amateur; the man of genius and the man of pleasure, all crowd to London as to the centre of attraction; where all that administers to intellectual gratification, refined taste, and elegant fancy, is to be found in the highest state of perfection; so that the internal life and gaiety of London, its intelligence, refinement, and splendour, correspond with its magnitude and importance, and place it above all other of the most celebrated cities of the world.

AN
ALPHABETICAL LIST
OF THE
STREETS, LANES,
PASSAGES,
Public Buildings and Bankers
IN THE METROPOLIS,
WITH REFERENCE TO THEIR SITUATION.

Note.—The figures prefixed to each Street, &c. refer to the same number of Division on the Plan, which the Publishers flatter themselves will be found of the greatest utility

Explanation of Abbreviations generally made use of through the List of Streets.

Al. alley	grt. great	O. Old	ter. terrace
bds. buildings	gt. gate	op. opposite	tn. town
bk back	h. or hl. hill	pas. passage	up. upper
bnk. bank	Hbn. Holborn	pl. place	Tot.ct. rd. Tottenham court road
Boro. Borough	l. or la. lane	r. row	ham court road
Ch. cr. Charing-cross	Lbth. Lambeth	rd. road	Vxhl. Vauxhall
cr. cross	lit. little	s. or sd. side	w. or wy. way
ct. court	lo. or low. lower	S. South	wh. wharf
E. East	mkt. market	sq. square	W. West
fds. fields	ms. mews	st. street	Westm Westminster
gdn. garden	Mdlx. Middlesex	Strd. Strand [wark]	yd. yard
gr. green	N. New or North	Swk. or Sthwk. South	

And many others which may be easily understood, as
Bfrs. Blackfriars--Blsby. Bloomsbury- Chps. Cheapside--Pic. Piccadilly--Rotherh. Rotherhithe--Tpl. b. Temple bar.

A

Ref. to Plan.
27..ABBEY place, end of Mary's-row, Bethnal-green-road
22..Abbey pl, 53, Great Coram st
22..Abbey rw, from Abbey pl, to White st
15..Abbey-st, near Bermondsey-sq
27..Abbey -st, 92, Bethnal-green-road
3..Abchurch ct, Gracechurch st
3..Abchurch-la, 68, Cannon-st
3..Abchurch-yard, 67, Cannon st
13..Abel's-bds, 94, Rosemary-lane
13..Abel's-ct, Rosemary-lane
35..Abingdon-bds 16 Abingdon-stWestms
24..Abingdon-pl, east side Abingdon-row

Ref. to Plan.
24..Abingdon-row, south end of Charles-st, Goswell-street-road
35..Abingdon-st,5, old Palace yd,Westm
35..Abingdon-st, (lit.) 10, Abingdon-st, Westminster
27..Abingdon-st, nr BelvedereBethnal-gr
45..Aboukir pl, Pleasant pl, Stepney gr
7..Academy-ct, 93, Chancery-lane
11..Acorn-ct, Bishopsgate-st, without
7..Acorn-st, 117, Roll's-bds, Fetter-lane
11..Acorn-st, 127 Bishopsgate-st, with
39..Acorn-st, Battlebridge
60..Acorn-yd, Trinity-st, Rother' c
32..Acton-pl, York-st, Walwo
2..Adam's-ct, 12, Broad-st

F.

Ref. to Plan.

12..Adam's-ct, Sharp's-bds, Duke's-pl
38..Adams'-mews, 21, Portman-square
52..Adams'-mews, South Audley-st,
    left of Grosvenor square
16..Adams'-pl, 187, High-st, Borough
70..Adams'-r, nrHenryst, Hampstead rd
33..Adam-st & mews, Edgeware-rd
46..Adam-st & place, Rotherhithe
46..Adam-st,from 93 Neptune-st,Rothrh
20..Adam-st, 72, Adelphi, Strand
53..Adam-st, 37, Manchester-sq
53..Adam-st, 8, Portman-sq
35..Adam-yd, Gt.Peter-st,Westminster
15..Adam & Eve-alley, Bermondsey-st
37..Adam & Eve-ct, 67, Oxford-st
13..Adam & Eve-ct, 106, Whitecross st,
    St. Luke's
38..Adam & Eve-ct, Tottenham-ct-rd
8..Adam & Eve-ct, West Smithfield
29..Adam & Eve-yd, Ratcliffe-highway
35..Addison's-yd, Peter-st, Westminstr
5..Addle-hill, 134, Upper Thames-st
2..Addle-st, 44, Wood-st, Cheapside
20..Adelphi, 72, Strand
20..Adelphi-terrace,Adelphi, 140, Strand
20..Adelphi-wharf, under Adelphi-ter.
12..Aggett's passage, Still-al,Houndsdh
13..Agnes-ct, Little George-st,Minories
26..Agnes-ct, Clare-fields, Hoxton
36..Air-st. 154, Piccadilly
23..Air-st-hill, Leather lane, Holborn
35..Akersty-yd, Gt. St. Ann-st, Limeh
13..Alarm-yard, Crutched-friars
36..Albany, 52, Piccadilly
48..Albany New rd, from the Wesleyan-
    chapel, Camberwell, to the Kent-rd
48..Albany-place, East-lane, Walworth
36..Albemarle-st & Mews,63, Piccadilly
24..Albemarle-st.83,St.John-st,Smithfd
1..Albion-bds, 150, Aldersgate street,
    Bartholomew-close
5..Albion-place & st, south, foot of
    bridge, Blackfriars road
48..Albion-place, 1, Smith's pl, East la,
    Walworth-common [St.George'sE
29..Albion-place, Lower Chapman-st,
33..Albion-place, Newington Butts
28..Albion-st, Bethnal-green
46..Albion-st, east of Paradise r, Rotherh
29..Albion ter, Commercial rd, a little
    west of Limehouse Church, Whcpl
35..Aloock's-rents, Bermondsey st
12..Alderman's-walk, 201 Bishopsgate-st
14..AldermanParson's-strs St.Catharines
2..Aldermanbury, 77, Lad-lane [wall
2..Aldermanbury-postern, 38, Loudon-
3..Aldermary Church yd, 37, Bow lane
1..Aldersgate-bds, 91, Aldersgate-st
1..Aldersgate-st, St Martin's le grand
    Goswell st
13..Aldgate, east end Leadenhall-st
10..Aldons-ct, Leonard-st, Finsbury sq
26..Alerton-st, near Walbrook place,
    Hoxton New town

Ref. to Plan.

15..Alexander gdns,3 Oak laHorselydwn
7..Alexander-yard, Water-la, Fleet-st
1..Alfred ct, Paul alley, Cripplegate
35..Alfred buildings, Castle la, Westmr
11..Alfred bds, Windmill st, north west
    corner of Finsbury square
38..Alfred mews, 200,Tottenham-ct-road
32..Alfred place, East lane, Walworth
38..Alfred place, Store st, Tot-ct-road,
    near Bedford-square
17..Alfred pl, 18, Gt. Surrey st,Black-
    friars road
17..Alfred pl, London road, opposite the
    Elephant and Castle
24..Alfred place, Goswell-st-road
61..Alfred pl, New road, Isle of Dogs
15..Alfred st, Limehouse wall
60..Alfred st, West India docks
13..Alie st, (Gt. & Lit.) Goodman's fds
35..Alingham st, Horseferry rd, Westm
30..Allard's hill, Rotherhithe wall
24..Allen st, 113, Goswell-st
23..Allen's bds, Bowlinggr la,Clerkenwl
13..Allen's ct, Harrow al, Houndsditch
3..Allen's-ct, Leadenhall-st
37..Allen's ct, nr Wardour st, Oxford-st
13..Allen's-rents, Leadenhall st
35..Allen-st, Vincent sq, Tothill fields
3..Allhallows' ct, 18, Gracechurch st
3..Allhallows' la, 153, Campion lane,
    Upper Thames st
3..Allhallows' stairs, 88, Up. Thames st
35..Almonry, (Gt. & Lit.)Dean st, Wstm
13..Alms alley, Arrow al, Middlesex-st
2..Almshouse yard, Coleman-st
35..Almshouse yard, Little Almonry
68..Alpha road & Cottages, Lissongreen
31..Alscot place, Grange-rd, Bermondsy
53..Alsop's buildings & terrace, near
    Baker st, 44, New rd, Marylebone
53..Alsop's pl,Baker st,New rd,Marylbn
13..Amble ct, Wellclose sq
67..Amelia place, Queen's Elms
5..Amelia row, St. George's place, St.
    George's-fields
33..Amelia row, Walworth
33..Amelia st, on the right, near the
    Elephant, and Castle, Walworth
7..Amen corner, near the end of Ave
    Maria-lane, Paternoster row
4..Amer's ct, near Maid la, Southwark
16..America pl, Great Guildford st
13..America square, 121, Minories
5..America st, Guildford st,Southwark
18..Amphitheatre row, 13, Standgate st,
    Westmr bridge road
29..Amsterdam ct, Upper Shadwell
16..Anchor alley, Mint st, Southwark
4..Anchor alley, Worcester place
30..Anchor&Hope alGreen bk, 120 Wapg
12..Anchor ct, Spitalfields
10..Anchor ct, 100, Old st, St. Luke's
4..Anchor lane, 8, Upper Thames st
10..Anchor st, Old st, St. Luke's

Ref. to Plan,

11..Anchor st, 54, Shoreditch
15..Anchor yd, Bermondsey sq
21..Anchor yd, Clare st, Clare market
35..Anchor yard, York st, Westminster
16..Anderson's alley, on the right from Union st, Southwark
9..Anderson's buildings, opposite the Orphan School, City road
34..Anderson's walk, nr Lambeth butts, Vauxhall walk
1..Angel alley, 40, Aldersgate-st
12..Angel al. Brick lane, Spitalfields
1..Angel alley, Charterhouse sq
4..Angel al Coal harbour 95 up Thames st
11..Angel alley, 133, Bishopsgate-st
2..Angel alley, 70, Coleman-st
3..Angel alley, Fenchurch-st
34..Angel alley, Fore st, Lambeth
1..Angel alley, Golden lane
23..Angel alley, Grays Inn lane
12..Angel alley, Houndsditch
13..Angel alley, Leadenhall-st
2..Angel alley, turn at 61, Fore st Little Moorfields
21..Angel alley, Long acre, near St. Martin's lane
15..Angel alley, Pepper al, Southwark
29..Angel alley, 61, Ratcliffe highway
3..Angel alley, Lower Thames-st
16..Angel al, 82, Redcross st, Southwark
7..Angel alley, Shoe lane, Fleet st
1..Angel alley, Whitecross-st
12..Angel all, 84, Whitechapel, High-st
2..Angel al, Long lane, Moorfields
2..Angel al, 95, Upper Thames-st
29..Angel ct, 235, Back la, Shadwell, St. George's East
20..Angel ct, Charing cr, left, nr the Strnd
3..Angel ct, 8, Friday st
21..Angel ct, Drury lane
4..Angel ct, Church st, Southwark
12..Angel ct, Dorset st, Spitalfields
16..Angel ct, 147, High st, Southwark
1..Angel ct, Angel alley, Aldersgate st
12..Angel ct, Camomile st
8..Angel ct, Charterhouse lane
16..Angel ct, Fowl lane, Borough
36..Angel ct, Great Windmill st
1..Angel ct, 67,.Grub st, Cripplegate
36..Angel ct, 20, King st, St. James's sq
3..Angel ct, 61, Leadenhall st
13..Angel ct, Minories
35..Angel ct, Prince's-st, near Storey's-gate, Westminster
29 Angel ct, Ratcliff highway
8..Angel ct, 24, Skinner-st, Snowhill
13..Angel ct, Stoney lane, nr Gravel-la, Houndsditch
20..Angel ct, 10, 173 & 335, Strand
2..Angel ct, 35, Throgmorton st
29..Angel-gdns, Back la, Shadwell
4..Angel passage, 94, upper Thames-st
18..Angel pl, Angel st, Blackfriars-rd
25..Angel row, next the Angel Inn, High st, Islington

Ref. to Plan.

11..Angel sq and st, 138, Bishopsgate without
18..Angel st, Broadwall, Lambeth
29..Angel st, St George's fields
1..Angel st, 15. St. Martin's le grand
2..Angel st, Moorfields
40..Angel terrace, opposite the Angel Inn, Islington
13..Angel & Sugar loaf yard, Minories
14..Anne alley & ct, East Smithfield
30..Anne's ct, Well st, Wapping
45..Anne's pl, a little on the left from Commercial rd, Limehouse
44..Anne's place, near the Ship, Stepney green
35..Anne's place, Duke st, St. George's
27..Anne's row, Bethnal green road
29..Anne st, New road, St. George's E
12..Anne st, Pelham st, Spitalfields
40..Anne st, 15, Henry-st, Pentonville
27..Anne st, N. W. of Wilmot sq, Bethnal green road
27..Anne st, Bethnal green road
22..Anson's alley, Broad st, Bloomsbury
14..Anson's gains, St.Catherine's,Tower
35..Antelope al, King st, Westminster
29..Anthony st, Lower Chapman st, new road, St. George's E.
32..Apollo bds, middle of East-lane, Walworth
17..Apollo buildings, St. George's fields
7..Apollo ct, 202, Fleet-st
15..Apollo ct Bermondsey-st
15..Appletree ct, 104, Bermondsey st
36..Appletree yd, near the Church, York st, St. James's sq
66..Arabella gardens, Chelsea
51..Arabella row, right of Buckingham gate, Pimlico
29..Arbour ter, Commercial rd, Whtchpl
36..Arcade, (Burlington) Piccadilly
21..Arch road, Lincoln's Inn fields
29..Arch yd,Harrison ct,Brook st Ratcliff
2..Archer's alley, Peter st, Bishopsgate
36..Archer st, 29, Rupert st, near the Haymarket
21..Archer st, Lincoln's Inn fields
12..Archibald ct, Fashion st, Spitalfields
37..Argyle st, 336, Oxford-st
23..Aris Builds,Bowling grn la, Clerkwll
53..Arklow pl, South West corner of Edgeware road
36..Arlington st, 160, Piccadilly
55..Arington st, Camden town
14..Arnold ct, New lane
1..Arnold ct, Barbican
33..Arnold pl, Francis st, Newington Bts
33..Arnold's paragon Francis st Newngtn
1..Arnold yard, Barbican
1..Arthur st, (Gt. & Little) Golden la turn at 10 Goswell st
15..Artichoke alley, Bermondsey st
11..Artichoke al, Holywell st,Shoreditch
3..Artichoke ct, 32, Cannon st
3..Artichoke ct, Walbrook

Ref. to Plan.

1..Artichoke ct, 19, Whitecross st
18..Artichoke ct, near Lambeth marsh
29..Artichoke hill, opposite Princes sq, Ratcliff highway
28..Artichoke lane, near the Fountain Mile end
17..Artichoke la, Newington causeway
29..Artichoke lane, Virginia st, Ratcliff nearly opposite the Haymarket
28..Artichoke row, Mile end road
17..Artichoke yd, Newington causeway behind the Inn
11..Artichoke yard, Shoreditch
1..Artillery ct, 54, Chiswell-st
15..Artillery ct, Fair st, Horselydown
10..Artillery ground, City-road and £3, Chiswell st
12..Artillery ground, Old Stewart st, Spitalfields part of Union st
15..Artillery la, Fair st, Horselydown
35..Artillery pl, Brewer's gr.Tothill fds
10..Artillery place, North corner of Finsbury square
12..Artillery st,.55, Bishopsgate-st
15..Artillery st, Bermondsey
15..Artillery st, Horselydown lane, near the E. end of Tooley st
36..Arundel st, N. end of the Haymarket
6..Arundel st, 189, Strand
24..Ashby ct, (Upper) Goswell st road
24..Ashby st, up & low. Northampton sq
39..Ashby st, Maiden la, Battle bridge
6..Ashentree ct, Temple
11..Ashentree ct, Shoreditch
21..Ashlin's place, Drury lane
39..Ashton square, Somerstown
60..Ashton st, Blackwall by the Dock Gt
10..Aske place & terrace, near Haberdashers Alms Houses, Hoxton
28..Assembly passage, 18, Assembly row Mile end
28..Assembly road, Mile end road
28..Assembly row, Mile end
18..Astley row, Lambeth
18..Asylum buildings, near the Obelisk Westminster rd
18..Asylum place, Westminster-road
1..Audley rents, Whitecross st
52..Audley sq,S.Audley st, Grosvenor sq
53..Audley st, N. & S. Grosvenor sq
31..Augustus row, near the site of the late Spa, Grange-road
2..Austin Friars, 67, Throgmorton st
2..Austin Friars passage, Austin Friars
11..Austin st, first from Shoreditch church
7..Ave Maria lane, 28, Ludgate-hill
51..Avery farm, place & row, Queen st, Pimlico op Ranelagh Walk
51..Avery green, Queen st, Chelsea
51..Avery row, Five fields, Chelsea
37..Avery ro, 3 Grosvenor stNewBond st
3..Axe alley, Leadenhall-st
1..Axe yard, Little Britain
16..Axe yard, Blackman st

Ref. to Plan.

1..Axe yard, south end of Grub-st
35..Axe yard, King st, Westminster
6..Axe yard, Norfolk st, Strand
24..Aylesbury st,103 St.John st,Clerknw
32..Ayliffe buildings, 5 Ayliffe-st
32..Ayliffe st, North of Harper st, New Kent-rd

B

16..Baalzephon st, 139 Long la,Southwk
16..Bab's alley, Mint st, Southwark
36..Babmay's mews, Well st. St.James
26..Bache's row, Charles square,Hoxton
39..Bachelor's place, Battlebridge.
23..Back alley, Back st, Hatton wall
15..Back al, Crown ct,King st,Tooley st
15..Back al, Rose al, Tooley-st
15..Back al, Bridge yard,Tooley st
35..Back al, Bowling al, Westminster
14..Back al, Gt Garden-st. St. Catherine's-lane
15..Back al, Church lane, Tooley-st
12..Back al, Church lane, Whitechapel
4..Back al, 3 Crane lane, Thames st
15..Back al, Church yard al, Tooley st
8..Back al, 22 Cloth fair, West Smithfild
15..Back al, King st, Tooley st
30..Back al, East lane, Bermondsey
1..Back al, St. Martin's le grand
31..Back al, Mill st, Dockhead
1..Back al, Playhouse yd,Whitecross st
18..Back al, Lambeth marsh
16..Back al, 3 Foxes ct, Long lane
30..Back al, East lane, Rotherhithe
34..Back al, Lambeth Butts
13..Back Change, 142 Swallows gardens Rosemary-lane
13..Back Church lane, Whitechapel
7..Back ct, Symond's Inn, Chancery-la
23..Back hill, Leather lane, Holborn
18..Back lane, Lambeth marsh
15..Back lane, 3 Hammer al, Tooley s
30..Back la, Elephant la, Rotherhithe
29..Back lane, Shadwell High st
29..Back lane, St. George's East continuation of the new road
27..Back lane, N of Globe pl, Bethnal gr
1..Back lane, Lit. Bartholomew-close
29..Back side, High-st, Shadwell
15..Back st, nr St.John's ch, Hoselydwn East end of Tooley-st
10..Back st, Old st square
8..Back st, Cloth fa r
34..Back st, Lambeth
19..Back walk, Narrow wall, Lambeth near upper Ground
2..Back yard, Angel al, Lit. Moorfields
30..Back yd, Marygold la, Bermoudsey
1..Back yard, Little Britain
20..Back yard, St. Clement's
9..Back yard, Brick lane, Old-st.
30..Back yard, Rotherhithe wall
60..Back yd,Ropemaker's fields, Limeh
29..Back yd,Shakespear's walk, Shadwl
45..Back yd, Shipwright st, Rotherhithe

Ref. to Plan.

2..Back yard, Short st, Moorfields
15..Back yard, Tooley st
16..Back yard, St. Margaret's hill, Swk
31..Back yard, St. Saviour's, Dockhead
10..Back yard,Stamford buildings,Old st
29..Back yard, Star st, Wapping wall
30..Back yard, Well alley, Wapping
60..Back yard,Three Colt ct, Limehouse
8..Back yard, Turnmill st, Cow cross
23..Back yard, Vine yd, Coldbath fields
12..Back yard, Wentworth st, Spitalfds
13..Back yard, White's yd, Rosemary la
12..Back yd, Woolpack al,Houndsditch
35..Back Cloister yd,Westminster abbey
11..Bacon alley, Shored-tch
15..Bacon ct, Bermondsey st
11..Bacon st, (great & liittle) 140 Brick
　　lane, Shoreditch
11..Bacon st, 160 Club row, Spitalfields
36..Badely ct, Well st, St. James's
8..Badger rents, St. John's square
8..Badger yard, 54 Red Lion st, St.
　　John's square
11..Badger yard, 43 Shoreditch
21..Bagnel's rents,Denmark st,StGiles's
23..Bagnigge marsh, Coldbath fields
23..Bagnigge wells, from opposite Cop-
　　pice row, Coldbath fields
23..Bagnigge wells road, from turnpike
　　opposite Coppice rw, Coldbath fds
8..Bagnio ct, 76 Newgate st
20..Bailey's al, Maiden la, Covent gardn
45..Bailey's ct, Cock hill, Ratcliff
7..Bailey's ct, Bell yard, turn at 204
　　Fleet st, Temple bar
20..Bailey's ct, nr Bedford st, Strand
12..Bailey's ct, Fashion st, Spitalfields
14..Bailey's pl,nr the Mint,LitTower hil
35..Bailey's yd,Broadway, Westminster
29..Bain's hill, Upper Shadwell
21..Bainbridge st, St. Giles's, south end
　　of Tottenham court road
5..Bakehouse ct, Doctors Commons
35..Baker al,Gardiner's la, Westminster
1..Baker's alley, Hart st, Cripplegate
1..Baker's alley, Goswell st
1..Baker's alley, Monkwell st
24..Baker's alley, St. John st
29..Baker's al, 45 Farmer st, Shadwell
12..Baker's alley, Church la,Whitechpl
20..Baker's alley, Strand
15..Baker's al, Stoney la, Boro market
13..Baker's Arms alley, Rosemary lane
2..Baker's buildings, Old Bethlem
62..Baker's Cottages, Park pl, Peckham
2..Bakers ct, Moorfields
11..Baker's ct, Half Moon al, Bishopsgt
11..Baker's ct, Cock la, Spitalfields
53..Baker's ct,92 East st,Manchester sq
12..Baker's ct,Baker's row,Whitechapel
7..Baker's ct, 149 Holborn bars
13..Baker's ct, 105 Rosemary lane
35..Baker's lane, Mill Bank
53..Baker's mews,5Baker st,Portman-sq

Ref. to Plan.

11..Baker's row, Hog la, Norton Falgate
23..Baker's row, Coldbath fie.ds
23..Baker's rw,Coppice rw,Clerkenwell
53..Baker's row, Portman square
12..Baker's row, 94 Whitechapel road
33..Baker's rw, Prospect rw, Walworth
　　High street
53..Baker st, 1 Portman square
53..Baker st, (Upper) Portman square
53..Baker st, North, continuation of
　　the last, New rd, Marylebone
23..Baker st, from op. Union Tavern,
　　end of Bagnigge wells road
20..Baker's yard, Milford lane, Strand
14..Baker's yard, Tower hill
29..Balaam's ct, Shadwell
3..Baldwin's ct, 18 Old Fish st hill
　　Cloak lane
16..Baldwin's ct, White st, Southwark
8..Baldwin's ct, Gray's Inn lane
8..Baldwin's gardens&sq, 77Leather la
8..Baldwin's pl, 48 Baldwin's gardens
15..Baldwin's yd, Stoney la, Tooley st
9..Baldwyn st, 104 Old st, St. Luke's
8..Bale's ct, Cow cross
3..Ball alley, Cannon st
11..Ball alley, Half Moon al, Bishopsgt
26..Ball alley, Kingsland road
3..Ball alley, Lime st
3..Ball alley, 50 Lombard st
2..Ball alley, London wall
11..Ball alley, Long alley, Moorfields
11..Ball alley, Little Cheapside.Moorfds
14..Ball alley, St. Catherine's lane, up-
　　per East Smithfield
3..Ball alley, 5 Sherbourn lane
11..Ball alley, Wheeler st, Spitalfields
3..Ball ct, 58 Cornhill
36..Ball ct, White Horse st, Piccadilly
14..Ball ct, St. Catherine's lane, upper
　　East Smithfield
13..Ball ct, 14 Jewry st
7..Ball ct, Old Bailey
8..Ball ct, 15 Giltspur st
1..Ball yard, Beech lane, Barbican
1..Ball's yd, 127 Golden la, Cripplegt
45..Ball's yd, Brook st, Ratcliff
11..Ballstag yd, Holywell row
9..Baltic ct, Baltic st, St. Luke's
9..Baltic pl, behind 20 Baltic st
9..Baltic st,Golden la,Old st,St.Luke's
21..Banbury ct, Long Acre
7..Bangor ct, 63 Shoe lane
16..Bangor ct, Church st, Blackman st
15..Bangor ct, Vine st, Southwark
3..Bank buildings, op. 102 Cornhill
37..Bank's ct, Knave's acre,Wardour st
4..Bank end, Southwark
4..Bank side,bank of the River, Sthwk
3..Bank st, opposite 14 Cornhill
10..Banner st, 80 Bunhill row
10..Banner sq, middle of Bonhill row
23..Banner's rents, Portpool lane
22..Bannister al, Broad st, Bloomsbury

y

Ref. to Plan.

1..Bannister ct, 67 Golden lane
6..Bannister yd, Water la, Blackfriars
23..Banshaw's rents, Portpool lane
7..Baptist ct, Carey street
1..BaptistHead ct,50WhitecrossstCripg
7..Baptist Chambers, 76 Chancery la
45..Barbadoes terrace, Stepney
12..Barber's al, Brown's la, Spitalfields
16..Barber's Pole al, St. Margaret's hill
1..Barbican,77 Aldersgate st
1..Barbican ct, 69 Barbican
5..Barge House alley, Up. Ground st,
     Blackfriars road
1..Barge House yd, Silver st, Wood st
3..Barge yard, near the Mansion house,
     Bucklersbury
1..Barker's rents, Redcross st
14..Barking alley, Gt Tower st •
14..Barking Church yard, Tower st
37..Barlam's mews,Bruton st,N Bond st
34..Barleymow al, Fore st, Lambeth
13..Barleymow ct,38Red Lion st, Whcpl
11..Barleymow ct, Fleet st, Spitalfields
8..Barleymow pas, 44 Cloth fair and 64
     Long lane, West Smithfield
5..Batlow's bdgs, Blackfriars road
21..Barlow ct, Coal yd, Drury lane
53..Barlow court, (great & little) 110
     High st, Marylebone
36..Barlow's mews,Bruton st,Berkley sq
7..Barnard's lun, 23 Holborn
2..Barnes' al turn at 49Brick la,Sptlfds
12..Barnes' bdgs, Castle la, Whitechpl
28..Barnes' place, Mile End road
13..Barnes' pl,James st,Lambeth marsh
13..Barnes' ter, 27 James st, Lambh st
35..Barnet's yd, Milbank
40..Barnsbury park, left, top of White
     Lion street, Islington
40..Barnsbury pl, near Barnsbury park
54..Barracks, *Horse Guards*, Blue, Re-
     gent's park
67.. Ditto, Knightsbridge
20.. Ditto, Tilt yard, Whitehall
35.. *Foot Guards*—Bird Bage walk
52.. Ditto, Knightsbridge
53.. Ditto, Orchard st, Portman sq
20.. Ditto, King's mews,Charing cross
15..Barrett's ct, Horselydown
37..Barrett's ct, Wigmore st, turn at 162
     Oxford street
45..Barrett's rents, Stepney causeway
17..Barron's bdgs,Webber st,Blackfrs rd
40..Barron st, Pentonville.and 33 White
     Lion st, Islington
26..Barossa terrace, Cambridge heath
1..Bartholomew close, 33 Litt'e Britain
12..Bartholomew ct, Houndsditch
2..Bartholomew ct, Throgmorton st
2..Bartholomew lane, opposite the
     Royal Exchange, near the Bank
26..Bartlett's bdgs, King st, Hoxton
7..Bartlett's buildings, 50 Holborn

Ref. to Plan.

7..Bartlett's pas, 60 Fetter la, Holborn
26..Barton ct, Hare walk, near the sign
     of the Hare, Hoxton
11..Barton rents, Shoreditch
35..Barton st, College st, Westminster
5..Bashaw rents, Love la, Bankside
26..Basing house oppos.te Union st,
     Kingsland road
3..Basing lane, 40 Bread st, Cheapside
2..Basinghall st, 1 Cateaton st
3..Basinghall st, (New) north end of
     Basinghall st, Cateaton st
1..Basket alley, 89 Golden lane
35..Bate's ct, King st, Westminster
29..Bates's st, Ratcliff highway
21..Bateman's bdgs, 127 Soho square
11..Bateman's row, Holywell st, 159
     Shoreditch
26..Bath-buildings, Hare walk, opposite
     the Ironmongers' Alms Houses,
     Kingsland road
23..Bath ct, 16 Coldbath sqnare
37..Bath pl, and row, Tottenham ct rd
23 .Bath row, 6 Coldbath sqnare
24..Bath st, (great & little) Clerkenwell
9..Bath st, Peerless pool, City road,
     turn at 56 Old street
38..Bath st, Hampstead rond
29..Bath st, Sun Tavern fields, Shadwell
16..Bath ter, E. side of Horsemonger
     lane Prison
66..Battersea fields, W. of 9 Elms,Surry
15..Battle bridge, Mill lane, Tooley st
39..Battle bdge,N. end of Gray's Inn la
15..Battle bridge stairs, Mill st, Tooley st
29..Batty's st, back Church la, Whchpl
29..Batty's gardens, back Church lane
20..Bayley's ct,Maiden la, Covent gardn
13..Bayley's ct,69 Cable st, Rosemary la
14..Bayley's pl, Little Tower hill
4..Baynard Castle st, Up. Thames st
23..Bayne's ct, 4 Coldbath square
23..Bayne's row, Coldbath fields, oppo-
     site the House of Correction
23..Beach row, Coldbath fields
35..Beadle's ct, Eagle st, Westminster
36..Beak st, 44 Swallow st
5..Bear alley, Addle hill
2..Bear alley, London wall
7..Bear alley, 28 Fleet market
5..Bear ct, Bear la, Blackfriars road
9..Bear ct, Butchers row,Ratcliff cross
52..Bear ct, Knightsbridge
4..Bear garden, Bank side, Southwark
5..Bear lane, George st, Blackfriars rd
3..Bear quay, 31 Lower Thames st
9..Bear st,13 Castle st, Leicester fields
34..Bear yard, Fore st, Lambeth
36..Bear yard, Silver st, Swallow st
21..Bear yard, Lincoln's Inn fields
21..Bear & Ragged Staff ct, Drury lane
52..Bear & Ragged Staff mews, Park la
1..Bear&Ragged Staff yd,176Whitecr st

Ref. to Plan.

37..Bearbinder lane, Oxford st
3..Bearbinder lane, near Post Office
8..Beauchamp st, Leather la, Holborn
20..Beaufort buildings, 95 Strand
20..Beaufort street, 89 Strand
31..Beaumont bds,BlueAnchor rd,Brmsy
28..Beaumont bdgs,New rd, Whitechpl
53..Beaumont mews, 22 Weymouth st,
　　　Marylebone
38..Beaumont pl,Tottenham court rd
53..Beaumont st, 16 Weymouth street,
　　　Marylebone
60..Beck row,Ropemaker's fields,Limeh
13..Beck's rents, Rosemary lane
32..Beckford's bdgs and row, Walworth
27..Beckford row, Bethnal green rd
20..Bedfordbury, 53 Chandos st,Cov gdn
20..Bedford ct, 64 Chandos st, Cov. gdn
2..Bedford ct, Basinghall st
22..Bedford ct, North st, Red Lion sq
20..Bedford ct, Angel ct, Strand
30..Bedford ct, Rusell st, Rotherhithe
32..Bedford ct, 5 Bedford st, Walworth
38..Bedford nursery, nr Euston square
38..Bedford pas,Charlotte st, Rathbn pl
22..Bedford pl, Russell square
29..Bedford pl, Commercial road
22..Bedford row, Red Lion st, Holborn
21..Bedford sq, Tottenham court rd
22..Bedford st, Red Lion square
32..Bedford st, Brandon st, Walworth
37..Bedford st, 268 Tottenham ct rd
20..Bedford st, 423 Strand
23..Bedford st, 17 Liquorpond st
32..Bedford st, Locksfields
29..Bedford st, Commercial road
1..Beech lane, 13 Beech st
1..Beech st, 64 Barbican
3..Beehive ct, Lit. St. Thomas Apostle
3..Beehive passage, Lime st
14..Beer lane, Tower st
32..Belgrade pl, nr East lane, Walworth
51..Belgrave buildings, Pimlico
51..Belgrave pl, up. & low, Chelsea rd
51..Belgrave st, Pimlico
51..Belgrave terrace, Pimlico
14..Bell alley, St. Catherine's lane
1..Bell alley, 14 Goswell st
2..Bell alley, Moorfields
3..Bell alley, Budge row, Cannon st
2..Bell alley, (Gt.&Lit.) 56 Coleman st
29..Bell alley, Dean st, Ratcliff
3..Bell alley, Fenchurch st
31..Bell alley, Dockhead
1..Bell alley, 4 Golden lane
15..Bell alley, Green alley, Tooley st
6..Bell alley, Great Carter lane
26..Bell alley, Kingsland road
4..Bell alley, Labour in vain hill
30..Bell alley, New stairs, Wapping
2..Bell alley, Old Bethlem
2..Bell alley, Austin friars
1..Bell alley, 14 Goswell st
3..Bell alley, Great Eastcheap
13..Bell alley, Minories

Ref. to Plan.

9..Bell alley, Old st
3..Bell alley, 47 Lombard st
8..Bell alley, Saffron hill
8..Bell alley, Snowhill
8..Bell alley, Turnmill st, Cowcross
14..Bell alley, St. Catherines
7..Bell's bds, Salisbury sq, Fleet st
15..Bell ct, and rents, Bermondsey st
3..Bell ct, Bow lane
5..Bell ct, Great Carter lane
21..Bell ct,175 Drury lane
2..Bell ct, 20 Foster lane, Cheapside
2..Bell ct, 79 Grub st, Moorfields
2..Bell ct, Little Moorfields
11..Bell ct, Long alley, Moorfields
15..Bell ct, 108 Bermondsey st
7..Bell ct, 22 Gray's Inn lane
3..Bell ct, 168 Fenchurch st
14..Bell ct, 26 Mincing lane, Tower st
3..Bell ct, Walbrook
11..Bell ct, 43 Wheeler st, Spitalfields
12..Bell la, Wentworth st, Whitechapel
16..Bell Inn yd, St. Margaret's hill
20..Bell Inn yd, Strand
7..Belle Sauvage yd, 37 Ludgate hill
2..Bell sq, Broker's row, Moorfields
2..Bell sq, 21 Foster la, Cheapside
68..Bell st, Paddington
18..Bell st, Lambeth marsh　　[Ratcliff
15..Bell whf, E. end of Shadwell High st
4..Bell wharf & pas, 78 Up Thames st
15..Bell yd, Bermondsey st
36..Bell yd, 60 Haymarket
2..Bell yd, Coleman street
34..Bell yd, Fore st, Lambeth
7..Bell yd, 204 Fleet st
5..Bell yd, Great Carter lane
13..Bell yd, Rosemary lane
16..Bell yd, St, Margaret's hill, Boro
16..Bell yd, Kent st, Borough
21..Bell yd, Little St. Martin's lane
11..Bell yd, Long alley, Moorfields
4..Bell yd, 13 Old Fish st hill
15..Bell yd, Stoney la, Southwark
15..Bell yd, Bermondsey
36..Bell yd, Vine st, Piccadilly
12..Bell yd, Whitechapel
29..Bell yd, White Horse st, Ratcliff
52..Bell yd, 58 Mount st, Grosvenor sq
37..Bell yd, 108 Oxford st
34..Belmont pl, Vauxhall turnpike
34..Belmont row, Vauxhall turnpike
8..Belt alley, Turnmill st, Clerkenwell
21..Belton st, 96 Long acre
17..Belvedere bdgs, 45 Belvedere pl,
　　　west of the King's Bench
17..Belvedere ct, 9 Belvedere rd, Lambh
17..Belvedere place, 15 Cobourgh pl,
　　　Borough road
27..Belvedere pl, & row, Bethnal green
19..Belvedere pl, Narrow wall, Lambth
1..Bember's rents, 107 Golden lane
44..Bencroft pl, & Almshouses,Mile end
60..Benege st, East India rd, Commrl rd
60..Bengal pl, East India rd, Commrl rd

Ref. to Plan.

32..Bengal st, New Kent road
32..Bengal terrace, New Kent road
8..Benjamin st,Red Lion st, Clerkenwl
33..Bennett's bldgs, nr Kennington lane
29..Bennett's ctCannon st road,St.Geo's
60..Bennett's ct, Limehouse causeway
16..Bennett's ct, 41, White st, Boro
21..Bennett's ct, Drury lane
12..Bennett's ct, Spicer st, Spitalfields
20..Bennett's ct, Strand
5..Bennett's hill, Doctors commons
27..Bennett pl, Pollard st, Bethnal gr rd
5..Bennett pl, Bennett st, Blackfriars rd
17..Bennett's row, Blackfriars road
5..Bennett st, 28, Stamford st,Blkfrs rd
5..Bennett st,83,Up.Ground Blckfrs rd
37..Bennett st,87,Charlotte st,Rathbn pl
38..Bennett st, Fitzroy square
35..Bennett st, Princess st, Westminstr
36..Bennett st, 54, St. James's
35..Bennett's yd, Tufton st, Westmnster
11..Benson's alley, Shoreditch
37..Bentinck mews, 27, Marylebone lane
37..Bentinck st, Cavendish square
37..Bentinck st, 81 Berwick st Soho
34..Bentinck st, West end of the Bridge
     road, Vauxhall
53..Berkeley mews, 74, Up. Berkeley st
36..Berkeley square, 146, New Bond st
34..Berkeley st, near Lambeth church
36..Berkeley st, 76, Piccadilly
53..Berkeley st, (up&low.)7,Portman sq
53..Berkeley st, West, Edgeware road
8..Berkeley st,18,St.John's laWSmthfd
31..Bermondsey bldgs, Bermdsy New rd
31..Bermondsey New road, leading from
     Bermondsey to Bricklayer's Arms
15..Bermondsey sq, south side of Ber-
     mondsey church
15..Bermondsey st, 63, Tooley st
30..Bermondsey wall, from Mill st, Ber-
     mondsey, to West st, Rotherhithe
22..Bernard st, & Mews, Brunswick sq
29..Berner st,Commercial rd,Whitechpl
37..Berner st & Mews, 54, Oxford road
23..Berry ct,Liquorpond st, Grays Inn la
2..Berry ct, Love la,Wood st, Cheapsd
37..Berwick sq, 373, Oxford st
46..Bethel pl,Canal bdgLowDeptford rd
32..Bethel place, Walworth turnpike
12..Bethlem (Old) 18, Bishopsgate
28..Bethnal green, nr Mile end turnpike
12..Bett's al, Anchor st, Spitalfields
29..Betts st, 164, Ratcliff highway
2..Bevis ct, Basinghall st
13..Bevis lane. Duke's place, Aldgate
13..Bevis marks, 30, St. Mary Axe
5..Bicker's pas, Broadwall, Blackfriars
16..Bicknels rents, 76 Kent st, Boro
38..Bidborough st,6,Mabledon plJudd-st
16..Bignold's ct, 77, Kent st, Boro
13..Bill alley, Billiter street
8..Bill alley, Turnmill st, Clerkenwell
3..Billingsgate, 18, Lower Thames st
13..Billiter ct, Billiter st
13..Billiter square, 12, Billiter st

Ref. to Plan.

13..Billiter st, 114, Fenchurch st
15..Bilton al, Freeman's la, Horseleydn
44..Bing st, op.Saville pl, Mile end rd
15..Bintou place, New st, Dockhead
3..Birchin lane, 62, Lombard st
12..Birds alley. Fashion st, Spitalfields
2..Birds ct, 22,Philip la, Aldermanbury
17..Bird st, West square, Lambeth
30..Bird st, N. side Wapping church
53..Bird st, 168, Oxford street
10..Birdcage al, Anchor st, Old st
16..Birdcage al, 172, High st, Boro
35..Birdcage walk, St. James's park,
     South side of Buckingham gate
27..Birdcage wk,Nag's head,Hackney rd
12..Birdcatcher al, Whitechapel
2..Bird in hand ct, 76, Cheapside
21..Bird in hand ct, 18, Long acre
24..Bishop's ct, 12, Aylesbury st
7..Bishop's ct, Brook st, Holborn
7..Bishop's ct, 78, Chancery lane
20..Bishop's ct, Durham yd, Strand
2..Bishop's ct, 6, Coleman st
2..Bishop's ct, Fore st, Cripplegate
7..Bishop's ct, 3, Old Bailey
2..Bishop's ct, Lothbury
34..Bishop's ct, Old st walk, Lambeth
11..Bishop's ct, King's head ct, Long al.
     Moorfields
9..Bishop's ct, 38, Old street
7..Bishop's head ct, 117Gray's Inn lane
34..Bishop's walk, 9 Stangate st,Lambth
53..Bishop's yd, S.E. corner Grosvnr sq
12..Bishopsgate church yd, Bishopsgt st
2..Bishopsgate st, within, 61, Cornhill
11..Bishopsgate st,wtht,103,NortonFalgt
16..Bist's gardens, Mint, Southwark
8..Bitt alley, 59, Turnmill st, Cowcross
8..Black alley, Turnmill street
14..Black al, Gt Garden la,St.Catharines
14..Black & White alley, Tower hill
12..Black Bell al,Middlesex st,Whitech
11..Black Bird al,St.John's st,Bethnal gr
8..Black Boy alley, Chick lane
15..Black Boy alley, Bermondsey
5..Black Boy alley, St. Peter's hill
13..Black Boy alley, Rosemary lane
13..Black Boy alley, Minories
16..Black Boy al'ey, Blackman st, Boro
34..Black Boy alley, Fore st, near the
     Church on the left, Lambeth
21..Black Boy court, Long acre
60..Black Boy la, Poplar, op.theHarrow
12..Black Bull al,Middlesex st,Whitech
35..Black Dog al, College st, Westmnstr
11..Black Dog yard, Shoreditch
12..Black Eagle st, op. 65, Brick lane
     Spitalfields
15..Blackfields, Horselydown
7..Blackfriars, Ludgate hill
6..Blackfriars bridge, end of New
     Bridge st, Blackfriars
5..Blackfriars rd, from Albion pl, foot
     of Bridge to the Obelisk
1..Black Horse alley, Barbican
7..Black Horse ct, 109, Fleet st

Ref. to Plan.

1..Black Horse ct, Aldersgate st
3..Black Horse ct, Old Change
10..Black Horse ct, Windmill st, Finsbry
13..Black Horse ct, Minories
16..Black Horse ct, White st, Borongh
11..Black Horse yd, Curtain road
12..Black Horse yd, 35 Aldgate
7..Black Horse yd, 52 Gray's Inn lane
1..Black Horse yd, 116 Goswell st
2..Black Horse yd, Fell st, Cheapside
7..Black Horse yd, Union buildings, Leather lane
13..Black Horse yard, Middlesex st
16..Black Horse yd, 174 Kent st, Boro
1..Black Horse yd, 30 Little Britain
37..Black Horse yd, Rathbone place
21..Black Horse yd, Tottenham ct rd
14..Black Horse yd, Tower hill
12..Black Horse yd, 88 Whitechapel
33..Black Prince row, 12 Staverton row Walworth
32..Black Prince pl, Walworth
3..Black Raven al, Leadenhall st
4..Black Raven alley, from 104 to Old Swan Stairs, Upper Thames st
3..Black Raven ct, 30 Leadenhall st
14..Black Raven ct, Seething lane
15..Black Raven ct, St. Olaves, Southwk
7..Black Raven passage, Fetter lane
8..Black Spread Eagle al, Turnmll st
16..Black Spread Eagle al, Blackman st
12..Black Swan al, Brown's la, Spitalfds
4..Black Swan al, 20 St.PaulsChurch yd
2..Black Swan al, lit. E. of Coleman st
16..Black Swan al, 34 St. Margaret's hill
14..Black Swan al, 61 Gt. Tower st
11..Black Swan al, Holywell st, Shdtch
15..Black Swan ct, Maze, Southwark
3..Black Swan ct, Cannon st, City
1..Black Swan ct, 58 Golden lane [hill
14..Black Swan ct,61,GtTower st,Tower
11..Black Swan ct, Shoreditch
12..Black Swan yd, Brown's la, Spitalfds
60..Black Swan yd, Ropemakers la Limb
15..Black Swan yd, 73 Bermondsey st
23..Blackburn ct, Portpool lane
37..Blackburn mews, 53 Upper Brook st Grosvenor sq
66..Blackland's lane, continuation of Blackland's to Brompton
66..Blackland's sq & ter, nr Sloane sq
66..Blackland's place, op. Symond's st, Chelsea common
30..Blackman's al, Rotherhithe wall
35..Blackman's ct, Gt. Peter st, Westmr
16..Blackman st, 156 High st, Boro
21..Blackmoor st, 100 Drury lane
60..Blackwall, near Limehouse
2..Blackwell hall ct, London wall
11..Blackwood al, Fleet st, Spitalfields
16..Black yd, end of Kent st, Borough
11..Blake's alley, Holywell la.Shoreditch
11..Blake ct, Catherine la, Shoreditch
29..Blake's ct 150 Old Gravel lane
40..Blakeney's head ct, 23 High st, Islington

Ref. to Plan.

1..Bland's bds, Frenchal, 21 Goswell st
21..Bland's ct, Great Wild st, Drury la
45..Bland's ct, Narrow st, Limehouse
13..Bland's yard, Minories
36..Blandford ct, Pall mall
36..Blandford place, 83 Pall mall
53..Blandford st, 14 Baker st, Portman sq
8..Bleeding heartyd,Charles st,Hatton g
37..Blenheim steps, Oxford st
37..Blenheim st, 351 Oxford st
7..Blewitt's buildings, 55 Fetter lane
8..B ind Beggar al, Cow cross st
11..Blinkford's buildings, King John court, Shoreditch
11..Block's ct, Phœnix st, near the end of Wheeler st, Spitalfields
35..Blood's ground, Marsham st, Westm
51..Bloody bridge, King's road, Chelsea
22..Bloomsbury ct, Bloomsbury market
22..Bloomsbury Market, Bloomsbury sq
22..Bloomsbury place, N. E. corner of Boomsbury square
22..Bloomsbury sq, 126 N. side, Holborn
22..Blossom ct & st, Whitelion st, Spitfd
10..Blue Anchor alley, 109 Bunhill row
45..Blue Anchor al,106, Brook st,Ratcliff
13..Blue Anchor al, Middlesex st
14..Blue Anchor al, St. Catherine's la
13..Blue Anchor al, Minories
9..Blue Anchor al, Old st
35..Blue Anchor al, York st, Westmr
15..Blue Anchor al, Tooley st
1..Blue Anchor al, Whitecross st
2..Blue Anchor ct, Coleman st
4..Blue Anchor ct, Maid la, Southwark
35..Blue Anchor ct, Gt Peter st, Westmr
31..Blue Anchor la, from the West end of Jamaica row, Bermondsey
31..Blue Anchor lane, Rotherhithe
2..Blue Anchor lane, London wall
35..Blue Anchor la, York st, Wesmr
34..Blue Anchor road, near Bricklayer's Arms Kent road
35..Blue Anchor yd, York st, Westmr
13..Blue Anchor yd, 48 Rosemary lane
16..Blue Ball al, Mint, Southwark
8..Blue Ball al, Saffron hill
16..Blue Ball ct, Lant st, Boro
38..Blue Ball ct, near Chenies st
3..Blue Ball ct, Cannon st
21..Blue Ball ct, Drury lane
37..Blue Ball ct, 62 Tottenham ct rd
21..Blue Ball ct, Hart st, Covent garden
7..Blue Ball ct, Salisbury sq, Fleet st
2..Blue Ball yard, Fell st, Wood st
36..Blue Ball yd, 62 St. James's st, Picdly
16..Blue Beard al, St. Margaret's hill
35..Blue Bell yd, York st Westminster
3..Blue Boar ct, Cannon st
37..Blue Boar ct, 61 Tottenham ct rd
13..Blue Boar ct, Middlesex st, Whitech
2..Blue Boar ct, Friday st, turn at 36 Cheapside
21..Blue Boar yd, 75 High Holborn
12..Blue Boar Inn yard, Whitechapel
8..Blue Coat bldings, 67 Butcher hall la

Ref. to Plan.
8..Blue Coat School, Newgate st
20..Blue Cross st, 7. St. Martin's lane
29..Bluegatefields, 95, Ratcliff highway
2..Blue Hart ct, Coleman st
60..Blue last ct, 31, Three colt st,Limeh
1..Blue Lion ct, Aldersgate st
22..Blunderbuss ct, Kingsgt st, Holborn
16..Blunderbuss ct, 298, Kent st, Boro
3..Blunderbuss ct, St. Thomas Apostle
11..Blunderbuss ct, Shoreditch church
26..Blyth's buildings, Hoxton
13..Boarded entry, Crutched friars
2..Boarded entry, London wall
20..Boarded entry, Snrry st, Strand
29..Boarded entry, 16,N Gravel la,Wapn
16..Boards buildings, 84, Kent st, Boro
12..Boar's Head alley, Whitechapel
16..Boar's Head alley, White st
15..Boar's Head ct,nrSt.Thomas's,Boro
7..Boar's Head ct, 66, Fleet market
3..Boar's Head ct, 80, Leadenhall mrkt
20..Boar's Head ct, St. Clement's lane
8..Boar's Head ct, 76, West Smithfield
16..Boar's Head pl, 25, Boro, High st
29..Bock's alley, Wapping wall
2..Bodd's ct, Philip lane, London wall
5..Boddy's brdg,60 Up.Ground st,Bkfrs
3..Boddington ct, Cloak lane,Cannon st
32..Bollingbroke row, Walworth
37..Bolsover street, 113, Oxford st
53..Bolston st, Park road, Marylebone
7..Bolt court, 152, Fleet street
20..Bolt in Tun alley, Strand
12..Bolt in Tun alley, Whitechapel
7..Bolt in Tun court, Fleet street
36..Bolton row, Bolton street
35..Bolton st, 179, Piccadilly
36..Bolton yard, 10, Bolton row
3..Bond court, Walbrook
35..Bond's ct,facing Rochester st,Westm
15..Bond's rents, Marygold st,Bermndsy
17..Bond st, 1 Grosvenor pl, Boro road
37..Bond st, (new) 307, Oxford st
36..Bond st, (old) 57, Piccadilly
27..Bond st, Hackney road
19..Bond st, 22, John st, Cornwall road
7..Bond's stables. 118, Fetter la,Fleet s
68..Bone's place, Harrow road
43..Bonner street, Bethnal green
43..Bonner's fields, Bethnal green
29..Book's alley, Wapping wall
1..Book's rents, Garter ct, 36, Barbican
3..Booker's gardens, 93, Leadenhall st
3..Boot alley, Abchurch lane
3..Boot alley, Nicholas lane
16..Boot alley, Kent street
5..Boot alley, Upper Ground st, Blkfrs
9..Boot st, Crown st, Old st road
26..Boot st, Hoxton market
12..Boot st, Brick lane, Whitechapel
12..Booth st, 50, Brick lane, Whitechapel
30..Booth yard, Wapping
37..Booth's ct,39, Wells st, Oxford st
4..Borough of Southwark, Surry side
    of London bridge

Ref. to Plan.
2..Boreman's blds, Bartholomew lane
16..Borough market, 276 High st, Boro
17..Borough road, from the Obelisk to
    the Stone's end, Borough
15..Borwick place, Fort pl, Bermondsey
38..Bosler's court, Tottenham ct road
4..Boss al, nr Trig wharf,97,Thames st
15..Boss al, 7,Gainsford st,Horselydown
15..Boss alley, Shad Thames
5..Boss ct, Peter's hill, 214, Upper
    Thames street
29..Bostock st, 156, Old Gravel lane, St
    George's East
7..Boswell ct, 18,Carey st, Chancery la
12..Boswell ct, Devonshire st,Bishopsgt
22..Boswell ct, nr North st, Redlion sq
66..Botanic gardens, op. 31, Paradise
    row, Chelsea
3..Botolph alley, Botolph lane
3..Botolph lane, Lower Thames st
3..Botolph wharf,91, Lower Thames st
2..Bottle alley, 183, near Old Bethlem
8..Bottle of Hay yard, 120, St. John st
27..Botwright's buildings, Hackney rd,
    opposite Middlesex hospital
11..Bough ct, behind 236, Shoreditch
17..Boundary road, Blackfriars road
36..Bourdon st, Davies st, Berkely sq
68..Bouverie gardens, Uxbridge road
7..Bouverie st, 63, Fleet street
3..Bow church yard, 54, Cheapside
59..Bow common, near Bow, Middlesex
60..Bow lane, Poplar
3..Bow lane, 58, Cheapside
59..Bow rd, & bridge, Bow, Middlesex
21..Bow st, 63, LongAcre,Covent garden
35..Bow st, near Westminster abbey
22..Bow st, 169, Bloomsbury
21..Bow st, Sutton st, Soho
21..Bow yard, 37, Broad st, St. Giles's
31..Bowl alley, St. Saviours dock
11..Bowl court, Shoreditch
21..Bowl yd, Brownlow st, Drury lane
1..Bowling al, 21,Whitecross st, Cripgt
4..Bowling alley, Thames st
15..Bowling alley, Tooley st
16..Bowling green, 49, King st, Boro
68..Bowling green, Lisson green
23..Bowling green la, 44, Coppice row,
    Clerkenwell
53..Bowling green lane, 27, High street,
    Marylebone
26..Bowling green row, Haberdasher's
    walk, Hoxton
7..Bowling pin alley, Bream's buildings
35..Bowling st, Dean's yd, Westminster
8..Bowling st, 10, Turnmill st,Clerknw
1..Bowman's buildings,140, Aldersgt st
7..Bowman's ct, Salisbury square
35..Bowman's ct, Gardiner's la, Westm
29..Bowyer's buildings, St. George's E
30..Bowyer's yard, Wapping st
29..Boxford ct, Wapping wall
7..Boxwood court, New st square
7..Boy court, 35, Ludgate hill

Ref. to Plan.

51..Boyd's walk, Avery.place, 5 Fields Chelsea
36..Boyle-st, Saville-row, Piccadilly
3..Brabant ct, Philpot-la, Fenchurch st
1..Brackley st, 8, Golden-la, Barbican
3..Bradley alley, Queen st, Cheapside
23..Bradshaw's rents, 42, Portpool lane
51..Bramah's lane, Chelsea road
45..Bran's ct, Narrow-st, Limehouse
11..Branch bds, 52, Tabernacle walk
13..Branch pl, 72, Cable-st, Rosemary la
26..Branch pl, Hoxton
45..Brand's ct, Narrow st, Limehouse
17..Brandon's row 67, Newington-causw
31..Brandon st, Bermondsey new road
37..Branstone st, [upper] 8, Oxford st
16..Brants ct, 183, High st, Boro
24..Brayne's row, Coppice row, Clerknw
13..Bray's rents, Rosemary lane
40..Bray st, 8, Lower road, Islington
15..Braze bridge, St. Olave st
7..Braziers buildings, 31, Fleet market
3..Bread st, 46, Cheapside
4..Bread st alley, Bread st hill
4..Bread st hill, 201, Upper Thames-st
7..Bream's bds, 31, Chancery lane
29..Breezer's hill, 60, lower E. Smith-field, Ratcliff highway
27..Brenan's pl, Gibraltar wk, Bethnal gr
11..Brett's bds, Long al, Moorfields
12..Brett's bds, Osborne st, Whitechapl
7..Brewer's alley, Shoe lane
20..Brewer's court, 34, Chandos st, Bedfordbury
2..Brewer's court, Basinghall st
37..Brewer's court, Oxford street
1..Brewer's court, 72, Golden lane
15..Brewer's ct, St. Thomas's st, Boro
15..Brewer's ct, near Bermondsey st
35..Brewer's green, Tothillfields
29..Brewer's la, Old Gravel la, Wappng
4..Brewer's lane, 83, Upper Thames st
12..Brewer's rents, Whitechapel
35..Brewer's row, Palmer's village, Tothill fields
39..Brewer st, near the Brill, Pancras
22..Brewer st, Museum st, Bloomsbury
51..Brewer st, Pimlico
36..Brewer st, Golden square
29..Brewer's st, 75, High st, Shadwell
8..Brewer's yard, Cow cross
8..Brewer's yd, 34, Long lane, W Smithfd
30..Brewhouse lane, 144, Wapping
7..Brewhouse yd, 33, Shoe la, Holborn
51..Brewhouse yd, Brewer-st, Pimlico
11..Briant's bdgs, behind 47, Shoreditch
27..Briant's bdgs, Hoxton
11..Briant's street, Shoreditch
12..Brick alley, Whitechapel
15..Brick buildings ct, Snowsfields
9..Brick court, Brick lane, Old st
35..Brick court, College st, Westmst
6..Brick ct, Middle Temple la, Fleet st
7..Brick ct, Gt Shire ln, Temple bar
9..Brick lane, 113, Old st, St. Luke's

Ref. to Plan.

12..Brick lane, Osborn st, Whitechapel
29..Brick lane, Ratcliffe
36..Brick st, 13, Park st, Piccadilly
17..Brick st, London rd, St. George's fds
12..Brick yd, Brick lane, Spitalfields
17..Brickell's bds, Newington causeway
4..Brickhill la, 75, Upper Thames st
2..Bricklington ct, Coleman st
7..Bride's passage, 82, Fleet st
7..Bride lane, 97, Fleet street
35..Bride la, Lt Peter st, Westminster
16..Bridewell alley, Boro High st
6..Bridewell precinct, New Bridge st
8..Bridewell row, Vine st, Hatton grdn
35..Bridge court, Westminster bridge
31..Bridge place, John st Hickman's folly
40..Bridge pl, Rawstorn st, Islington rd
15..Bridge rents, Fair st, Horselydown
19..Bridge rd, Surry side, Westm bridge
50..Bridge road, Vauxhall
51..Bridge row, Chelsea bridge
6..Bridge st, Blackfriars bridge
15..Bridge st, Tooley st
35..Bridge st, Westminster bridge
30..Bridge st, King st, Wapping
4..Bridge st, Southwark
50..Bridge st, Vauxhall bridge
6..Bridge st, (lit.)op.8, Bridge st, Blkfrs
15..Bridge yd, Tooley st
1..Bridgewater ct, 38, Bridgewater grdn
1..Bridgewater grdns, Bridgewater sq
1..Bridgewater sq, Princess st, Barbica
39..Bridgewater sq, Somerstown
1..Bridle la, 8, Brewer st, Golden la
37..Bridle la, Silver st, Golden sq
12..Brigg's alley, Thrale st [Kent road
32..Brighton pl, 1, Weymouth st, New
39..Brighton st, 107 Cromer st
39..Brill crescent, Pancras
39..Brill place, Pancras
33..Brill road, Pancras
39..Brill row, Somers town
39..Brill terrace, Pancras
13..Brimstone ct, Rosemary lane
51..Brissenden bds, Brewer st, Pimlico
4..Bristol place, Bristol st
4..Bristol st, St. Andrew's hill, Upper . Thames st
5..Bristow st, 18 St. Andrews hill
1..Britain (little) 176 Aldersgate st
29..Britains ct, 178 Ratcliffe highway
1..Britannia court, 30, Golden lane
26..Britannia gardens, upper end of Glo'ster terrace, Hoxton
18..Britannia row, Lambeth marsh
39..Brittania st, Battle bridge
26..Brittannia ter, Glo'ster pl, Hoxton
26..Britannia walk, Glo'ster pl, Hoxton
15..Briton's al, Freeman's la, Horselydn
29..Briton's ct, Princes sq, Ratcliff hwy
7..Briton's ct, 18 Water la, Fleet st
26..Britt's bds, Glo'ster pl, Hoxton
30..Britt's st, Gt Hermitage, Wapping
29..BroadBridge, 87 np. Shadwell, High st
1..Broad arrow ct, 88, Grub st, Cripplg

Ref to Plan.

21..Broad court, 43 Drury lane
29..Broad bridge lane, Upper Shadwell
21..Broad ct, Bow st, Covent garden
12..Broad ct, Duke's pl, Houndsditch
21..Broad ct, 69 Long acre
37..Broad ct, Dean st, Soho
8..Broad ct, Turnmill st, Cow cross
11..Broad place, back of the Church, Shoreditch
21..Broad st, Bloomsbury, N end of Holb
36..Broad st, 36, Berwick st, Carnabymkt
15..Broad st, Horselydown
2..Broad st, [old & new] 53, Threadneedle st
34..Broad st, from Lambeth butts to the Thames
37..Broad st, Poland st
45..Broad st, Ratcliff cross
50..Broad st, Worcester st, O Gravel la
2..Broad st bds, Old Bethlem
2..Broad st pl, 36 Broad st buildings
5..Broad wall, now Angel st, opposite 1, upper Stamford st, Blackfriars
6..Broadway, 19, Ludgate hill, near Apothecaries' hall
15..Broadway, 24 New st, Princes st, Boro
19..Broadway, Privy grds, Whitehall
35..Broadway, W end of Tothill st, Westminster
61..Broadway, Deptford
16..Broad yd, 69 Blackman st, Southwark
11..Broad yd, Holywell la, Shoreditch
29..Broad yd, Milk yd, Wapping
8..Broad yd, St. John st, Smithfield
1..Broad yard, Whitecross st
5..Broad yd, Up Ground, Blackfriars
8..Broad yd, 65 Turnmill st, Clerkenwl
4..Broken wharf, 40 Upper Thames st
21..Broker's alley, 25, Drury lane
2..Brokers row, Moorfields
38..Bromley pl, Conway st, Fitzroy sq
67..Brompton, W end of Sloan st, Chlsea
67..Brompton crescent, Brompton
67..Brompton grove, Brompton
67..Brompton mews, Brompton
67..Brompton park, Brompton
67..Brompton row, Brompton
67..Brompton terrace, Knightsbridge
1..Brook alley, Noble street
18..Brook court, 8 Lambeth marsh
4..Brook court, Thames st
7..Brook's court, Brook's mrkt, Holbrn
13..Brook's court, Minories
4..Brookes's lane, op. 212 up Thames st
7..Brook's market, 140, Holborn
37..Brook's mews, 51, Brook st, Bond st
36..Brooks's mews, 50, Davis st Berkly sq
23..Brook's place, Bagnigge wells
33..Brook's place, Kennington cross
38..Brook's pl, Mary st, Tottenham ct rd
1..Brook's rents, Fore st
38..Brook st, (gt & lit.) Tottenham ct rd
33..Brook st, Walcot pl. Lambeth
37..Brook st, Hanover st
7..Brook st, 142 Holborn

Ref. to Plan.

53..Brook st, (up & lwr) Grosvenor sq
33..Brook st, Lambeth
45..Brook st, Sun Tavern flds, Ratcliffe
4..Brook's wharf, 14, Gardiners lane, Upper Thames st
34..Brook's yard, Fore st, Lambeth
4..Brook's yd, 211 up Thames st
13..Broom alley, 53, Whitechapel
61..Broomfield place, Deptford
11..Broomstick alley, Long al, Moorflds
37..Brother's bds, Ogle ct, Foley st
34..Brother's row, High st, Lambeth
11..Brown alley, Norton Falgate
14..Brown Bear al, 120 up. E. Smithfield
15..Brown's bds, Joiner st, Tooley st
37..Brown's bds, 201 Holywell st, Shord
13..Brown's bds, Prince st, Rosemary la
13..Brown's bds, St. Mary Axe
5..Brown's buildings, 47, Green st, Friars st, Blackfriars rd
21..Brown's buildings, 27, Stanhope st, Clare market
36..Brown's court, 24 Carnaby market
13..Brown's ct, 49 Gt, Alie st, Whitechpl
53..Brown's ct, 10 Green st, N Audley st
68..Brown's court, 81, Edgeware road
12..Brown's court, Hounsditch
13..Brown's court, Biliter st
12..Brown's ct, op. 55 Brick la, Spitalfld
14..Brown's court, St. Catherine's la
13..Brown's court, Crutched friars
3..Brown's court, Gracechurch st
53..Brown's court, North rd, Grosv sq
11..Brown's court, Long al, Moorfields
7..Brown's court, Shoe lane
36..Brown's ct, Titchborne st, Haymrkt
30..Brown's ct, King & Queen stairs, Roth
12..Brown's lane, Brick la, Spitalfields
7..Brown's court, Old Bailey
53..Brown's pas, 57 Green st, N Audley st
34..Brown's place, Lambeth walk
14..Brown's rents, St. Catherine's lane
1..Brown st, 60, Bunhill row
53..Brown st, Bryanston sq
53..Brown st, 36 Duke st, Grosvenor sq
68..Brown st, 26 upper George st, Edgeware road
11..Brown's yard, nr Holywell st
1..Brown's yard, Whitecross st
14..Brown Bear al, 1 up, East Smithfield
21..Brownlow st, 19, Drury lane
7..Brownlow st, 50 Holborn
21..Brownlow st, Long acre
13..Brownson's ct, Alie st, Goodman's fd
5..Brunswick ct, Brunswick st, Christ Church, Surrey
15..Brunswick ct, Crucifix la, Bermonds
53..Brunswick mews, gt, Cumberland st
22..Brunswick mews, Brunswick sq
9..Brunswick place, City road
22..Brunswick place, Queen sq, Bloomsb
5..Brunswick pl, 117, Brunswick st, Blackfriars road
27..Brunswick place, Hackney road
32..Brunswick pl, cornr East la, Kent rd

Ref. to Plan.

35..Brunswick rd, Horseferry rd, Westm
22..Brunswick sq, near Foundling hosp
27..Brunswick st, Hackney road
5..Brunswick st, 22 Stamford st, Blkfrs
11..Brunswick st, Webb sq, Shoreditch
14..Brush all, 61 up E. Smithfield
36..Bruton st, 22, Berkeley square
53..Bryanstone mews, Bryanstonesq
53..Bryanstone sq, 14, up. Humberstone
st, Marylebone
53..Bryanstone st, 19. Portman square
19..Bryants lane, 9 Stangate
21..Brydges st, Covent garden
13..Buck's rents, Rosemary lane
3..Buck's head court, Great Distaff la
Friday st, Cheapside
20..Buckingham court, 36, Charing cross
36..Buckingham gate, St. James's park
36..Buckingham house & gate, Pimlico
35..Buckingham row, nr York st, Westm
38..Buckingham st, Fitzroy square
20..Buckingham st, 39, Strand
32..Buckingham st, Kent road
38..Buckingham st, Up Titchfield st
13..Buckle st, Redlion st, Whitechapel
30..Buckler's rents, Rotherhithe wall
3..Bucklersbury, 90, Cheapside
16..Buckneler court, Kent st, Southwrk
3..Budge row, Watling st
15..Bull alley, Tooley st
9..Bull alley, Brick lane, Old st
16..Bull alley, Kent st, Southwark
2..Bull alley, Broad st, London wall
34..Bull alley, Fore st, Lambeth
5..Bull alley, Upper ground, Blkfriars
3..Bull al, Nicholas la, Lombard st
8..Bull alley, Turnmill st
15..Bull bridge, Horselydown
45..Bull bridge, Fore st, Limehouse
8..Bull court, 15 Giltspur st
26..Bull court, 60 Kingsland road
16..Bull court, 290 Kent st, Borough
2..Bull court, Bishopsgate st
12..Bull court, 78, Whitechapel
15..Bull court, Tooley st
22..Bull & Gate yard, 243 Holborn
7..Bull Head court, 188, Fleet st
16..Bull Head court, 291, Kent st
1..Bull Head ct, Jewin st, Aldersgate st
2..Bull Head ct, London wall
8..Bull Head ct, 19, Peter st, Cow cross
37..Bull Head ct, 101, Tottenham crt rd
8..Bull Head ct, 80, Newgate st
15..Bull Head ct, Tooley st
21..Bull Head ct, Queen st, Lincoln's Inn
2..Bull Head ct, 94, Wood st, Cheapside
8..Bull Head ct, Cow lane, Smithfield
35..Bull Head ct, Gt Peter st, Westmns
2..Bull Head passage, 94 Wood st,
Cheapside
3..Bull Head passage, 81 Gracechurch st
16..Bull Head yard, Blackman st, Boro
38..Bull Head yd, 101, Tottenham-ct-rd
20..Bull Inn court, Strand
3..Bulliford ct, Fenchurch st
G.

Ref. to Plan

15..Bull's rents, Freeman's la, Horsleyd
18..Bull's rents, Lambeth marsh
5..Bull stairs, 16, Upr ground, Southwk
12..Bullstake ct, 58, Whitechapel
44..Bull lane, Stepney
66..Bull Wall, 18 Paradise row, Chelsea
4..Bull wharf la, 63, Upper Thames st
1..Bull & Mouth st, 4, St. Martin's le gd
45..Bull yd, Whitehorse st, Commercl r d
Limehouse
23..Bull yard, 82 Grays Inn lane
8..Bull yard, Back hill, Leather lane
1..Bull yard, Bridgewater gdn, Barbican
11..Bull yd, Dunning's alley, Bishopsgte
2..Bullock's court, Old Bethlem
13..Bullock's court, Minories
11..Bullock's yard, Shoreditch
28..Bully row, Bethnal green
53..Bulstrode st & mews, 28 and 32,
Marylebone lane
12..Bunch alley, Thrall al, Spitalfields
10..Bunhill court, 54, Bunhill row
1..Bunhill ro, 63, Chiswell st, Finsburysq
32..Burdett place, Kent road
32..Burdett st, Walworth
35..Burdett st, Asylum, Westminster rd
2..Burgess ct, Wood st, Cheapside
20..Burleigh st & ct, 365, Strand
36..Burlington arcade, Piccadilly
36..Burlington gardens, Old Bond st
36..Burlington mews, 129, Swallow st
32..Burlington pl, 97 Broad st, Ratcliff
36..Burlington st, (Old) 148, Swallow st
Burlington gardens
36..Burlington st, (New) 120, Swallow st
14..Burr st, 58, East Smithfield
5..Burrow's bdgs, Blackfriars road
15..Bursar st. Tooley st   [Coram st
38..Burton crescent, Marchmont st,
36..Burton place, Berkeley square
11..Burton's rents, Holywell la, Shored
38..Burton st & pl, Tavistock sq
36..Burton st & mews, Berkeley sq
13..Bury ct, 20, St. Mary Axe
53..Bury ct, Barlow ct, Marylebone
21..Bury st, Hart st, Bloomsbury
66..Bury st, Chelsea common
8..Bury st, Lit Sutton st, Goswell st
13..Bury st, St. Mary Axe
37..Bury st, Portland Chapel, Oxford st
53..Burying ground pass, 49, Paddington st
53..Burying ground pass, 11 Paradise st,
Marylebone
11..Busby ct, Busby st, Shoreditch
11..Busby st, Shoreditch
14..Bush alley, near St. Catherine's
14..Bush al, St. Catharine's, Tower hill
3..Bush lane, 22, Cannon st, City
16..Bush yard, Kent st, Southwark
2..Bushel ct, Lothbury   [Wapping
30..Bushell's rents, 17, Gt Hermitage st
8..Butcher's alley, St. John's st, Smth f
8..Butcher hall la, 82, Newgate st
29..Butcher row, 61, Broad st, Ratcliffe cr
14..Butcher row, 82, up. E. Smithfield

Ref. to Plan.
17..Butcher st, St. George's fields
2..Butler's alley, Little Moorfields
14..Butler's bdgs, 5 up. E. Smithfield
15..Butler's bdgs, Crucifix lane, Boro
2..Butler's ct, 87, Fore st, Cripplegate
12..Butler's court, Houndsditch
12..Butler st, Spitalfields
61..Butt lane, Deptford
34..Butt st, Lambeth
1..Butterfly court, Grub st
2..Button', al, Ropemaker st, Moorfields
45..Button's entry, Whitehorse st, Stepn
34..Buxton place, Canterbury pl, Lambeth
26..Byng's buildings, Hoxton

C

16..Cabbage alley, 37 Long la, Southwark
12..Cabinet ct, Duke st, Spitalfields
13..Cable place, 55 Cable st, Rosemary la
13..Cable st, 75 Rosemary lane
19..Caddick's row, opposite the Admiralty, near Whitehall
52..Cadogan place, 76 Sloane st, Chelsea
52..Cadogan sq, Sloane st, Chelsea
52..Cadogan ter, 110 Sloane st, Chelsea
13..Cæsar's head ct, Crutched friars
4..Cain's alley, Bankside, Southwark
13..Cain's pl, Church la, Cable st, Whtchpl
5..Cair place, Blackfriars road
21..Calendar ct, Drury lane
11..Calendars ct, Long alley, Moorfields
15..Calico bdgs, Printer's pl, Bermondsy
53..Calmel bds, 9 Orchard st, Portman sq
66..Calthorp pl, 12 Paradise row, Chelsea
16..Calvert's bds, St. Margaret's hill
3..Calvert's court, Fenchurch st
29..Calvert st, Old Gravel lane
63..Camberwell green, Camberwell, 3 miles from London Bridge
38..Cambridge ct, Upper Cleveland st
27..Cambridge crescent, Hackney road
27..Cambridge heath, Hackney road
27..Cambridge place, Cambridge heath
37..Cambridge st, 15 Broad st, Carnaby mk
1..Camden ct, 94 Grub st, Cripplegate
27..Camden place, Bethnal green
27..Camden gardens, Bethnal grn, a little E. of Wilmot st
32..Camden st, East lane, Walworth
28..Camel row, Mile End
12..Camomile st, Bishopsgate st, facing Bevis Marks
35..Campion al, Market st, Millbnk st
4..Campion lane, 153 Upper Thames st
16..Camperdown pl, Bermondsey st, King st, Snowsfields
2..Canada ct, Little Cheapside, Morfds
20..Canary ct, Exeter st, Strand
47..Canal place, 200 yards E. of the Surry Canal Bridge, Kent road
15..Canal row, Eastlane, Bermondseywall
28..Cannon place, Whitechapel road
35..Cannon row, 9 Bridge st, Westminstr
3 Cannon st, 28 Great East Cheap
29..Cannon st, 143 Ratcliffe highway

Ref. to Plan.
16..Cannon st, Mint st, 109 Blackman st, Southwark
29..Cannon st road, continuation of ditto, St. George's East
1..Canon al, 63 St. Paul's Church yard
34..Canterbury bds, Lambeth terrace, near the Church
5..Canterbury ct, St. Andrew's hill, Blackfriars
18..Canterbury pl, op the Stags, Lambeth
32..Canterbury pl. East la, Walworth
33..Canterbury row, Kennington road
15..Canterbury sq, Dean st, Tooley st
34..Canterbury walk, 15 Lambeth terrace
60..Canton pl, East India road, Poplar
30..Canton row, Wapping
2..Capel ct, Bartholomew la, Bank
8..Car ct, West Smithfield
1..Car sq, 7 Moor la, Cripplegate
13..Car yd, Blue anchor yd, Rosemary la
38..Carburton st, Cleveland st, Fitzroy sq
33..Cardigan place, Kennington cross
33..Cardigan st, Kennington lane
4..Cardinal cap al, Bankside, Boro
1..Carey lane, 32 Gutter la, Cheapside
18..Carey pl, 27 Oakley place, Carey st, Lambeth marsh
35..Carey st, Vincent sq, Westminster
18..Carey st, Lambeth marsh
7..Carey st, 98 Chancery lane
18..Carlisle la, Westminster bridge road
18..Carlisle pl, Carlisle la, Lambeth
18..Carlisle row, Lambeth
18..Carlisle sq, 18 Carlisle row, Lambeth
37..Carlisle st, 37 Soho square
36..Carlton palace, Pall Mall
36..Carlton pl, St. Ann's st, Pall Mall
18..Carlton pl. Carlisle la, Lambeth
38..Carmarthen sq, Tottenham ct road
38..Carmarthen st, Tottenham ct road
37..Carnaby market, Carnaby st
11..Carnaby row, Spitalfields
37..Carnaby st, 28 Gt Marlborough st
8..Caroline ct, 18 Gt Saffron hill, Holbrn
24..Caroline pl, op. 43 St. John's st road
23..Caroline pl, Foundling hospital
9..Caroline pl, op. Fountain pl, City rd
21..Caroline st & mews, 116 Great Russel st, Bedford square
27..Caroline st, Hackney road
18..Caroline st, Lambeth
2..Carpenter's bds, 75 London wall
13..Carpenter's rents, Jewry st
52..Carpenter's st, Mount st, Grosvn sq
35..Carpenter st, 44 Vine st, Millbank
16..Carpenter yd, Up Ground, Blkfriars
16..Carpenter's yard, Blackman st
8..Carpenter's yd, Long la, W Smithfld
2..Carpenter's yard, Coleman court
1..Carpenter's yard, Beech lane
21..Carreer st, Lawrence st, St. Giles's
52..Carrington pl, 17 Hertford st, Picdlly
36..Carrington st, (lit) Hertford st, Mayfr
36..Carrington st & mews, Curzon st
15..Carter lane, 243 Tooley st

Ref. to Plan.

5..Carter la, (gt & lit.) Doctors Commons and 42 St. Andrews hill
12..Carter st, 167 Brick lane, Spitalfields
1..Carthusian st, Charter house sq
14..Carthusian st, Pickle Herring st
35..Cartwright st, Broadway, Westminst
13..Cartwright st, 31 Rosemary lane
13..Cartwright sq, Rosemary lane
11..Cash alley, near Shoreditch church
3..Castle alley, 99 Cornhill
4..Castle al, Lambeth hill, UpThames st
12..Castle alley, 124 Whitechapel
16..Castle alley, 249 Kent st, Southwark
3..Castle court, 23 Birchin lane
3..Castle ct, Budge row, 10 Watling-st
7..Castle ct, 23 Fullwood's rents, Holbn
21..Castle ct, Long acre   [Boro
16..Castle ct, E. side of Castle la, Mint,
11..Castle ct, Castle st Shoreditch church
20..Castle ct, 8 Chandos st, Covent grdn
1..Castle ct, Aldersgate st
20..Castle ct, 110 Strand
12..Castle ct, Houndsditch
1..Castle ct, 54 Whitecross st
20..Castle ct, St. Martin's lane
2..Castle ct, Lawrence lane
12..Castle ct, Old Castle st, Whitechapel
4..Castle la, 13 Redcross st, Borough
4..Castle la, Lambeth hill, UpThames st
35..Castle la, James st, Buckingham gate
21..Castle la, Castle st, Long acre
12..Castle la, Castle place, New Castle street, Whitechapel
35..Castle pas, Castle st, James st, Westm
36..Castle st, Air st, Piccadilly
10..Castle st, Artillery place, City road
11..Castle st, Austin st, Shoreditch
21..Castle st, Hart st, Bloomsbury
1..Castle st, (New)Falcon sq. Aldersgt st
7..Castle st, 34 Fleet Market
8..Castle st, 40 Turnmill st, Clerkenwel
7..Castle st, 12 nr Middle row, Holborn
20..Castle st, Howard st, Strand
12..Castle st, 47 Houndsditch
20..Castle st, 14 GtNewport st, Lester sq
21..Castle st, Long acre
37..Castle st, (Up&Low) Oxford market
4..Castle st, 13 Redcross st, Borough
4..Castle st, 222 Upper Thames st
12..Castle st, 120 High st, Whitechapel
35..Castle st, Chapel st, Westminster
5..Castle yard, Gravel lane, Southwark
35..Castle yard, Dacre st, Westminster
6..Castle yard, Saffron hill
22..Castle yard, East st, Bloomsbury
12..Castle yard, Houndsditch
4..Castle yard, Upper Thames st
2..Cateaton st, 16 Milk st, nr Guildhall
35..Catherine bds, William st, Pimlico
3..Catherine ct, Threadneedle st
14..Catherine ct, Tower hill
35..Catherine ct, Gt. Peter st, Westmr
14..Catherine sq, St. Catherine's Tower
14..Catherine st, near the Tower
29..Catherine st, Commercial rd Whitech

Ref. to Plan.

35..Catherine st, Palace st, Pimlico
45..Catherine st, Stepney fields
20..Catherine st, 342 Strand
15..Catherine wheel al, Snowsfields
13..Catherine wheel al, Middlesex st
2..Catherine wheel al, 44 Bishopsgate st
16..Catherine wheel al, 248Kent st, Boro
12..Catherine wheel ct Essex st, Whitech
1..Catherine wheel ct 14Bridgewater gds
12..Catherine wheel yd, Widegate st
36..Catherine wheel yd, Cleveland row St. James's
68..Cato st, John st, Edgeware road
8..Cats alley, Long lane, Smithfield
28..Cats row, Dog row, Mile end
35..Cat's Head ct, 44 Orchard st, Westmr
14..Catshold ct, St. Catherine's
45..Causeway ct, Stepney causeway
35..Causton st, Tothill fields
12..Cavendish ct, 91 Houndsditch
37..Cavendish sq, Oxford st
37..Cavendish st, (Old) 141 Oxford st
37..Cavendish st, 82 Great Portland st
20..Cecil ct, 92 St. Martin's lane, Strand
20..Cecil st, 84 Strand
29..Chad's row, near the Turnpike, Battle bridge, Gray's Inn lane
13..Chain al, Crutched Friars
7..Chain ct, Ship yard, Temble bar
16..Chaingate, 297 High st, Boro
18..Chalcrof ter, Gt. Charlotte st, Blkfrs
60..Chalkstone, Poplar marsh
29..Chamber sq, 95 Lower E. Smithfield
13..Chamber st, Goodman's fields
35..Champion al, Vine st, Milbank Westm
4..Champion la, Upper Thames st
11..Chancellor ct, Church st, Shoreditch
7..Chancery lane, 192 Fleet st
35..Chandler's al, Orchard st, Westmnstr
5..Chandler's rents, 7Addle st, Blackfrs
37..Chandler st, Davies st, Grosvenor sq
37..Chandos st, N.Ecorner of Cavendish sq
20..Chandos st, turn at 423 Strand
9..Change al, 23 Cornhill and 17 &[71 Lombard st
20..Change ct, 365 Strand
35..Channel row, Bridge st, Westmstr
60..Chapel ct, Poplar
16..Chapel ct, 124 Borough High st
21..Chapel ct, 130 Long Acre
36..Chapel ct, 50 Swallow st
11..Chapel ct, Holywell st, Shoreditch
3..Chapel ct, Miles lane, Cannon st
52..Chapel ct, South Audley st, south side of the Chapel
53..Chapel ct, 23 North Audley st
22..Chapel ct, Gilbert st, Bloomsbury
37..Chapel ct, Henrietta st, Cavendish sq
7..Chapel ct, Clement's lane
1..Chapel ct, 63 Wood st, London wall
21..Chapel ct, King st, Golden sq
53..Chapel place, 148 Oxford st
7..Chapel pl, Fetter la
39..Chapel path, 35 Wilsted st, Somerstwn
22..Chapel pl, Lit. Coram st, Russell sq

Ref. to Plan.
40..Chapel pl, Chapel st, Pentonville
67..Chapel row, Rawstorne st, Brompton
23..Chapel row, west side of the Chapel, Exmouth st, Spafields
7..Chapel stair, Lincoln's Inn
52..Chapel st, May fair
20..Chapel st, Covent garden
37..Chapel st, 395 Oxford st
23..Chapel st, Bayne's row, Spafields
35..Chapel st, Broadway, Westminster
35..Chapel st, Charlotte st, Pimlico
29..Chapel st, Chapman st, Cannon st rd
11..Chapel st, 56, Curtain rd, Shoreditch
52..Chapel st, (E. & W.) Curzon st
52..Chapel st, 26 Grosvenor pl, Hyde Park
1..Chapel st, 14 Grub st, Cripplegate
22..Chapel st, Lamb's Conduit st
68..Chapel st, Lissongrove, 100 Edgware road, Paddington
37..Chapel st, 95 Portland st, Oxford st
52 Chapel st, (E. & W)64 South Audley st
37..Chapel st, Tottenham court road
11..Chapel st, Wheeler st, Spitalfields
37..Chapel st, Wardour st, Soho
40..Chapel st, Pentonville
11..Chapel yard, Spitalfields
29..Chapman st, St. George's East
15..Chapman's rents, Bermondsey st
40..Chapman st, Pentonville
40..Chapman pl, Chapman st
29..Chapman st, Cannon st road
13..Chapman's yard, Goodman's fields
7..Chapterhouse yd, 67 St Paul's chrch yd
35..Chapter st, Tothill fields
29..Chargaur row, New rd, St. George's E
20..Charing cross, 487 St. Martin's la, Strd
34..Charing cross yd, Fore st, Lambeth
20..Charing place, Charing cross
15..Charity al, St. Thomas st, Boro
1..Charles ct, Bartholomew close
29..Charles ct, Charles st, Old Gravel la
20..Charles ct, St. Martin's la, Strand
20..Charles ct, 27 Strand
23..Charles pl, Baker's row, Coldbath sq
26..Charles pl, Charles sq, Hoxton
26..Charles sq, Hoxton
29..Charles st, Back la, Ratcliff
28..Charles st, Baker's rw, Whitechpl rd
36..Charles st, Berkeley sq
5..Charles st, 37 Blackfriars road
1..Charles st, Bridgewater sq 17 Barbican
26..Charles st, Charles sq, Hoxton
28..Charles st, Church la, Whitechapel
39..Charles st, Somerstown
20..Charles st, Covent garden
11..Charles st, Curtain road, Shoreditch
21..Charles st, 174 Drury-lane
24..Charles st, Goswell st road
53..Charles st, 33 George st, Portman sq
29..Charles st, Greenfield st, Comrcl rd
53..Charles st, Grosvenor sq
8..Charles st, 24 Hatton garden
15..Charles st, Horselydown
21..Charles st, 85 Long Acre
53..Charles st, 47 Thayer st, Manchestr sq

Ref. to Plan.
37..Charles st, Middlesex hospital
24..Charles st, Northampton sq
29..Charles st, Old Gravel la, St Geo. E.
35..Charles st, 8 King st, Westminster
18..Charles st, or Carey st, Lambeth mrsh
36..Charles st, St. James's sq
37..Charles st, Soho square
38..Charles st, (little) facing the Water-works, Hampstead road
18..Charles st, Westminster bridge road
10..Charles st, Willow walk, Old st rd
27..Charles st, Wilmot sq, Bethnal gr rd
68..Charles st, Lisson grove, Paddington
24..Charles st, 93 Up. Goswell st road
66..Charles st, Sloane sq, Chelsea
10..Charles st, Old st road
37..Charles st, Hanover square
23..Charlotte bdgs, 17 Gray's Inn lane
29..Charlotte ct, Charlotte st, Cannon st rd
5..Charlotte ct, Willow st, Bankside
1..Charlotte ct, 27 Redcross st, Cripplegt
22..Charlotte mews, Castle st, Bloomsby
38..Charlotte mews, 74 Charlotte street, Fitzroy square
17..Charlotte place, Borough road, near the King's Bench
18..Charlotte place, Lambeth marsh
68..Charlotte row, Lisson green turnpike
16..Charlotte row, West end of Welling-ton row. Long lane, Bermondsey
32..Charlotte row, High st, Walworth
46..Charlotte row, Surry canal, Rotherh
3..Charlotte row, 27 Poultry
48..Charlotte row, Camberwell turnpike
39..Charlotte st, Battle bdge, Grays Inn la
21..Charlotte st, 103 Great Russell street Bedford square
17..Charlotte st, Surry chapel, Black-friars road
18..Charlotte st, (Great) Blackfriars
67..Charlotte st, Brompton road
66..Charlotte st, Hans place, Sloane sq
27..Charlotte st, New road, Bethnal grn
12..Charlotte st, Fieldgate st, turn at 266 Whitechapel
10..Charlotte st, Old st road
37..Charlotte st, Portland pl, Marylebone
37..Charlotte st, (Up, & Lower) Rath-bone place
26..Charlotte st, Hoxton
35..Charlotte st, (Gt & Lit) Stafford row
11..Charlotte st, Church st, Shoreditch
38..Charlotte st, Fitzroy square
15..Charlotte terrace, east side of Gre-gorian Arms, Jamaica row, Bermd
18..Charlotte ter, New Cut, Blackfrs rd
39..Charlton ct, 15 Charlton st, Somerstwn
40..Charlton place, Islington
37..Charlton st, Titchfield st, Marylebone
39..Charlton st, Somerstown, near the Turnpike, Battle bridge
2..Charlton st, Whitecross st, Moorfields
40..Charlton st, Lower Islington
29..Charlton st, New rd, Commercial rd
8..Charterhouse lane, Charterhouse sq

Ref. to Plan.

8..Charterhouse sq, Aldersgate st
8..Charterhouse st, 23 Long lane, West Smithfield
9..Chatham gdns, Peerless pool, City rd
6..Chatham pl, N:foot of Blackfrs brdge
21..Chatham pl, Broad st, Bloomsbury
11..Cheapside (Lit) Long al, Moorfields
16..Cheapside (Little) Mint. Southwark
2..Cheapside, St. Paul's
12..Cheeseman's ct, Brick la, Whitechpl
66..Chelsea, South W of Buckingham gt
66..Chelsea college, one mile and half from Hyde Park corner, Chelsea
66..Chelsea common, Chelsea
66..Chelsea market, 27 Lower Sloane st,
66..Chelsea reach and creek, Chelsea
51..Chelsea road, from Pimlico to Chelsea
51..Chelsea Water works, Chelsea road
35..Chelsea Water-works (New & Old) near the Neat Houses, Millbank
18..Cheltenham place, Asylum, Lambeth
27..Chenies alley, Shoreditch
38..Chenies st and Mews, Gower street, Bedford square
20..Chemister ct, 16 Bedfordbury
10..Chequer alley, 98 Bunhill row
1..Chequer al, Whitecross st,Cripplegat
20..Chequer ct, Charing cross
13..Chequer yard, 1 Aldgate, High st
3..Chequer yard, Bush lane, Cannon st
3..Chequer yard, 45 Dowgate hill
27..Cherrington row, Wilmot square
30..Cherrygarden st & stairs,Rotherhithe
10..Cherry tree alley, Bunhil row
1..Cherry tree ct, 53, Aldersgate street
1..Cherry tree ct, 183Golden la, Barbicn
45..Cheshire's rents, Shipwrights row, Rotherhithe
27..Chester place, Bethnal green road
33..Chester place, Kennington cross
7..Chester place, Fleet market
52..Chester st, 36 Grosvenor place,Hyde Park Corner
33..Chester st,opposite 6 Guildford place Kennington
53..Chesterfield st, Marylebone
66..Cheyne row, Cheyne walk, Chelsea
66..Cheyne walk, Chelsea
7..Chichester rents, 83 Chancery lane
8..Chick lane, West Smithfield
12..Chicksand st,GtGarden st,Whitechpl
29..Chigwell hill, 5 Ratcliff highway
35..Child's ct, Tothill st, Westminster
7..Child's pl, 2 Fleet st, nr Temple bar
20..Chilton's st,Bedfordbury.Covent gdn
18..China ct, near the Asylum, Lambeth
46..China Hall, Deptford Lower road
34..China walk, Buxton place, Lambeth
34..China row,nr the three Stags,Lambth
1..Chiswell st, Finsbury sq
29..Choppen's st,25OldGravel la,Wapng
8..Christ Church pass, 92 Newgate st
31..Christian st, New road, Rotherhithe
2..Christopher all,38 Wilson st,Moorfds

Ref. to Plan,

13..Christopher ct, Lambeth st
32..Christopher row, East lane, Walwth
11..Christopher st, 1 Wilson st, Finsbury square
8..Christopher st, 16 Back la,Hatton gd
11..Christopher st, Austin st, Shoreditch
2..Church alley, Cateaton st, Guildhall
3..Church alley, Old Jewry
6..Church alley, St. Andrew's hill
3..Church alley,St.Mary hill,Billingsgt
2..Church ct, Basinghall st
35..Church ct, Chapel st, Westminster
3..Church ct, Clement'sla, Lombard st
3..Church ct, Friday st, Cheapside
2..Church ct, Lothbury
36..Church ct, (St. James)200 Piccadilly
20..Church ct, (St. Martin's) 466 Strand
3..Church ct, Walbrook, near the Mansion House
6..Church entry, Shoemaker row,Blkfrs
30..Churches gardens, Tench st
45..Church lane, Limehouse church
12..Church lane,Middlesex st, Whitechpl
20..Church lane,(St.Martin's)457 Strand
12..Church lane, 71 Whitechapel
13..Church lane, Cable st, Rosemary la
28..Church lane, Mile end, Old town
2..Church passage, Guildhall
21..Church passage, Monmouth st
36..Church passage, 200 Piccadilly
33..Church place, Newington Butts
12..Church place, Whitechapel church
29..Church rd, Commercial rd, and Back lane, St. George East
13..Church row, 8 High st, Aldgate
27..Church row, Bethnal green road
13..Church row, Fenchurch st
45..Church row, Limehouse church
39..Church row, place &terrace, Pancras
15..Church row, Horselydown, east side of St John's Church
45..Church row, Stepney church yard
9..Church row, Ironmonger row, Old st
12..Church st, Baker's row, Whitechapel
5..Church st, 22 Blackfriars road
29..Church st, Brook st, Sun Tavern filds
21..Church st, Lawrence st, St. Giles
34..Church st, Lambeth
13..Church st, Minories
68..Church st, Paddington green
68..Church st, (New) Edgeware road
30..Church st, side of the Church Rotherhithe
16..Church st, from St. George's Church to White st Southwark
35..Church st, (St. John's) Westminster
4..Church st,(St.Saviour's)Southwark
11..Church st, Shoreditch
21..Church st, (St. Ann's) Soho
12..Church st, Spitalfields
30..Church st, 96 Wapping
39..Church way,Charlton st, Somerstwn
15..Church yard alley, 247 Tooley st
4..Church yard alley, 119 Up Thames st
15..Church yard ct, St. Thomas st

G 2

Ref. to Plan.

6..Church yard ct, Temple
33..Church yard row, Newington Butts
20..Chymister's alley, 16 Bedfordbury
29..Cinnamon st, Old Gravel lane
13..Circus, Minories
38..Circus, Marylebone
68..Circus st, Lisson green, Marylebone
38..Cirencester st, Fitzroy square
2..City Chambers, 119 Bishopsgate st
1..City Greenyard, Whitecross st
9..City road, Finsbury sq to Islington
9..City ter, 1 Caroline ter, City road
21..Clare court, 104 Drury lane
44..Clare Hall place, Stepney green
21..Clare market, Portugal st, near Lincoln's Inn fields
9..Claremont place, City road
24..Claremont terrace, Pentonville road
21..Clare passage, Clare market
43..Clare st, Cambridge heath, Hackney
21..Clare st, Clare market
46..Clarence garden,Clarence st,Rotherh
39..Clarence pas, N.side Smallpox hosptl
27..Clarence place, Hackney road
40..Clarence place, Pentonville
39..Clarence place, Pancras
30..Clarence st, near Rotherhithe church
39..Clarendon place, Clarendon square
39..Clarendon square, Somerstown
36..Clarges st, 84 Piccadilly
12..Clark's alley,Camomile st, Bishopsgt
8..Clark's buildgs, 52 Skinner st,Snowh
8..Clark's ct, Vine st, 76 Gt Saffron hill
7..Clark's ct, Little Turnstile, Holborn
2..Clark's ct, 58 Bishopsgate st within
30..Clark's orchard,355 near Rotherhithe church
15..Clark's place,Worcester st, Borough
24..Clark's st, Allen st, Goswell st
29..Clark's terrace, Cannon st road, from the Turnpike Cannon st, to the Chapel
5..Clark's yd, Upper Ground st, Blakfrs
53..Clay st, Dorset st, Portman square
33..Clayton place, Kennington road
33..Clayton st, Upper Kennington green
33..Cleaver st, Kennington cross
2..Clement's ct, Milk st, Cheapside
7..Clement's la,13 Pickett st,Temple br
3..Clement's lane, 29 Lombard st
21..Clement's Inn passage, east side of Ditto to Clare market
24..Clerkenwell close, back of Clerkenwell church
24..Clerkenwell green, south side of the church, Clerkenwell
36..Cleveland ct, St. James's palace
36..Cleveland place, St. James's palace
36..Cleveland row,op.St.James's palace
..Cleveland mews, 16 Cleveland street, Fitzroy square
38..Cleveland st, Fitzroy square
36..Cleveland st, St. James's
36..Cleveland yd, King st, St. James's sq
7..Clifford's Inn, 187 Fleet st

Ref. to Plan.

7..Clifford's Inn passage, 183 Fleet st
66..Clifford row, Queen st, Chelsea
37..Clifford st, 14 New Bond st
66..Clifford st, Battersea fields
11..Clifton st, Finsbury square
4..Clink st,nr St. Saviour's church,Boro
38..Clipstone st, Fitzroy square
3..Cloak lane, Dewgate hill
8..Cloath st, 88 Long lane W Smithfld
6..Cloisters temple
8..Cloth fair, 60 West Smithfield
11..Club row, Spitalfields
18..Coad's row, Westminster bridge road
21..Coal yard; 185 Drury lane
6..Cobb's ct, Shoemaker row, and Broadway, Blackfriars
12..Cobb's yard,Middlesex st,Whitechpl
23..Cobham row, opposite the House of Correction, Coldbath square
31..Cobourg road, near the Lord Wellington, Kent road
4..Cock alley, near Pepper alley, Boro
14..Cock alley, Upper East Smithfield
11..Cock alley, 33 Norton falgate
11..Cock alley, near Shoreditch turnpike
37..Cock ct, Hopkin st, Carnaby market
13..Cock ct, Jewry st, Aldgate
7..Cock ct, 19, Ludgate hill
1..Cock ct, St. Martins le grand
8..Cock ct, 75 Snowhill
8..Cock ct, Turnmill st, Clerkenwell green
11..Cock hill, Anchor st, Spitalfields
45..Cock hill, 124 Upper Shadwell
14..Cock hill, Catharine alley
11..Cock lane,24 Holywell st, Shoreditch
8..Cock lane, 4 Giltspur st,WSmithfield
35..Cock yard, Tothill-st, Westminster
12..Cock's buildings, Stoney la, Midlx st
21..Cockpit alley, Drury-lane
4..Cockpit ct, Maid lane, Southwark
7..Cockpit ct, Poppin's ct, Fleet st
22..Cockpit yard, Little James st, Bedford row
20..Cockspur st, 67 Charing cross
1..Cock & Crown ct, nr Falcon square
12..Cock & Hoop yard, 138 Houndsditch
4..Coffee-house alley, 56 Up Thames st
26..Coffee-house walk and Gardens, near Bacchus walk, Hoxton
13..Colchester st, Redlion st, Whitechpl
13..Colchester st, Savage gdns,Tower h.
23..Coldbath square, Spafields, south side the House of Correction
8..Cole's blds, 30 Long lane, Smithfield
16..Cole's place, White Bear yd,Kent st
10..Colebrook place, Farmer's square, Glo'ster terrace, Hoxton
24..Colebrook row, New River,Islington
26..Colebrook square, near Glo'ster-ter. Hoxton
4..Cole harbour lane, 99 Up Thames st
26..Cole harbour row, Haggerstone lane, Hackney road
10..Coleman's alley, 83 Bunhill row

Ref. to Plan.

2..Coleman's ct, Castle lane, Maidlane, Borough
2..Coleman's place, Ratcliffe row, St. Luke's, Ironmonger row
15..Coleman's yard, 110, Bermondsey
2..Coleman st, 1 Fore st, and 42, Cateaton-street
10..Coleman st, 46 Banner st, Bunhill row
29..Coleman st, 150 New Gravel lane, Wapping
2..Coleman st buildings, 72 Coleman-st
29..Colet place, Commercial-road
18..Collate st, Glocester st, Lambeth
8..College ct, 5 Cowcross st, Smithfield
3..College hill, op. 75 Up Thames st
35..College mews, College st, Westmstr
55..College st, Camden town
33..College st, Newington Butts
66..College st, (Great & Little) Chelsea
19..College st, Narrow wall, Lambeth
15..College st, 140 Tooley-st, Borough
35..College st, 18 Abingdon st, Westmstr
66..College terrace, Chelsea common
16..College yd, Counter st, St. Margaret's hill, Borough
44..Collet place, White Horse st, Stepny
1..Collier ct, Charles st, Bridgewater sq, and 12 Golden lane, Barbican
11..Collier's ct, Fleet st, Spitalfields
15..Collier's ct, 39 Mill-lane, Tooley st, Borough
16..Collier's rents, 39 White st. High-st. Borough
40..Collier's st, Rodney-st, Pentonville
9..Collingwood place, Trafalgar street, - City-road
11..Collingwood-st, Mount-st, Shoredh
28..Collingwood st, Dog row, Mile end
17..Collingwood st, Charlotte st, Blackfrs
29..Collin's ct, 44 Farmer st, Shadwell
33..Collitch place, Cross st, Newington
22..Colonade & Mews, Upper Guildford street, Foundling-hospital
37..Colvill ct, Charlotte st, Oxford st
5..Commerce row, op. Surry Chapel, Blackfriars road
29..Commercial place, south side Commercial road
32..Commercial place, Kent road
29..Commercial road, turn at Whitechapel church
19..Commercial road, the south foot of Waterloo bridge, Surry
29..Commercial terrace, Commercial rd, Whitechapel
24..Compton passage, 61 Compton st, St. John's-st
24..Compton st, 24 St. John's st, Smithfld
21..Compton st, (Old & New) Soho
22..Compton st, Tavistock square
21..Conduit ct, Long Acre, a few doors on the right from St. Martin's lane
37..Conduit st. 23 New Bond st
36..Constitution hill, Green park, St. James's park

Ref. to Plan.

23..Constitution row, from op. Sidmouth place to Chad's row, Gray's Inn la
53..Connaught place, a little on the left from Tyburn turnpike, Edgeware-rd
53..Connaught terrace, Edgeware-road
53..Conway ct, 10 Paradise st, Marylebn
38..Conway st, Upper, Fitzroy square
38..Conway st, 12 Fitzroy place, New road, Marylebone
17..Cooke st East, Borough rd, Southwk
12..Cook's ct, 15 Primrose st, Bishopsgt
7..Cook's ct, 36 Carey st, Lincoln's Inn fds
11..Cook's place, Long alley, Moorfields
13..Cooper's ct, Blue Anchor yard, Rosemary-lane
23..Cooper's ct, 27 Portpool-lane
36..Cooper's ct, Great Windmill-street
37..Cooper's ct, Salisbury mews
9..Cooper's ct, Steward st, Goswell st
1..Cooper's ct, 63 Whitecross st, Cripplg
27..Cooper's gardens, Gascoigne-place, Hackney road
13..Cooper's row, Upper East Smithfield
13..Cooper's row, Trinity sq, Tower hill
35..Cooper st, Orchard st, Westminster
45..Copenhagen pl, Salmon la, Limehouse
23..Coppice row, near Coldbath square, Clerkenwell
14..Coppin ct, St. Dunstan's hill
2..Copthall buildings, from Copthall chambers to Bell alley, Throgmorton-street
2..Copthall ct, 30, Throgmorton st
20..Coral ct, nr Southampton st, Strand
22..Coram place, Little Coram st
22..Coram st, (Great & Little) 10 Tavistock-square
3..Corbet's ct, 5 Gracechurch st
12..Corbet's ct, 36 Brown's lane, Sptalfds
36..Cork-st, Burlington gardens, New Bond street
36..Cork st mews, 12 Cork st
35..Corkcutter st, Princes-st, Westmtsr
34..Corket's alley, High st, Lambeth
32..Cornbury place, near the Deaf and Dumb Asylum, Kent road
3..Cornhill, extends from the Mansion-house to Leadenhall st
18..Cornwall road, Commercial rd, Lmbh
29..Cornwall st, St. George's East, near Cannon st Turnpike
4..Corny Cap alley, Bank side, Borough
17..Coronation place, south end of Little Surry street, Blackfriars
24..Corporation ct, Clerkenwell
24..Corporation la, St. James's, Clrknwl
24..Corporation row, 137 St. John's st
35..Cottage pl, Horseferry road, Westmr
16..Cottage place, Long lane, Borough
32..Cottage place, Harper st, New Kent rd
18..Cottage place, Hercules bds, Lambeth
32..Cottage place, Lion st, New Kent rd
35..Cotton gardens, Old Palace yard, Westminster
16..Counter alley, 254 High st, Borough

Ref. to Plan
16..Counter st, Borough, High-st
16..Countin's alley, Kent-st, Borough
15..County row, Mill-st, Tooley-st
32..County terrace, (Webb's) New Kent road
28..Court st, 110 Whitechapel
4..Cousin's lane, 84 Upper Thames-st
13..Couzen's rents, Rosemary-lane
20..Covent garden, Southampton st
36..Coventry ct,12 Coventry st,Haymrkt
36..Coventry st, 4 Haymarket
27..Coventry st, Camden gardens
30..Cow ct, 333 Church-st, Rotherhithe
30..Cow ct, Jamaica st, Rotherhithe
8..Cowcross st, 87 St, John's st, West Smithfield
9..Cowlane, 93 West Smithfield
61..Cow lane,Trinity-st, Greenland dock
45..Cow lane, near Stepney church
39..Cow lane, 97 New Gravel lane, Shadwell
23..Cow yard, Liquorpond-st, Gray's Inn lane
4..Cowden's rents, Trinity-lane
1..Cowheel alley, 168, Whitecross-st, Old-street
11..Cowley rents, Long alley Moorfields
35..Cowley st, nr College st, Westmstr
3..Cowper's ct. 32 Cornhill
1..Cox ct. 160 Aldersgate st
12..Cox's sq,Wentworth st,Whitechapel
5..Coy's ct, Green walk, Blackfriars rd
27..Crabtree row, Hackney road, near the Turnpike
1..Cradle ct, 50 Aldersgate st
1..Cradle ct, 51 Redcross st, Cripplegt
13..Cradle st, 21 St, Mary Axe
20..Craig's ct, 20 Charing cross
20..Cranbourn alley, Cranbourn-st, Leicester square
20..Cranbourn passage, 16 Cranbourn st
20..Cranbourn st, opposite 8 Castle st, Leicester square
7..Crane ct, 174 Fleet-street
4..Crane ct, St. Peter's hill
13..Cranford ct, Rosemary lane
24..Cranford passage, Baker's row, Clkwl
26..Craven buildings, Charles sq,Hoxton
21..Craven buildings, 94 Drury lane
20..Craven ct, 34 Craven st, Strand
26..Craven ct, Charles square, Hoxton
26..Craven st, 11 Strand
21..Craven yard, 97 Drury lane
53..Crawford st,44 Baker's st,Portman sq
13..Creechurch lane, 86 Leadenhall st
7..Creed lane, 15 Ludgate street
3..Creed lane, Leadenhall st
32..Crescent, Salisbury pl, Lock's fields
13..Crescent, 102 Minories
13..Crescent mews, Vine st, Minories
38..Crescent place, Burton crescent
39..Crescent place, Somerstown
27.Crescent place, 12 Clarence place, Hackney-road
1..Crescent, 10 Jewin st, Aldersgate st

Ref. to Plan.
17..Crescent place, near the Obelisk, Lambeth road
31..Crimscott place, Grange rd, Bermdsy
1..Cripplegate buildings, 63 Wood st, Cheapside, and Fore st
12..Crispin st, 23 Union st, Bishopsgate
29..Cromhie's or Doran's row, Commercial road, Whitechapel
39..Cromer's st,14 Judd st,Somer's town
34..Crooked alley, High st, Lambeth
3..Crooked lane, 49 Cannon st, and Fish st hill
2..Crooked billet ct, Little Cheapside, Moorfields
26..Crooked billet yd, 53 Kingsland rd
11..Crosby bldgs, Norfolk pl, Shoredh
16..Crosby row, White st, Borough
32..Crosby row, Walworth
2..Crosby square, 28 Bishopsgate st
7..Cross alley, Shoe lane, Fleet-st
30..Cross alley, Upper Gun alley
20..Cross ct, Beaufort buildings
21..Cross ct, Broad ct, Drury lane
37..Cross ct, Carnaby market
3..Cross lane, Bush lane, 22 Cannon st
14..Cross lane, Harp lane
21..Cross lane, 106 Long acre
35..Cross lane, Millbank st
21..Cross lane, Newton st, Holborn
3..Cross lane, St. Mary at hill
45..Cross lane, Ratcliff sq
44..Cross row, Stepney green
29..Cross st, Back lane, Sun Tavern flds
27..Cross st, Camden gardens
5..Cross st, 14 Blackfriars road
37..Cross st, Carnaby st
30..Cross st,Cherry gardens, Rotherhithe
9..Cross st, near Trafalgar st, City road
11..Cross st, 17 Church st, Shoreditch
2..Cross st, 29 Finsbury place
9..Cross st, near Trafalgar place
26..Crosast, Gloucester st, Hoxton
66..Cross st, Han's place, Sloan st
8..Cross st, 43 Hatton garden, Holborn
29..Cross st, Humberstone st
30..Cross st, 10 King st, Rotherhithe
11..Cross st, Leonard st, Shoreditch
33..Cross st, Newington nr the Elephant and Castle
15..Cross st, 25 Fair st, Horselydown
31..Cross st, Webb street, Bermondsey New road
8..Cross st, 5 Gt. Sutton st, Wilderness row, St. John's st
13..Cross-gun ct, 112, Rosemary lane
16..Crosskeys alley, Blackman st, Boro
15..Crosskeys alley, 266 Bermondsey st
2..Crosskeys ct, 12 London wall
1..Crosskeys sq. Little Britain, 75 Aldersgate st
1..Crow alley, Whitecross st, Fore st
11..Crown alley, Crown st, Finsbury sq
11..Crown alley, Curtain road, near Holywell lane, Shoreditch
16..Crown alley yd, Wycomb pl, Boro

Ref. to Plan.
8..Crown & Cushion ct, 1 West Smithfd
36..Crown & Sceptre ct,36 St. James's st
1..Crown ct, near Jewin st
4..Crown ct, near Thames st, Bankside
2..Crown ct, White's alley, Coleman st
2..Crown ct, Broad st, Royal Exchange
1..Crown ct, 5 Butcherhall lane
13..Crown ct, Cartwright st,Rosemary la
7..Crown ct, 221 Chancery lane,Fleet st
1..Crown ct, 7 Charterhouse lane
2..Crown ct, 64 Cheapside
8..Crown ct, 70 Chick lane, Smithfield
12..Crown ct, Church lane, Whitechapel
35..Crown ct, Crown st, Westminster
37..Crown ct,nr Oxford st, Dean st,Soho
11..Crown ct, Dunning's al, Bishopsgate
6..Crown ct, Dorset st, Salisbury sq
7..Crown ct, near Water lane, Fleet st
1..Crown ct, French alley, Goswell ct
1..Crown ct, 16 Golden lane, Barbican
30..Crown ct, Great Hermitage st
1..Crown ct, 85 Grub st, Cripplegate
11..Crown ct, Holywell lane, Shoreditch
15..Crown ct, Horselydown lane
13..Crown ct, 12 Jewry street, Aldgate
23..Crown ct, 5 Gray's Inn lane, Liquorpond street
11..Crown ct, Little Pearl st, Spitalfields
21..Crown ct, Lit Russell st, Covent gdn
7..Crown ct, Little Shire lane
19..Crown ct, near Vine st, Narrow wall
3..Crown ct, Old Change
7..Crown ct, Picket st
23..Crown ct, Portpool lane
21..Crown ct, 22 Lit Princess st, Soho
11..Crown ct, 29 Wheeler st, Quaker's-
 street, Spitalfields
29..Crown ct, Queen's row, King st
14..Crown ct, Seething lane, turn at 55
 Great Tower st
36..Crown ct, Pall Mall
11..Crown ct, Church st, Shoreditch
36..Crown ct, 10, Gerrard st, Golden sq
21..Crown ct, Short's gardens
3..Crown ct, 45 Threadneedle st
4..Crown ct, Trinity lane, Bread st
8..Crown ct, 37 Warwick la, Newgate
 street
12..Crown ct, 99 Wentworth st
2..Crown ct, White's alley, Coleman st
2..Crown ct, Wilson st,Finsbury square
36..Crown mews, Swallow st
6..Crown Office row, Temple
13..Crown place, nr King-st,Rosemary la
20..Crown pl, Crown ct, op. 218 Strand
44..Crown row, Mile end road
32..Crown row, a short distance south
 from Cross st, Newington, Walwth
11..Crown st, S. E. corner Finsbury sq
10..Crown st, Hoxton square
35..Crown st, King st, Westminster
21..Crown st, 440 Oxford st, Soho
16..Crown sq. 269 High st, Borough
16..Crown yard, nr Wycomb pl, Kent st
53..Croyden st, Upper Seymour place
15..Crucifix lane, 50 Bermondsey st

Ref. to Plan.
13..Crutched friars, 64 Mark lane
60..Cuckold's point & stairs, 126Rotherh
4..Cuckold's ct, near Castle lane, Boro
3..Cullum st, 135 Fenchurch st
11..Cullum st, Shoreditch
3..Culver ct, 120 Fenchurch st
17..Cumber's ct, (Great & Lit) near 53
 Horsemonger lane [nal green
11..Cumberland ct, Blackwood all,Beth-
53. Cumberland crescent, Durweston sq
53..Cumberland gate, op the south end
 of Edgeware road, Oxford st
53..Cumberland mews, Adam's st, West,
 Up Seymour st, Portman square
53..Cumberland mews, North gate, Cumberland st, top of Oxford st
53..Cumberland mews, Up Bryanstone
 street, Edgeware road
40..Cumberland pl, 11 Pullens row, High
 street, Islington
32..Cumberland pl,Kent row, nr Surry sq
53..Cumberland pl, near Durweston sq
68..Cumberland pl, near Lisson green
39..Cumberland row, south side of the
 turnpike, Battle bridge
31..Cumberland row, Blue Anchor fields
33..Cumberland row, Kennington green
11..Cumberland st, 77 Curtain road
27..Cumberland st, (gt & lit)Hackney rd
37..Cumberland st, 23 Goodge st,Totten-
 ham court road
53. Cumberland st, 245 Oxford st
5..Cumberland st,63John st,Blackfra rd
68..Cumberland st, near Lisson green
52..Cumberland st, Blackland's lane
20..Cumming's pl, Southampton street,
 Pentonville
39..Cumming st, west side of the chapel
 Pentonville
19..Cuper's bridge & stairs, Narrow wall
 Lambeth, nr Waterloo bdge, Surry
1..Cupid's ct, op.47 Golden la, Barbicn
2..Currier's ct, nrWood st,London wal
7..Cursitor st, 38 Chancery lane
11..Curtain road, 250 Shoreditch
36..Curzon st, May fair, Clarges st,Picdl
2..Cushion ct, 10 Old Broad st, Royal
 Exchange
14..Custom House ct, Beer lane, Great
 Tower street
12..Cutler st, Houndsditch
34..Cut-throat lane, nr Lambeth palace
45..Cut-throat lane, Brook st, Comrcl rd

D

35..Dacre st, 25 New Tothill st, Westmr
1..Dacre's rents yard, 16 White Cross-
 st, Cripplegate
15..Daffy's rents, St, Thomas's st, Boro
16..Dagger all, St. Margaret's hill, Boro
11..Dagger ct, N. E. corner of Long-
 alley, Moorfields
2..Daggett's ct. Broker's row,Moorflds
24..Dalby terrace, Sidney st, City road
29..Dalgleish place, Commercial road
28..Daniel st, Redman's row, Mile end

Ref. to Plan.

35..Darby court, Cannon row
36..Darby ct, Jermyn st, St. James's
13..Darby st, 37 Rosemary lane
14..Dark entry, 59 Lower E Smithfield
3..Darkhouse lane, 15 Lower Thames-street, Billingsgate
4..Darkhouse lane, Queenhithe
28..Darling place, Dog row, Mile end
13..Dart's alley, nr Plough st, Whitechpl
35..Dartmouth st, Tothill st, Westminstr
53..David st, York pl, Portman square
53..David st, Marylebone
13..David & Harp alley, Whitechapel
37..Davies st, 294 Oxford-st
36..Davies st & mews, north side of Berkeley square
66..Davis place, Chelsea
16..Davis's rents, Kent st, Boro
15..Deadman's place, Barclay's Brew-house, Park st, Boro
11..Deal's ct, Fleur-de-lis st, Brick lane Spitalfields
28..Deal st, Mile end
11..Deal st, Pelham st, Spitalfields
32..Dean's buildings, Lock's fields, near Apollo buildings, Walworth
5..Dean's ct, Doctors Commons, and 5 St. Paul's church yard
10..Dean's ct, 48 Kingsland road
7..Dean's ct, 50 Old Bailey
20..Dean's ct, New Round ct, Strand
18..Dean's pl, near the Asylum, Lambeth
33..Dean's row, Amelia st, High st, Walworth
29..Dean st, Commercial road
35..Dean st, Dean yard, Westminster
14..Dean st, 95, Upper East Smithfield
7..Dean st, 43 Fetter lane
11..Dean st, Finsbury square
45..Dean's st, Gold's hill
5..Dean st, Friar st, Blackfriars road
22..Dean st, 92 High Holborn
36..Dean st, Park st, Piccadilly
37..Dean st, Soho sq, 400 Oxford st
15..Dean st, 200 Tooley st, Boro
37..Dean st, (Little) 44 Dean st, Soho
11..Dean's yard, Shoreditch
35..Dean's yard, south west corner of Westminster abbey
39..Deer's place, Brill row, Somers twn
35..Deluhay st, 34 Gt St, George st
35..Delap ct, York st, Westminster
21..Denham's ct, Drury lane
14..Denham court, East Smithfield
20..Denmark court, 382 Strand
29..Denmark st, 154 Ratcliff highway
21..Denmark st, opposite Church st, High-st, St, Giles's
16..Dent's alley, Redcross st, Southwrk
66..Denton's bldgs, New road, Sloane st
39..Denton's buildings, Chapel path, Somerstown
39..Denton st, St. Pancras
21..Denzel st,48 Stanhope st,Clare mrkt
61..Deptford between Rotherh &Greench

Ref, to plan.

36..Derby st, 22 Curzon st, Mayfair
35..Derby st, 49 Parliament st,Westmstr
7..Devereux ct,216 Strand,nr Temple br
11..Devonshire buildings, 21 Worship street, Finsbury square
8..Devonshire ct, Long la, Smithfield
37..Devonshire mews, (east) Portland pl
37..Devonshire mews, (W) Portland pl
37..Devonshire pl & mews, Wimpole st
45..Devonshire pl, Cow lane, Stepney
28..Devonshire pl, Globe la, Mile end
34..Devonshire pl, up. Kennington lane
37..Devenshire row, Portland place
12..Devonshire sq, end of Devonshire st, Bishopsgate street
12..Devonshire st, 18 Bishopsgt st, w tht
34..Devonshire st, Kennington lane
53..Devonshire st, New rd, Paddington
37..Devonshire st, Portland place
28..Devonshire st, Globe road
22..Devonshire st, Queen sq, Foundling hospital
53..Devonshire terrace, Edgware road
28..Devonshire terrace, Globe lane
11..Diamond ct,21 Gt Pearl st,Spitalfilds
8..Diamond ct, 6Hosier lane, Smithfield
44..Diamond st, Stepney green, near the Church
38..Diana place, opposite Upper Conway street, New road, Fitzroy square
3..Dice quay lane and wharf, 23 lower Thames st, near Billingsgate
16..Dickson's alley, Long la, Southwark
17..Dickson's place, Newington butts
20..Dirty lane, 15 Strand, opposite Southampton street
16..Dirty lane, 90 Blackman st, Borough
11..Dirty lane, 73 Shoreditch
3..Distaff lane, (Great & Lit) Friday st, Cheapside
11..Distiller's yard, Shoreditch
10..Ditchman's gardens, Old st road
3..Dobb's ct, Swithin's lane, Cannon st
40..Dobney's ct, Pentonville
40..Dobney's pl, Pentonville
31..Dock head, Shad Thames
29..Dock st, Ratcliff highway
29..Dock st, Commercial rd,Whitechapel
13..Dock st, Rosemary la, Tower hill
5..Doctors Commons, St. Paul's
46..Dodd's place, Hanover st,Rotherhith
60..Dodd's row, Three Colt lane, Beth-nal green
28..Dog row, Mile end turnpike
15..Dog & Bear yard, 127 Tooley st
37..Dog and Duck alley, New Bond st
61..Dog and Duck stairs,Greenland dock
37..Dollason's buildings, 2 Tottenham-court road, near Hanway st
16..Dolphin al, Blackman st, Boro
11..Dolphin alley, Long lane, Moorfields
22..Dolphin ct, 299 High Holborn
7..Dolphin ct, 12 Ludgate hill
1..Dolphin ct, 40 Noble st, Foster lane
10..Dolphin ct, 135 Old st

Ref. to Plan.
12..Dolphin ct, 53 Whitchapel road
12..Dolphin ct, Widegate st
12..Dolphin ct, Lombard st, Spitalfields
16..Dolphin yard, Blackman st, Boro
9..Domingo st, 15 Old st
29..Dorans row, W. side the Half way House, Commercial road
34..Doris st, near Prince's pl, Lambeth
23..Dorrington st, near the House of Correction, Coldbath fields
7..Dorrington st, 87 Leather la, Holborn
35..Dorset ct, or sq. Cannon row, turn at 46 Parliament st
7..Dorset ct. Salisbury sq. Fleet st
53..Dorset mews, Dorset st, Portman sq
53..Dorset mews, (West) Dorset st, Portman square
39..Dorset pl, Pancras, Churen row, nr Gray's Inns lane
53..Dorset sq, New rd, Paddington
53..Dorset st, Portman sq
6..Dorset st, Salisbury sq. Fleet st
53..Dorset st, 28 Manchester st, Manchester sq
12..Dorset st. nr the church Spitalfields
35..Dorset st, Tothill fields
14..Dotteridge st. St, Catherine's lane
23..Doughty mews, Doughty st
34..Doughty place, Lambeth Butts
23..Doughty st, (Up & Low) near the Foundling Hospital, Guildford st, Gray's Inn lane
34..Doughty st, Lambeth walk
35..Douglas st, Tothill fields
5..Dove ct, Addle hill, Thames st
28..Dove ct, Dog row, Mile end
4..Dove ct, Labour in vain hill
2..Dove ct, Gutter lane, Cheapside
3..Dove ct, Lombard st, Cornhill
4..Dove ct, Old Fish st hill
2..Dove ct, Old Jewry
16..Dove ct, near Redcross st, Boro
1..Dove ct, 20 St. Martins le grand
3..Dove ct, St. Swithin's lane
43..Dove pl and rw, Hackney fields
32..Dove pl, Greenwich road
32..Dover pl, Surry sq, Kent road
32..Dover pl, nr Paragon, New Kent rd
16..Dover st, (Great) 1 Blackman st, Boro
36..Dover st, 68 Piccadilly
8..Dowgate hill &ct, op 83 Up Thames st
4..Dowgate stairs, Conzin lane
4..Dowgate wharf, 83 Up Thames st
36..Down st, Piccadilly, E. of Park lane
35..Downing st, W. corner of Whitehall Parliament st
12..Dowson place, Osborn place, 20 Brick la, Whitechapel
52..D'Oyles st, Sloan terrace
22..Drake st, Red Lion sq
13..Draper al, Cooper's row, Tower hill
2..Draper's bds, 60 London wall
38..Draper's bds, Burton crescent
2..Draper ct, Lothbury

Ref, to Planr
9..Draper pl, facing 33 Old st
13..Drum ct, Plough st, 50 Whitechapel
20..Drury ct, 318 Strand
21..Drury la, from 171 Broad st, Bloomsbury, to New church Strand
37..Duchess mews, Duchess st
37..Duchess st, Portland pl, Marylebone
37..Duck lane, Edward st, Soho
8..Duck lane, West Smithfield
35..Duck lane, Orchard st, Westminster
4..Duck's Foot la, 145 Up Thames st
36..Duckpond mews, South side, Shepherd st, Mayfair
28..Ducking pond row, near turnpike, Whitechapel road
21..Dudley ct, 52 High st, St Gile's
68..Dudley grove, Harrow road, Paddington, near the Green
37..Duffour pl, 21 Broad st. Carnaby mkt
7..Duke alley Castle st, Holborn
21..Duke's court, Drury lane
17..Duke's ct, Duke st, Charlte st, Bkfrs
36..Duke's ct, Duke st, Piccadilly
35..Duke's ct, Gt Almonry, Westminster
35..Duke's ct, op. York st, James's st, Westminster
26..Duke's ct, nr, Turnpike, Kingsland r
20..Duke's ct, 134 St Martin's lane
36..Duke's ct, Pall mall
21..Duke's ct, Seven Dials
12..Duke's place, Duke's st, Hounsdtch
38..Duke's road, Tavistock square
51..Duke's row, Pimlico
39..Duke's row, Somers town
20..Duke st, Adelphi, 32 Strand
13..Duke st, Aldgate
29..Duke st, Chapman st, St, George's E
17..Duke st, Charlotte st, Blackfriars rd
6..Duke st, Commercial road, Lambeth
35..Duke st, St, George's st, Westminstr
21..Duke st, 42 Gt Russel st, Bloomsbury
53..Duke st, Grosvenor sq
21..Duke st, Lincoln's Inn fields
53..Duke st, 8 Manchester sq
16..Duke st, Mint st, Boro
37..Duke st, Portland pl, Marylebone
17..Duke st, Obelisk, St. George's fields
36..Duke st, St. James', 182 Piccadilly
12..Duke st, Union st, Bishopgate st
8..Duke st, 56, West Smithfield
11..Duke st, Worship st. Finsbury
12..Duke st, Church st, Whitechapel
12..Duke st, Spitalfields
20..Duke st, York buildings, Strand
15..Duke's head ct, New st, Boro
8..Duke's Head passage, 22 Ivy lane, Newgate st
24..Duncan pl, & ter. nr the New river, City road
20..Duncan pl, 14 Leicester pl, Leicester sq
13..Duncan st. Redlion st, Whitechapel
11..Duncomb ct, 'Cock lane, Church st, Shoreditch
30..Dundee Arms wharf, 253 Wapping
12..Dunk ct, Dunk st, Mile end, N w Twn

Ref. to Plan.

12..Dunk st, Whitechapel road
11..Dunning's al, 151 Bishopsgate without
7..Dunstan's ct, 187 Fleet st
7..Dunstan's ct, 20 Old Bailey
14..Dunster ct, Mincing lane
29..Dunstone place, Sun Tavern fields
18..Durham pl, Asylum, Lambeth
66..Durham pl, Gt Smith st, Chelsea
27..Durham pl, (N. and S.) Hackney rd
27..Durham pl, (East) Hackney road
20..Durham st, 65 Strand
20..Durham yard, Strand
8..Durham yard, West Smithfield
11..Durton st, Curtain road
53..Durweston mews, Crawford st, Portman square
53..Durweston sq, new end of Great Cumberland place, Oxford road
53..Durweston st, 45 Baker st, Portman sq
23..Dutton st, Lucas st, Gray's Inn lane
17..Dyer's st. William st, Blackfrs road
7..Dyer's buildings, 19 Holborn
29..Dyer's buildings, near Judd pl. (East)
2..Dyer's ct, Aldermanbury
1..Dyer's ct, 34 Noble st, Foster lane
12..Dyer's ct, 53 Whitechapel
39..Dyer's place, Judd pl, East, Somers Town
33..Dyer's pl, Parsonage pl, Newington
11..Dyer's pl, Long alley, Moorfields
12..Dyer's yard, Old Bethlehem
13..Dyer's yard, Whitechapel

E

22..Eagle ct, Dean st, Redlion sq, Holbn
8..Eagle ct, 5 St John's la, Clerkenwell
21..Eagle ct, White Hart yd, 33 Drury la
20..Eagle ct, Catherine st, Strand
12..Eagle st, Brick la, Spitalfields
36..Eagle st, 212 Piccadilly
45..Eagle st, Stepney fields
22..Eagle st, 65 Redlion st, High Holbn
28..Eagle pl, Mile End, quarter of a mile below the turnpike
12..Eagle pl, Princes-st, Whitechapel road, Back lane, Poplar
7..Eagle & Child alley, 61 Fleet market
34..Eagle & Child alley, Fore st, Lmbth
36..Eam's yard, 21 Picdlly, op. GreenPark
21..Earl ct, Gt. Earl st, Seven Dials
21..Earl ct, Cranbourne st, Leicester sq.
67..Earl's ct, Old Brompton
6..Earl st, north foot Blackfriars bridge
11..Earl st, Finsbury market
17..Earl st, London rd, St. George's flds
21 : Earl-st, (Gt. and Lit.) Seven Dials, 106 Long Acre
5..Earl-st, Gt. Surry st
35..Earl st, Horseferry rd, Westminster
52..Earl st, Sloane st, Knightsbridge
35..Earl st, Marsham st
21..Earl's yard, Castle st, Long acre
3..Eastcheap Gt. 46 Cannon st
3..Eastcheap Little, 48 Fish st Hill to Little Tower st

Ref. to P an.

31..East lane, nr Dock head, Horselydn
32..East lane, Kent road, extending to Walworth
30..Eastlane stairs, Bermondsey, nearly opposite Union stairs, Wapping
37..Eastley's mews, 24 Wigmore street, Cavendish square
34..East mews, East st, Lambeth
8..East Passage, Cloth Fair, Long Lane, West Smithfield
29..East passage, Wellclose square
32..East place, Upper Prior pl, East la, Walworth
17..East pl, West sq, Lambeth
34..East pl, East st, Lambeth
40..East pl, Chapel st, Pentonville
9..East row, Winksworth's bds, City-rd
44..East st, Smart st, Bethnal green
53..East st, Manchester sq.
32..East st, first on the right in East la, Kent road
34..East st, Lambeth, third on the right from the Stags towards Kenningtn
66..East st, Chelsea common
22..East st, Redlion sq, Holborn
12..East st, Spitalfields market, middle of east side to Redlion st
32..East st, Walworth, part of East la, next to Walworth High st
68..East st, Devonshire pl, Edgware rd
7..East Harding st, Shoe lane
3..East India chambers, 23 Leadenhall st
14..East Smithfield, Tower hill
12..Eastman's ct, Wentworth st
23..Easton ct, 20 Easton st
23..Easton st, Exmouth st, Spafields
51..Eaton lane, Pimlico, third on the right from Buckingham gate
51..Eaton pl, Lit. Eaton st, Pimlico
18..Eaton st, New Cut, Lambeth
17..Ebden ct, Pearl row, first on the right from Blackfriars rd
33..Ebenezer place, west side of Kennington lane
12..Ebenezer sq, Stoney la, Petticoat la
9..Ebenezer st, Plumber st, Peerless pool, City road
51..Ebury Farm row, Ebury square
51..Ebury square, Chelsea road
51..Ebury st & pl, Five fields, Chelsea
13..Eccles yard, Minories
51..Eccleston st, Five fields, Pimlico
51..Eccleston st, fifth on the right from Buckingham gate
51..Eccleston place, Chelsea road
7..Eden ct, Shoe lane, Fleet street
38..Eden ct, Hampstead road
53..Edgware road, west end of Oxford street on the right
53..Edgware st, Oxford st
27..Edith's gardens and place, Birdcage walk, Hackney road
21..Edmond's ct, 27 Princes st, Soho
29..Edmond's st, Up. Maidenhead lane Battle Bridge

Ref. to Plan.
27..Edmond's st, Hackney road
1..Edmund pl, 28 Nelson st, Long lane
37..Edward ct, 14 Edward st, Cavdsh sq
53..Edward's mews, 37 Duke st,Oxfd st
24..Edward place, St. John's st road
27..Edward place, Weymouth terrace
53..Edward place, Up. Seymour place
36..Edward st, Oxendon st
5..Edward st, Blackfriars road
11..Edward st, 23 Hare st, Bethnal grn
38..Edward st, Hampstead road, first
   north of the chapel
37..Edward st,Margaret st,Cavendish sq
45..Edward st, Nelson st, Stepney,near
   the Church
10..Edward st, Old st
45..Edward st,(Up&Lw) Stepney fields
37..Edward st, 95 Wardour st, Soho
37..Edward st, Wigmore st.
33..Edward st, Chester st, Lambeth
   Edward st, 23 Berwick st, Soho
21..Eight bell's yard,opposite St.Giles's
3..Elbow passage, Dowgate hill
35..Elder lane, Upper Millbank
11..Elder st, Norton Falgate
23..Eldon buildings, Bagnigge Wells
30..Elephant lane,nr Church, Rotherhth
  ..Elger's sq, Essex st, Whitechapel
7..Elim ct, 100 Fetter lane, Fleet st
10..Elim ct, Helmit ct, Old st
7..Elim pl, 105 Fetter la, Fleet st
16..Elim st, Baalzephon st, Long lane,
   Bermondsey
12..Elison st, Middlesex st, Whitechpel
51..Eliza st, Belgrave place
12..Elizabeth ct, Phœnix st, Spitalfields
1..Elizabeth la 135Whitecross stOld st
33..Elizabeth place, Kennington cross
35..Elizabeth pl, Gt Peter st, Westmstr
34..Elizabeth place, Vauxhall walk
27..Elizabeth st, Hackney road, between Durham pl, & James pl
66..Elizabeth st, 46 Hans pl, Sloane st
68..Elkins row, Uxbridge road ·
7..Elliott ct, 21 Old Bailey
17..Elliott's ct, Elliott's row
17..Elliott's row, 17 Prospect place, St
   George's fields
28..Ellis's buildings, Dog row,Mile end
28..Ellis's row, White st, Bethnal green
33..Ellis's sq, middle east side of Penton st, Walworth
52..Ellis's st, Sloane st, Knightsbridge
32..Elm ct, Saville row, Walworth
6..Elm court, Middle Temple
29..Elm row, Sun Tavern fields
23..Elm st, & ct, 81 Gray's Inn lane
16..Eltham pl, Kent st, Borough
7..Ely court, 117 Holborn hill
7..Ely place, 102 Holborn hill
17..Ely place, Prospect pl, nearWest sq
36..Engine st, near Park lane, Piccadlly
13..Enoch ct,Goodman's yd,60Minories
28..Epping pl, near Mile end turnpike
44..Ernest st,Whitehorse la,Mile end rd

H

Ref to Plan.
55..Eschol place, north of Wilfred place
   Hampstead road
12..Essex alley, Essex st, Whitechapel
12..Essex ct, Essex st, Whitechapel
6..Essex ct, back of Brick court, middle Temple lane
7..Essex st, Bouverie st, Fleet st
29..Essex st, Charlotte st, New road,
   St. George's East
26..Essex street, half a mile left from
   Shoreditch Church, Kingsland rd
6..Essex st. 210 Strand
12..Essex st, 106 High st, Whitechapel
44..Essex st, Globe lane, Mile end
32..Etham place, 141 Kent road, near
   the Turnpike   [Old st
9..Europa pl, 10 John's row, Brick la,
38..Euston crescent, Somerstown
38..Euston grove, Somers town
38..Euston place, Euston st
38..Euston sq, 28 New road, Tot ct rd
38..Euston st, Euston square
12..Euston st, Spitalfields
2..Evan's ct, 45 Basinghall st
1..Evan's rents, Grub st, Cripplegate
6..Evangelist ct 3Lit. Bridge st,Blckfrs
37..Evelyn's buildings, Rathbone place,
   Oxford street   ·
13..Everard place, west side of Church
   lane, Whitechapel
22..Everett st, 48 Berner's st, Brunswick square
39..Eversham buildings, Charlotte st,
   Somers town
39..Eversham bildgs, (Up) Somer's twn
17..Ewer st, Gravel lane, Southwark
28..Ewing's buildings, Mile end road,
   near Bencrofts Alms houses
3..Exchange al, 17 & 71 Lombard st
20..Exeter Change, 355 Strand
20..Exeter ct, adjoining east side of
   Exeter Change
52..Exeter place, Exeter st, Hans Town
   Sloane street
20..Exeter st, 304 Catherine st, Strand
52..Exeter st, Sloane st, to New street,
   Brompton
23..Exmouth st, Brayne's row,Spafields
29..Exmouth st, Commercial rd, Whitch
23..Eyre place, Eyre st
23..Eyre st, Leather-lane, Holborn

F

15..Fair st,St. John's church, Horselyd
34..Faircloth ct, High st, Lambeth
16..Falcon ct, 176 High st, Boro
7..Falcon ct, 84 Shoe lane
16..Falcon ct, 39White st, Longla,Boro
23..Falcon place, Portpool lane
23..Falcon pl, Coppice row, Clerkenwll ·
1..Falcon square, east end of Falcon-
   st, Aldersgate st
21..Falconbridge ct, Crown st, Soho
21..Falconer ct, Sutton st, Soho square
8..Falconer ct, Cowcross st, Smithfild

Ref. to Plan.

16..Falstaff yd, 140 Kent st, Borough
1..Fan ct, first on the left of Fan st Goswell street
3..Fan ct, Miles's lane, Cannon st
1..Fan st, east side of Aldersgate st, between 106 & 1, Goswell st
36..Farm mews, Hill st, Berkely sq
36..Farm st, Berkeley sq, continuation of the mews to Union st
21..Farmer's rents,top of Crown st,Soho
11..Farmer's rents, Sun st, Bishopsgate
45..Farmer row, St. Anne's place
10..Farmer's sq. Glo'ster ter, Hoxton
29..Farmer st, 30 High st, Shadwell
7..Farrar's buildings, Inner Temple lane, Fleet street
13..Farthing alley, 9 Up East Smithfield
30..Farthing alley, Jacob st, Dockhead, Bermondsey
15..Farthing alley, Tattle alley
29..Farthing fields, 40 New Gravel la
11..Farthing st, Phœnix st, Spitalfields
12..Fashion st, 194 Brick la, Spitalfds
15..Feamore's rents, Roper la, Horslydn
7..Featherbed la, 19 Fetter la, Fleet st
21..Feather's ct, 88 Drury la, Strand
23..Feather's ct, Fox ct, Gray's Inn la
2..Feather's ct, Milk st, Cheapside
21..Feather's ct,Gate st,Lincolns Inn fds
22..Featherstone buildings, 63 Holborn
22..Featherstone ct, 101, City road
10..Featherstone st, 60 Bunhill row
18..Felix st, 32 Stangate st, Lambeth
37..Felix st, Hackney road
1..Fell ct, Fell st, Wood st
1..Fell st, 70 Wood st, Cheapside
26..Felton st, Hoxton
13..Fen ct, 124 Fenchurch st
3..Fenchurch bldgs, 108 Fenchurch st
3..Fenchurch st, 66 Gracechurch st
22..Fenwick ct, 291 High Holborn
15..Ferguson's rents, Snow fields, near Bermondsey street
34..Ferry st, High st, Lambeth
7..Fetter lane, 179 Fleet st
22..Field ct, south west corner of Gray's Inn square
7..Field lane, 84 Holborn bridge
39..Field place, south end of Field terrace, Battle bridge
39..Field row, Battle bridge
39..Field st, first on the right from the turnpike, Battle bridge
12..Fieldgate st, 268, Whitechapel rd
11..Fife's ct, Fleet st, Spitalfields
39..Fifteenfeet la, Gray's Inn lane, near Battle bridge
39..Pig lane, Pancras
1..Figtree ct, 4 Barbican
6..Figtree ct, Temple lane, Temple
5..Finch bdgs, Ewer st, Duke st, Boro
3..Finch lane, 80 Cornhill
31..Findal st, Grange road, Bermondsey new road
35..Fines st, Vincent square

Ref. to Plan.

31..Finmore ct, Blue Anchor yd, Rosemary lane
10..Finsbury ct,N E corner of Finsby sq
11..Finsbury market, East end of Christopher st, Finsbury square
2..Finsbury place, from Moorfields to Finsbury square
11..Finsbury sq, N. side of Moorfields
2..Finsbury pavement, Moorfields
1..Finsbury st, 35 Chiswell st
9..Finsbury terrace, op. Featherstone street, City road
12..Fireball ct, 132 Houndsditch
4..Fish st (Old) S. end of Old Change
3..Fish st hill, 36 Upper Thames st, London bridge
6..Fisher's alley, 62 Dorset st,Salisby sq
12..Fisher's alley, Petticoat la, Whitech
22..Fisher's ct, Eagle st, Redlion square
22..Fisher's st, Kingsgate ct, Redlion square, Holborn
3..Fishmonger's alley, 118 Fenchurch st
16..Fishmonger's alley, High st, Boro
17..Fishmongers' almshouse, Elephant and Castle
1..Fitchet's ct, Noble st, very near Falcon square
38..Fitzroy market, Grafton st,Tot ct rd
38..Fitzroy pl,13 New rd, Fitzroy sq
38..Fitzroy row, Fitzroy pl,New rd
38..Fitzroy sq,end of Grafton st,Tot ct rd
38..Fitzroy st, S.E. corner of Fitzroy sq
2..Five bell alley, Little Moorfields
51..Five fields row, Chelsea
4..Five feet lane, 203 Up.Thames st
12..Five Inkhorn ct, 91 Whtchpl High st
51..Flask lane, Five fields, Chelsea
51..Flask place, Chelsea road
7..Fleet lane, 17 Fleet market
7..Fleet market, 105 Fleet st
23..Fleet row, 15 Eyre st,Leather lane
11..Fleet st, Brick lane, Spitalfields
7..Fleet st, from Temple bar to New Bridge st
11..Fleet st hill, John st, Bethnal green
14..Flemish st, east side of Tower hill
7..Fleur-de-lis ct, 178 Fleet st
12..Fleur-de-lis ct, 112 Houndsditch
23..Fleur-de-lis ct, 84 Gray's Inn lane
15..Fleur-de-lis ct, Tooley st, Borough
8..Fleur-de-lis ct, Turnmill st, Clknwl
11..Fleur-de-lis st, 10 Shoreditch, near White Lion st
34..Flint st, East lane, Walworth
5..Flint st, Higler's st, Blackfriars rd
68..Flood st, Westminster
12..Flower and Dean st, 200 Brick lane, Spitalfields
35..Fludyer st, 6 King st, Westminster
2..Flying horse ct, Maiden la, Wood st
2..Flying horse ct, Rose & Crown ct, N. E. corner of Moorfields
2..Flying horse yd, 54 Grub st, Cripplgt
37..Foley pla, 33 Portland st, Oxford st
38..Foley st, 27 Gt Titchfield st

Ref. to Plan.
31..Folley buildings, Bermondsey
1..Fore st, Cripplegate, from 26 S.W.
corner of Moorfds to Redcross st
34..Fore st, nr Church, Lambeth
45..Fore st, Three Colt st, Limehouse
17..Fort place, West square, Lambeth
31..Fort place, Grange road, Bermdsy
11..Fort st, Spital square
11..Forster bdgs, nr Holywell lane
1..Forster's bdgs, 123 Whitecross st,
St Luke's
44..Fosesket's bdgs, Bethnal green
2..Foster lane, 148 Cheapside
11..Foster st, Bishopsgate st
2..Foster st, Flying horse yd, Moorfds.
2..Founder's ct, Lothbury, a short distance east of Coleman st
3..Foundry ct, nr Friday st,Cheapside
26..Foundry row, Bowling green row,
Hoxton
2..Fountain ct, Aldermanbury
4..Fountain ct, nr Castle la, Southwark
20..Fountain ct, 104 Strand, near Charing cross
13..Fountain ct, 19 Minories
3..Fountain ct, 29 Cheapside
15..Fountain ct, New st, Horselydown
20..Fountain ct, St. Martin's la
12..Fountain ct, Old Bethlem,Bishopsgt
7..Fountain ct, Shoe lane, Holborn
20..Fountain ct, nr Beaufort buildings
6..Fountain ct, Middle Temple lane,
Fleet street
30..Fountain dock, Bermondsey
9..Fountain pl, City rd, nr Finsbury sq
30..Fountain stairs, Bermondsey walk,
west end of Salisbury st
14..Fowkes's bldgs, Gt Tower st
16..Fowl la, Borough
34..Fox alley, Prince's st, Lambeth
37..Fox's bdgs, Kent st, Borough
55..Fox's ct, High st, Shadwell
7..Fox's ct, 11 Gray's Inn lane
23..Fox ct, near the Green, Ray street,
Clerkenwell
36..Fox ct, St. James's st, Piccadilly
1..Fox ct, Newgate st, Cheapside
29..Fox's lane, 55 High st, Shadwell
29..Fox and Goose yd, Coleman st,New
Gravel lane, Wapping wall
3..Fox and Knot ct, Sharpe's alley,
West Smithfield
3..Fox Ordinary ct, Nicholas la, a few
doors on the right from Lombard st
35..Frances place, opposite the Asylum,
Waterloo bridge road
66..Frances st, Chelsea common
35..Francis pl, Palmer's village, Wmstr
20..Francis ct,33Maiden la, Cov, garden
8..Francis ct, Berkley st, Clerkenwell
38..Francis pl, Francis st,three doors on
the right from Tottenham ct rd
37..Francis pl, Marylebone st
18..Francis pl, Westminster rd
18..Francis st, Westminster road

Ref. to Plan.
38..Francis st, nearly op.Newington ch
38..Francis st, 191 Tottenham ct rd
51..Franklin's row, east side of Chelsea
hospital
5..Frazer's ct, Green walk, Blackfriars
33..Frederick pl, 10 High st,Newington
3..Frederick pl, Old Jury, Cheapside
38..Frederick place, Sol's row
24..Frederick pl row, Goswell st road
38..Frederick st, Sol's row
35..Frederick st, 16 Calthorpe pl
34..Freeman's ct, Princes st, Lambeth
2..Freeman's ct, Cheapside
3..Freeman's ct, 83 Cornhill
15..Freeman's lane, Back st, Horselyda
15..Freeschool st, Horselydown
1..French alley, 24 Goswell st
9..French alley, north east corner of
Old st, St. Luke's
12..French ct, Wentworth st
9..French hospital, Ratcliff row
9..French row, nr Ratcliff row,City rd
23..French yard, Bowling gn la,Clrknwl
5..Friar st, Blackfriars road
12..Friar's mount,Church st,Spitalfields
2..Friday st, 36 Cheapside
28..Friendly pl, Mile end
29..Friendly pl,Chapel st,St.George'sE.
10..Friendly pl, Castle st, City road
32..Friendly p', nr Asylum, Kent road,
near Elephant and Castle
..Friendly pl, Brondwall, Lambeth
21..Frith st, 30 Soho square
8..Frogwell ct, 4 Charter house lane,
St. John street
12..Frosty ct, Old Montague st, Spitlfds
13..Fryer's ct, Trinity square
30..Fryer's ct, Gt Hermitage st
30..Fryer's hill, Gt Hermitage st
6..Fryer's st, Shoemaker row, Creed
lane, Ludgate hill
1..Fryingpan al, 60 Turnmill st,Clrkwl
29..Fry's al, Shakespeare wk, Shadwell
35..Fugeon row,Palmer'svillage,Wstmr
67..Fulham road, Brompton
14..Fuller's ct, 35 Upper East Smithfd
11..Fuller's st, 37 Hare st, Bethnal grn
35..Fulmer's row, Palmer's village
7..Fullwood's rents, 34 Holborn
7..Furnival's Inn, 134 High Holborn
7..Furnival's Inn ct, 128 Holborn
7..Furrier's alley, Shoe lane, Fleet st
35..Fynes st, Tothill fields

G

14..Gainsford st, 34 Horselydown
47..Galley walk, op. Blue Anchor road
9..Galway st, Bath st. City road
16..Garden ct, 58 Blackman st, Borough
18..Garden ct,Mason st,Bridge rd,Lmblh
1..Garden ct, Paul's al, Cripplegate
13..Garden ct, George yd, Whitechapel
6..Garden ct, Middle Temple lane,
Fleet street
22..Garden ct, Gt Turnstile, Holborn

Ref. to Plan.

7..Garden ct, 15 Baldwin's gardens, Gray's Inn lane
27..Garden ct, Union st, Bethnal green
12..Garden place, Chicksand st, Mile end New Town
17..Garden pl, nr King's Bench, Boro
17..Garden pl, S. end of Temple st, Surry
19..Garden pl, Vine st, Narrow wall, Lambeth
9..Garden row, 209 City road
17..Garden row, London road
33..Garden row, Newington
33..Garden row, New Hampton st, Walw
27..Garden row, Gibraltar wk, Bethnl grn
18..Garden row, 12 Stangate st, Lambeth
52..Garden row, Sloane st
66..Garden row, west end of Turk's row, Chelsea
33..Garden st, Temple st, Newington
35..Garden st, Totbill fields
12..Garden st, Whitechapel road, near the Church
10..Garden walk, Willow walk, Tabernacle square
35..Gardiner's la, King st, Westmstr
4..Gardner's lane, High Timber street, first on the left Up Thames st
29..Garford st, Ratcliff cross
3..Garlick hill, 191 Up Thames st
32..Garmouth row, nr Asylum, Kent rd
1..Garter court, Barbican
27..Gascoigne pl, Crabtree row, Bthnl gn
9..Gastigny pl, Bath st, City road
21..Gate st, Lincoln's Inn fields
10..Gateward buildgs, Hill st, Finsbury
17..Gaywood st, 9 London road
31..Gelding st, Dockhead
53..Gee's ct, 163 Oxford road
24..Gee st, 52 Goswell st road
39..Gee st, north west corner of Clarendon square, Somers town
7..George alley, 69 Fleet market
21..George alley, Holles st, Clare market
3..George alley, 52 Lombard st, Cornhill
3..George alley, Swan la, London bridge
4..George alley, 96 Old Fish st hill
20..George ct, Duke st, Adelphi
4..George ct, 5 Bennet's hill, Upper Thames street
35..George ct, Gt St Anne st, Westmstr
8..George ct, Little Saffron hill
35..George ct, Old Pye street
36..George ct, 40 Piccadilly
20..George ct, Prince's st, Leicester sq
8..George ct, Redlion st, Clerkenwell
13..George ct, Stoney la, Petticoat la
4..George ct, nr Lambeth hill
16..George ct, 35 White st, Long la, Boro
3..George lane, Botolph lane
3..George lane, Gt Eastcheap
17..George pas, Brick lane, Borough rd
66..George pl, Paradise row, Chelsea
32..George row, nr Lockfields, Walworth
9..George row, Ratcliff row, City road
17..George row, Nelson sq, Blackfrs rd

Ref. to Plan

10..George's st, nr Hoxton square
20..George's st, York blds, Adelphi, Strd
21..George st, 26 Broad st, Bloomsbury
37..George st, Hanover square
53..George st, up. 441 Edgware road
68..George st, James's st, Lisson green
9..George st, nr Nelson st, City road
44..George st, Stepney lane
15..George st, Freeschool st
46..George st, nr Greenland dock
30..George st, Nutkins corner
23..George st, Battle brg, op. Weston st
23..George st, Lucas st, Gray's Inn lane
27..George st, Union st, Bethnal green
5..George st, Blackfriars road
12..George st, Gt Garden st
45..George st, Stepney fields
11..George st, Fleur-de-lis st
37..George st, Foley st, Q. Anne st, E.
1..George st, 28 Foster lane, Cheapside
13..George st, 84 Minories
13..George st, Trinity square
53..George st, nr North Audley st
53..George st, Portman square
36..George st, St James's st, Westmr
35..George st, Palace st, Pimlico
66..George st, (Up&Lw) Sloane sq
38..George st, Old Mint st, Tottenham court rd, first E. of Hampstead rd
17..George st, Borough
32..George st, Trafalgar st, Walworth
27..George st, Bethnal green road
11..George st, 208 High st, Shoreditch
11..George st, Spicer st, Spitalfields
44..George st, near Whitehorse street, Commercial road
53..George st, Manchester square
52..George st, Up. north east corner of Sloane square, Chelsea
12..George st, Wentworth st, Spitalfields
45..George ter, Commercial rd, Limeh.
3..George yd, Bow lane, Cheapside
2..George yd, 56 Coleman st
3..George yd, 56 Lombard st
7..George yd, Seacoal la, Fleet market
8..George yd, Snowhill
12..George yd, 63 Whitechapel High st
1..George yd, 46 Golden lane, Barbican
9..George yd, 108 Old st, St. Luke's
21..George yd, Crown st, Soho
37..George yd, 39 Duke st, Grosvenor sq
21..George yd, Macclesfield st, Soho
16..George yd, nr Old Mint st, Southwrk
34..George yd, Fore st, Lambeth
36..George yd, 32 Piccadilly
35..George&Plough yd, York st, Wstmr
21..Gerrard st, Princes st, Soho
15..Gibbon's rents, Bermondsey st
17..Gibraltar pl, Prospect pl, Newington
17..Gibraltar row, Prospect pl, 238 Kent street, Borough
27..Gibraltar row, Hackney road
17..Gibraltar row, nr West sq, Lambeth
27..Gibraltar walk, Church st, Bethnal gn
35..Gibson's ct, 39 Marylebone st, Piccdly

Ref. to Plan.
18..Gibson's st, op. west side of the Cobourg Theatre
22..Gilbert st, Bury st, Bloomsbury sq
34..Gilbert's buildings, west side of Vauxhall gardens
18..Gilbert's buildings and row, near the Asylum, Westminster bridge road
21..Gilbert's passage, Clare market
21..Gilbert st, Clare market
30..Gilham's ct, Milpond brdg, Rotherh
11..Gilham's fields, 5 Worship st,Finsby
31..Gilham's rents, Hickman's folly
29..Gill st, Coml. rd, Limehouse church
15..Gimber's rents, Snowsfields, Boro
8..Giltspur st, 125 West Smithfield
11..Gingerbread ct, Lamb al, Bishopsgt
37..Glanville mews, Up Rathbone pl
23..Glass ct, Mutton la, Hatton wall
34..Glasshouse bdgs, nr Vauxhall gardns
34..Glasshouse court, Glasshouse street, Vauxhall walk
34..Glasshouse st, Vauxhall walk
36..Glasshouse st, Swallow st, Piccadly
1..Glasshouse yd, 108 Goswell st
1..Glasshouse yd, Aldersgate st
13..Glasshouse yd, Goodman's yd, Mins
5..Glasshouse yd, Gravel la, Southwk
5..Glasshouse yd, Playhouse yd, Water lane, Blackfriars
20..Glastonbury ct, Rose st,Covent gdn
45..Glazier's rents, Fore st, Limehouse
15..Gleen alley, 160 Tooley st
4..Globe ct, 22 Fish st hill
34..Globe ct, Lambeth walk
30..Globe ct, Gt Hermitage st
30..Globe ct, 57 Wapping st
44..Globe lane, Mile end road
44..Globe place, 78 Ratcliff highway, Bethnal green, Hackney road
18..Globe pl, Westmr bridge rd, Lambh
44..Globe road, Mile end
45..Globe stairs, 104 Rotherhithe st
44..Globe terrace, Globe la, Bethnal grn
36..Gloucester ct, St.James's st,Piccdly
1..Gloucester ct, 114 Whitecross st, Old street
53..Gloucester mews, West George st, Portman square
53..Gloucester pl, New rd, Marylebone
53..Gloucester place, Montague square
53..Gloucester place,41 Portman square
17..Gloucester place,Walworth common
32..Gloucester pl, east end of Prospect row, Walworth
45..Gloucester pl, St. Ann's place
47..Gloucester pl, Kent road
34..Gloucester pl, Vauxhall walk, near the gardens
11..Gloucester pl, 94 Curtain road,Shrdh
68..Gloucester row, Edgware road
26..Gloucester row,Gloucester st,Hoxn
17..Gloucester row, Newington
32..Gloucester row, Prospect row,Walw
6..Gloucester st, a short distance on the left from Old st road, Hoxton

Ref. to Plan.
18..Gloucester st, Lambeth
18..Gloucester st, Oakley st, Lambeth
34..Gloucester st, Vauxhall walk
53..Gloucester st, 41 George street, Portman square
27..Gloucester st, Hackney fields
22..Gloucester st, Queen st, Bloomsby
45..Gloucester st, St. Anne's pl, Limeh
28..Gloucester st, Charlotte st,Whitechl
10..Gloucester terrace, Hoxton, continuation of Haberdasher's walk
29..Gloucester ter, Cannon st rd, Wbpl
4..Goat stairs, Bankside
15..Goat st, Freeschool street
16..Goat yd, 24 Blackman st, Borough
11..Goddard rents, Webb's sq. Shoredh
18..Godney's row,Westminster br rd
5..Godliman st, Paul's chain, St. Paul's church yard
45..Gold's hill, nr Cock hill, Shadwell
44..Gold st, Stepney green
29..Gold st, Old Gravel la, Wapping
1..Golden ct, 117 Golden la,Barbican
1..Golden lane, 30 Barbican
36..Golden sq, top of Air st, Piccadilly
21..Golden Ball ct, Wild st, Drury lane
13..Golden Fleece ct, 2 Minories
1..Golden Lion ct, 21 Aldersgate st
16..Golden Lion ct,St.George's ch,Boro
21..Golden place, 138 Drury lane,
33..Golden pl, Market st, Lambeth
7..Goldsmith row, part of south side of east Harding st, Fetter lane
7..Goldsmith's ct, 20, Great New st, Fetter lane
27..Goldsmith's row, opposite Nag's Head, Hackney road
7..Goldsmith st, East Harding st
2..Goldsmith st, 124 Wood st,Cheapside
7..Goldsmith st, Shoe lane, Gough sq, Fleet st
27..Goldsmith place, Hackney road
60..Goldsworthy place, short distance right from Paradise row, Deptford
37..Goodge st, 64 Tottenham court road
13..Goodman's fields, Swan st,Minories
27..Goodman's gardens, Middlesex pl, Hackney road
35..Goodman's gardens, Palmer's village, Tothill fields, Westminster
12..Goodman's stile, Church st, Whcpl
13..Goodman's yard, 60 Minories
20..Goodwin's ct, 55 St. Martin's lane, Charing cross
5..Goodwyn's sq, Bear la, Blckfrs rd
1..Goose yd,near Old st,Whitecross st
1..Goswell st, from 107 Aldersgate st, to Islington
24..Goswell st rd, end of Goswell st
1..Goswell terrace, Goswell st
18..Gould ct, near Stangate st, Lambeth
13..Gould square, Crutched Friars
7..Gough square, from 145 and 151 Fleet street
12..Gouldstone sq, N end Gouldstone st

H 2

Ref. to Plan.

12. Gouldstone street, 140 Whitechapel
28..Govey pl, near the Three Mackerel, Mile end road   [Bedford sq
38..Gower mews, south end of Gower st,
38..Gower place, Upper Gower st
38..Gower st, N E corner of Bedford sq
12..Gower walk, Church la, Whitechapel
13..Gowers row, Mill yard, Cable st
13..Grace's alley, Wellclose square, Ratcliff highway
3..Gracechurch lane, 1, Leadenhall st
3..Gracechurch st, Cornhill
53..Grafton ct, Paradise st, Marylebone
38..Grafton ct, Fitzroy square
38..Grafton mews, 119 Grafton street, Tottenham court road
36..Grafton st, Old Bond st
21..Grafton st, Soho, near continuation of Gerrard st
38..Grafton st East, Tottenham court rd
21..Granby buildings, 111 Drury lane
31..Granby buildings, Vauxhall walk
18..Granby pl & bldgs, Lambeth Butts
11..Granby row, Abbey st, Bethnal green
27..Granby row, White st, Bethnal grn
11..Granby st, St. James's st, Spitalflds
68..Grand Junction canal, Paddington
68..Grand Junction st & wharf, Whitefrs
68..Grand Junction water works and reservoir, Paddington
46..Grand Survey or Croydon canal, Rotherhithe
7..Grange ct, Carey st, Chancery lane
31..Grange road, Bermondsey
31..Grange walk, Bermondsey square
32..Grantham pl, 91 Park st, Piccadilly
1..Grasshopper ct, 217, Whitecross st, Cripplegate
12..Gravel lane, 148, Houndsditch
5..Gravel lane, east end of Holland st, Blackfriars road
1..Gravel wlk Blue Anchor al Bunhill rw
53..Gray's buildings, 38 Duke street, Manchester square
7..Gray's Inn, op. Middle rw, Holborn
7..Gray's Inn lane, 152 Holborn
23..Gray's Inn lane rd, Gray's Inn lane
22..Gray's Inn passage, Red Lion sq
22..Gray's Inn passage, Bedford row
22..Gray's Inn square, south side of Gray's Inn lane
5..Gray st, Blackfriar's road
33..Gray st, Duke st, Manchester square
34..Gray's walk, Lambeth walk, near the Church
1..Gt Arthur st, New ct, Goswell st
35..Gt Almonry, Dean st, Westminster
35..Gt Anne st, Westminster
53..Gt Barlow st, 110 High st, Maryleba
8..Gt Bartholomew close, 33 W Smthfd
23..Gt Bath st, Coldbath square
27..Gt Cambridge st, Hackney road
5..Gt Carter lane, Doctors Commons
37..Gt Castle st, Oxford market
37..Gt Chapel st, 305 Oxford st

Ref. to Plan.

17..Gt Charlotte st, Blackfriars road
22..Gt Coram st, Brunswick square
53..Gt Cumberland pl, Up Seymour st
53..Gt Cumberland st, 246, Oxford st
53..Gt Cumberland st, N Portman sq
16..Gt Dover st, 1 Blackman st, Boro
21..Gt Earl street, 106 Seven Dials, Long Acre
3..Gt Elbow lane, College hill, Upper Thames street
14..Gt Garden ct, St. Catherine's lane
12..Gt Garden st, 49 Whitechapel road
35..Gt George st, 1, King st, Westmr
17..Gt Guildford st, 35 Queen st, Boro
30..Gt Hermitage st, from Hermitage Bridge, London Docks
13..Gt Holloway st, Union st, Whitechpl
22..Gt James st, Bedford row
68..Gt James st, Lisson grove, Padingtn
5..Gt Knightrider st, Doctors Commons
16..Gt Lamb ct, 34, Blackman st, Boro
34..Gt Lemon ct, Princess st, Lambeth
37..Gt Marlbro st, Poland st, Oxford st
37..Gt Marylebone st, 51 Harley street, Cavendish sq,   [Charing cross
20..Gt May's buildings 49 St. Martins la
15..Gt Maze ct, Maze pond, Snow's flds
7..Gt New st, Shoe lane
21..Gt Newport st, St. Martin's lane, opposite Long Acre
22..Gt Ormond st, Lambs Conduit st
11..Gt Pearl street, continuation of Fleur de lis street, Spitalfields
35..Gt Peter st, nr Bowling st, Westm
37..Gt Portland st, 8 John st, Oxford st
13..Gt Prescot st, Goodman's flds Swan st
36..Gt Pulteney st, 15 Brewers street, Golden square
53..Gt Quebec st, Marylebone
21..Gt Queen st, north west corner of Lincoln's Inn fields
21..Gt Queen sq, Lincoln's Inn fields
36..Gt Rider st, St. James's st, Piccadilly
21..Gt Russell st. Bloomsbury
21..Gt Russell st, Covent garden
21..Gt St. Andrew's st, Seven Dials
35..Gt St. Anne's ct, Gt St. Anne's st
35..Gt St. Anne's st, Orchard st, Westmr
35..Gt St. George, 1 King st, Westmr
12..Gt St. Helen's, Bishopsgate st
8..Gt Saffron hill, north end of Field la, Holborn bridge
20..Gt Scotland yard, Whitehall
21..Gt Shire lane, Lincoln's Inn fields
35..Gt Smith st, continuation of Dean st, Westminster
30..Gt Somerset st, near Hermitage, do
16..Gt Suffolk st, 52 Blackman st, Boro
16..Gt Suffolk st East, Blackman ot
5..Gt Surry st, Albion place, south foot of Blackfriars Bridge
8..Gt Sutton st, 128 Goswell st
37..Gt Titchfield st, Oxford market
21..Gt Turnstile, 293 Holborn
16..Gt Union st, Borough High st

Ref. to Plan.

23..Gt Warner st, Coldbath square
19..Gt Waterloo st, Waterloo bridge rd
7..Gt White alley, 33 Chancery lane
21..Gt White Lion st, Seven Dials, 1st
   on the left in Monmouth st
21..Gt Wild st, Gt Queen st, Lincoln's
   Inn fields
2..Gt Winchester st, Broad st, Royal
   Exchange
36..Gt Windmill st, north end Haymkt
53..Gt Woodstock st, Paddington st
53..Gt York Mews, York pl,Portman sq
11..Greaves ct, George yd,Whitechapel
15..Greek ct,Bermondsey st,nr Webb st
21..Greek st, Soho square
30..Green bank, Old Gravel lane,
   Wapping church
15..Green bank, near 31 Tooley st
18..Green's buildings, Lambeth marsh,
   3d turning left from Blackfriars rd
37..Green ct, Little Pulteney st, Soho
2..Green ct,1 Coleman st, London wall
5..Green ct, Holland st, Blackfriars rd
44..Green pl, Green st, Bethnal green
5..Green st, Bear lane, Blackfriars rd
53..Green st, Grosvenor square
20..Green st, 30 Leicester square
22..Green st,Theobald's rd, RedLion sq
5..Green walk, nrChrist ch,Blackfrs rd
5..Green walk, Christchurch, Surrey,
   2nd turning right, near Holland st,
   Blackfriars road
13..Green yard, New Martin ct
4..Green Arbour ct, 5 doors right of
   the Old Change, Lambeth hill
2..Green Arbour ct, 15 Lit. Moorfields
7..Green Arbour ct, 16 Old Bailey
14..Green Church yd, St. Catherine's st
45..Green Dragon al, Narrow st, Limeh
30..Green Dragon al, 194 Wapping
8..Green Dragon al43Cow la W Smithfd
2..Green Dragon ct, 103 Fore st,Crplgt
12..Green Dragon ct, 10 Whitechapel
16..Green Dragon ct, York st, High st,
   Borough
8..Green Dragon yard, Giltspur st,
   Newgate st
21..Green Dragon yd, 199 High Holbn
29..Greenfield st, White Horse lane,
   Commercial road
8..Greenhill's rents, 94 St. John st
5..Greenhouse row, Blackfriars road
30..Greenland pl, Lucas st, GraysInn la
61..Greenland docks, Rotherhithe
1..Green Lettuce ct,170 Fore st,Crplgt
3..Green Lettuce la, 51Cannon st,City
4..Greenwich st, Brickhill lane
14..Greenwood's ct, 25 Nightingale la,
   East Smithfield
12..Greg's al, Essex st, Whitechapel
15..Gregory place, Maze, Borough
24..Gregory pl, 20 Wingrove pl, Clknwl
47..Grenada place, New Peckam, op
   posite Canal place, Kent road
45..Grenada pl, Commercial rd,Stepney

Ref. to Plan.

45..Grenada ter,Commercial rd,Stepney
22..Grenville st, Brunswick square
39..Grenville st,Somer's town, opposite
   Clarendon square
37..Gresse st,Rathbone place, Oxford st
27..Gretton pl, near Patriot square
39..Greville st, Brook st, Holborn
7..Greville st, Hatton garden
35..Greycoat buildings, Tothill fields
35..Greycoat st, Vincent square
12..Grey Eagle st, Phœnix st, Spitalfds
3..Greyhound alley, St. Mary Axe
8..Greyhound court, Chick lane
20..Greyhound ct, Milford lane, Strand
14..Greyhound ct, St. Catherine's lane,
   Tower hill
28..Greyhound lane, 104 Whitechapel
7..Greystock pl, 101 Fetter la, Holborn
34..Grey's walk, Lambeth walk
28..Griffin pl, Dog row, Bethnal green
29..Griffin st, 61 Shadwell High st
15..Griffith's rents, Bermondsey st, near
   Tooley st
13..Grig's ct, Goodman's yard
31..Grimscott st, Grange road
31..Grimstead place, near Alscott place
11..Grocer's ct, 55 Kingsland road
3..Grocer's hall ct, 36 Poultry
45..Grog ct, north end of Nightingale la,
   Limehouse
52..Grosvenor gate, Park la, Piccadilly
36..Grosvenor market, 23 S Molton st
38..Grosvenor mews, south side from
   Grosvenor square
52..Grosvenor place, Hyde park corner
17..Grosvenor place,opposite south end
   of Pearl row, Borough road
68..Grosvenor row, Edgeware road
66..Grosvenor row, near the Hospital,
   Chelsea
36..Grosvenor square, New Bond st
36..Grosvenor st, Grosvenor square
35..Grosvenor st, 6 Millbank rw, Westm
51..Grosvenor st, up Eaton st, Pimlico
16..Grotto gdn, Cannon st,Mint st,Bore
53..Grove, James st, first on the left
   from Lisson grove
39..Grove place, Somer's town
24..Grove place, Goswell st road
28..Grove place, Mile end road, near
   the turnpike
53..Grove place, Lisson grove
35..Grove row, Palmer's village
28..Grove st, near turnpike, Mile end
68..Grove st, Lisson green, Paddington
61..Grove st, Deptford
29..Grove st, Commercial rd, Whitechpl
1..Grub st,14 Fore st, Cripplegate
35..Grub st, 33 Vine st, Westminster
4..Grub's yd, Castle lane, Southwark
22..Guildford mews, Upper Guildford st
22..Guildford st, 28 Grays Inn lane
24..Guildford place, Spafields
24..Guildford st East, Spafields
3..Guildhall alley, Basinghall st

Ref, to Plan.

2..Guildhall, north end of King st, Chpsd
15..Gun alley, 34 Bermondsey st
30..Gun al, Up.&Low Wapping church
2..Gun alley, Little Moorfields
29..Gun alley, Queen st, Ratcliff cross
13..Gun ct, Cable st, Rosemary lane
8..Gun ct, near Wilderness row, St. John st, Clerkenwell
60..Gun lane, Three Colt st, Limehouse
12..Gun square, 151, Houndsditch
12..Gun st, 20 Union st, Bishopsgate st
5..Gun st, Higler's lane, Blackfriars rd
16..Gun yard, Pepper al, Boro. High st
34..Gunhouse al &stairs, Princes st, Lmbh
7..Gunpowder alley, 95 Shoe lane
2..Gutter lane, 134 Cheapside
26..Gwynn's buildings, Goswell st rd, Islington, near the Angel
53..Gwynn's pl, Lisson grove, Paddngtn
24..Gwyn's place, Goswell st road

H

10..Haberdashers Almshouses, north end of Pitfield st, Old st road
6..Haberdasher's ct, 27 Nicholas lane
10..Haberdasher's place, adjoining the Almshouses
1..Haberdasher's sq, Grub st, Cripplegt
10..Haberdasher's st, Hoxton
10..Haberdasher's walk, continuation of Pitfield
32..Hackney pl, Lion st, New Kent rd
11..Hackney road, from Shoreditch Church to Hackney Turnpike
27..Hackney road crescent, Hackney rd
27..Hackney road terrace, Hackney rd
26..Haggerston or Agoston, Kingsland rd
15..Haglin's gateway, 44 Tooley st
13..Hairbrain st, Blue Anchor yard, Rosemary lane
33..Hall place, a few doors right from Newington, Kennington lane
14..Hall's rents Helmet ct St. Catherine's
60..Hall st, Poplar
1..Half Moon al, 138, Jewin st
11..Half Moon al, Bishopsgate without
30..Half Moon al, 8 High st, Wapping
2..Half Moon al, 17 Little Moorfields
13..Half Moon al, Whitechapel High st
1..Half Moon al, 46 Whitecross st, Cripplegate
1..Half Moon ct, 138 Aldersgate
30..Half Moon ct, Hermitage bridge
11..Half Moon ct, Long al, Moorfields
23..Half Moon ct, 20 Portpool lane
3..Half Moon pass, 89 Gracechurch st
36..Half Moon st, 86 Piccadilly
11..Half Nichol's st, Church st, Shoredh
39..Halford row, Britannia st
6..Half paved ct, Dorset st, Salisbury sq
31..Halfpenny hatch, Bermondsey chrch
46..Halfpenny hatch, Deptford, Lower road to Greenland dock
14..Halifax st, Mile end, New town
52..Halkin st, Grosvnr pl, Hyde pk tnrpk

Ref. to Plan.

36..Ham yard, 37 Gt Windmill st
44..Hampden place, Bonner's fields
39..Hampden st, Clarendon square, Somers town
4..Hamer's la, Maid la, Southwark
39..Hamilton place, Britannia-st
52..Hamilton place, near Hyde park corner, Piccadilly
45..Hammer & Crown ct, 80 Broad st Ratcliff
13..Hammet st, 100 Minories
14..Hammond's ct, 23 Mincing lane
26..Hammond sq, Hoxton
38..Hampstead rd, north, continuation of Tottenham court road
33..Hampton st, three turnings from the Elephant & Castle, Walworth
52..Han's place, Sloane st
27..Han's row. Wilmot square
63..Han's st, Sloane st, Knightsbridge
13..Hanam court, Aldgate
11..Hand al, 42, Long al, Moorfields
1..Hand ct, 71 Golden lane, Barbican
22..Hand ct, 58 High Holborn
20..Hand ct, 26 Maiden la, Covent gdn
2..Hand ct, 25 Philip la, London wall
4..Hand ct, 151 Upper Thames st
5..Hand & Crown ct, Orchard st, Westr
14..Hand & Pen ct, 35 Tower hill
3..Hand and Pen ct, near Creed-church lane, 64 Leadenhall st
8..Hand & Pen ct, Long la, Smithfield
7..Hangingsword al, Water la, Fleet st
1..Hanover ct, 74 Grub st, Cripplegate
13..Hanover ct, 103 Minories
46..Hanover gardens, Hanover st, Roth
37..Hanover square, 132 Oxford st
37..Hanover st, Hanover square
21..Hanover st, 97 Long Acre
46..Hanover st and stairs, Rotherhithe
33..Hanover st, Walworth
37..Hanway st, 23 E end of Oxford st
27..Harbour row, Bethnal green
6..Harcourt buildings, Middle Temple
53..Harcourt st, Lisson grove
7..Harding st, Gough square
35..Harding's al, York st, Broadway
11..Hare al, Holywell, Shoreditch
1..Hare ct, Aldersgate st
11..Hare ct, Hare st, Spitalfields
26..Hare ct, Kingsland road
7..Hare ct, Ship place, Temple Bar
8..Hare ct, Inner Temple lane
11..Hare marsh, Hare st, Spitalfields
11..Hare st, Bethnal green
26..Hare st, Hoxton road
26..Hare walk, Hoxton road
37..Harewood place, 124 Hanover sq
21..Harford buildings, 115 Drury lane
33..Harleyford pl, Kennington common
33..Harleyford st, nr the Horns, Keningtn
37..Harley mews, Cavendish square, Wigmore st
53..Harley place, New rd, Marylebone
37..Harley st, Cavendish square

Ref. to Plan.
28..Harlow place, Mile end turnpike
16..Harmer buildings, Horsemonger la
7..Harp alley, 82 Fleet market and
13 Shoe lane
8..Harp alley, Saffron hill
14..Harp lane, Lower Thames st
34..Harper's walk, High st, Lambeth
22..Harpur st, 47 Theobald's road
13..Harrard's alley, Wellclose square
30..Harrol's row, Green bank, Wapping
12..Harriet place, 56 Passion, Spitalfds
45..Harris's ct, 115 Brook st, Ratcliff
29..Harris's ct, 112 Ratcliff highway
37..Harris's place, 363, Oxford st
7..Harrison's ct, Gray's Inn lane, near
Acton st
13. Harrow alley, 62 Aldgate st
13..Harrow al, White st, Houndsditch
68..Harrow road, Paddington, near
Tyburn turnpike
68..Harrow st, Lisson green
4..Harrow st, St. Peter's hill
16..Harrow st, Mint st, Borough
37..Hart st, Duke st, Grosvenor square
21..Hart st, King st, Bloomsbury
21..Hart st, Covent garden
1..Hart st, 63 Wood st, Cheapside
13..Hart st, 64 Crutched Friars
32..Hart st, Weymouth st, New Kent rd
1..Hart st, Cripplegate
21..Hartford place, Drury lane
33..Hartford place, East la, Walworth
32..Hartly pl, opposite Deaf and Dumb
Asylum, Kent road
1..Hartshorn ct, 82 Golden la, Barbican
3..Hartshorn ct, 94 Fenchurch st
2..Hartshorn ct, 17 Moor la, Cripplegt
2..Hat & Tun yard, Hatton wall
4..Hatchet ct, Little Trinity lane,
Bread st, Cheapside
5..Hatfield's bdgs, Stamford st, Blkfrs
17..Hatfield pl, near the Obelisk, St.
George's fields
1..Hatfield place, 26 Goswell st
5..Hatfield st, Stamford st, Blackfrs rd
5..Hatfield st (Lower) Stamford st
8..Hatton ct, 138 Saffron hill
3..Hatton ct, 49 Threadneedle st
8..Hatton garden, 106 Holborn hill
23..Hatton wall, end of Hatton garden,
or 75 Gt Saffron hill
37..Haunch of Venison yd, Brook st,
Grosvenor square
3..Hawkin's ct, Mile's lane, Cannon st
13..Hawkin's ct, 82 Rosemary lane
36..Hay hill, Berkley square
13..Haydon ct, Haydon square
13..Haydon square, Minories
13..Haydon yard, 40 Minories
36..Haymarket, east end of Piccadilly
to Pall Mall
66..Haymer place, Chelsea hospital
86..Hay st, nr John st, Berkley square
21..Hay's ct, Gerrard st, Soho
36..Hay's mews, Charles st, Berkley sq

Ref. to Plan.
10..Hazlewoodct, Twister's al, Bnhill rw
43..Heath place, Hackney turnpike
13..Heath's rents, Church la, Rosemy la
45..Heath row, Stepney causeway
45..Heath st, Commercial road, near
Stepney causeway
20..Heathcock ct, nr Bedford st, Strand
20..Heathcock st, Strand
23..Heathcote st, Mecklenburg square
36..Heddon ct, 131 Swallow st, Piccadilly
36..Heddon st, Swallow st
40..Hedge row, Back lane, Islington
29..Helen ct, Ratcliff square
29..Helmet ct, Butcher row, Up E. Smhfd
12..Helmet ct, 12 & 13, Wormwood st,
Bishopsgate st
14..Helmet ct, St. Catherine's
2..Helmet ct, Wormwood st
2..Helmet ct, nr Basinghall st
5..Helmet ct, nr Addle hill
20..Helmet ct, 278 Somerset pl, Strand
7..Helmet ct, Carey st, Lincoln's Inn
10..Helmet row, 17 Old st, St. Luke's
20..Hemming's row, 118 St. Martin's la,
Charing cross
66..Hema terrace, nr Chelsea hospital
7..Hen & Chicken's ct, 185 Fleet st
3..Hencage la, Duke's pl, Leadenhall st
12..Henneage lane, Bevis Marks
27..Henrietta lane, Hackney road
20..Henrietta mews, Henrietta street,
Brunswick square
22..Henrietta st, Brunswick square
37..Henrietta st, Cavendish square
53..Henrietta st, Duke st, Manchester sq
20..Henrietta st, Covent garden
27..Henrietta st, Hackney road, half a
mile from Shoreditch church
38..Henry pas, Henry st, Tottnhm ct rd
32..Henry pl, Monmouth pl, Surry sq.
35..Henry pl, Castle st, Westminster
23..Henry st, John's st, Gray's Inn la
10..Henry st, 80 Old st, St. Luke's
40..Henry st, Pentonville, continuation
of White Lion st
38..Henry st, James's chapl, Hampst rd
29..Henry st, Ratcliff highway
37..Henry st, Tottenham court road
19..Henry st, Waterloo road
14..Henry yd, St. Catherine's
20..Herbert's pass, Foundling ct, Strand
18..Hercules bdgs, nr Asylum, Lambh
29..Hereford ct & pl, Cannon st road,
Commercial road
53..Hereford st, Park st, Grosvenor sq
39..Hereford st, Skinner st, Somers twn
29..Hereford st, Turner st, Commrl rd
40..Hermes st, 9 Henry st, Pentonville
67..Hermitage, Yeoman's row, Brompta
30..Hermitage bridge, Wapping
30..Hermitage yd, Gt. Hermitage st
13..Hern's ct, Dock st, Rosemary lane
38..Hertford st, Fitzroy square
36..Hertford st, Mayfair, Down st, Picdly
39..Hertford st, Skinner st, Somers town

Ref to Plan.
26..Hervey st, Hoxton
20..Hervey's bds, Bedford st, Strand
20..Hewitt's ct, 462 Strand
31..Hickman's folly, Dockhead
15..Hickman's rents,Russell st,Bermd st
36..Hide's ct, King st, Golden square
35..Hide place, Tothill fields
56..Highbury, Islington
21..High Holborn,from the top of Drury
    lane to Gray's Inn lane
52..High row, op. Sloane st, Knightsbg
12..High st, Gt Garden st, Whitechapel
34..High st, near Church, Lambeth
53..High st, Marylebone lane
33..High st, near Church, Newington
21..High st,St. Giles's, between the end
    of Oxford st and Broad st
29..High st, Up Shadwell
52..High st, Kensington
53..High st, Marylebone, Thayer st,
    Manchester square
16..High st, from 322 Boro, London bg
13..High st, Aldgate
 4..High Timber st, Up Thames street,
    Broken wharf
17..Higler's lane, Blackfriars road
 5..Hill's (Rev. Rowland) Alms-houses,
    middle of Rochester row,Blkfrs rd
51..Hill's bdgs,Avery farm row,Pimlico
29..Hill's ct, Old Gravel lane
11..Hill ct, nr Webb sq, 51 Shoreditch
36..Hill st, 41 Berkley square
27..Hill st, Bethnal green
10..Hill st, 5 Paul st, Finsbury square
29..Hilliard's ct, 15 Old Gravel lane
 7..Hind ct, 147 Fleet street
 1..Hinde ct, Noble st, Foster lane
53..Hinde mews, 61 Marylebone lane
53..Hinde st,Bentinck st, Manchester sq
53..Hinton st, New rd, Marylebone
17..Hitchcock's yd,Newington causewy
30..Hobb's rents, Marygold st, Rotherh
34..Hobb's row, Lambeth
15..Hobson's bldgs, Russell st,Bermnsy
15..Hobson's ct, Tooley st, Borough
13..Hobson's pl, Pelham ct, Mile end
33..Hodson st, Francis st, Walworth
11..Hog lane, Norton Falgate
13..Hog yd, White's yd, Rosemary la
 7..Holborn extends from Snowhill to
    Broad st, Bloomsbury
 7..Holborn bridge, 87 Snowhill
 7..Holborn hill, 84 Holborn bridge
 7..Holborn ct, entrance to Gray's Inn
 7..Holborn pl, 76 Holborn hill
21..Holborn row, Lincoln's Inn fields
38..Holbrook blds, 127 Tottenham ct rd
 8..Hole in the Wall pas, 24 Baldwin's
    gardens, Leather lane, Holborn
 7..Hole in the Wall ct, 160 Fleet st
 6..Holiday yd, Creed la, Ludgate hill
 6..Hollwell st, 266 Strand
 5..Holland st, Surry side Blackfrs bdge
35..Holland st, Horseferry rd, Westmsr
37..Hollen st, 130 Oxford st

Ref. to Plan.
37..Holles st, Cavendish square
21..Holles st, Clare market
34..Holyfield row, Elizabeth pl, Lambh
11..Holywell ct, Holywell st, Shoredh
11..Holywell la, 110 Curtain rd,Shoredh
11..Holywell mount, Shoreditch
11..Holywell row, Worship st, Shoredh
35..Holywell st, Millbank
35..Holywell st, Westminster
53..Homer pl, Lisson green, Paddington
53..Homer row, Lisson green
53..Homer st, Lisson green
29..Homerton st, Commercial rd, Whpl
10..Honduras st,24 Old st, Goswell st
29..Honduras ter,Commercial rd,Whcpl
 2..Honey lane, 11 Cheapside
 2..Honey lane market, Cheapside
 2..Honeysuckle ct, Moor la, Cripplegt
13..Hooker's sq, 82 Leman st, Good-
    man's fields
14..Hooper's ct, 28 Up East Smithfield
52..Hooper's ct, North st, Han's pl
12..Hooper's ct, Pelham st
 8..Hooper's st, Gt. Sutton st
20..Hop gdns, St.Martin's la,Charng cr
12..Hope st, Quaker st, Brick la,Sptlfds
27..Hope town, Church st, Bethnal grn
37..Hopkin's st, 51 Broad st, Berwick st
53..Horace pl, Lisson green
 1..Horn alley, 40 Aldersgate st
 3..Horn alley, 30 Liquorpond st
 1..Horn ct, Salter's ct. Shoreditch ch
35..Horseferry road, 118 Rotherhithe ch
45..Horseferry rd,Narrow st,Limehouse
33..Horse and Groom yd, 20 High st,
    Newington
32..Horsely st, Mount st, Walworth
15..Horselydown,from the end of Tooley
    street to Dockhead
15..Horselydown lane, near east end of
    Tooley street
16..Horsemonger la, Newington causw
16..Horsemonger prison,Horsemonger la
 4..Horseshoe alley, Bankside, Borough
10..Horseshoe alley, 99 Old st
13..Horseshoe alley,Middlesex st,Whcpl
 2..Horseshoe alley,Wilson st, Moorfds
35..Horseshoe al,York st, Broadway,
    Westminster
 7..Horseshoe & Star ct, 185 Fleet st
21..Horseshoe ct,Carey st,Lincoln's Inn
21..Horseshoe ct, Clement's lane, or 11
    Carey street, Lincoln's Inn
 7..Horseshoe ct, 32 Ludgate hill
13..Horseshoe st,Middlesex st, Whchpl
 8..Hosier lane, West Smithfield
66..Hospital row, Chelsea
21..Houghton st, Clare market
12..Houndsditch,from 4 High st,Aldgate
24..Howard's alley, Clerkenwell close
 9..Howard's green, City road, back of
    Anderson's buildings
27..Howard's pl, Hackney rd, nr turnpk
 9..Howard st, Howard's green
20..Howard st, Arundel st, Strand

Ref. to Plan.

3..Howford's blds, 148 Fenchurch st
34..Howick pl, Vauxhall road
34..Howick ter, Vauxhall road
38..Howland's mews, west, Howland street, Fitzroy square
38..Howland st, 94, Tottenham ct rd
10..Hoxton market, Crown st, Old st
10..Hoxton road, end of Curtain road
10..Hoxton square, Old st road
26..Hoxton town, first on' the right in Old st road, Shoreditch
9..Hoxton new town, City road
11..Hudson's ct, 22 Wheeler st, Sptlfds
20..Hudson's ct, op. Northumberland st Strand
33..Hudson st, Francis st, Newington
4..Huggin ct. east side Huggin lane, in Little Trinity Lane
4..Huggin lane, 200 Up. Thames st
2..Huggin lane, 110 Wood st, Cheapside
17..Hughes's ct, Newington causeway
6..Huish ct, 9 Earl st, New Bridge st, Blackfriars
9..Hull pl, John's row, Brick la, Old st
60..Hull st, nr East India dock
9..Hull st, John's row, Brick la, Old st
29..Humberstone st, Commercial road, second on the left from Cannon st rd
45..Humber st, White horse lane, Commercial road
20..Hungerford mkt, Hungerford st
20..Hungerford st, 20 Strand
15..Hunt's ct, Queen st, Horselydown
20..Hunt's ct, 19 Castle st, Leicester sq
12..Hunt's ct, Hunt's st, Spitalfields
20..Hunt's ct, St. Martin's lane, first on right from the Strand
12..Hunt's st, Spitalfields
22..Hunter's mews, Henrietta street, Brunswick square
22..Hunter's st, north west corner of Brunswick square
22..Hunter's st, 16 Etham pl, op. the Bull, Gt. Dover rd, Borough
16..Hunter st, (Lit.) 141 Kent st, Boro
26..Huntingdon st, first turning on the left from Kingsland road
37..Husband st, Hopkins st, Carnaby market. Shoreditch
3..Hurle's bldgs, Garlick hill, Upper Thames st
32..Hyde park, Lock's fields
52..Hyde park, west end of Piccadilly, and Oxford st
52..Hyde park corner, end of Piccadilly
..Hyde place, Hoxton
35..Hyde pl, nr Vincent st, Tothill flds
21..Hyde st, Lyon st Bloomsbury
13..Hylord's court, 46 Crutched friars, Savage gardens

I

14..Idle lane, Gt. Tower st
60..India (East) dock, Blackwall
3..India (East) house, Leadenhall st

Ref. to Plan.

60..India (East) rd, E. end Commercial rd
60..India row, nr East India dock
60..India (West) docks, Poplar
35..Infirmary, Horseferry rd, Westmstr
3..Ingram ct, 166 Fenchurch street, St. Mary Axe
12..Innage lane, Bevis marks
19..Inner Scotland yd, Whitehall
6..Inner Temple lane, Temple
44..Ireland row, nr Stepney green
5..Ireland yd, St. Andrew's hill, Blkrs
13..Irish ct, Whitechapel High st
53..Ironmonger lane, Edgeware road
3..Ironmonger lane, 91 Cheapside
9..Ironmonger row, 91 Old st, St. Luke's
9..Ironmonger st, nr Old st square
39..Isaac's place, Wilstead st, Somers tn
7..Isaac's rents, Shoe lane, Holborn
35..Isabella row, 22 William st, Pimlico
29..Island pl, Commercial rd, Limehs
61..Isle of Dogs, opposite Deptford, nr Limehouse
40..Islington, near Pentonville
24..Islington rd, St. John st, Smithfield
t..Ivy lane, 30 Paternoster row
22..Ivy st, George st, Broad st, Blmsby

J

6 Jackson's ct, Bristol place
2..Jackson's pl, Long alley, Moorfields
8..Jacob's ct, 2 Turnmill st, Clerkenwll
53..Jacob's mews, 14 Charles st, Manchester square
30..Jacob st, near Dock head
1..Jacob's well ct, 21 Barbican
1..Jamaica ct, Golden la, Barbican
60..Jamaica place, Commercial road, near the church, Limehouse
17..Jamaica pl, Borough road, a few yards left from the Obelisk
31..Jamaica row, nr Grange wk, Bermdsy
30..Jamaica st, Rotherhithe
9..James's ct, 101 Golden la, Barbican
27..James's pl, Birdcage wk, Hackney rd
15..James's pl, Salisbury st, Jamaica row, Bermondsey
30..James's pl, Silver st, King st, Wapps
38..James's pl, Hampstead road, a short distance on the right from Tot ct rd
9..James's rents, near Old st road
17..James's row, op. 16 Gravel la, Boro
17..James's row, Gt. Suffolk st, Boro
36..James's st, (Lower) 12 Golden sq
37..James's st, Brook st, Grosvenor sq
35..James's st, from Buckingham gate to York st
20..James's st, 43 Long Acre
36..James's st, 18 Haymarket
11..James's st.52 Leonard st, Shoreditch
17..James st, Dover st, Blackfr'ars rd
44..James st, nr Trafalgar sq, Stepney
20..James st, Duke st, Adelphi
36..James's market, 52 Haymarket
60..James st, Isle of Dogs
68..James st, (Gt) 19 Stafford st, Mary'bn

Ref. to Plan.

37..James st, 165 Oxford st
68..James st, Lisson green, Paddington
18..James st, 32 New cut, Lmbth marsh
45..James st, Limehouse walk
11..James st, Leonard st
29..James st, St. George's, East
36..James st, St. James st, 164,Picadilly
9..James st, Old st
37..James st,near Duke st, Oxford st
39..James st, West st, Somer's town
53..James st, Manchester square
36..James st, 12 Lower Golden square
32..Jane place, nr the Asylum, Kent rd
32..Jane place, Kent road
29..Jane st, Commercial road, 2nd on
    the right from Cannon st road
17..Jane st, Collingwood st. Blackfriars
29..Jane st,Commercial rd,Whitechapel
11..Jane Shore alley, Shoreditch church
37..Jee's ct, 164, Oxford st
35..Jeffery's buildings, Great Almonry,
    Tothill fields
13..Jeffry's sq, St. Mary Axe, Leaden-
    hall street
36..Jermyn ct, Jermyn st
36..Jermyn st, 46, Haymarket
3..Jerusalem ct, 59 Gracechurch st
24..Jerusalem court, 89 St. John's st,
    Smithfield
24..Jerusalem passage, St. John's sq
17..Jetson st, Bennett's row,Blackfriars
1..Jewin court, 10 Jewin st
1..Jewin st, 45 Aldersgate st
13..Jewry st, Aldgate, Leadenhall st
66..Jew's row, near Chelsea hospital
27..Jew's walk, N. side of Bethnal gr rd
52..Jobbin's ct, Knightsbridge
22..Jockey's fields, 25 King's rd, Bed-
    ford row, Holborn
26..John's buildings, Gt Peter st,Westm
29..John ct, Charlton st, Somer's town
36..John ct, Lower John st
1..John ct, St. Martin's le grand
19..John's ct, Church lane, Cable st
..John's ct, opposite 26, Wingrove pl,
    Clerkenwell
14..John's ct, 54 E. Smithfd, Tower hill
36..John's ct, Farm st,
37..John's ct, Hanway st
14..John's ct, 55 Upper East Smithfield
15..John's ct, Three Oak la
13..John's ct, Somerset st, Whitechapel
37..John's ct, Wigmore st
22..John's mews, Little James st
9..John's pl, John's row, Old st, a
    few doors on the left, opposite
    Shoreditch church
9..John's row, Brick lane, Old st
20..John's st, 34 Ratcliff highway
20..John st, 143, Adelphi, Strand
48..John st, Cambridge heath
5..John st, Blackfriars road
10..John st, Charles st, Willow walk
29..John st, near Doran's row
29..John st, Cross st, Sun Tavern fields

Ref. to Plan.

22..John st, 7 Sion pl, East la,Walworth
68..John st, 78 Edgeware road
15. John st, Free School st
36..John st, 21 Brewers st,Golden sqr
45..John st, Stepney fields
45..John st, Whitehorse lane, Stepney
36..John st, Grosvenor mews
31..John st, Hickman's folly, Dock head
36..John st,15 Hill st, Berkley square
5..John st, Holland st, Blackfriars rd
32..John-st, New Kent road, second
    turning left, below the Brick-
    layers Arms
28..John st, near Dog row, Mile end
22..John st, 7 King's rd, Gray's Inn la
11..John st, Leonard st, Finsbury
12..John st, Brick la, Whitechapel
13. John st, 121 Minories
37..John st, 102 Oxford st
53..John st, New rd, Marylebone
29..John st, Cannon st road
29..John st, New Gravel lane
43..John st, Bonner's st, Bethnal green
36..John st, St. James's square
35..John st, St. John's church, Westmr
24..John st, 21 Yardley st, Spafields
38..John st, Tottenham court road
34..John st, Union st, Walcot pl,Lmbth
15..John st, Webb st, Bermondsey st
12..John st, Brown's lane, Spitalfields
28..John terrace, Dog row, Mile end
34..Johnson's bldgs, nr Lambeth church
13..Johnson's buildings, Rosemary lane
17..Johnson's buildings, Blackfriars rd
20..Johnson's ct, Charing cross
7..Johnson's ct, 164 Fleet st
13..Johnson's ct,LitAlie st Goodman's fds
35..Johnson's ct, Great Peter st
17..Johnson's ct, Blackfriars road
35..Johnson's row, New Ranelagh
35..Johnson's st, Millbank
30..Johnson's st, 156 Old Gravel lane
29..Johnson's st, Sun Tavern fields
39..Johnson's st. Somer's town
18..Joiner's al, Westminster bridge road
4..Joiner's al, Upper Thames st
15..Joiner's ct, 241 Tooley st
4..Joiner's Hall bdgs, 79 Up. Thames st
4..Joiner's st, Upper Thames st
5..Joseph's al, Gravel la, Southwark
39..Joseph st, Lucas st, Gray's Inn lane
29..Joseph st, Sun Tavern fields
29..Jubilee pl, Crombie's row
66..Jubilee pl, Royal Hospital row,
    Chelsea
66..Jubilee st, Chelsea common
39..Judd pl, (East) Somers town, west
    side the road to Marylebone
39..Judd pl, (West) continuation of
    Judd pl, (East)
39..Judd st, op Judd pl, Brunswick sq
68..Junction pl, Harrow road
16..Juniper ct, Park st, Boro market
18..Juston st, Hooper's st, near the
    Asylum, Lambeth

K

12..Keat st, Flower & Dean st
12..Keate st, 208 Brick lane, Spitalfields
33..Keen's row, Walworth High st, half
right from Elephant & Castle
9..Keep's al, Brick la, Old st
37..Kemp's ct, 90 Berwick st, Soho
53..Kendall's mews, 18 George street,
Portman square
18..Kendal st, 14 Stangate st
30..Kenning bdgs, Swan la, Rotherhth ch
49..Kennington comnon, Surry
33..Kennington, from the Cross to the
Horns Tavern
33..Kennington la, leading to Vauxhall
49..Kennington oval, nr Kennington com
33..Kennington pl, Kennington green
34..Kennington pl, Kennington lane
33..Kennington rd, leading to Kngtn com
34..Kennington row, 14 Kennington,
opposite the Common
38..Kenrick pl, Thornaugh st
67..Kensington gardens, Hyde park
67..Kensington Gore, nr Knightsbridge
68..Kensington gravel pits, on the Uxbridge rd, W. end of Oxford st
35..Kensington pl, Holywell st, Millbank
35..Kensington pl, Holywell st, Westmr
32..Kent pl, nr Asylum, Kent road
32..Kent road, from the Bricklayers'
Arms to New Cross
16..Kent st, nr St. George's church, Boro
16..Kentish bdgs, 90 High st, Boro
22..Kenton st, Brunswick sq
22..Keppel mews, N Keppel st, Bedfd sq
4..Keppel st, Gt Guilford st, Southwk
29..Keppel st, 71 Old Gravel lane
65..Keppel st, Chelsea common
22..Keppel st, Russel square
67..Keppel row, nr Crescent, Brompton
38..Keppels row, 4 Portland road, New
road, Marylebone
15..Key alley, near Tooley st
43..Key ct, Little St. Thomas Apostle
37..Key's mews, top of Marylebone lane
67..Kimbolton st, Fulham road
3..King's Arms passage, 27 Cornhill
16..King's ct, Gt. Suffolk st, Borough
10..King's ct, 22 Blue Anchor al, Banhill r
9..King's ct, 33 Lombard st
1..King's Head ct, 26 St. Paul's ch yd
16..King's gardens, Blackman st
20..King's mews, Charing cross
22..King's mews, 2 King's rd, Grays Inn la
17..King's pl, 62 Blackman st, near the
King's Bench
36..King's pl, 58 Pall Mall
32..King's pl, Walworth
22..King's road, 103 Gray's Inn lane
51..King's Private road, Chelsea
26..King's road, Hoxton
66..King's rd ter, King's rd, Chelsea
67..King's rd, op. Queen's row Brompton
31..King's rd, Grange rd, Bermondsey

I

28..King's row, Dog row, Bethnal green
14..King's row, Gainsford st
40..King's row, nr Chapel, Pentonville
51..King's row, nr Arabella row, Pimlico
26..King's row, Hoxton
11..King's sq, 165 Brick la, Whitechapel
9..King's st, 19 Bath st, Old st
30..King's st, 60 Wapping st
17..King st, 6 Belvedere pl, Boro rd
32..King st, Bermondsey New road
16..King st, 111 High st, Borough
11..King st, Brick la, Spitalfields
2..King st, Cheapside
8..King st, Clothfair, West Smithfield
24..King st, 96 Goswell st, Clerkenwell
20..King st, N. W. corner of Cov. gar.
3..King st, Gracechurch lane
21..King st, 165 Drury lane
32..King st, East lane, Walworth
53..King st, 54 Edgeware road
53..King st, West, Edgeware road
51..King st, Ebury st, Five Fields row,
Chelsea
37..King st, Golden square
29..King st, (Old) 17 Gravel lane
11..King st, Finsbury market
30..King st, Gt Hermitage st
22..King st, 120 High Holborn
10..King st, 20 Old st road, leading to
Hoxton square
34..King st, Lambeth walk, nr Church
16..King st, Mint st, Borough
53..King st, Park st, Oxford st
9..King st, Pesthouse row, St. Luke's
53..King st, 69 Baker's st, Portman sq
12..King st, Gt Garden st, Whitechapel
27..King st, nr Bethnal green
30..King st, 375 Rotherhithe st
6..King st, nr Shoemaker row, Blackfrs
36..King st, St. James's square
21..King st, Seven Dials
21..King st, nr St. Ann's Church, Soho
8..King st, late Cow lane, Snowhill
14..King st, on the right, near Rosemary lane, Tower hill
11..King st, Austin st, Shoreditch
35..King st, nr Parliament st
29..King st, Commercial rd, Whitechpl
33..King st mews, Park st, Grosvenor sq
32..King Arthur's row, East la, Walwth
29..King David's la, High st, Shadwell
6..King Edward st, Bridge st, Blackfrs
12..King Edward st, Gt Garden st
14..King Henry's yd, Nightingale lane,
East Smithfield
11..King John's ct, New Inn yd, Shoredh
2..King's Arms bdgs, Wood st, Cheapsd
12..King's Arms ct, 29 Whitechapel
29..King's Arms gardens, Sun Tavern
fields, Shadwell
37..King's Arms pl, nr Whitfield chapel,
Tottenham court road
59..King's Arms row, Old Ford rd, Bow
2..King's Arms yd, 51 Coleman st
34..King's Arms yd, Princes st, Lambh

Ref. to Plan.

38..King's Arms yd, 81 Tottenham ct rd
17..King's Bench al, Margaret's hill, Bor
17..King's Bench row, south side King's
 Bench prison
17..King's Bench walk, Bennett's row,
 Blackfriars road
6..King's Bench walk, Temple
22..King'sgate st, Holborn
1..King's Head ct, Beech st, 42 Barbicn
3..King's Head ct, 35 Fish st hill
7..King's Head ct, 25 Gray's Inn lane
2..King's Head ct, 14 Gutter la, Cheaps
7..King's Head ct, 68 Fetter lane
35..King' Head ct, John st, Westmstr
6..King's Head ct, Carter lane
11..King's Head ct, Long al, Moorfields
13..King's Head ct, Petticoat la, Whchpl
12..King's Head ct, Rose lane
1..King's Head ct, 18 St. Martin's le gnd
7..King's Head ct, 18 Shoe lane, leading to Gough square
11..King's Head ct, 244 High st, Shoredh
15..King's Head ct, 178 Tooley st
35..King's Head ct, Tothill st, Westmr
1..King's Head ct, 42 Whitecross st,
 Cripplegate
21..King's Head yard, Duke st, Lincoln's Inn fields
34..King's Head yd, High st, Lambeth,
 near the church
45..King John st, nr Spring gdns, Stepny
26..Kingsland road, Old st road to the
 end of Shoreditch
42..Kingsland town, near Shoreditch
37..King's sq ct, Carlisle st, Soho sq
8..Kirby st, Charles st, Hatton garden
37..Kirkman's pl, 54 Tottenham ct rd
27..Kittesford pl, Hackney road
13..Kittleby court, Blue Anchor yard,
 Rosemary lane
30..Knight's ct, Tench st, Wapping
5..Knight's ct, Green walk, Holland st,
 Blackfriars road
5..Knightrider ct, 1 Doctors' Commons
5..Knightrider st, (Gt) 1 Doctors' Com.
5..Knightrider st (Lit.) 100 ldFish st hill
52..Knightsbridge, from Hyde park
 corner towards Kensington
4..Knowles' ct, 10 Little Carter lane

L

4..Labour in vain hill, Old Fish st hill
29..Labour in vain st, Shadwell market
16..Lackson ct, Long lane, Borough
2..Lad lane, 20 Wood st, Cheapside
15..Lamb alley, nr 185 Bermondsey st
16..Lamb alley, 34 Blackman st, Boro
11..Lamb al, 144 Bishopsgate st without
24..Lamb ct, 23 Clerkenwell green
11..Lamb ct, Lamb al, Sun st, Bisnopsgt
12..Lamb ct, Red Lion st, Spitalfields
10..Lamb's buildings, Cherry Tree alley,
 Bunhill row
6..Lamb's buildings, Inner Temple la
 Fleet street

Ref. to Plan.

22..Lamb's ct, Lamb's Conduit st, op
 the Foundling Hospital
12..Lamb's ct, 65 Whitechapel road
15..Lamb green, Lamb la, Bermondsey st
43..Lamb lane, London fields
1..Lamb passage, 75 Chiswell st
22..Lamb's passage, Red Lion sq, Holbn
11..Lamb's st, continuation of Spital sq
22..Lamb yd, Lamb's Conduit st
1..Lamb's Chapel ct, Monkwell st,
 Wood street
22..Lamb's Conduit passage, Red Lion sq
22..Lamb's Conduit st, Foundling hospu
34..Lambeth buildings, Lambeth
34..Lambeth Butts, between Vauxhall
 walk and Lambeth walk
5..Lambeth hill, 212 Up Thames st
18..Lambeth marsh, Westminr bridge rd
36..Lambeth mews, end of Clarges st,
 Piccadilly
34..Lambeth palace, S. end Bishop's wk
18..Lambeth rd, near the Obelisk, St.
 George's fields
13..Lambeth st, Alie st
34..Lambeth terrace, nr Church, Lambh
34..Lambeth walk, Paradise row, near
 Lambeth church
37..Lancashire ct, New Bond st
20..Lancaster ct, 473 Strand
38..Lancaster st, Leigh st, Burton crescnt
8..Land yd, 46 Turnmill st, Clerkenwell
3..Langbourn chambers, Fenchurch st,
2..Langburn ct, Lit. Bell al, Colemn st
29..Langdale st, James st, New road,
 St. George's East
37..Langham pl, Portland pl
28..Langley folly, Mile end road
29..Langley pl, Commercial road, north
 side, near Greenfield st
21..Langley st, 116 Long Acre
22..Lansdown mews, Foundling hosptl
22..Lansdown pl, Brunswick square
16..Lant st, 111 Blackman st, Borough
21..Lascelles ct, Broad st, Bloomsbury
21..Lascelles pl, Broad st, Bloomsbury
39..Latham's place, Somer's place, near
 Somer's town
16..Laton's bldgs, 143 High st, Borough
35..Laundry yd, Gt Peter st, Westmar
45..Lavender lane, nr Cuckold's point
34..Lawn, S. Lambeth, near the Vauxhall turnpike
2..Lawrence lane, 97 Cheapside
21..Lawrence st, St. Giles's
3..Lawrence Pountney la, 37 Cannon st,
 Upper Thames st
3..Lawrence Pountney lane, 140 Cannon street road [Inn lane
22..Laystall st, Liquorpond st, Gray's
16..Layton's grove, 137 High st, Boro
16..Layton's bdgs, 144 Borough High st
21..Lazenby ct, Long Acre
12..Lead yd, Plough st, Whitechapel
3..Leadenhall bdgs, 80 Gracechurch st
3..Leadenhall market, 5 Leadenhall st

Ref. to Plan.
3..Leadenhall st, from 60 Cornhill
66..Leader place, Chelsea common
66..Leader st, Chelsea common
66..Leader terrace, Chelsea common
29..Leading st, Fox's lane, Shadwell
7..Leather lane, 128 Holborn
2..Leatherseller's bdgs,51 London wall
11..Leblond's bds, William st, Shoredh
14..Lee's ct,St. Catharine's la,Tower h
53..Lee's mews, North Audley street, Grosvenor square
17..Lee's row, Hatfield pl, St. George's fields. near the Obelisk
21..Legg alley, 34 Long acre
11..Legg alley, 240 Shoreditch
35..Legg ct, Gt Peter st, Westminster
11..Leg of mutton garden, near the turnpike, Kingsland road
20..Leicester ct, Leicester square
20..Leicester pl, Leicester square
20..Leicester sq, Coventry st, Haymkt
20..Leicester st,21Castle st, Leicester sq
36..Leicester st, Swallow st, Piccadilly
38..Leigh st, Burton crescent, Tavistock square
22..Leigh st, Red Lion sq, Holborn
13..Leman rw,Leman st,Goodman's fds
13..Leman st, Goodman's fields, Red Lion st, Whitechapel
34..Lemon ct, Prince's st, Lambeth
20..Lemon tree yd, 3 Bedfordbury
36..Lemon tree yd, corner of Haymarkt, Piccadilly
10..Leonard's ct, 44 Paul st, Finsbury
10..Leonard's sq, 81 Paul st, Finsbury
10..Leonard st, (Lit.) 4 Paul st
8..Leopard's ct, Baldwin's gardens
33..Lestock place, King st, East street, Walworth
26..Leverington pl, Charles st, Hoxton
9..Lewington's bds, near the turnpike, Peerless pool, City road
34..Lewer row, Lambeth Butts, near Lambeth walk [street, Westm
35..Lewisham st, Dartmouth st,Princes
9..Ligonier st, Ratcliff row, City road
1..Lilliput lane, Noble st, Foster lane
8..Lilly st, 40 Gt Saffron hill
3..Lime st, 21 Leadenhall st
3..Lime st passage, leading to Leadenhall st, Lime st
3..Lime st sq, Lime st, Fenchurch st
45..Limehouse, nr West India docks
60..Limehouse causeway, Three Colt st
60..Limehouse hole, continuation of Three Colt st
19..Limetree ct, Narrow wall, Limehs
7..Lincoln's Inn, op. 40 Chancery lane
21..Lincoln's Inn fields, Holborn
7..Lincoln's Inn passage, Serle st
7..Lincoln's Inn New sq,Lincoln's Inn
21..Linny ct, Queen st, Bloomsbury
17..Lint st, St. George's road
66..Linton pl, Bell st, Paddington, nr Edgeware road

Ref to Plan.
21..Lion st, 140 High Holborn, near Bloomsbury market
32..Lion st, second turning on the right from Elephant and Castle
23..Liquorpond st, 69 Gray's Inn lane, Holborn
28..Lisbon st, Dog row, Mile end
20..Lisle st, Leicester square
68..Lisson green, Paddington
68..Lisson grove, near the turnpike, Lisson green
68..Lisson grove lane, Lisson green
53..Lisson mews, Southampton row, Edgeware road
68..Lisson place, Lisson green
53..Lisson row, Lisson grove
68..Lisson st, Lisson green
21..Litchfield st, nr Gerrard st, Soho
35..LittleAbingdon st,10GtAbingdon st, Westminster
35..Little Almonry, east end of Gt Almonry st, Tothill st
12..Little Anchor st, Bethnal green
37..Little Argyle st, 99 Oxford st
1..Little Arthur st, Goswell st
12..Little Ayliffe st, Red Lion st,Whiteh
11..Little Bacon st,140 Brick la,Spitlfds
23..Little Baynes's st, Coldbath square
2..Little Bell alley, London wall
6..Little Bridge st, op. Bride's passage
1..Little Britain, 176 Aldersgate st
38..Little Brook st, Tottenham ct rd
37..Little Brook st,nr Brook st,New rd, Fitzroy square
5..Little Brunswick st, Stamford st, Blackfriars road
36..Little Bruton st, Berkeley square
13..Little Buckle st,Red Lion st,Whchpl
14..Little Burr st, King Henry yard
3..Little Bush lane, 23 Bush lane
52..Little Cadogan place, east side of Cadogan square
27..Little Cambridge st, Hackney road
18..Little Canterbury pl, Asylum,Lmbh
5..Little Carter la, from 3 Paul's chain
20..Little Catherine st, 11 Catherine st, Strand
37..Little Chapel st, S end of Oxford st
35..Little Chapel st, Broadway,Westmr
38..Little Charles st, 33 George st, Portman square
16..Little Charlotte row, White st,Bore
37..Little Charlotte st, Up.Rathbone pl
2..Little Cheapside, 168 Whitecross st, St. Luke's
11..Little Cheapside, Long all, Moorfds
37..Little Chesterfield st,Gt.Marylebn st
10..Little Coleman st, Bunhill row
35..LittleCollege st,9 College st,Westm
21..Little Compton st, Greek st, Soho
22..Little Coram st, 10 Tavistock pl
20..Little ct, Castle st, Leicester sq
16..Little Cumber ct, two doors south of Gt Cumber court
21..Little Dean st, Soho

Ref. to Plan.

35..Little Dean's yd,Westminster abbey
3..Little Distaff lane, Distaff lane
20..Little Drury lane, Strand *
13..Little Duke's pl, 29 Aldgate
21..Little Earl st, Seven dials
51..Little Eaton st, Pimlico, second from Buckingham gate
3..Little Eastcheap, 48 Fish st hill
3..Little Elbow lane, 176Up Thames st
20..Little Essex st, first on the right in Essex st, Strand
16..Little Falcon ct, Redcross st, Boro
4..Little Friday st,42Friday st,Cheapsd
9..Little Galway st, Bath st, City road
27..Little George st, Bethnal green
13..Little George st, George st, Minors
35..Little George st, Westminster
38..Little George st, Hampstead road
53..Little Gloucester st, a short distance on the right from Baker st, Portman square
23..Little Gray's Inn la,72Gray's Inn la
36..Little Grosvenor st, 63 Grosvenor st
22..Little Guildford st, 49 Bernard st
16..Little Guildford st, op. Gt Guildford st, Union st, Borough
30..Little Hermitage st, GtHermitage st
13..Little Holloway st, continuation of Holloway st
38..Little Howland st, Howland st
32..Little James row, in Gt James's st, Bedford row
22..Little James st, Bedford row
36..Little Jermyn st, W end of Jermyn st
22..Little Keppel st,Keppel st,Russel sq
36..Little King st, west end ot King st, St. James's square
5..LittleKnightrider st,10 Old Fish st hl
16..Little Lamb al, St. George's ch, Bor
16..LittleLant st,continuation of Lant st
            [Lombard st,Boro
16..Little Lombard street, north end of
Blackman st
2..Little Love lane, 37 Love lane
37..Little Maddox st, op. Gt Maddox st
37..Little Marlborough st, King's st, Oxford street
37..Little Marylebone st, 23 Marylebone
20..Little May's bdgs, Bedfordbury
15..Little Maze ct,Maze pond,1st on left
12..Little Middlesex st, in Middlesex st, Aldgate
3..Little Mitre ct, 19 Fenchurch st
2..Little Moorfields,82 Fore st,Cripplgt
18..Little Moor pl, south end of Moor place, Asylum, Lambeth
17..Little New st, second on the right Borough road,
7..Little New st, 89 Shoe la, Fleet st
20..Litle Newport st, continuation of Newport st, Leicester square
24..Little Northamptpn st, St. John st
22..Little Ormond st, Queen square, Foundling hospital
33..Little Park st, Kennington cross, west continuation of Park st

Ref. to Plan.

12..Little Paternoster row, 41 Paternoster row, Spitalfields
11..Little Pearl st, Spitalfields
35..Little Peter st, continuation. of Wood st,from 63 Millbank,Westm
37..Little Portland st, 122 John street, Oxford street
13..Little Prescot st, continuation of Mansell street
37..Little Pulteney st, Gt Windmill st
53..Little Queen st, Edgeware road
21..Litle Queen st, 223 High Holborn
35..Little Queen st, Prince's st,Westmr
32..Little Richmond pl, East st,Walwh
36..Little Rider st, St. James st
21..Little Russell st, 60 Drury lane
20..Little Russell st, Covent garden
8..Little Saffron hill, continuation of Great Saffron hill
21..Little St. Andrew st, Seven dials
35..Little St. Anne's la, Gt Peter st
36..Little St. James's st, Piccadilly
21..Little St. Martin's lane, Long Acre
3..Little St. Thomas Apostle,35 Bow la
20..Little Scotland yard, Whitehall
7..Little Shire lane, Temple bar
35..Little Smith st, Bowling st, Westmr
66..Little Smith st, 22 Gt Smith st, King's road, Chelsea
13..Little Somerset st, 22 Somerset st, Whitechapel
29..Little Spring st, four doors from. the end of the church yd,Shadwell
52..Little Stanhope st,Hertford st,Mayfr
16..Little Suffolk st, 80 Blackman st
20..Little Suffolk st, Haymarket
17..Little Surrey st, Blackfriars road
24..Little Sutton st, a few yards north: of Gt Sutton st
2..Little Swan alley, 71 St. John's st, Clerkenwell
2..Little Swan st, Coleman st
14..Little Thames st, adjoining St. Catherine st, Lower E. Smithfield
37..Little Titchfield st, 20 Gt Portland st
12..Little Tongue yd, nr Fieldgate st
14..Little Tower hill, end of the Minors
3..Little Tower st, Eastcheap
32..Little Trafalgar pl, Lock's fields
3..Little Trinity lane,9 Bow lane,Chpsd
35..Little Tufton st, Tufton st
7..Little Turnstile, 244 Holborn
36..Little Vine st, nr St. John's church, Vine st, Piccadilly
23..Little Warner st, continuation of Ray st, Clerkenwell
37..Little Welbeck st, Cavendish sq
21..Little White Lion st, continuation of White Lion st
7..Little White's alley, Chancery lane
21..Little Wild st, second on the left in Gt Wild st, Lincoln's inn fields
2..Little Winchester st,in Broad st,City
37..Little Windmill st, continuation of Gt Windmill st, Haymarket

Ref. to Plan.
9..Lizard st, Bath st, Old st
21..Lloyd's ct, Crown st, St Giles's
33..Lock pl, York st, Walworth High st
39..Lock pl, Fitzroy pl, Totenham ct rd
33..Lock's fields, E side Walworth
8..Lockwood ct, Gt Saffron hill
17..Loman's pond, Gravel la, Southwk
37..Loman's st, E end of Loman's pond, Gravel lane
3..Lombard st, 23 Gracechurch st
7..Lombard st, 55 Fleet street, near Bouverie street
16..Lombard st, end of Mint st, Boro
12..Lombard st, Mile end New Town, third on the right from Brick lane, Whitechapel
3..London Bridge, bottom of Fish st hill
38..London mews, London st, Fitzry sq
17..London rd, op. the Obelisk, end of Gt Surrey st
42..London fields, Hackney
31..London st, Dockhead, Horselydown
13..London st, 59 Fenchurch st
38..London st, Fitzroy square
17..London st, London rd, St George's fds
29..London st, Queen st, Radcliff cross
37..London st, 108 Tottenham ct rd
27..London terrace, Hackney road, op. Gt. Cambridge street
29..London terrace, Commercial road
3..London wall, Moorfields
1..London house yd, 74 St Paul's ch yd
21..Long acre, 40 Drury lane
11..Long alley, N. E. corner of Moorfds
11..Long alley, 29 Crown st, Finsby sq
8..Long lane, 67 Smithfield
16..Long lane, White st, St. George's church yard, Borough
31..Long walk, Bermondsey square
22..Long yard, Lamb's Conduit st, Foundling hospital
1..Long's bdgs, Whitecross st, Cripplgt
20..Long's ct, 1 St. Martin's lane, Leicester square
30..Long's ct, nr Rotherhithe church
37..Looker's ct, King st, Oxford st
21..Lord's ct, Crown st, Soho
2..Lothbury, near the Old Jewry
7..Love ct, George alley, Fleet market
8..Love ct, Mutton la, Clerkenwell grn
45..Love lane, Cock hill, Shadwell
3..Love lane, Lower Thames st
30..Love la, 160 Old Gravel la, Wapping
30..Love lane, 384 Rotherhithe st
5..Love lane, Willow walk, Bankside
2..Love lane, 36 Wood st, Cheapside
13..Love lane, 120 Petticoat lane
15..Love lane, 157 Tooley st
2..Love la, (Lit) 37 Wood st, Cheapsd
3..Love lane, 103 Little Eastcheap
29..Love lane, 117 Up Shadwell
8..Lovel's ct, 20 Paternoster row
5..Lowdell's passage, Broadwall
29..Lower Chapman st, New road, St. George's East

Ref. to Plan.
24..Lower Charles st, Goswell st road
14..Lower East Smithfld, London docks
51..Lower George st, Sloane st
51..Lower Grosvenor place, Pimlico
30..Lower Gun al, Greenbank, Wapping
36..Lower James st, Golden square
36..Lower John st, Golden square
45..Lower Queen st, nr Greenland dock
29..Lower Shadwell, Ratcliff cross
37..Lower court, Carnaby market
18..Lower Lambeth marsh, Westminster bridge rd turnpike to Blackfriars rd
8..Lower West st, West Smithfield
24..Loyd's row, Spafields
37..Lucas place, Fitzroy pl, Marylebone
45..Lucas pl & st, Commercial rd, Stepney
30..Lucas st, Millpond bridge, Rotherh
23..Lucas st, near Gray's Inn lane, name changed to Cromer st
7..Ludgate hill, 1 Fleet market
7..Ludgate st, 80 St. Paul's church yd
10..Luke st, 86 Paul st, Finsbury
21..Lumber court, Seven dials
20..Lumley ct, 401 Strand
12..Luntley st, Osborne pl, Brick la, Whitechapel
17..Lynn st, Gaywood st St George's fds
6..Lyon's Inn, 20 High st, Strand

M

39..Mabledon place, Burton crescent, Tavistock square
21..Macclesfield st, Gerrard st, Soho
29..Macord's rents, String st, Old Gravel la, Wapping   [Hanover sq
35..Maddox st, Great George street,
44..Madman's row, nr Bancroft's Almshouses, Mile end road
13..Magdalen row, Prescot st, Goodmans fields
15..Magdalen st, 148 Tooley st
12..Magpie al, nearly op. Wentworth st
1..Magpie ct, 180 Aldersgate st, Shrdh
7..Mag's place, Fetter lane
5..Maid la, Gravel la, Southwark bridge
68..Maida field, Edgeware road
68..Maida hill, Paddington
61..Maida pl, near Danby's turnpike, Deptford Lower road, Rotherhithe
68..Maida terrace, Edgeware road
5..Maiden ct, Broadwall, Blackfriars
3..Maiden la, 37 Queen st, Cheapside
20..Maiden lane, Southampton street, Covent garden
2..Maiden la, 110 Wood st, Cheapside
39..Maiden lane, North of Gray's Inn la, Battle bridge
39..Maiden place, Battle bridge
30..Maidenhead ct, 102 Wapping, a few doors left of the London docks
29..Maidenhead ct, 61, Farmer street, Shadwell
1..Maidenhead ct, 30 Aldersgate st
13..Maidenhead ct, Great Garden court, St. Catherine's lane

Ref to Plan.
2..Maidenhead ct, 1 Cripplegt, Moorla
29..Maidenhead ct, near Wapping ch
11..Maidenhead ct, 67 Wheeler street, Spitalfields
34..Maidenhead ct, Shakespeare's walk
4..Maidenhead ct, Lit. St. Thos. Apostle
5..Maidenhead yard, 24 Addle hill
13..Maidstone buildings, Goodman's fds
16..Maidstone buildings, 145 Borough
36..Major Foubert's passage, Swallow st
14..Malaga ct, 36 Nightingale la, East Smithfield
35..Manchester buildings, Cannon row, Westminster
53..Manchester mews, Manchester sq
53..Manchester square, North end of Duke st, Oxford st
53..Manchester st, North West corner of Manchester square
19..Manning pl, Portugal st, Lambeth
35..Mann's bdgs, near Grey coat school
66..Manor buildings, opposite Robinson's lane, King's road, Chelsea
33..Manor place, Walworth, 6th turning on the right from the Elephant and Castle
66..Manor place, King's road, Chelsea
66..Manor row, Robinson's la, Chelsea
3..Manor row, 49 Tower hill
33..Manor row, south side of Manor pl, Walworth
61..Manor row, south side the Seven Houses, Deptford lower road
66..Manor st, Cheyne walk
66..Manor terrace, King's road, Chelsea, near Manor's place
13..Mansell st, Swan st, Minories
3..Mansion house place, Lombard st
17..Mansfield pl, near Obelisk, Boro
37..Mansfield st, Portland st, Marylebn
3..Mansion house st, 1 Lombard st, or 25 Bucklersbury
33..Mansion house st, Kennington road
44..Map's rw, Stepney green, nr Mile end
31..Marble st, Webb st, Bermondsey st
22..Marchmont place, Little Coram st, Brunswick square
22..Marchmont st, 44 Great Coram st, Brunswick square
43..Mare st, Hackney
16..Margaret's hill, (St.) Town hall, High st, Borough
37..Margaret ct, 60 Margaret street, Cavendish square
43..Margaret place, Hackney fields
16..Margaret's rents, Weston street, Snows fields, Borough
38..Margaret st, Euston sq, Somerstown
37..Margaret st, Cavendish square, and 63 Well st
23..Margaret st, 2 Spring pl, Bagnigge-wells road
43..Margaret st, Hackney fields
23..Margaret st, Spafields
29..Margrave buildings, New Gravel la

Ref. to Plan.
30..Marigold st, near Cherry Garden st, Rotherhithe
31..Marine crescent, north side the Neckenger road, Bermondsey
34..Mariner's alley, Forest, Lambeth ch
13..Mark lane, 53 Fenchurch st
10..Mark st, 54 Paul st, Finsbury sq
37..Market ct, 99 Oxford market
29..Market hill, 65 Shadwell High st
36..Market lane, St. James's market
33..Market lane, 14 White hart place, Kennington lane
35..Market st, Millbank st
21..Market st, W. side Newport market
37..Market st, 87 Oxford st
37..Market st, east side St. George's market, London road
33..Market st, Walcot place, Lambeth
24..Market st, 1 St. John's st road
66..Markham place, King's rd, Chelsea
36..Marlborough ct, 82 Pall Mall
37..Marlborough ct, 24 Carnaby st
66..Marlborough crescent, Chelsea
36..Marlborough place, near the Palace. Pall mall
32..Marlborough place, Walworth
33..Marlborough pl, Kennington cross
48..Marlboro pl, Southampton st Cmbrwl
35..Marlborough square, corner of Great Peter st, Westminster
17..Marlborough st, Great Charlotte st, Blackfriars
29..Marmaduke st, William st, New rd, St. George's East
29..Marman st, James st, Cannon st road
18..Marsh place, 13 New cut, Lambeth
37..Marshall st, Carnaby market
17..Marshall street, London road, St. George's fields
16..Marshalsea prison, 150 Boro High st
35..Marsham st, near Dean's st, Westmr
26..Marson st, Union st, Hoxton, Nwtwn
43..Martha st, 1st right from Cambridge Heath turnpike, Hackney road
29..Martha st, Cornfields, St. George's E
29..Martin's buildings, New Gravel lane
9..Martin's bldngs, 69 Old st, St. Lukes
29..Martin's ct, 197 Ratcliff highway
3..Martins lane, 42 Cannon st
29..Martin st, Cross st, Sun Tavern fds
9..Martin street, Westmoreland place, City road
12..Martin st, Essex st, Whitechapel
21..Martlett's ct, 31 Bow st, Covent gran
38..Mary place, Mary st, Charles st
37..Mary's row, Bethnal green road
37..Mary st, Charles st, Tottenham ct rd
2..Mary st, 66 Aldermanbury
29..Mary st, 75 Whitechapel road
90..Marygold ct, or Southampton place, 372 Strand
81..Marygold stairs, opposite 86 Upper Ground, Blackfriars
81..Marygold st, Jamaica row

Ref. to Plan.

37..Marylebone ct, 27 Weymouth street, Marylebone
53..Marylebone lane, High st, Marylebn
37..Marylebone mews, 50 Gt Marybn st
54..Marylebone park, Regent's park, New road, Marylebone
37..Marylebone pas,68Well st,Oxford st
36..Marylebone st, 17 Brewer st,Gldn sq
37..Marylebone st,(Up)54 Gt Portland st
37..Marylebone st, (Gt) 51 Harley st, Cavendish square
2..Mason's alley, Basinghall st
11..Mason's ct, opposite Thrawl st
11..Mason's ct, Montague ct,nrSpital sq
11..Mason's ct, near Shoreditch church
18..Mason st, Westminster bridge road
39..Mason st, Brill place, Somerstown
32..Mason st, near the Deaf and Dumb Asylum, Kent road
36..Mason's yard, Duke st, St.James's
35..Mason's Arms yard, Maddox street, Hanover square
13..Matilda place, N. E. Wellclose sq
32..Matilda place, Kent road
30..Matthew's ct, Redmaid la, Wapping
27..Matthew's pl, nr Hackney turnpike, Hackney road
10..Matthew's st,Mark st,Paul st,Fnsby
14..Maudlin's rents, Nightingale lane, Wapping
11..Maxwell ct, Long alley, Moorfields
36..Mayfair,N. side Piccadilly, nrPark la
36..May's buildings, Brick st, Piccadilly
20..May's buildings, (Great) 40, St. Martin's lane, Charing cross
60..May's row, New cut, Limehouse
29..Mayfield's buildings,Princes square, Ratcliffhighway
21..Maynard st, Buckeridge st, High st, St. Giles's
52..Mayorrow,op.Knightsbridge chapel
16..Maypole al, 208 High st, Borough
30..Maypole ct, East Smithfield
15..Maze, or The Maze, 194 Tooley st
15..Maze pond, south end of New st, Joiners st, Borough
37..Mead's ct,Old Bond st, Piccadilly
18..Mead place, near Asylum, Lambeth
11..Mead st, Turvill st
32..Meadow row. 2nd turning from the Elephant and Castle, New Kent rd
37..Meards ct, Wardour st, Soho
23..Mecklinburgh terrace, opposite the Barracks, Grays Inn lane
23..Mecklinburgh sq, nr Foundling hos
24..Medcalf place, Pentonville road
35..Medway pl, Horseferry rd, Westmr
61..Medway pl, Deptford Lower road
30..Meeting house al, Greenbank, Wpng
21..Meeting house ct, nr Broker's alley
15.Meeting house ct, 18 Gainsford st, Horseleydown
15..Meeting house ct, Tooley st
11..Meeting house ct, Long al, Moorfds
16..Meeting house walk,4 Snowfds,Boro

Ref. to Plan.

15..Meeting house walk,near Weston st, Snowsfields
31..Meeting house yard, Dockhead
16..Meeting house yard, Redcross st
18..Melina place, nr the Asylum, Lmbth
15..Melior st, Weston st,Snowsfields
7..Mellin's rents, Shoe lane
9..Memel st, Downing st, near Old-street turnpike
3..Mercer's ct,St.Mary at hill,Tower st
29..Mercer's rw, nr 110Shadwell,High st
21..Mercer st, 125 Long acre
24..Meridith st, 2 Wingrove pl, Clrknwl
23..Merlin's place, back of Upper Rosoman st, Spafields
10..Mermaid ct 63 near King st, Boro
16..Mermaid ct, 119 Borough High st
15..Mermaid row, Sun st, Snowsfields
11..Merrett's buildings, Peter st, Sun st, Bishopsgate
29..Merton ct,nearPell st,Ratcliff hghwy
16..Mestaer's rents, near canal, Rotberh
67..Michael buildings,nrBrompton crsnt
67..Michael's grove, near the Stones, Brompton
67..Michael's place, commencement of the Brompton road
7..Middle row, op Gray's Inn la, Hlbrn
17..Middle row, 24 Rockingham row, New Kent road
52..Middle row, Knightsbridge
21..Middle row, 37 St. Giles's
8..Middle st, 25 Cloth fair, W. Smithfd
7..Middle New st, Shoe lane
19..Middle Scotland yard, Whitehall
29..Middle Shadwell, Pope's hill, Shadwell market
6..Middle Temple buildings, Temple
6..Middle Temple, Fleet st
7..Middle Temple la, Temple bar
27..Middlesex buildings, Middlesex pl, Hackney road
15..Middlesex buildings, Tooley st
21..Middlesex ct, 36 Drury la
68..Middlesex pl, Lisson green,Padngtn
13..Middlesex st, (Lit.) Middlesex st
13..Middlesex st, or Petticoat lane, 41 Aldgate, High st
39..Middlesex st, Somerstown
37..Middleton bds. Foley st, Marylebone
24..Middleton st, op. 36 Rosoman st
24..Middleton terrace, by Middlesex chapel, Hackney road
35..Milbank row, Abingdon st, Westmr
35..Milbank st, continuation of Abingdon st, Westminster
3..Mildred's ct, 36 Broad st, Cheapside
3..Mildred's ct, 27 Poultry
28..Mile End, from Whitechapel turnpike to Bow
28..Mile end corner, Dog row, Mile end
28..Mile End green, near the London Hospital, Whitechapel
28..Mile End row, nr Mile End turnpike
3..Miles's lane, 129 Upper Thames st

Ref. to Plan.

16..Miles's rents, near Bermondsey st, Long lane, Borough
20..Milford st, 199 Strand
36..Milford place, Tottenham court rd
2..Milk st, 115 Cheapside
32..Milk st, near Queen's row, Walwth
7..Milk yard, Poppin's ct, Fleet st
29..Milk yard, New Gravel lane
15..Mill lane, Tooley st, Borough
31..Mill st, Dock head
37..Mill st, Maddox st, Hanover square
18..Mill st, Lambeth walk, north side the Windmill, leading to Pratt st
13..Mill yd, 80 Cable st, Rosemary lane
37..Mill hill mews, Wimple street, Marylebone
35..Millbank, near Westminster abbey
2..Miller's ct, 39 Aldermanbury
22..Millman pl,Gt James st, Bedford rw
23..Millman st, New Guildford st, a few doors on the left from Gray's Inn lane
44..Millman's row, Stepney green
23..Millman st, Bedford rw, Red lion sq
32..Mill's buildings, Knightsbridge, half a mile from Hyde park corner
13..Mill's ct, Middlesex st, Whitechpl
10..Mill's ct, Charlotte st, Old st road
29..Mill's place, Commercial rd, Limehouse, a short distance from the Church
30..Millpond bridge, Rotherhithe
30..Millpond st, Bermondsey
8..Millard's ct, Duke's ct, Chick lane, West Smithfield
60..Millwall, Limeho.reach, Isle of Dogs
18..Milner place, Lambeth marsh
13..Mincing lane, 43 Fenchurch st
17..Minor place, 19 Belvidere buildings, King's st, King's Bench
13..Minories, 81 High st, Aldgate
16..Mint square, Mint st, Borough
16..Mint street, opposite St. George's church, Borough
68..Mitcham st, Lisson green
9..Mitchell court, Mitchell st, Old st, St. Lukes
9..Mitchell st, 63 Brick lane, Old st, St. Lukes
2..Mitre ct, Milk st, Cheapside
3..Mitre ct, 19 Fenchurch st
6..Mitre court buildings, Temple
3..Mitre ct, 71 St. Paul's church yard
7..Mitre ct, 9 Ely place, Holborn
7..Mitre ct, 44 Fleet st
2..Mitre ct, 14 Cheapside
8..Mitre ct, 145 St. John street, West Smithfield
6..Mitre ct, Temple
17..Mitre st, 22 Short st, Gt. Surrey st
13..Mitre st, 29 Aldgate
18..Mitre st, near Coburgh Theatre
3..Modifort ct, 40 Fenchurch st
9..Moffatt st, continuation of Trafalgar st, City road

Ref. to Plan.

29..Moffling's ct 26 New Gravel la, Wpng
18..Mole hill lodge, Lambeth
18..Mole hill pl,near Hercules buildings
53..Molyneux st,Queen's st,Edgware rd
37..Monday's ct, north east corner of Carnaby market
13..Money Bag alley, Blue Anchor yard, Rosemary lane
26..Moneyers st, Cross street, Hoxton New Town
26..Monk's bdgs, Coffee house walk
1..Monkwell st, 13 Falcon square, Aldersgate st
1..Monkwell st, Cripplegate
21..Monmouth ct, Monmth st, St.Giles'
36..Monmouth ct, Whitcomb st, second turning on the right from Chering Cross
32..Monmouth st, Surry square
21..Monmouth st, second east of the Church, St. Giles's
11..Monmouth st, Quaker st, Spitalfilds
29..Monmouth st hill,High st, Shadwell
51..Monster row, St. George's row, Chelsea bridge
11..Montague ct, 94 Bishopsgt without
1..Montague ct, 32 Little Britain
4..Montague close, near St. Saviour's Church, Borough
53..Montague mews, south, 4 Upper George st, Portman square
53..Montague mews, north, Montagueplace, Portman square
53..Montague mews, west side of Montague square
22..Montague place, Russell square
45..Montague pl, City canal, Limehouse
12..Montague pl, opposite Brown's la, Brick lane, Spitalfields
53..Montague place, Portman square
53..Montague sq 12 Montague st,Marybn
22..Montague st, Russell square
12..Montague st, (Old) Whitechapel
53..Montague st, Up. Berkeley square
12..Montague st, Wentworth st
3..Monument yard, 40 Fish st hill
11..Moon al, 103 Bishopsgate without
16..Moonraker's al, Gt. Suffolk st,Boro
34..Moore hall place, Vauxhall
11..Moor's alley, 33 Norton Falgate, nearly opposite Spital square
12..Moor's ct, Essex st, Whitechapel
11..Moor's gdns, Long alley, Moorfields
2..Moorfields,Finsbury sq,north side of London wall
2..Moor lane, 86 Fore st, Cripplegate
18..Moor pl, near Asylum, Lambeth
2..Moor sq, Moor lane, Cripplegate
53..Moor st, Queen st, Edgware road
21..Moor st, Seven Dials, in Comptonstreet and Greek st
4..Moor's yard, Old Fish st
20..Moor's yard, St. Martin's lane, Charing cross
15..Morgan's lane, 79 Tooley st, Boro

Ref. to Plan.

44..Morgan ct, Mile end, a few yards east of Stepney green
29..Mergau st, Commercial rd, second left of Cannon st road
38..Mornington place, Hampstead road
15..Morris's ct, New sq, Horselydown
14..Morris's ct,Nightingale laE.Smthfd
4..Morris's wlk, Castle la,Maid laBoro
38..Mortimer's market, 169 Tot ct road
37..Mortimer st, Cavendish square
34..Morten place, North st, Lambeth
17..Morton st, Newington causeway
13..Moses and Aaron alley, near the turnpike, Newcastle st, Whtchpl
43..Mosman's place, Hackney rd, near the turnpike
5..Moss's al, Willow st, Bankside
16..Moss's ct, Queen st row, the fourth door from Union st
11..Motley ct, Motley st, Curtain road
11..Motley place, Motley st, Curtain rd
11..Metley st, 50 Curtain rd, Shoreditch
1..Mouldmaker's row, Foster la,Chpsd
12..Mount ct, Narrow al, Houndsditch
34..Mount ct, Lambeth
33..Mountford place, Kennington green
18..Mount gardens, 8 Mount st, Westminster bridge road
36..Mount pas, Mount st, Grosvenor sq
11..Mount place, Mount st, Shoreditch
12..Mount place, Whitechapel road
9..Mount pleasant, Winkworth hdngs, City road
23..Mount pleasant, Elm st
36..Mount row, Davis st, Berkeley sq
32..Mount row, New Kent road, north side between the Bricklayers Arms and the Paragon
32..Mount row, nr Mount st, Walworth
27..Mount sq, 67 Mount st, Bethnal grn
36..Mount st, 35 Berkley sq
32.. Mount st, Walworth, High st, opposite Montpellier gardens
52..Mount st, Grosvenor square
18..Mount st, Westminster bridge road
28..Mount st, (Old) 206 Whitechapel rd
28..Mount terrace, Cannon st road, east side, adjoining Whitechapel road
22..Mud's ct, 54 Lambs conduit street, Foundling hospital
29..Mud's ct, Broad st, Ratcliff crescent
4..Muggeridge bds,Castle st, Southwk
4..Mulberry ct, 28Castle st, Southwark
16..Mulberry ct, Long la, Bermondsey, second left from the Church
12..Mulberry court, 99 Petticoot lane
11..Mulberry ct, Horse shoe al,Moorfds
12..Mulberry gardens, King Edward st, Whitechapel
30..Mulberry gdns,Nightingale la,Wpng
24..Mulberry pl,Charles st,Goswell st rd
12..Mulberry st, Sion square
32..Mullin's buildings, Blue Anchor rd, Bermondsey
7..Mullin's rents, Shoe lane, Holborn

Ref. to Plan.

2..Mumford ct, Milk st, Che pside
37..Munday's ct, 22 Carnaby market
30..Murten's rents, Wapping
14..Muscovy ct, Trinity sq, Tower hill
21..Museum st, 169 High Holborn, Bloomsbury
29..Music house ct, 53 Shadwell High st
2..Mutton ct, Malden lane, Wood st, Cheapside [the turnpike
28..Mutton lane, Mile end road, near
8..Mutton lane, Vine st, Hatton garden
43..Mutton and Cat lane, Hackney
10..Myrtle street, Gloucester terrace, Hoxton town

N

3..Nagshead alley, Fenchurch st
16..Nagshead alley, St. Margaret's hill
21..Nagshead ct, 118 Drury lane
1..Nagshead ct, 87 Golden la, Barbican
3..Nagshead ct, 33 Gracechurch st
8..Nagshead ct, 40 Leather lane
27..Nag's yd, near Bridcage wlk, Hkny
37..Nailer's yd, Silver st, Golden sq
34..Naked Boy al, Princes st, Lambeth
3..Naked Boy ct, 6 Timber st
7..New Boy ct, 34 Ludgate hill
45..Narrow st, from Ratcliff cross stairs to Fore st, Limehouse
19..Narrow wall, continuation of Pedlars acre, Lambeth
29..Nassau place, Commercial road
21..Nassau st, 13 King st, Soho
37..Nassau st, Goodge st, Tot ct road
60..Naval row, Blackwall
21..Neale's passage, Gt Earl st, 7 Dials
21..Neale's yd, Queen st, Seven Dials
12..Neat Boy's ct, 54 Fashion st,Sptlfds
51..Neathouse row, near the Bridge at Pimlico
31..Neckinger road, Bermondsey
21..Nelson's ct, Drury lane
13..Nelson's ct, opposite Old Gravel la, Ratcliff highway
53..Nelson place, Circus st, Marylebone, first on the right from the New rd
47..Nelson place, New Kent road
9..Nelson pl, Peerless pool, City road
34..Nelson's pl, near Flint st, Walworth
16..Nelson's pl, 100 Blackman st, Boro
27..Nelson's pl, Nelson st, Hackney rd
32..Nelson's pl, nr Swan st, Kent road
5..Nelson pl, 8 Gravel lane, Borough
17..Nelson sq, 12 Surrey road, near the Obelisk
29..Nelson st, Cannon st road, first north of the Commercial road
11..Nelson st, Castle st, Shoreditch
27..Nelson st, Hackney road, half a mile right from Shoreditch
9..Nelson st, between Windsor place and Po el's pl, City road
16..Nelson st, 57 Long lane, Borough
44..Nelson st, north side the Church yd, Stepney

Ref. to Plan.

13..Nelson st, Redlion st, Whitechapel
9..Nelson terrace, City road, nearly opposite Sidney st
7..Nelson terrace, Hackney road
18..Neptune pl, Lambeth marsh, north of the Home Brewery
30..Neptune st, Church st, near the Church, Rotherhithe, towards Narrow wall
32..Neptune st, Lock's fields, Walworth
13..Neptune st, Wellclose square
7..Nevill's ct, 38 Fetter lane, Fleet st
16..New al, 155 High st, Borough
16..New alley, 1 White st, Borough
60..New al, 63 Three Colt st, Limehouse
3..New Basinghall st, London wall
22..New Bolton st, Brownlow st
37..New Bond st, Oxford st
7..New Boswell ct, 18 Lincoln's Inn fds
2..New Broad st, Royal Exchange
36..New Burlington st, Piccadilly
2..New bldngs, Lit. Bell al, Coleman st
14..New bds, Sun yd, East Smithfield
60..Newby pl, near Almshouses, Poplar
7..Newcastle ct, opposite 218 Strand
24..Newcastle place, Clerkenwell close
3..Newcastle st, 8 Bridge row
7..Newcastle st, 33 Fleet market
16..Newcastle st, 98 Kent st, Borough
20..Newcastle st, 309 Strand
13..Newcastle st, 120 High st, Whtchpl
37..New Cavendish st, Portland st
21..New Compton st, St. Giles's
8..New ct, Cloth fair, second left from 60 West Smithfield
20..New ct, 205 Strand
7..New ct, 24 Gt New st, Fetter lane
24..New ct, Allen st, 10 Goswell st
11..New court, Angel sq, near Sun st, Bishopsgate
3..New ct, Bow lane, 5 Cheapside
2..New ct, Broad st, a few doors from Threadneedle st
12..New ct, 34 Brown's la, Spitalfields
21..New ct, 99 Carey st, Lincolns inn fds
4..New ct, Castle lane, 8 doors on the left from Castle st, Southwark
35..New ct, Chapel st, Westminster
11..New ct, Crown st, Finsbury square, west side of Maxwell court
13..New ct, 45 Crutched friars
35..New ct, Duck lane, near Orchard st, Westminster
12..New ct, Fashion st, Spitalfields
7..New ct, 20 Fleet market
1..New ct, 121 Fore st, Cripplegate
12..New ct, George yard, Whitechapel
1..New ct, 10 Goswell st
7..New ct, Great New st, Shoe lane
11..New ct, 34 Great Pearl st. Spitalfds
11..New ct, 18 Holywell st, Shoreditch,
3..New ct, King st, Creechurch lane, Leadenhall st
2..New ct, Lit. Cheapside, Moorflds
2..New ct, Moor la, Fore st, Cripplegt

Ref. to Plan.

12..New ct, New st, first on the right from Fieldgate st
35..New ct, Orchard st, Westminster
33..New ct, High st, Newington, a few doors left of the Church
30..New ct, Nightingale lane, East Smithfield, near the London Dock entrance
7..New ct, 50 Old Bailey
8..New ct, Peter st, Saffron hill
23..New ct, Portpool la, 50 Grays inn la
11..New ct, Quaker st, Spitalfields
24..New ct, 124 St. John's st, Smithfield
13..New ct, Duke's place, Aldgate
14..New ct, St.Catherines, nr the Tower
8..New ct, St. Peter's lane, St. John's street, West Smithfield
3..New ct, St. Martin's la, Cannon st
6..New ct, Temple
2..New ct, nr the Bank, Throgmorton st
12..New ct, Wentworth st, Spitalfields
1..New ct, Whitecross st, Cripplegate
3..New ct, 10 St. Swithin's lane
30..New crane, 198 New Gravel lane, Wapping
15..New cut, Bermondsey
60..New cut, Limehouse
17..New cut, Lambeth marsh
61..New Deptford and Greenwich road, Isle of Dogs
20..New Exchange ct, 418 Strand
8..Newgate market, 20 Newgate st
8..Newgate st, Cheapside
16..New George yd, Kent st
34..New Gloucester st, Vauxhall walk
12..New Gouldstone st, 140 Whitechapel
29..New Gravel la, 23 Shadwell High st
59..New Grove, Mile end road
33..Newington Butt's District, in the neighbourhood of the Fishmongers Almshouses
17..Newington causeway, south end of Blackman st, Borough
33..Newington pl or row, Kennington rd
20..New Inn, Wych st, a few doors on the right from St. Clement's ch
38..New Inn, 187 Tottenham court rd
20..New Inn bldngs, 30 Wych st, Strand,
21..New Inn passage, Clare market
21..New Inn sq, Bateman's rw, 159 Shrdh
11..New Inn st, New Inn yd, Shrdtch
11..New Inn yd, 175 Shoreditch turnpike
32..New Kent road, from the Elephant and Castle to Bricklayer's Arms, Kent road
14..New lane, 102 Shad Thames
16..New Lant st, Lant st, Borough
38..New London st, 108 Tottenham ct rd
13..New London st, 59 Fenchurch st
3..Newman's ct, Corn hill
37..Newman's mews, 74 Oxford st
12..Newman's rents, Whitechapel
21..Newman's row, north east corner of Lincoln's inn fields
15..Newman's row, 117 Bermondsey st

Ref. to Plan.

37..Newman st, East end of Oxford st
37..Newman st, 34 Oxford st
20..Newmarket st, 157 Wapping
43..Newmarket ter, Cambridge heath, Hackney turnpike
13..New Martin ct, White's yd, turn at 96 Upper East Smithfield
1..New Medal row, Goswell st
22..New Millman st, a few doors on the left from Grays inn lane
11..Newnham pl,133 Bishopsgt without
15..Newnham row, 117 Bermondsey st
53..Newnham st, Queen st,Edgeware rd
11..New Nicol's ct, Cock la, Bethnalgreen, Shoreditch
22..New North street, continuation of North st,Redlion square
22..New Ormond st, Lamb's conduit st
35..New Palace yd, 33 Parliament st, Westminster
30..NewParadise st,Millpond br,Rothrh
4..New Park st, north east corner of Great Guildford st, Borough
35..New Peter st, Gt. Peter st, Westmr
21..Newport market, west end of Great Newport st
21..Newport st,(Gt&Lit)St.Martin's la, opposite Long acre
35..New Pye st, Orchard st, Westmnstr
53..New Quebec st, 69 Up. Berkeley st
35..New Ranelagh, Millbank, near the Bridge
24..New Riverhead, nr Saddlers wells, Spafields
24..New River ter, City rd, Islington
38..New road, Marylebone, from 81 Edgware road, to the Adam and Eve, Tottenham court road
28..New road, Mile end to Hackney
68..New road, Edgware road, Paddington, to Primrose hill, Hampstead and Highgate
38..New rd, from Portland rd, through Regent's park, to Primrose hill
29..New road, St. George's East, Cannon st, to Whitechapel road
66..New road,back of Sloane st,Chelsea
31..New rd, Grange rd, Bermondsey
39..New road, Somerstown
20..New Round court, 448 Strand
13..New square, 129 Minories
36..New square, 37 Orchard street, Westminster [Horselydown
15..New sq, New la, 102 Shad Thames,
21..New sq, Lincolns inn, Chancery la
30..New st, 96 Adam st. Rotherhithe ch
53..New st, Baker st, (N) Marylebone, a little on the left of the New rd
12..New st, 30 Bishopsgate st
46..New st, Bonner's fds, Bethnal green
19..New st, Princess st, Lambeth
37..New st, 46 Broad st, Carnaby mrkt
67..New st, Brompton
8..New st, Cloth fair, West Smithfield
20..New st, 58 St. Martin's lane

Ref. to Plan.

21..New st, George st, St. Giles's, near 28 Great Russell st
15..New st, Fair st, Horselydown
12..New st, Fieldgate st, Whitechapel
1..New st, 126 Aldersgate st, leading to Cloth fair
39..New st, Judd st, Burton crescent
28..New st, Mile end road
9..New st, French row, Peerless pool
37..New st, Hanover square
32..New street, Camden st, East lane, Walworth
32..New st, Bridge st, Southwark
33..New st, Kennington road
32..New st,Newington, a short distance on the left south from the Church
29..New st, 67 High st, Shadwell mrkt
29..New st, New rd, St. George's East
9..New st,92 Old st
34..New st, Union st, Lambeth, third on the left from Walcott place
14..New st, St.Catherine's la,E.Smthfd
14..New st, 66 Lower East Smithfield
17..New st, opposite. Obelisk st, St. George's fields
15..New st, St. Thomas's Gt. Borough
6..New st, Shoemaker's row, Blkfrs
20..New st, Spring grdns, Charing cross
11..New st, Turk st, Shoreditch
32..New st, Union st, Lambeth
35..New st, Regent pl, Westminster
7..New st hill, 89, Shoe lane
7..New st square, Shoe lane, opposite Dean st, Fetter lane
15..New st maze, first on the right from 196 Tooley st
21..New Sawyer's yd, Clare market
66..New terrace, Sloan square
10..New terrace, Tabernacle row, first on the left from 36 City road
21..Newton st, 207 High Holborn
33..Newton terrace, Kennington lane
35..New Tothill st, Westminster, near the Abbey
21..New Turnstile, 232 High st, Hlbrn
21..New Turville st, Cock la, Shoredch
21..New Tyson street, Church street, Bethnal green [Horselydown,
15..New walk, Thomas st, Gainsford st
35..New way, Orchard st, Broadway, Westminster
13..Nicholl's ct, Rosemary lane
3..Nicholl's ct, Nichol's lane
3..Nichol's lane, 59 Cannon st, or.24 Lombard st
11..Nicholl's row, Church st, Shoredch
1..Nichol's square, 18 Castle st, near Falcon square
14..Nightingale ct, Swan la, E Smthfd
14..Nightingale la, 110 Up. East Smthfd
45..Nightingale la,60 Fore st,Limehouse
32..Nile pl, Weymouth st, N Kent road
9..Nile st, second on the left of Winckworth buildings, City road
9..Nile terrace, City road

Ref. to Plan.
50..Nine Elms, near Vauxhall turnpike
29..Noah's Ark al, Queen st, Ratcliff cr
18..Noah's Ark ct, op 17 Amphitheatre rw
1..Noble st, from Foster lane, Cheapside, to Falcon square
60..Noble st, first turning west of the East India Almshouses, Poplar
9..Noble st, 53 Goswell st
37..Noel st, 67 Berwick st, Oxford st
31..Noel st, 6 Bermondsey new road
11..Norfolk pl, Bateman's r, Shoreditch
11..Norfolk place, third turning on the left from Old st, Curtain road
17..Norfolk pl, opposite Fishmongers Almshouses, St. George's fields
31..Norfolk place, Marygold street, Jamaica row, Bermondsey
33..Norfolk place, Newington
44..Norfolk pl, Globe lane, Mile end rd
66..Norfolk pl, and street, Chelsea com
34..Norfolk row, Church st, Lambeth, first east of High st
29..Norfolk st, Cannon st road, second north of the Commercial road
17..Norfolk st, Loman's pond
53..Norfolk st, near Oxford st, Park la
37..Norfolk st, Charles st, Tot ct road
20..Norfolk st. Strand, near St. Clement's church
39..Norfolk st, Battle bridge, Gray's Inn lane
26..Norfolk st, Kingsland rd, nr Shrdch
25..Norfolk st, 7 Norfolk pl, Lower rd, Islington
17..Norfolk st, Lit. Guildford st, Boro, from 75 Queen st
9..Norman's buildings, Wenlock street, Helmet row, St. Luke's
13..Norman's ct, near Wellclose square
9..Norman st, 41 Cable st, Wenlock st, Old street
14..Norris's court, 26 Nightingale lane, Upper East Smithfield
36..Norris st, 56 Haymarket
9..Norris st, Old st, St. Lukes'
11..Norris st, Spitalfields
38..North crescent, Tottenham court rd
22..North mews, Little James's row
38..North mews, North st, Fitzroy sq
23..North mews, Gray's Inn lane
10..North pl, Banner st, Bunhill row
43..North pl, Globe st, Bethnal green
23..North place, near Liquorpond st
13..North pl, Wellclose sq Ratcliff hwy
38..North place, Hampstead road
23..North pl, op. 80 Gray's Inn lane
25..North road, Hoxton
43..North row, Hackney fields
32..North row, East st, Walworth
52..North row, Park st, Grosvenor sq
36..North row mews, Grosvenor sq
18..North st, near the Three Stags, Asylum, Lambeth
38..North st, Charlotte st, Fitzroy sq
10..North st, near Old st rd, City road

Ref. to Plan.
44..North st, Whitechapel, Mile end road turnpike
32..North st, East st, Walworth
52..North st, a few doors on the right in Sloane st
53..North st, Paradise st, Marylebone
40..North st, 6 New road, Pentonville
2..North st, Ropemaker's st
35..North st, St. John's church, Wstmr
-12..North st, 11 Lambs st, Spitalfields market
32..North st, 26 Salisbury pl, Locks fds
60..North st, Poplar
28..North st, 154 Whitechapel road
52..North st, Knightsbridge
22..North st, 32 Red Lion sq, Holborn
35..North st, St. John's st, Westminstr
43..North ter, Bonner's fields, Hackney
53..North Audley st, 263 Oxford st
52..North east ct, South Audley st
13..North east passage, north east corner of Wellclose square
37..North Harley mews, Harley st
53..North Portman mews, 1 Gloucester st north side of Portman square
39..Northam's buildings, Welstead st, Somerstown
24..Northampton buildings, Rosomond-street, Clerkenwell
24..Northampton ct, 31 Northampton st, Clerkenwell, Islington road
8..Northampton pl, 1 St. John's st, West Smithfield
32..Northampton place, Kent road
27..Northampton place, near Bird cage walk, Hackney road
32..Northampton place, North st
24..Northampton rw Brayne's rw, Spafds
24..Northampton square, west end of Charles st, Goswell st road
24..Northampton st, 2 Compton st, St John's st road
24..Northampton st, (Lower) 33 Percival st, St. John's st road
32..Northampton st, near Surry square
24..Northampton ter, west side City rd
27..Northampton walk, Hackney road
3..Northumberland al, 78 Fenchurch st
8..Northumberland court, Compton st, West Smithfield
7..Northumberland court, Southampton buildings, High Holborn
20..Northumberland court, 2 Strand
53..Northumberland mews, New row, Marylebone
32..Northumberland place, Walworth
45..Northumberland pl, Commercial rd
24..Northumberland place, 64 Compton st, Clerkenwell
53..Northumberland st, 18 Paddington
20..Northumberland st, 4 Strand
32..Northumberland st, Walworth
11..Norton Falgate, 103 Bishopsgate street without
37..Norton st, Marylebone st

Ref. to Plan.
29..Norway place, Commercial road,
    Whitechapel, near the Church
1..Norway st, 20 Old st road
24..Norway st, Northampton pl,City rd
27..Norwell place, Bethnal green road,
    near the turnpike
14..Norwich ct, 24 Up. East Smithfield
7..Norwich ct, 93 Fetter lane, Fleet st
21..Nottingham ct,Short's gdns.Drury la
53..Nottingham mews, 58 High street,
    Marylebone
53..Nottingham pl,New rd,Marylebone,
    between High st & Northumber
    land street
28..Nottingham pl, 5Charlotte st,Whcpl
53..Nottingham st, 61 High st, Marylebn
40..Nowel's bds, Back la, Islington
2..Nun's ct,74 Coleman st,London wall
32..Nursery place, corner of East lane,
    Kent road
17..Nursery place, near West square,
    St. George's fields
17..Nursery row, nr West sq, Lambeth
32..Nursery row, Lock's fds, Walwth rd
30..Nutkin's corner,Jacob's st,Dock hd

O

28..Oak pl, 123 Whitechapel road
66..Oakham st, Chelsea common
27..Oakley's ct, 35 Hare st, Bethnal grn
27..Oakley's row,Thomas st,Bethnal grn
18..Oakley st, Westminster bridge road
1..Oat la, 12 Noble st, Foster lane
15..Oatmeal yard, Dog and Bear yard,
    Tooley st; Borough
44..Ocean row, near Church, Stepney
44..Ocean st, Cow lane, Stepney
33..Octagon pl, W.side Kenningtoncom
25..Oddy row, Islington
20..Off alley, Villiers st, Strand
38..Ogle ct, Foley st, Fitzroy square
7..Old Bailey, 26 Ludgate hill
21..Old Belton st, continuation of Har-
    court street
12..Old Bethlem,148Bishopsgt stwithout
36..Old Bond st, 56 Piccadilly
7..Old Boswell ct, Picket st
21..Old bds, Lincoln's Inn, Chancery la
36..Old Burlington st, 148 Swallow st,
    Burlington gardens
12..Old Castle st, Wentworth st, Whcpl
37..Old Cavendish st, Cavendish sq
5..Old Chain, 34, St. Paul's Church yd
3..Old Change, 10 Cheapside
2..Old City chambers, Bishopsgate-
    street, within
4..Old Fish st,south end of Old Change
4..Old Fish st hill, 36 Up. Thames st
44..Old Ford lane, near Bethnal green
15..Old George yd, 241 Kent st, Boro
29..Old Gravel la, 65 Ratcliff highway
3..Old Jewry, 42 Poultry, Cheapside
12..Old Montagu st, Osborn st, Whtcpl
12..Old Nichol's street, Cock lane,
    Bethnall green

K

Ref. to Plan.
22..Old North st, 32Redlion sq,Holborn
35..Old Palace yard,south side of West-
    minster hall, Westminster
30..Old Paradise st, Millpond bridge
35..Old Pye st,in New Pyest,Orchard st
    Westminster
20..Old Round court, 437 Strand
20..Old Round ct, 14 Strand
21..Old square, Lincoln's Inn
45..Old sq, near Church, Stepney
29..Old Star yard, Old Gravel lane
9..Old st, St. Lukes, 38 Goswell st
10..Old st rd, 120 Shoreditch, to 46
    City road
9..Old st sq, north end of Henry st,
    St. Lukes
4..Old Swan lane, 97 Upper Thames st
11..Old York st, Church st, Shoreditch
35..Oliver st, Bowling st, Dean's yard,
    Westminster
20..One Tun al,Hungerford mkt,Strand
20..One Tun ct, 25 Strand
8..Ounslow st, Vine st, Hatton wall
14..Orain's ct, Water lane, Tower st
20..Orange ct, 17Orange st,Leicester sq
21..Orange ct, 130 Drury lane
7..Orange ct, Clement's Inn
20..Orange ct, St. Martin's lane
13..Orange ct, Whitechapel
30..Orange ct, 23 Wapping st, near
    Hermitage bridge
16..Orange garden's, Blackman st
33..Orange row, Kennington road
20..Orange st, 35 Leicester square, St.
    Martin's st
46..Orange st, lower road to Deptford,
    nearly opposite China walk
17..Orange st, Loman's pond, Gra-
    vel lane, Borough
22..Orange st,Redlion sq and20 King st,
    Holborn
29..Orange st, Sun Tavern fields
11..Orange st, 55 Swallow st, Picdly
53..Orchard st, 197 Oxford street and
    Portman square
35..Orchard st, Broadway, Westminster
9..Orchard st, Ironmonger row, Old st
    St. Lukes
60..Ord st, near West India Docks
36..Ormond mews, Duke st, Picdadilly
22..Ormond mews, Great Ormond st
22..Ormond pl, Great Ormond st
22..Ormond st, (New) 31 Lambs Con-
    duit street
36..Ormond yd, York st, St. James's sq
44..Orton st, near Trafalgar square
4..O'Ryan's bds, Castle st, Borough
12..Osborne pl, Brick lane,Whitechapel
12..Osborne st, 74 Whitechapel church
12..Osborne ter, Osborne pl, Whcpl
52..Osnaburg row,bottom of Grosvenor
    square, Hyde park corner
38..Osnaburg st, near Regent's park
39..Ossulton st,continuation of Wilsted
    street, Somers town

Ref. to Plan.

39..Ossulton st (North) Somers town
24..Owen's ct, Owen's pl, Goswell st
24..Owen's pl, Goswell st road
40..Owen's row, 54 Goswell st road
20..Oxendon st, 26 Coventry st, Hmkt
37..Oxford bdgs, 299 Oxford st
3..Oxford ct. Cannon st, Watling st
37..Oxford ct. 317 Oxford st
37..Oxford market, 86 Oxford st
17..Oxford pl, Obelisk, St. George's fds
32..Oxford row, nr Asylum, Kent road
37..Oxford st, from High st, St. Giles's
     to Edgeware road
28..Oxford st, Whitechapel road
15..Oxley st. Parker's row, Dock head,
     Bermondsey

P

2..Packer's ct, Lothbury, Coleman st.
     Old Jewry   [Thames street
3..Pack's al, nr Bread st hill Upper
68..Paddington canal, Paddington
68..Paddington green, Paddington, nr
     the church
68..Paddington Beast market,Paddingtn
53..Paddington st, 80 High st, Marybn
35..Page st, Tothill fields
31..Page's walk, King st rd, Bermondsy
29..Paget's ct, Bluegate fields, Rat-
     cliffe highway   [cliffe cross
45..Painter's rents, 66 Broad st, Rat-
36..Palace row, Tottenham ct, Tot ct rd
35..Palace st,Charlotte st, Stafford row,
     Pimlico
29..Palatine place, White horse lane,
     Commercial road
36..Pall Mall ct, 102 Pall Mall
36..Pall Mall W. St. James's, S end of
     the Haymarket
40..Palmer pl, Back rd, Islington
15..Palmer's rents, Snow's fields, near
     Bermondsey
56..Palmer's terrace, Holloway road
35..Palmer's village, Brewers green,
     Westminster
7..Palsgrave pl, 222 Strand
3..Pancras lane, Bucklersbury, Cheaps
39..Pancras pl, Battle br, Gray's Inn la
38..Pancras st, 174 Tottenham ct rd
20..Panton sq, 25 Haymarket
20..Panton st, Covent garden, Haymkt
1..Panyer alley, 50 Newgate st
6..Paper buildings, west side Kings
     Bench walk, Inner Temple
36..Paper row, near New Ranelagh
27..Paradise buildings, Bethnal green
23..Paradise ct, Paradise st, Battle brdg
27..Paradise ct or bds, Bethnal green
53..Paradise pl, High st, Marylebone
10..Paradise pl, 44 Tabernacle walk,
     Finsbury
17..Paradise pl, Gravel lane, Southwark
66..Paradise pl, Paradise row, Chelsea
10..Paradise pl, Paul st, Finsbury
34..Paradise pl and row, Lambeth walk

Ref. to Plan.

39..Paradise rw, Paradise st,Battle brdg
27..Paradise rw,west side Bethnal green
17..Paradise row, Gravel lane, Borough,
     a few doors south of Charlotte st
66..Paradise row, Chelsea hospital
34..Paradise row, High st, Lambeth,
     first on the left from the Church
37..Paradise row, Brook st, Bond st
29..Paradise row, Old Gravel lane
35..Paradise row, Palmer's village,
     Westminster
30..Paradise row, first south from Lu-
     cas st, to Deptford lower road,
     Rotherhithe
39..Paradise st, Britania st, Battle brdg
30..Paradise st, (Old & New) Rotherh
53..Paradise st, 82 High st, Marylebone
10..Paradise st, 30 Paul st, Finsbury sq
40..Paradise terrace, Islington
66..Paradise walk, opposite 18 Para-
     dise row, Chelsea
32..Paragon buildings, New Kent road
32..Paragon pl, Locks fields, Walworth
32..Paragon place, New Kent road
32..Paragon row, 4 Victory place,
     Locks fields
24..Paragon passage, St John's st
16..Parain st, Kent st, Southwark
15..Paratalia place, Snowsfields, 6th
     on the right from 109 Boro High st
30..Pardhee pl, Millpond st, Rotherh
8..Pardon passage, Wilderness row,
     54 St. John's st, Clerkenwell
1..Paris ct, Golden lane, Old st
68..Paris pl, Chapel st, Lisson green
15..Parish st, Tooley st, last on the
     right from London bridge
40..Park lane, Back road, Islington
52..Park lane,Hyde park corner,toTy-
     burn turnpike
32..Park place, East lane, Walworth
     4th on the right from the Kent rd,
33..Park place, Kennington cross, op-
     posite the White hart
52..Park place, Knightsbridge, east end
     of the Barracks
53..Park place, Marylebone fields
36..Park pl, 60 St. James's Piccadilly
60..Park place, Limehouse causeway
28..Park place, Mile end road
52..Park prospect, west end of Cannon
     Brewery, Knightsbridge
33..Park row, Kennington cross
31..Park row, Bermondsey
53..Park st, 256 Oxford st
33..Park st, near Kennington cross
53..Park st, Baker st, (North)Marybone
53..Park st, New st, Marylebone
35..Park st, Westminster, north end of
     Cartaret st
53..Park st, Grosvenor square
33..Park st, Kennington cross, opposite
     the White Hart
4..Park st,northern end of Redcross st
     Borough market

Ref. to Plan.

8..Parker's alley, Clerkenwell green, Turnmill st
31..Parker's buildings, Grange road, third on the right from Bermondsey New road
2..Parker's ct,46Coleman st,Old Jewry
1..Parker's rents,Whitecross st,Crplgt
7..Parker's rents, 45 Shoe lane
31..Parker's row, Hickman's folly, Dockhead
21..Parker's st, 161 Drury lane
8..Parker's yard, King st, Cloth fair, West Smithfield
12..Parliament ct, Artillery lane, turn at 55 Bishopsgate st
27..Parliament place, Bethnal green, opposite the Nursery grove
35..Parliament place, Old Palace yard, Westminster
35..Parliament st, north west of Whitehall, Westminster
27..Parliament street, Bethnal green, Parliament place
28..Parliament st, Dog row
35..Parliament sq, Westminster Abbey
53..Parr's bds, 20 North rw, Grosvnr sq
1..Parrot al, Playhouse yard, turn at 50 Golden lane
7..Parson ct, Bride lane, turn at 97 Fleet street
6..Parson's ct, 116 Holywell st, Strand
40..Parson's ct, 22 High st, Islington
27..Parson's pl, New rd, Bethnal green
11..Parson's square, 114 Holywell st, Shoreditch
30..Parson's stairs, Rotherhithe
14..Parson's stairs, 82 Lower Smithfield
14..Parson's street, 50 Lower East Smithfield
33..Parsonage place, Newington
33..Parsonage row, 8 Queen head row, Newington church
33..Parsonage walk, near Newington ch
11..Parsonage yard, Shoreditch, three doors from the Church
12..Partridge ct, 129 Houndsditch
30..Pasfield's rents, Millpond brdg Roth
8..Passing alley, 49 St. John's lane, Clerkenwell
1..Paternoster alley, Paternoster row, St. Paul's
1..Paternoster row, 3 Cheapside
12..Paternoster row, continuation of Union st, Spitalfields
12..Paternoster row,(Lit)41Paternoster-row, Spitalfields
11..Patience st,north end of Wheeler st, Spitalfields
43..Patriot pl, Patriot st, Bethnal green
43..Patriot row, Bethnal green, adjoining Patriot square
43..Patriot square, a few yards from Bethnal green,towards Hackney rd
29..Patriot st. James's st, New rd, St. George's East

Ref. to Plan.

13..Patterson's gards,Church laCable st Commercial road
11..Patty's ct, second on the left in Holywell st, from 195 Shoreditch,
1..Paul's alley, 9 Paternoster row
1..Paul's alley, Redcross st, Cripplegt
3..Paul's alley, Sherbourn lane,Lombard street
2..Paul's alley, Wood st, Cheapside
5..Paul's chain,16 St.Paul's Church yd
1..Paul's ct, 71St. Paul's Church yard
2..Paul's ct, Hugginlane, Wood st
10..Paul sq, Paul st, Finsbury square
10..Paul st, 25 Providence row, Finsbury square
6..Paul Baker's ct, Godliman street, Doctors commons
2..Paul's College court, 2 St. Paul's Church yard, side of St. Paul's
3..Paul's Head court,155 Fenchurch st
8..Paved alley, Newgate market
36..Paved alley, 66 west end Pall mall
2..Pavement, west side Moorfields
1..Paved alley, 30 Paternoster row
5..Paved pl, 30 Gravel lane, Borough
51..Pavilion row, Five fields, Pimlico
55..Pavilion row, Battersea fields
52..Pavilion st, Sloane st, Chelsea
16..Paviors alley, Union st, Southwark
37..Paviours Arms court,50 Wardour st, Soho
29..Pavior st, Ratcliff highway
30..Paxton's ct, near Swan la, Rotherh
38..Paxton place, Tottenham court rd
1..Payne's place, 142 Aldersgate st
27..Peacock ct, 42 Minories
12..Peacock's place, north west corner of Bethnal green
33..Peacock st, 16 High st, Newington
12..Peahen ct,75 Bishopsgate st
28..Pearl pl, nr Redman's row,Stepn gr
17..Pearl row, Blackfriar's road
11..Pearl st, (Gt & Little) Spitalfields
29..Pearl st, 62 Shadwell High st
22..Pearl st, Silver st, Bloomsbury mkt
29..Peartree al, 46 High st Shadwell
24..Peartree court, 5 Coppice row, Clerkenwell green
11..Peartree ct, near Shoreditch chur
29..Peartree ct, 132 High st, Shadwell
1..Peartree ct, 42 Aldersgate st
18..Peartree row, 1 Charlotte terrace, New cut, Lambeth
9..Peartree st, 13 Brick lane, Old st
9..Peartree st, a short distance above Peerless pool, City road
6..Peck's buildings, Kings Benchwalk,Temple
19..Pedlar's acre, Bridge rd, Westminster bridge
29..Peel alley, nr Fox's lane, Shadwell
1..Peel ct, Glasshouse yd,Aldersgate st
9..Peerless row, Peerless pool, City rd
9..Peerless pool,Baldwyn st, City road
12..Pelham st, Brick lane, Spitalfields

Ref. to Plan.
1..Pelican court, 60 Little Britain
29..Pell place, Pell st, Ratcliff highway
13..Pell st, 194 Ratcliff highway
7..Pemberton row, 18 Fetter lane, Gough square, Fleet st
53..Pendrey's yd, 23 Marylebone lane
34..Peniel pl, South st, Lambeth
34..Penitentiary prison, Millbank
35..Penitentiary road, Westminster
34..Penlington place, Lambeth
29..Pennington st, 18 Ratcliff highway
60..Penny fields, High st, Poplar
40..Penton grove,44 Whitelion stPutnvl
33..Penton place, Francis st, Newington
23..Penton place, Pentonville
40..Penton st, 11 Henry st, Pentonville, 2nd right from Angel Inn, Islington
1..Pentoll's rents, Chiswell st
33..Penton st, Newington butts
40.'.Pentonville, from the Angel Inn, Islington, to Battle bridge
15..Pepper alley, west side London-bridge foot
17..Pepper st, Duke st, Charlotte st, Blackfriars road
24..Percival st, Northampton square, Goswell st road
37..Percy mews, 26 Rathbone place
26..Percy st, Kingsland road
37..Percy st, 38, Tottenham court rd
35..Perkin's rents, old Pye street
29..Perriwinckle ct, Turk's row, nearly opposite Sloan st, Chelsea
29..Perriwinckle st, Sun Tavern fields
37..Perry's place, 29 Oxford st
27..Perry's rents, Middlesex place, Hackney road
29..Perry's rents, 40, New Gravel lane
39..Perry st, Pancras
39..Pershore pl, Judd pl, E Somerstwn
9..Pesthouse row, west end of St. Luke's Hospital, Old st
24..Peter court, St, John's st
13..Peter ct, 28, Rosemary lane
20..Peter ct, 111 St. Martin's lane
8..Peter la, 69 John's st, W. Smithfd
21..Peter st, Hart st, Bloomsbury
16..Peter st 45 Redcross st, Union street, Borough
8..Peter st, Saffron hill
11..Peter st, Church st, Shoreditch
37..Peter st, Wardour st, Soho
8..Peter & Key ct, Peter's lane, St. John's street
8..Peter's st 7, Turnmill st Clerkenwell
3..Peter's alley, 55 Cornhill
4..Peter's st hill, 216 up. Thames st
7..Peterborough court, 136 Fleet st
12..Petticoat lane, now Middlesex-st, 148, Hight st, Whitechapel
37..Petty's court, Hanway st, Oxford st
37..Petty's place, near Rathbone place
8..Pewtner's ct, 20 Charterhouse lane, West Smithfield
2..Phillip's ct, Addle st, Aldermanbury

Ref. to Plan.
2..Phillip lane, 8 London wall
3..Philip lane, 8, Leadenhall st
29..Philip st, Cross st, Shadwell
11..Philip st, Curtain road, Shoreditch
1..Phillip's ct, Brackley st, 10 Golden-lane, Cripplegate
1..Phillip's ct, 65 Grub st, Cripplegate
12..Phillip's bds, Houndsditch
39..Phillip's bds, Wilsted st, Somerstwn
38..Phillip's gardens, Tottenham ct rd
15..Phillip's rents, Maze pond, Boro
38..Phillip's row, Tottenham court rd
26..Phillip's st, Hoxton
3..Phillpot lane, 13 Little Eastcheap, Fenchurch st
68..Phillpotter, near Church st, Padngtn
11..Phipp's ct, Phipp's st, Curtain road
60..Phœbe st, Limehouse causeway
21..Phœnix alley, 54 Long Acre
14..Phœnix ct,38,Butcher row, E Smthfd
8..Phœnix ct, 3, Newgate st
3..Phœnix ct, 27 Old Change
1..Phœnix ct, 73 West st, West Smthfd
17..Phœnix row, Blackfriars road, near Webber street
11..Phœnix st, Brick lane, Spitalfields
21..Phœnix st, Bedford square
39..Phœnix st,Clarendon sq,Somerstwn
22..Phœnix st, Plumbtree st, Broad st, Bloomsbury
21..Phœnix st, Crown st, near Compton st, St. Giles's
32..Phœnix st, South st, East la, Walwth
37..Phœnix yard, 126 Oxford st
36..Piccadilly, from Coventry st, Hay-market, to Hyde park corner
17..Pichegru place, London road, St. George's fields
60..Pickering pl, nr East India Dock rd
36..Pickering pl, St. James's st, Picdly
7..Picket st, 245, Strand
14..Pickle Herring st, Morgan's-lane, Tooley street
40..Pierpoint row, Islington
17..Pilgrims st, 2 Ludgate hill
14..Pillory lane, 7, Little Thames st
35..Pimlico, from Buckingham gate to Chelsea
10..Pimlico gardens, Haberdashers walk Hoxton
7..Pindar st, a few doors south of Britannia st, Gray's Inn lane
35..Pine Apple ct, Castle st, Westmnst
9..Pink's row, near Peerless pool, City road
7..Pinnor ct, 35 Gray's Inn lane
2..Pinnor ct. 54 Old Broad st, Royal Exchange
35..Pipe alley, Broadway, Tothill st, Westminster
45..Pipemaker's al, 32 Narrow st, Limeh
45..Pipemaker's al, 35 White Horse st, Ratcliffe
20..Pipemaker's ct, 35 Bedfordbury
12..Pitch ct, Crispin st, Spitalfields

Ref. to Plan.

2..Pitches ct, Lit. Bell al, Coleman st
10..Pitfield st, 1st turning in Old st road, from the City road
17..Pit ct, Prospect place, Newington
32..Pitt place, Kent road, nearly opposite the Bricklayer's Arms
5..Pitt place, Maid lane, Southwark
5..Pitt place, Gt. Guildford st, Boro
32..Pitt st, Kent road, 1st turning below the Bricklayer's Arms
28..Pitt st, near Chester pl, Bethnal grn
17..Pitt st, 11 Prospect pl, Newington
27..Pitt st, Camden row, Bethnal green
38..Pitt st, Charlotte st, Rathbone pl, Tottenham court road
52..Pitt's head mews, Park lane
9..Pittman's bds, John's row, Brick-lane, Old street
31..Pittman's pl, Neckinger rd, Brmndsy
6..Playhouse yd, 36 Water la, Blackfrs
1..Playhouse yard, 50 Golden la, Brbcn
5..Pleasant ct, 33, Broadwall, Blackfrs rd
27..Pleasant place, near Wilmot square, Bethnal green road
43..Pleasant pl, Bonner's st, Bethnal grn
40..Pleasant pl, Pleasant row, Pentonvl
45..Pleasant place, west end of Prospect place, Stepney green
33..Pleasant pl, Upper Kennington lane
33..Pleasant pl, Elliott's row, Newingtn
5..Pleasant place, Zoar st
18..Pleasant retreat, Webber row, Blackfriars road
32..Pleasant row, East st, Walworth
45..Pleasant row, Globe alley, 54 Fore-street, Limehouse
26..Pleasant row, Kingsland road, half a mile on the left from Shrdtch ch
12..Pleasant row, Mile End, New town, continuation of Pelham st
32..Pleasant row, near Camden street, East, Walworth
44..Pleasant row, 5 Stepney causeway
11..Pleasant row, Wm. st, 137 Shrdtch
40..Pleasant row, Winchester st, Pentvl
30..Plough al, Gt Hermitage st, Wpng
1..Plough alley, 52, Barbican
21..Plough ct, 22, Carey st, Lincoln's inn fields
7..Plough ct, 48 Fetter lane, Holborn
13..Plough & Harrow yard, 84 Kent st, Borough
3..Plough court, 37, Lombard st
13..Plough st, 44 High st, Whitechapel
15..Plough yard, 79 Bermondsy
13..Plough yard, Seething lane
11..Plough yard, 223 High st, Shoreditch
15..Plough & Harrow yard, 99 Tooley st
29..Plumber's row, Whitehorse lane, Commercial road, Whitechapel
22..Plumber's ct, 111 High Holborn
9..Plummer st, opposite Fountain pl, City road
7..Plumtree ct, Shoe lane
21..Plumtree st, 62 Broad st, Bloomsby

K 2

Ref. to Plan.

35..Poet's corner, Old Palace yard
10..Pointer's buildings, Old st road, near Fuller's Almshouses
31..Poitiers pl, 8 Bermondsey new road
37..Poland st, 366 Oxford st
27..Pollard st, near Wilmot square, Bethnal green road
37 .Pollin st, Maddox st, Hanover sq
39..Polygon, Clarendon square, Somer's town
66..Pond st, Chelsea common
5..Pond yd, Bankside, Southwark
52..Pont st, Cadogan pl, Sloane st
18..Pontypool row, Webber st
23..Pool's bds, Mt. Pleasant, Colbath sq
9..Pool ter, north side of Peerless pool, City road
3..Pope's Head alley, 19 Cornhill
11..Pope's head ct, Quaker st
7..Pope's head court, 20 Bell yard, Temple bar
21..Pope's head yd, Lincoln's Inn
29..Pope's hill, 76 Shadwell High st
60..Poplar, near Blackwall
60..Poplar, High st, from the Commercial road, by the West India Docks to Blackwall
32..Poplar row, New Kent rd
60..Poplar terrace, Poplar
7..Poppin's ct, 111 Fleet st
9..Porridgepot al, 107, Brick la, Old st
41..Porter's place, Holloway road
21..Porter st, 14, Great Newport street, Long acre
11..Porter st, Norton Falgate
37..Portland mews, 20 Portland st
37..Portland place, Oxford st
32..Portland place, near Queen's row, Walworth common
24..Portland place, 16, Market street, St. John's st road
37..Portland road, opposite 4 Conway st, New road, Marylebone
37..Portland st, Wardour st, Soho
53..Portland st, 8 John st, Oxford st
68..Portman place, 14 Edgware road
53..Portman place, Portman square
53..Portman sq, 79, Upper Berkley st
53..Portman st, 219 Oxford st
20..Portobello passage, 33 Lisle street, Leicester square
23..Portpool lane, 54 Gray's Inn lane
33..Portsmouth place, Kennington lane
21..Portsmouth st, Portugal st, Lincoln's Inn fields
21..Portugal st, near the south east corner of Lincoln's Inn fields
28..Portugal pl, Dog row, Mile End
19..Portugal st, Lambeth
36..Portugal street, Mount street, Grosvenor square
14..Postern row, 31 Tower hill
3..Post Office General 11 Lmbrd st, Cornh
3..Post Office, Twopenny (General) Lombard st, Cornhill

Ref. to Plan.
21..Post Office, Twopenny (General) 38, Gerrard st, Soho
27..Pott st, Camden rd, Bethnal green
15..Potter's fields, Back st, Horselydwn
43..Potter's row, Cambridge heath
31..Potter's st, Bermondsey new road
3..Poultry, 77 Cheapside
3..Pountney lane, 30 Cannon st, City
16..Powell's al, 296 Kent st, Borough
43..Power st, Cambridge heath
·32..Powis place, 50, Great Ormond st
52..Powis place, Knightsbridge
33..Pownal ter, Kennington cross
68..Praed st, Edgware road
39..Pratt pl,Battle bridge, Gray's Inn la
29..Pratt's bds,36 New Gravel la,Shdwl
34..Pratt st, Church st, Lambeth
13..Prescot st, Goodman's fields
9..Prevost st, Plummer st
37..Price's alley, Little Pulteney street, Grosvenor square
16..Price's buildings, King st, Boro
5..Price's ct, 90 Queen st, Southwark
5..Price's pl, Bear la, Blackfriars rd
5..Price's st, Bear la, Blackfriars rd
14..Priest alley, 47 Great Tower st
1..Priest ct, Foster la, Cheapside
15..Primrose alley, Church st,Boro mkt
11..Primrose ct, Long alley, Moorfields
20..Primrose hill, Salisbury sq, Fleet st
43..Primrose st, near Three Colt lane, Bethnal green
11..Primrose st110Bishopsgate without
30..Prince's al, 15 Princes st, Rotherh
10..Prince's ct,6 Banner st, Bunhill row
53..Prince's ct, 81 Edgware road
2..Prince's ct, Coleman st, Old Jewry
36..Prince's ct, Duke st, St. James's, Piccadilly
21..Prince's ct,144op.Broad ct, Drury la
20..Prince's ct, Leicester square
21..Prince's ct, east side Newport mkt
34..Prince's ct, Prince's st, Lambeth
35..Prince's ct, Great George st,Westm
35..Prince's ct, Stafford place, near Buckingham gate
11..Prince's ct, Virginia st, Shordch ch
19..Prince's ct, corner of Broad wall, Commercial road, Lambeth
36..Prince's place, Kennington cross
36..Prince's pl, 40 Duke st, St.James's
29..Prince's place, St. George's East
12..Prince's place, Great Garden st
51..Prince's place, Prince's st, Pimlico, 3rd left of Buckingham gate
33..Prince's rd, 10 Prince's pl, Kennington cross
33..Prince's sq, Kennington common
29..Prince's sq,Prince's st, Ratcliff hwy
2..Prince's sq, Finsbury
30..Prince's stairs, 40 Rotherhithe st
1..Prince's st, 42 Barbican
2..Prince's st, Bank of England
37..Prince's st, Cavendish square ·
21..Prince's st, Drury lane

Ref to Plan.
27..Prince's st, Gibraltar walk
53..Prince's st, 119 Oxford st
12..Prince's st, 186 Brick la, Whitechpl
12..Prince's st, Great Garden st
35..Prince's st, Gt George st, Westmr
30..Prince's st, Great Hermitage st
37..Prince's st, Hanover square
34..Prince's st, Fore st,Lambeth church
20..Prince's st, Leicester square
35..Prince's st, George st, Westminster
21..Prince's st, LitQueen st,High Hlbrn
17..Prince's st, London road
29..Prince's st, 27 Old Gravel lane
32..Prince's st, Queen's st, Locksfields Walworth
29..Prince's st, 173 Ratcliff highway
51..Prince's st, Queen's row, Pimlico
19..Prince's st, Commercial rd, Lmbth
22..Prince's st, Red Lion square
30..Prince's st,350 Rotherhithe st
11..Prince's st, Tyson st, Bethnalgreen
13..Prince's st, Rosemary lane, 3rd on the left from the Minories
11..Prince's st, Wilson st, Finsbury sq
44..Prince's stWhitehorse laMileEnd rd
12..Prince's st, Spitalfields
7..Printer st, Lit. New st, Shoe lane
7..Printer's ct, Eagle and Child alley, Fleet market
31..Printer's pl, Neckinger road
6..Printing house lane, Blackfriars
6..Printing house sq,33Water la,Blkfrs
6..Printing st, 9 Earl st, Blackfriars
13..Priors ct, Chamber st,Goodmans fds
32..Prior pl, opposite Apollo buildings, Walworth
5..Prior pl, Gravel lane, Southwark
15..Pritchard's al, Fair st,Horselydown
19..Privy gardens, Whitehall
19..Privy garden terrace, Whitehall
29..Produce st, Lower Turning Shdwl
47..Prospect pl, Canal bridge, Kent rd
29..Prospect pl, Back la, Sun Tavern fds
43..Prospect place, Cambridge heath, Hackney road
30..Prospect place, Blue Anchor road, Bermondsey
27..Prospect place, Bethnal green
66..Prospect place, Chelsea
33..Prospect place, Newington green
17..Prospect pl, from the Elephant and Castle, to the Philanthropic
44..Prospect pl, Trafalgar square
44..Prospect pl, Stepney green, third on the right from Mile End
40..Prospect pl,6 Henry st, Pentonville
31..Prospect row, Neckinger road
32..Prospect row, Walworth, 2nd left from the Elephant and Castle
7..Prospect ter, near Sydney street, Gray's Inn lane
68..Pross garden, Bell st, Paddington
32..Providence buildings, New Kent rd, near the Elephant and Castle
33..Providence buildings, Kennington

Ref. to Plan.
53..Providence ct, George st, Oxford st
35..Providence ct, Gt Peter st, Westm
27..Providence gardens, Hackney road, third left from Shoreditch church
23..Providence place, Coldbath square
15..Providence place, 5 Crosby row, Snowsfields
16..Providence pl, Baalzephon st
12..Providence pl,Midelesex st,Whchpl
32..Providence row, Westmorland row
10..Providence row, N. E. corner of Finsbury square
17..Providence row, Bennett's row, Blackfriars road [tonville
40..Providence row, Pleasant row, Pen-
43..Provdience row, top of New road, to Hackney
35..Providence rw, Palmer's vil,Westm
9..Providence st, 426 City road
26..Provost sreet, Cross street, Hoxton New town
7..Prujean square, 64 Old Bailey
29..Prussian Island, Cinnamon st, Old Gravel lane
29..Pudding lane, 3 Little East Cheap
6..Puddle dock hill, Great Carter lane, opposite Earl st, Blackfriars
40..Pullen's row, opposite the Green, High st, Islington [sqr
37..Pulteney ct, 1 Cambridge st, Golden
36..Pulteney st,15 Brewer's st,Goldn sq
10..Pump al, Coleman's al, Bunhil row
1..Pump ct, Bridgewater gardens, Aldersgate street
17..Pump ct, Duke st, Charlotte street, Blackfriars road
16..Pump court, 12 Long la, Borough
15..Pump ct, 62 Snowsfields
8..Pump ct, White's yd, 24, Great Saffron hill
14..Pump ct,32 Dean's st, up E Smthfd
2..Pump ct, 2 Moor lane, Cripplegate
6..Pump ct, Mid. Temple la, Fleet st
10..Pump row, opposite the Vinegar yd, Old street road
27..Punderson row, S side of Bethnal gr
28..Purim pl, Dog row, Mile end
3..Purse court, 40 old Change, Cheapsd
8..Pye corner, Giltspur st, corner of Cock lane
35..Pye gardens, Willow st, Bankside

Q

36..Quadrant, Regent street
11..Quaker st, Brick la, Spitalfields
7..Quality ct, 47 Chancery la
53..Quebec mews, new Quebec st, Oxford street
53..Quebec st, 237 Oxford street
53..Quebec st, (Old,) 235 Oxford st
53..Quebec st,(New,)69 up.Berkeley st
4..Queenhithe, 59 Upper Thames st
67..Queen's buildings, left side Brompton, near Knightsbridge
35..Queen's buildings, Pimlico

Ref. to Plan.
28..Queen's court, near Dog row
17..Queen's ct, Great Suffolk st, Boro
22..Queen's court, Red Lion square
20..Queen's ct, 30 King st, Covent gdn
35..Queen's ct, Queen road, Pimlico
21..Queen's ct, 58 Great Queen st, Lincoln's Inn fields
16..Queen's ct, 40 Queen st, Mint st, Borough
29..Queen's ct, Queen st, Ratcliff cross
16..Queen's ct, Union st, Borough
13..Queen's ct, North side the Circus, Minories
21..Queen's ct, 247 High Holborn
27..Queen's ct, 21 King st, Bethnal grn
67..Queen's elms, Brompton
67..Queen's gardens, Brompton, third on the left from Knightsbridge
36..Queen's gardens, Pimlico
16..Queen's gdns, Crosby row, Boro
36..Queen's palace, St. James's park
35..Queen's pl, Peter st, Westminster
66..Queen's pl, Queen st, Chelsea
16..Queen's place, 19, King st, Boro
67..Queen's row, Brompton
33..Queen's row, Newington
28..Queen's row, Dog row, Bethnal gra
34..Queen's row, near Lambeth walk
30..Queen's row, King st, near 17 Old Gravel lane
33..Queen's row, 14 Kennington road, opposite the Common
60..Queen's row, Poplar
66..Queen's row, Chelsea
24..Queen's row, Pentonville, near the Angel, Islington [Barracks
51..Queen's row, Pimlico, opposite the
48..Queen's row,nr Camberwell turnpk
35..Queen's r, Palmer's village, Westm
26..Queen's row, nr Hoxton Madhouse
1..Queen's square, 138 Aldersgate st
2..Queen's sq. nr Wilson st, Moorfields
22..Queen's sq, Southampton row,Bisby
2..Queen's sq, 12 Moorfields
35..Queen sq, nr Broadway, Westmnst
35..Queen sq, pl, Queen sq, Westmstr
67..Queen sq, Brompton, fourth on the left from Knightsbridge
59..Queen st, Bryanstone square
3..Queen st, 61 Cheapside
51..Queen st, Ranelagh wlk, nr Chelsea
12..Queen st, Church st,Whitechapel rd
36..Queen st, Curzon st, Mayfair
35..Queen st, Dartmouth st,Westmnstr
53..Queen st, 60 Edgware road
14..Queen st, Gainsford street
53..Queen st, Grosvenor square
36..Queen st, 18 Windmill st, Haymarkt
21..Queen st, Great Russell street
10..Queen st, Hoxton market, Hoxton
16..Queen st, 20 King st, Borough
16..Queen st, Mint st, Borough
30..Queen st, King st, 17 Old Gravel la
34..Queen st, Prince's road, Lambeth
18..Queen st, near Cobourg Theatre

Ref to Plan.

37..Queen st, 71 Oxford st
11..Queen st, Worship st, Moorfields
40..Queen st,39 Percival st,Islington rd
33..Queen st, Prince's sq, nr Newingtn
11..Queen st, Quaker st, Spitalfields
29..Queen st, continuation of Broad st, from Ratcliff cross
30..Queen st, Old Paradise st, Rotherh
21..Queen street, Seven Dials
21..Queen st, 340 Oxford st
13..Queen st, 1 Rosemary la, Tower hil
32..Queen st, York st, Walworth
66..Queen st, King's road, Chelsea
66..Queen st, Cheyne walk, Chelsea
34..Queen st, Vauxhall walk
37..Queen Anne's mews, Chandos st Cavendish square
28..Queen Anne st, Ducking pond row, opposite Count st, Whitechapel rd
37..Queen Anne st, Harley st
5..Queen's Arms ct, Upper Ground-st, Blackfriars
48..Queen Catherine st, 23 Brooke-st, Ratcliffe
30..Queen's Head alley, 122 Wapping
8..Queen's Head ct, Giltspur st
23..Queen's Head ct, Gray's Inn lane
18..Queen's Head ct, near Stangate st
20..Queen's Head ct, 405 Strand
36..Queen's Head ct, 24 Great Wind-mill st, Haymarket
1..Queen's Head pas, Paternoster row
18..Queen's Head sq, 22 upper Lam-beth marsh
38..Quickset row, 16 New Road nearly opposite Fitzroy-square

R

7..Racquet court, 115 Fleet street
24..Radcliff terrace, Goswell st road
9..Radnor st, 42 Bath st, City road
23..Ragdale street, Millman-street
19..Ragged row, Narrow wall, Lambeth
21..Ragged Staff ct, 12 Drury-lane
9..Rahere st, York st, City road
11..Ram alley, Spicer-at, Spitalfields
30..Ram alley, 217 Rotherhithe st
6..Ram alley, Cow cross,W Smithfield
7..Ram court, 47 Fleet st
32..Ramsden's yard, 20 Beckford row, Walworth
30..Randall causeway, Rotherhithe
35..Ranelagh gardens, Millbank near the Bridge
51..Ranelagh gardens, nr Chelsea bridge
51..Ranelagh place, Pimlico, a short distance right of Arabella row
51..Ranelagh st,lower Grosvenor place, Pimlico
51..Ranelagh st, Chelsea road
51..Ranelagh walk, Chelsea bridge
29..Ratcliffe ct, 115 Ratcliff highway
29..Ratcliff cross, opposite the end of Butcher row, Ratcliff

Ref. to Plan.

29..Ratcliff highway, from the end of Shadwell High st, to Limehouse
9..Ratcliffe rw,36 Bath st,Peerless pool
29..Ratcliff sq, Broad st, Ratcliff cross
9..Ratcliff's layer, Brick la, Old st
37..Rathbone place, 2 Oxford st
7..Raven court, 110 Fetter lane
28..Raven row, nr Whitechapel trnpike
12..Raven row, Widegate st [sey sq,
15..Raven &Sunyd,Russell st,Bermond-
67..Rawston st, Brompton
24..Rawstorn place, in Rawstorn st
24..Rawstorn st, 24 Islington road
23..Ray ct,Onslow st,Vine st,Hatton wl
23..Ray st, 63 Clerkenwell green
66..Rayner place, N side Chelsea hosptl
37..Rebecca ct, Wells st, Oxford st
4..Red Bull yd, 93 Upper Thames st
28..Red Cow lane, Mile end road
16..Red Cow lane, 105 Kent st, Boro
16..Redcross alley, near Wycombe place Borough High st
16..Redcross alley, Kent st, Borough
16..Redcross ct, 37 Redcross st, Boro
8..Redcross ct, (now King st) W Smfd
13..Redcross ct, Tower st
16..Redcross pas, Whitecross st, Boro
1..Redcross sq, Jewin st, Aldersgate at
14..Redcross sq, Park, Southwark
14..Redcross sq, 59 Great Tower st
1..Redcross st, Fore st, Cripplegate
14..Redcross st, Nightingale la, Wping
16..Redcross st, Union st, Borough
13..Redgate court, 79, Minories
66..Redhouse, Battersea fields,
61..Red house, Vict. office, Deptford
13..Red lion alley, nearly opposite the Minories
8..Red lion al, 71 Cow cr, West Smthfi
13..Red lion alley, 30, Whtchpl, High st
3..Red lion ct, 20 Basing la, Cheapside
6..Red lion ct. Addle hill
15..Red lion ct. 44 Bermondsey st, near Crucifix lane
7..Red lion ct, Castle st, Holborn bars
8..Red lion ct, 10 Charter house lane, St. John st
8..Redlion ct, op 19 Cock la, Snowhill
7..Redlion ct, 169 nr Fleet st, Fetterla
11..Redlion ct, Holywell la, Shoreditch
26..Redlion ct, Huntingdon st, Hoxton, nearly op the Britannia Asylum
10..Redlion ct,63 Kingsland road
2..Redlion ct, 37 London wall
16..Redlion ct, St. Margaret's hill
11..Redlion ct, Long al, Moorfields
30..Redlion ct, Red lion st, Green bank, Wapping
7..Redlion ct, 43 Shoe lane
12..Redlion ct, Redlion st, Spitalfields
14..Redlion ct, St. Catherine's lane
8..Redlion ct,57 St John's st, Smithfield
2..Redlion ct,7 Silver st, nr Cheapside
3..Redlion ct, 11 Great Saffron hill
21..Redlion ct, White Hart yd,Drury la

Ref. to Plan.
1..Redlion mkrt, 207 Whitecross st,
St. Luke's
39..Redlion passage, Battle bridge, west
side the Small Pox Hospital
22..Redl on pass, Redlion sq, Holborn
7..Redlion passage, Fleet st
8..Redlion passage. Clothfair, Smithfild
1..Redlion pass, 213 Whitecross st, St.
Luke's
68..Redlion place, Edgware road
22..Redlion sq, High Holborn
16..Redlion st, 263 High st, Borough
8..Redlion st, S. side of Clerkenwell gr
30..Redlion st, near Wapping church
22..Redlion st, 71 Holborn
12..Redlion st, Spitalfields church
13..Redlion st, 30 Whitechapel, High st
7..Redlion yd, 255 Holborn
23..Redlion yd, 46 Coppice rw, Cierkwl
8..Redlion yd, 70 Red lion st, Clkenwl
8..Redlion yd, 8 Long la, W. Smithfild
34..Redlion yd, Church st, Lambeth
23..Redlion yd, 62 Swallow st, Piedilly
8..Redlion yard, Long lane, Smithfield
21..Redlion yd, up King st, Bloomsby
37..Redlion yard, Old Cavendish st
12..Redlion yd, Houndsditch
30..Red Maid la, Great Hermitage st
28..Redman's row, Stepney green
1..Redrose alley, turn at 56 Whitecross st, Cripplegate
10..Reeve's bdgs, King's rd, Hoxton
53..Reeve's mews, Park st, Grosvenor sq
5..Regency place, 14 Gt Surrey st
35..Regent pl, Vincent sq
38..Regent's circus, Portman place
37..Regent's circus, 11 Oxford st
54..Regent's park, north of the New
road, Hampstead, Marylebone
66..Regent's pl, Chelsea common
60..Regent st, west end of Caulker st,
Blackwall causeway
66..Regent st, Chelsea common
33..Regent st, Princes st, Kenningtn cros
35..Regent st, Vincent square
36..Regent st, continuation of Waterloo
place, Pall Mall, op. Carlton palace
11..Reliance pl, New Inn yd, 175 Shoredh
66..Remos pl, King's rd, Chelsea
15..Renney's rent's, 29 Maze Boro
1..Renon's ct, Whitecross alley, Wilson st, Moorfields
16..Rephidim st, 11 Potier st, Bermdsey
26..Reputation row, Ironmonger's Alms
houses, Kingsland road
33..Respenden st, Kent rd
17..Revel row, Blackman st, Borough,
near the King's Bench prison
34..Retreat, Lambeth, first on the left
from Vauxhall turnpike
12..Ran's ct, Church la, Whitechapel
44..Rhode's well, east of the Church,
Stepney
45..Rich st, Commercial rd, Limehouse
7..Richard's ct, 72 Shoe lane, Holborn

Ref. to Plan.
29..Richard ct, Commercial rd, Whchpl
40..Richard st, Pentonville
60..Richard st, nr Limehouse church
45..Richard st, Anchor fields, Stepney
7..Richardson's blds, 73 Shoe la, Hlbn
16..Richardson's st, north side, Loug la,
Borough
22..Richbell ct, Lamb's Conduit street,
3..Riche's ct, 50 Lime st, Fenchurch st
37..Richmond bdgs, Dean st, Soho
37..Richmond mews, Dean st, Soho
32..Richmond pl, part of East la, Walw
9..Richmond st, Pesthouse row, near
St. Luke's hospital, Old st
21..Richmond st, 25 Rupert st, Soho
32..Richmond ter, East la, Walworth
2..Rockington's ct, Coleman st
37..Ridinghouse la, Gt. Portland st
23..Riley st, 90 Cromer st, Gray's Inn la
4..Riloch yd, New Park st, Borough
8..Rising Sun alley, St. John's st
30..River st, Gt Hermitage st
66..Robert's buildings, Chelsea
51..Robert's bdgs, Avery Farm row
20..Robert's st, Adelphi, Strand
67..Robert's st. Brompton
16..Robert st, 112 Kent st, Borough
5..Robert st, George st, Blackfriars rd
22..Robert st, Little James's st
38..Robert st, 14 Hampstead road
29..Robert st, William st, Cannon st rd
3..Robin Hood ct, Bow la, Cheapside
2..Robin Hood ct, Milk st, Cheapside
7..Robin Hood ct, Shoe la, Fleet st
1..Robin Hood ct, Bell alley, Golden
lane, Barbican
15..Robin Hood ct, 23 Mill la, Tooley st
51..Robinson's bdgs, Flask lane
66..Robinson's lane, Cheyne walk
51..Robinson's lane, Flask lane
29..Robinson's pl, Farmer st, Shadwell
35..Rochester row, west end of the
bridge, Vauxhall road
16..Rochester st, Borough market
35..Rochester st, Tothill fields
35..Rochester ter, op. Rochester row
32..Rockingham pl, New Kent road
32..Rockingham row, op. 12 Brighton
place, New Kent road
52..Rodney buildings, New Kent road,
near the Elephant and Castle
52..Rodney place, Knightsbridge
39..Rodney pl, 30 High st, Shadwell
32..Rodney row, Rodney buildings
40..Rodney st, east side the chapel,
Pentonville
8..Roebuck ct, 29 Turnmill st, Cerkwl
7..Roll's bdgs, 118 Fetter lane   [st
7..Roll's ct, Chancery la, tr at 192 Flee
35..Romney row, Marsham st, Westmr
35..Romney terrace, Horseferry road
3..Rood lane, 23 Fenchurch st
30..Roopes Tenements, 391 Rotherhith st
2..Ropemakers' alley, south side of
Ropemakers st, Moorfields

60..Ropemakers' fields, Limehouse
3..Ropemakers's st, 19 Pavement
15..Roper la, St. John's ch, Horselydn
12..Roper's bdgs,Petticoat la,Harrow al
15..Roper's la, Russell st, Bermondsey
40..Rosamond st, Islington
24..Rosamond st, east end of Bowling
      green lane, Clerkenwell
22..Rose alley,Eagle st, Redlion square
14..Rose al, Butcher row, E. Smithfd
12..Rose al, Fashion st, Spitalfields
7..Rose al, Fleet lane, Old Bailey
1..Rose al, Golden la, Barbican
4..Rose al, 35 Maid la, near Castle la,
      Borough
12..Rose al, Bishopsgate st without
8..Rose al, 64 Turnmill st
21..Rose al, 88 High Holborn
2..Rose ct, Aldermanbury
14..Rose ct, Aldermanbury
14..Rose ct, Beer la, Gt Tower st
13..Rose ct, Blue Anchor yd,Rosemy la
3..Rose ct, Bow la, Cheapside
1..Rose ct, Fore st, Cripplegate
31..Rose ct,Hickman's folly, Dock head
21..Rose ct,Long acre, a few yards right
      from St. Martin's lane
11..Rose ct, Wheeler st, Spitalfields
11..Rose ct, William st, Shoreditch
12..Rose lane, Wentworth st, Spitalfds
29..Rose lane,9 White horse st, Ratcliffe
44..Rose pl, Globe la, Mile End road
28..Rose pl, Turk st, Bethnall green
9..Rose st, 49 Brick lane, Old st
11..Rose st, 44 Church st, Shoreditch
21..Rose st, 12 Long acre
8..Rose st, 20 Newgate st, leading to
      the market
21..Rose st, Greek st, Soho square
20..Rose st, 23 King st, Covent garden
11..Rose yd, nr Holywell st, Shoreditch
..Rose yd, 85 Redcross st, Borough
2..Rose and Crown alley, Moorfields
12..Rose & Crown ct, Essex st, Whchpl
2..Rose & Crown ct, Foster lane
40..Rose & Crown ct, 126 St.John's st,
      West Smithfield
2..Rose & Crown ct, Broad st bldgs,
      Moorfields
14..Rose & Crown ct, St. Catherine's
      lane, east Smithfield
12..Rose & Crown ct, Booth st, Spitlfds
7..Rose & Crown ct, 27 Shoe la, Hlbrn
16..Rose & Crown ct, 114 Long la,Boro
7..Rose & Crown ct, Gray's Inn lane
13..Rose & Crown yd, Whitechapel
13..Rosemary Branch aly, Rosemary la
13..Rosemary lane, 10 Sparrow corner,
      Tower hill
45..Rosetta st, Blue Anchor fds, Stepny
30..Rotherhithe, from Dockhead to
      Greenland Dock
30..Rotherhithe wall, from the east side
      of St. Saviour's dock to West la
1..Rotten row, 29 Goswell st
2..Round ct, Moor la, Cripplegate

Ref. to Plan.
20..Round ct, 448 Strand
..Round ct, Whitechapel
20..Rowit court, 13 Chandos st
8..Rowit alley, Cowcross st, W Smthd
1..Rowit ct, 34 St. Martin's le grand
20..Rowit passage, 14 Chandos st
44..Rowland row, Stepney gr, M End
15..Rowlandsons street, Russell sreet,
      Bermondsey st
36..Royal arcade, Pall Mall
15..Royal ct, Horselydown lane
3..Royal Exchange, 90 Cornhill
16..Royal Oak ct, 282 Kent st, Boro
36..Royal Oak ct, Beak st, Swallow st
45..Royal Oak ct, 20 Broad st, Ratcliffe
10..Royal Oak wk, Haberdasher's walk
15..Royal Oak yd, 173 Bermondsey st
5..Royal Oak yard, Maid la, Southwrk
18..Royal row, Stangate st, Lambeth
16..Royal Tent ct, 294 Kent st, Boro
11..Ruddick's bds, Long al, Moorfields
2..Rumbal's al, Lit. Cheapside, Mrfds
20..Rupert st, 6 Coventry st,Haymarket
13..Rupert st, little Alie st,Goodmn's fds
5..Russell buildings, 72 Wapping
21..Russell ct, 75 Drury lane
20..Russell ct, Brydges st, Covent grdn
36..Russell ct,Cleveland rw, St.James'
68..Russell court, Lisson green
29..Russell ct, near Old Gravel lane,
      Ratcliff highway   [mary lane
13..Russell ct, Blue Anchor road,Rose-
22..Russell ct, Little Coram st
36..Russell mews, Cleveland r, St. Jas.
38..Russell mews, Howland st,Fitzr. sq
21..Russell pl, Bow st, Covent garden
38..Russell pl, London st, Fitzroy sq
15..Russell pl, near Addle hill
30..Russell bds, Russell st, Bermondsey
22..Russell square, near Queen sq
15..Russell st, 90 Bermondsey st,Sthwk
21..Russell st, Covent garden
61..Russell st, Greenland dock
29..Russell st, 120 Ratcliffe highway
3..Russia ct, Leadenhall st
2..Russia ct, Honey lane mkt, Chpside
43..Russia lane, near Hackney turnpike
2..Russia row, Milk street
8..Rutland lane, Charterhouse square
      Aldersgate street
4..Rutland place, 239 Upper Thames st
29..Rutland st, Cannon st road
21..Ryder ct, Newport market
29..Ryder ct, 152 Old Gravel lane
36..Ryder st, 26 James's st
45..Rye loaf ct, 119 Cock hill, Ratcliffe

S

36..Sackville st, 48 Piccadilly
36..Sadler's Arms yard, 147 Swallow st
24..Sadler's Wells row, Spafields, on
      the left of Islington road
8..Saffron ct, 67 Great Saffron hill
8..Saffron hill, Charles st, Hatton grdn
8..Saffron pl, 57 Great Saffron hill

Ref. to Plan.

6..Saffron st,Peter st,30 GtSaffron hill
8..Saffron terrace, 100 Gt Saffron hill
10..St. Agnes crescent, Old st road
10..St. Agnes le Claire, Old st road
10..St. Agnes st, Wood st, Old st road
10..St. Agnes terrace, Tabernacle walk
2..St. Alban's ct, 94 Wood st, Cheapsd
68..St. Alban's place, Edgware road
7..St. Andrew's st, Holborn hill
5..St. Andrew's hill, 13 Earl st, Blkfrs
37..St. Anne's ct, Dean st, Soho, and
31 Wardour st
1..St. Anne's lane, 59 Foster lane, St.
St. Martins le Grand
36..St. Anne's lane, (Little) 39 Old
Pye st, Westminster
1..St. Anne's pas,41 Noble st,Foster la
35..St. Anne's pas, Smith st, Westmr
45..St. Anne's pl,Commercial rd, Limeh
45..St. Anne's row, Limehouse church
45..St. Anne's st, Comrcial rd, Limeh
35..St. Anne's st, 33 Orchard street,
Westminster
3..St. Antholen's Church yd,Watling st
7..St. Bride's Church yd, Fleet st
7..St. Bride's ct, 4 New Bridge st
14..St. Catherine's, Little Tower hill
14..St. Catherine's st, Trinity square
14..St. Catherine'sNew ctSt.Catherines
14..St. Catherine's lane, Tower hill
14..St. Catherine's sq, St. Catherine's
7..St. Dunstan's alley, 187 Fleet st
7..St. Dunstan's ct, 161 Fleet st
6..St. Dunstan's hill, 13 Earl street,
Blackfriars
14..St. Dunstan's hill, Tower st
14..St. Dunstan's pas, St.Dunstan's hill
35..St. Ermin's hill, Chapel st, West
29..St. George's court, William street,
Cannon st road
18..St. George's cres, Westmr brdg rd
18..St. George's mall, Westmr brdg rd,
near the Asylum
17..St. George's market, east side the
London road
37..St. George's market, 289 Oxford st
51..St. George's pl, St. George's row,
south side of Chelsea bridge
51..St. George's row, south side of
Chelsea bridge
29..St. George's row, Back la, Shadwl
17..St. George's row, Tower st, Westminster rd, near the Obelisk
53..St. George's row, on the right near
Tyburn turnpike
44..St. George's st, Worse la, Stepney
17..St. George's New town, the open
space before the Elephant and
Castle, London road, Southwark
31..St. George's row, Hickman's folly
5..St. George's pl, east side of Surry
Chapel, Blackfriars road
34..St. George's yd, West sq, Lambeth
21..St. Giles's, Broad st, Holborn
2..St. Helen's pl, 44 Bishopsgt within

Ref. to Plan.

46..St. Helena, south side, ear the
halfway house. Deptford Lower rd
24..St. Helena pl, op. the New River
Waterworks, Spafields
24..St. James's bds, 51 Rosamond st
36..St. James's market, 52 Haymarket
36..St. James's park, back of the Admiralty, Charing cross
23..St. James's pl, east side the Church,
Clerkenwell green
36..St. James' pl, 66 St. James's st
38..St. James's pl, Hampstead road, on
the right from Tottenham ct road
43..St. James's pl, near Patriot square
36..St. James's square, north side of
Pall Mall
36..St. James's st, 164 Piccadilly
35..St. James's st, Pimlico
24..St. James's st, St. James's place,
Clerkenwell church
24..St. James's walk, Clerkenwell grn
35..St. John's Church yd,Westminster,
near Horseferry road
14..St John's ct, 55 Up. East Smithfd
8..St. John's la, 68 St.John's st,Smthfd
68..St. John's place, Lisson green
24..St. John's st row, 25 Northampton-
street, Clerkenwell
37..St. John's row, Marylebone st
8..St. John's square, north end of St.
John's lane, Clerkenwell
11..St. John's st, 106 Brick la,Spitalfds
35..St. John's st, Westminster
8..St. John's st, 96 Smithfield Bars
68..St.John's Wood row, Lisson green
9..St. Martin's buildings, 69 Old st,
St. Luke's
16..St. Margaret's hill, the open space
opposite the Town hall, Borough
20..St. Martin's Ch. yd,St. Martin's la
20..St. Martin's ct, 89 St. Martin's la
20..St. Martin's ct, 16 and 10Castle st,
Leicester square
7..St. Martin's ct, 18 Ludgate hill
20..St. Martin's la, 487 Charing cr oss
1..St. Martin's le grand, Newgate st
17..St. Martin's st, Blackfriars road
20..St. Martin's st, 40 Leicester square
3..St. Mary at hill, 97 or 27, Little
Eastcheap, Lower Thames st
12..St. Mary's st, Whitechapel church
12..St. Mary Axe, 116 Leadenhall st,
or 56 Houndsditch
37..St. Marylebone. north of Oxford st
3..St. Michael's alley, 42 Cornhill
3..St. Mildred's ct, 27 Poultry
4..St. Nicholas, (Olaves) Church yd,
Bread st hill
1..St. Paul's Church yd, 4 Cheapside
32..St.Paul's al,&pl,Walworth common
3..St. Peter's alley, 55 Cornhill
5..St. Peter's hill, 5 Little Knightrider-
street, Doctors commons
8..St. Peter's lane, Cow cross street,
Smithfield, and 69 St. John's st

Ref. to Plan.

33..St. Peter's place, opposite the St Paul's Head, Walworth common
32..St. Peter's st, near Walworth comn
4..St Saviour's Church yd, 296 Boro
35..St. Stephen's ct, east side of New Palace yard, Westminster
3..St. Swithin's lane, Lombard st, and 81 Cannon st
3..St. Thomas Apostle, 25 Bow lane, Cheapside
15..St. Thomas's rents, east end of St. Thomas st, Borough
43..St. Thomas's square, Hackney
15..St. Thomas's st, 42 Boro High st
28..St. Thomas's st, Ducking pond row, turn at 105 Whitechapel
24..St. Vincent row, Sidney st, City rd
1..Salisbury ct, W. Cross st, Cripplegate
34..Salamanca st, Lambeth walk
7..Salisbury ct, 81 Fleet st
82..Salisbury crescent, Lock's fields, and Pitt st, Kent road
30..Salisbury la, near Mill stairs, Brmdsy
53..Salisbury mews, back of Salisbury pl, Marylebone
53..Salisbury place, John st, New rd, Marylebone
32..Salisbury pl, east end of Nelson pl, Lock's fields, Walworth
15..Salisbury pl, Salisbury st, 2nd on the right from Bermondsey
15..Salisbury pl, Salisbury st, Bermndsy
7..Salisbury sq, Salisbury ct, Fleet st,
34..Salisbury st, Jamaica row
20..Salisbury st, 78 Strand
29..Sally's al, 44 London st, Ratcliffe
10..Salmon & Ball ct, 94 Bunhill row
45..Salmon ct, Salmon la, Limehouse
45..Salmon lane, Commercial road, Limehouse
45..Salmon st, Salmon la, Limehouse
3..Salter's ct, Bow lane, Cheapside
11..Salter's ct, near Shoreditch church
3..Salter's Hall court, Oxford court, Cannon street
27..Salter's rents, Hackney road
24..Salutation ct, Broad st, Bloomsbury
3..Salutation ct, 101 Lower Thames st
2..Sambrook ct, 25 Basinghall st
30..Samson's gardens, Gt Hermitage st
12..Samuel st, Booth st, Spitalfields
45..Samuel st, Stepney
29..Samuel st, 2nd west of Cannon st rd
35..Sanctuary, near Tothill st
8..Sand yard, Turnmill st, Clerkenwell
36..Sander's ct, Gt Peter st, Westmr
26..Sanders gardens, 60 Kingsland rd
12..Sandy st, Artillery la, Bishopsgt st
12..Saracen's Head yd, 8 Camomile st
29..Sarah's ct, 145 New Gravel lane, Wapping
27..Sarah st, 30 Church st, Bethnal grn
30..Sarn's alley, 37 Rotherhithe st
27..Satchel's rents, 32 Church street, Bethnal green road

Ref. to Plan.

19..Saunder's st, Portugal st, Lambeth
12..Savage ct. 30 Widegate st, Bishopsgt
13..Savage gdns, Trinity sq, Tower hill
26..Savannah pl, Essex st, Kingsland rd
44..Saville buildings, 17 Aldgate
34..Saville place, Canterbury pl, Lambeth church
36..Saville pl, Conduit st, Swallow st
44..Saville place, near Bancroft's Alms Houses, Mile End road
36..Saville row, Burlington gardens, Old Bond st
44..Saville row, near Bancroft's Alms Houses, Mile End road
32..Saville row, Walworth, near the Elephant and Castle
36..Saville st, Burlington gds, Old Bond st
20..Savoy steps, 107 Strand
20..Savoy st, 125 Strand
3..Sawyers ct, (new) 60 Clements lane
11..Sawyers bds, Phœnix st, Spitalfields
11..Scalter's st, Anchor st, Shoreditch
4..Schoolhouse al, Upper Thames st, near Queen st
45..Schoolhouse la, 104 Cock hill, Shdwl
4..Schoolhouse pas, 183 Up. Thames st
24..Schoolhouse yard, Aylesbury street, Clerkenwell
29..Schooner's al, nr Star st, Wpng wall
7..Scotch court, Cross lane, Holborn
19..Scotland yard, Whitehall
3..Scott's yd, Bush lane, Cannon st
5..Scrubb sq, Bennet st, Stamford st Blackfriars road
11..Seabright place, Hackney road
40..Seabrook place, 10 Whitelion street, Pentonville
7..Seacoal la, 14 Skinner st, Snow hill
14..Seething la, 54 Great Tower st
7..Sergeant's Inn, 4 Chancery lane, Fleet street
21..Serles pl, Lincoln's Inn
21..Serle st, 50 Carey st, Lincoln's Inn fds
24..Sessions house, W. side Clknwl grn
35..Sessions house, near Westmr abbey
7..Sessions house, 54 Old Bailey
16..Session house, St. Margaret's hill, Borough
5..Sermon lane, Little Carter lane, Doctor's commons
25..Sermon lane, Islington
45..Sermon lane, Farmer row
21..Seven Dials, Monmth st, St. Giles's
29..Seven Star al, 82 Ratcliff highway
13..Seven Star ct, 23 Rosemary lane Tower hill
30..Seven Step al, Princess st, Rotherh
43..Severn st, Three colt lane
11..Severn st, Splidts fields
9..Sewart st, 83 Goswell st
8..Sexton ct, Long la, West Smithfield
20..Seymour ct, 45 Chandos st, Covnt gdn
32..Seymour crescent Lock's fields
36..Seymour crescent, Euston square
36..Seymour mews, 5 Low. Berkeley st

Ref. to Plan.

53..Seymour mews, Seymour street
39..Seymour pl, Charlton st, Somrstwn
53..Seymour pl, Park lane
53..Seymour place, Durweston square
32..Seymour place, York st, Walworth
52..Seymour place, op. 48 Curzons-
 street, Mayfair
38..Seymour place, near Euston square
52..Seymour steps17Pitt's mewsMayfair
53..Seymour st,40Portman st,Portmn sq
53..Seymour ter, Edgeware road
11..Shacklewell st,Tyson st, Church st,
 Shoreditch
14..Shad Thames,Dockhead, Horselydn
29..Shadwell High st,fromRatcliff highway to 1 Cock hill
29..Shadwell gap, 161 High st, Shadwl
29..Shadwell mkt. near Shadwell ch
 3..Shaft's court, 133 Leadenhall st
 1..Shaftsbury pl, 34 Aldersgate st
34..Shakespeare walk, Vauxhall walk
13..Shakespeare's walk,47 Upper Shadwell, High st
15..Shakespeare's walk, Bermoudsey sq
 8..Sharp's al, 58 Cow cross st, Smthfd
 4..Sharp's ct, Little Trinity lane
12..Sharp's buildings, Duke's place,
 Rosemary lane
21..Shaw ct, Charles st, Drury lane
16..Shaw's ct, St. Margaret's hill, Boro
15..Sherrard court, near Joiners st,
 Tooley st
 7..Sheen's place, 90 Holborn
21..Sheffield st, west side of Clare mrkt
20..Shelton court, 44 Bedfordbury,
 Covent garden
16..Shepherd court, Borough
37..Shepherd st, nr Bond st, Oxford st
36..Shepherd st, Shepherd's market
 4..Shepherd's alley, 64 Up Thames st
 7..Shepherd's ct,King's Hd ct,Shoe la
53..Shepherd's ct,8UpperBrook street,
 Grosvenor square
36..Shepherd's market, Mayfair, north
 end of White horse st
27..Shepherd's row, Bethnal green rd,
 Wilmot square
36..Shepherd's sq,38 Curzon st,Mayfair
 9..Shepherd's walk, opposite Shepherd
 and Shepherdess,City road
 3..Sherbourne lane, 2 St. Swithin's la
37..Sherrard st, Golden sq, first right
 in Tichborn st
36..Sherrold st, 36 Brewer st,Golden sq
29..Ship al, 62lower East Smithfield
45..Ship alley, Fore st, Limehouse
35..Ship alley, Gardiner's lane, Kings-
 street, Westminster
11..Ship al, Phœnix st, Spitalfields
13..Ship alley, Wellclose square
15..Ship & Mermaid court, Snowsfields
 7..Ship court, 66 Old Bailey
35..Ship court, York st, Westminster
30..Ship st, King st, Wapping
 3..Ship tavern pas, 75 Gracechurch st

L

Ref. to Plan.

45..Shipwright st,Globe stairs,Rotherh
15..Ship yard, Greenbank, 81 Tooley st
 1..Ship yard, 38 Redcross st, Cripplegt
 7..Ship yard, 1 Picket st, Temple bar
15..Ship yard, 33 High st, Borough
13..Ship yard, 32 Minories
 7..Shire lane, Temple bar, & 6 Carey st
 7..Shoe lane, 130 Fleet st
 6..Shoemaker row, 8 Broadway,Blkfrs
13..Shoemaker's row, Aldgate
11..Shoreditch, 21 Norton Falgate
21..Short's gardens, Drury lane
26..Short st 7 Huntingdon stKingsld rd
11..Short st, Cumberland st, Shoreditch
 2..Short st, leading to 15 Pavement,
 Moorfields
13..Short st, Middlesex st, Whitechpl
 2..Shorter's court, Throgmorton st,
 Royal Exchange
13..Shorter st, Cable st, Wellc'ose sq
45..Shoulder of Mutton alley, 52 Fore-
 street, Limehouse
53..Shouldham st, John st, Edgware rd
12..Shovel alley, Great Garden st
29..Shovel al, New rd, St. George's E.
 2..Shovel ct, 120 Wood st, Cheapside
25..Shropshire pl, Pancras pl, corner
 of Upper Thornaugh st, Islington
 2..Shuter ct, 32 Basinghall st
 7..Sidmooth mews, 9 Gray's Inn lane
23..Sidmouth pl, Gray's Inn lane road
20..Sidney alley, Princes st,Leicester sq
24..Sidney place, Sidney st, City road
66..Sidney place, King's road, Chelsea
29..Sidney place. Commercial road
24..Sidney st, 29 Dalby ter, City road
39..Sidney st, Somer's town
29..Sidney st, Commercial road
 1..Silk st,west sideGrub st,Chiswell st
21..Silver st,Southampton st,Bloomsby
 7..Silver st, Bouverie st, Fleet st
23..Silver st, Clerkenwell, north end of
 Turnmill st
44..Silver st, Mile End, New Town,
 from 62 Brick lane
37..Silver st,14Cambridge st, Golden sq
30..Silver st, King st, Old Gravel lane
17..Silver st, Loman's pond, Borough
45..Silver st, Lower Queen st, Greenland Dock, Rotherhithe
12..Silver st, Pelham st, Spitalfields
44..Silver st, Stepney, 2nd right from
 Redman's row, Mile End
15..Silver st, Vine st, Tooley st
 2..Silver st, 81 Wood st, Cheapside
66..Simmons st,Sloane square, Chelsea
35..Simon's bds, 55 Old Pye st, Westm
27..Simon's pl, Bridge walk,Bethnl grn
68..Simon st, Lisson green
16..Sion court, 122 Bermondsey st
 2..Sion garden, 44 Aldermanbury
32..Sion place, East lane, Walworth
12..Sion sq, Union st, Whitechapel ch
30..Sir William Warren's sq, Wapping
19..Sir st, Portugal st, Lambeth

Ref. to Plan.

3..Sise lane, 10 Bucklersbury
3..Sise yard, 22 Whitechapel road
39..Skinner's pl,Skinner st,Somer's twn
11..Skinner's st, nr Sun st, Bishopsgt
66..Skinner st, Sloane st
8..Skinner st, Snow hill, from Fleet-
market to the Old Bailey
39..Skinner st, 17 Somer's town
2..Slade's buildings, Angel alley,
Long alley, Moorfields
16..Slater's ct, Redcross st, Borough
13..Slater's ct,Bl.Anchor ydRosemary la
24..Slater's place, 4 Little Sutton st
8..Sheep's alley, St. John's st, Smithfd
52..Sloane place, North st, Brompton,
2nd right from Sloane st
66..Sloane square, Chelsea
52..Sloane st, Knightsbridge, first on
the left from Hyde Park corner
52..Sloane ter, D'Oyles st, Sloane st
2..Slutter's ct, Basinghall st, Fore st
39..Smallpox hospital, Battle bridge
21..Smart's buildings, 185High Holbrn
43..Smart's court, Bonner's fields,
Bethnal green
1..Smith's buildings, Chequer alley,
89 Bunhill row
11..Smith's bds, 130 Bishopsgt without
7..Smith's buildings, Holborn hill
11..Smith's buildings, Lamb ct, Sun st
7..Smith's bldngs, bot Gray's Inn lane
3..Smith's buildings, 76 Leadenhall st
2..Smith's buildings, Long la,Moorfds
16..Smith's buildings, Long la,Bermdsy
9..Smith's buildings, City road
12..Smith's court, 64 Whitechapel road
1..Smith's court, Brackley st, Golden-
lane,Barbican
36..Smith's court, Great Windmill st,
Haymarket
29..Smith's court, Lower Chapman st
17..Smith's court, Gibraltar row, St.
George's fields
30..Smith's place, 65 Wapping st
4..Smith's rents,16 Bankside, Borough
16..Smith's rents, 165 Bermondsey st
8..Smith's rents, St.John st, Smithfield
35..Smith's rents, York st, Broadway,
Westminster
35..Smith square, 32 Millbank,Westmr
66..Smith st, King's road, Chelsea
24..Smith st, Northampton square
39..Smith st, Smallpox hospital
35..Smith st, south continuation of
Dean's st, Westminster
14..Smithfield (East) Tower hill
8..Smithfield (West) fromthe south end
of Smithfield Bars to Giltspur st
8..Smithfield Bars, south end of St.
John st, Smithfield
36..Snead's ct, Engine st, Piccadilly
7..Snowhill, on a line with Holborn-
bridge, north side of Skinner st
15..Snowsfields,42King st, Boro High st
35..Snows rents, York st, Westminster

Ref. to Plan.

11..Socrates pl,New Innst,New Inn yd,
Shoreditch
21..Soho square, Charles st, Oxford st
38..Sols row,west side of Hampstead rd
35..Somers place, Palmers village
25..Somers place, 20 Lower st, Islington
39..Somers pl, East Somers town
39..Somers town, Pancras
46..Somersetpl, near the Blue Anchor,
Blue Anchor road
20..Somerset place, Strand
53..Somerset place, Portman st
49..Somerset pl, 35 Kennington comon
53..Somerset rw,5 Orchard st,Oxford st
53..Somerset street, 45 Duke street,
Manchester square
13..Somerset st, Whitechapel, High st
29..Somerwood st, Wm. stCannon st rd
53..South mews, 7 South st, Mnchstr sq
2..South pl, N. side of Moorfields
52..South st,South Audley st,Grosvnr sq
34..South st,op. the Three Stags,Lmbth
12..South st,23 Paternoster row,Sptlfds
32..South st, Lock's fields
2..South st, Finsbury
53..South st, 195 Whitechapel road
36..South st, Berkeley square
17..South st, West sq, St. George's fds
7..Southampton bds, 319 High Holborn
7..Southampton ct, Southampton bds
22..Southampton ct, Southampton row
36..Southampton ct,topTottenham ct rd
38..Southampton mews, New road,
Tottenham court road
22..Southampton row, Bloomsbury
68..Southampton row, 82 Edgware rd
39..Southampton st, 29 New road,
Pentonville
20..Southampton st, 387 Strand
21..Southampton st, 126 High Holborn
22..Southampton st, Bloomsbury sq
48..Southampton st, Camberwell
52..South Audley st, Grosvenor sq
36..South Bruton mews, Bruton st
33..South Lambeth Waterworks, Kennington lane
37..SouthMolton la,Brook stGrosvnr sq
37..South Moulton row, Oxford st
37..South Moulton st, 295Oxford st
53..South Portman mews, Portman sq
2..South Sea court, Broad street,
Royal Exchange
16..South Sea court, Mint st, Borough
4..Southwark, S. side of London bridge
4..Southwark bridge bottom of Queen-
street, 181 Upper Thames st
4..Southwark square, Bridge st, and
Union st, Southwark
29..Southwick's rents, Betts st
24..Spafields, north of Clerkenwell,
towards Islington
29..Spa place, Brayne's row, Spafields
31..Spa place, Spa road, Bermondsey
24..Spa terrace nr New River head
47..Spangle place, Kent road

Ref. to Plan.
53..Spanish pl, opposite 12 Charles st, Manchester square
39..Span place, Brill pl, Somers town
37..Sparkle court, Little Portland st
13..Sparke's court, Duke's pl, Aldgate
15..Sparrick's row, Weston st
15..Sparrow buildings, Potter's fields
13..Sparrow corner, 84 Minories
23..Sparrow's rents, Portpool lane, Leather la, Holborn
39..Speldhurst st, Judd st, Somers twn
24..Spence row, Goswell st road, west side near the turnpike
39..Spencer st, Battle bridge
29..Spencer st, Back la, St. George's E.
24..Spencer st, Northampton square, Goswell st road
35..Spencer st, Horseferry road, west
11..Spicer st, 82 Brick la, Spitalfields
18..Spillers court, Webber row, Webber street, Blackfriars road
13..Splidts bds, Back la, Welloiose sq
12..Splidts fields, Whitechapel
11..Spital sq, 104 Bishopsgt st, without
12..Spitalfields market, Union street, Bishopsgate
11..Spotted Horse ct, 197 Shoreditch
30..Spread Eagle ct, 1 Church st, Roth
3..Spread Eagle ct, Finch la, Cornhill
7..Spread Eagle ct, 27 Gray's Inn la
3..Spread Eagle ct, Threadneedle st
44..Spring garden ct, Mile end, near Globe lane
20..Spring garden mews, Charing cross
20..Spring garden pas, Charing cross
45..Spring garden place, Bull lane, Stepney church
20..Spring gardens, 52 Charing cross
44..Spring gardens, near Globe lane, Mile End
20..Spring garden ter, Charing cross
24..Spring place, 1 Margaret street, Bagnigge wells
24..Spring st, 2 Spring place, Bagnigge wells road
53..Spring st, Dorset st, Portman sq
29..Spring st, Shadwell church, near the Church
20..Spur st, 33 Princes st, Leicester sq
36..Stable yd, W. end St. James's palace
21..Stacey st, Monmouth st, St. Giles's
35..Stafford row, Palace st, Pimlico
68..Stafford st, Lisson green
36..Stafford st, Old Bond st, Piccadilly
2..Staining lane, Maiden lane, Wood st, Cheapside
32..Stamford pl, opposite the Albion, East lane, Walworth
5..Stamford st, 16 Blackfriars road
5..Stamford st road, Stamford st
15..Standing ct, Stoney la, Tooley st
31..Standgate bds, Bermondsey New rd
19..Stangate, Lambeth, a few yards on the right from Westminster bridge
18..Stangate pl, 36 Stangate st, Lambeth

Ref. to Plan
18..Stangate st, opposite 8 Upper Lambeth marsh
16..Stanhope row, Long la, Bermondsy
21..Stanhope st, Clare market
52..Stanhope st, Mayfair, first in South Audley st
16..Staple ct, 166 Bermondsey st
7..Staples Inn, Middle row, Holborn
7..Staples Inn bds, 3 Holborn bars
30..Staples rents, New Paradise st, Hlbn
16..Staple st, Long lane, Borough
2..Stapleton ct, Ropemakers st, Mrfds
15..Star alley, Bermondsey
14..Star alley, 9 East Smithfield
16..Star alley, Harrow st, Borough
13..Star alley, 53 Fenchurch st
31..Star corner, op. 1 Bermondsey sq
2..Star court, Cheapside
15..Star court, near Bermondsey st
3..Star ct, 54 Bread st, Cheapside
7..Star ct, 114 Chancery lane
21..Star ct, Lit. Compton st, Soho
21..Star ct, Cross la, Newton st, Holbrn
3..Star ct, 6 Great Eastcheap
1..Star ct, 17 Grub st, Cripplegate
4..Star ct, Huggin la, Up. Thames st
14..Star ct, Nightingale la, Wapping
4..Star court, Old Fish st
29..Star st, Wapping wall
21..Star yard, opposite 1 Carey st, Lincolns Inn fields
16..Star yard, 96 Blackman st, Borough
29..Star yard, 103 Old Gravel lane
29..Star & Garter yard, 89 Ratcliff hwy
1..Starch al, Rotten row, Goswell st
7..Stationers ct, 35 Ludgate st
12..Statute Hall ct, Whitehorse lane, Commercial road
30..Stave yard, 332 Wapping
33..Staverton row, Newington Butts
11..Staymakers alley, Spitalfields
45..Steborn heath, near Salmon lane, Ratcliffe
8..Steel alley, St. Johns st, Smithfield, near Corporation row
13..Steel yard, 38 Great Tower hill
3..Steel yard, 88 Upper Thames st
1..Steers pl, 9 Barbican, Aldersgate st
4..Stene lane, 8 Gardeners la, Upper Thames street
37..Stephens mews, Gresse st, Rathbn pl
37..Stephen st, 28 Tottenham court rd
68..Stephen st, Lisson grove
45..Stepney, nr Mile End & Limehouse
45..Stepney causeway, 38 Brooks st, Ratcliffe
45..Stepney fields, Commercial road
44..Stepney green, Mile End turnpike
45..Stepney lane, Mile end road
45..Stepney sq, Whitehorse la, Stepney
13..Sterry place, Minories
68..Stevens bldngs. Bell st, Paddington, near Lisson green
24..Stewards ct, 33 Clerkenwell green
12..Stewards st, Union st, Bishopsgate

Ref. to Plan.

21..Steward's rents, 129, Drury lane
29..Still al, Bluegate fields, Ratcliff
12..Still al, 196, Bishopsgate without
12..Still alley, 104, Houndsditch
15..Stillwell ct, 25, Maze, Tooley st
26..Stone bridge la, Haggerston
21..Stone buildings, Lincoln's Inn, opposite 56, Chancery lane
7..Stone ct, New st, Fetter lane
45..Stone stairs ct, 30, Broad st, Ratcliff
17..Stones end, nr King's Bench, Boro
1..Stone's yard, 77, Bunhill row
21..Stonecutter's al, Lincoln's Inn fds
21..Stonecutters bds, Lit Queen-st Hlbrn
21..Stonecutter's ct, Little Martin's la Long Aere
9..Stonecutters ct, 89, Old st, St. Luke's
7..Stonecutter st, 75, Fleet market
16..Stonecutter yard, 24, Kent st, Boro
13..Stoney lane, Middlesex st, Whchpl
15..Stoney lane, 95, Tooley street
15..Stoney st, Borough market
37..Store st, Bedford square, and 227, Tottenham court road
35..Storey's gate, W. end Great George st
40..Stratham pl, nr Chapman st, Islington
20..Strand, Temple bar to Charing cross
20..Strand lane, op. Newcastle st, Strand
37..Stratford mews, 160, Oxford st
37..Stratford pl, nr Bond st, Oxford st
36..Stratton st, 78, Piccadilly
21..Streaham st, Charlton st, Bedford sq
66..Streathaven place, Chelsea
16..Steel's gardens, Horsemonger la
36..Street's bds, Mount st, Grosvenor sq
16..Stringer's bds, Lant st, Boro
30..Stringer's row, Millpond bridge, Rotherhithe
60..Strong bds, nr East India docks
27..Stout place, Hackney road
35..Strutton ground, Broadway, Chapel street, Westminster
8..Stubb's rents, Charterhouse lane
16..Suffolk ct, Harrow st, Borough
3..Suffolk lane, 152, Upper Thames st
37..Suffolk mews, west side of Middlesex hospital
27..Suffolk place, Hackney road
28..Suffolk st, New road, Whitechapel
16..Suffolk st, [Gt.] 52 Blackman street
16..Suffolk st, [Little] 80, Blackman st
39..Suffolk st, Battle bridge
40..Suffolk st, 74, Whitelion st, Islngtn
40..Suffolk st, Baron st, Pentonville
15..Sugar Loaf court, Bermondsey st
2..Sugar Loaf court, Bishopsgate st
7..Sugar Loaf ct, Dorset st, Fleet st
12..Sugar Loaf ct, Essex st, Whitechpl
4..Sugar Loaf ct, 14, Garlick hill
3..Sugar Loaf ct, 50 Leadenball st
2..Sugar Loaf court, Lit. Cheapside, Moorfields
13..Sugar Loaf ct, Swan st, Minories
30..Sugar Loaf hill, Gt. Hermitage st
23..Summer st, Eyre st, Liquorpond st

Ref. to Plan.

12..Summers ct, 20, Bishopsgate without
14..Sun alley, Butcher row, E. Smithfd
1..Sun alley, 32, Golden la. Barbican
3..Sun court, 68, Cornhill
8..Sun ct, 40, Cloth fair, W. Smithfd
12..Sun court, Lit Swan al, Coleman st
13..Sun ct, 18, Aldgate, High st
12..Sun court, Whitechapel
24..Sun pl, nr Holfield rd, Vauxhall
..Sun square, 19, Sun st
32..Sun row, New Kent road
11..Sun st, 105, Bishopsgate st
32..Sun st, East lane, Walworth
15..Sun st, Snowsfields, Bermondsey
36..Sun st, Shepherd's market
14..Sun yard, 28, Nightingale la, Wpng
29..Sun tavern fields, Shadwell High st
32..Surry place, 30, Surry st, Strand
32..Surry pl, (East) Kent road
17..Surry row, 15, Great Surry st
32..Surry square, 1st on the right from East lane, Kent road
20..Surry st, 172 Strand
11..Susannah row, 42, Curtain road, Shoreditch [Bricklayer's Arms
47..Sussex pl, Kent road, near the
39..Suter's bdgs, Chapel path, Smrstwn
2..Sutton's court, 79, Bishopsgate
15..Sutton st, 40, Great Maze pond, Snow's fields
68..Sutton st, Lisson green, Paddington
21..Sutton st, 21 Soho square
29..Sutton st, Commercial rd, Whtchpl
8..Sutton st, (Gt.) 129 Goswell st
1..Sutton st, (Little) 123, Goswell st
13..Swallow gardens, 127 Rosemary la
37..Swallow passage, 324 Oxford st
36..Swallow st, 45 Piccadilly
2..Swan alley, Coleman st
14..Swan al, 102 upper East Smithfield
8..Swan al, St. John's st, West Smithfd
3..Swan & Hoop pas, nr Mansion house
7..Swan's ct, 6 Bream's bds, Chancery la
2..Swan ct, Bartholomew lane
16..Swan court, Great Dover st, Boro
13..Swan ct, 20 Whitechapel
19..Swan ct, Narrow wall, Lambeth
17..Swan ct, William st, Blackfriars
13..Swan ct, nr White's yd, Rosemary la
11..Swan st, 2 Blackman st, Shoreditch
30..Swan la, 310 nr Rotherhithe church
4..Swan lane, 103 upper Thames st
4..Swan lane, (Old) 97 up Thames st
28..Swan pl, Epping place, Mile End
32..Swan place, Kent road
11..Swan st, Shoreditch
32..Swan st, Kent road
13..Swan st, 47 Minories
14..Swan st, Nightingale la, East Smthfd
66..Swan walk, Paradise row, Chelsea, near Botanic gardens
16..Swan yard, 34, Blackman st, Boro
40..Swan yard, 20, High st, Islington
44..Swan yd, near Jews Burial Ground, Mile End

Ref. to Plan.

13..Swan yard, Minories
20..Swan yard, 335 Strand
35..Swan yard, Tothill st, Westminster
12..Swan yard, 20 Whitechapel, High st
3..Swede's court, Trinity lane
2..Sweeden's pas, 25, Moor st, Criplgt
12..Sweedland ct,50Bishopsgt at without
13..Sweedland ct, Trinity square
3..Sweet Apple ct, Trinity lane
11..Sweet Apple ct, 2d Austin st
12..SweetApple ct,Bishopsgt st,without
3..Sweeting's al, 88 Cornhill
3..Sweeting's rents, Royal Exchange
39..Swinton st, 58 Gray's Inn lane, near Acton st
3..Swithin st, 26 Cannon st
24..Sydney grove, Goswell st road
66..Sydney pl, King's rd,Sloane square
33..Sydney place, Kennington green, Lambeth
43..Sydney st, Bonner's fields
24..Sydney st, top of the City road
7..Symond's Inn, 23 Chancery lane
66..Symonds st, Chelsea common

T

3..Tabernacle alley, 127 Fenchurch st
10..Tabernacle row, 35, City road
10..Tabernacle sq, 62, Paul st,Finsbury
10..Tabernacle walk, continuation of Windmill st, Finsbury
3..Talbot ct, 56 Gracechurch st
23..Talbot court, Portpool lane
16..Tan alley, Long lane, Borough
6..Tanfield ct, east side of Lamb's buildings, Temple
35..Tanner's yard, Marsham st
18..Tarling's court, near Joiner's place, Lambeth road
23..Tash court, Tash st
23..Tash st, 43 Gray's Inn lane
15..Tattle alley, 246 Bermondsey st
32..Tatum st, East lane, Walworth
20..Tavistock ct, south east corner of Covent garden
22..Tavistock mews, 7 Little Coram st
21..Tavistock mews, 5Tavistock street, Bedford square
38..Tavistock place, 16 Tavistock sq
20..Tavistock row, S. side Covnt grdn
36..Tavistock sq, 29, Woburn place
20..Tavistock st, Southampton street, Strand
38..Tavistock st, 260, Tottenham ct rd
26..Taylor's bds,west side Kingsland rd
20..Taylor's bds, 1, Bedfordbury
20..Taylor's bds, 45 Chandos st
20..Taylor's bds, 32, St. Martin's lane, Charing cross
3..Taylor's ct, 30 Bow lane, Cheapside
29..Taylor's court, 58 Farmer st
26..Taylor's ct, 4Hare walk,Kingslnd rd
40..Taylor's ct, 13 Islington road
36..Taylor's passage, Swallow st
40..Taylor's row, 30 Islington road

L 2

Ref. to Plan.

4..Taylor's yard, 6 Whitehind al, Boro
6..Temple [The] 6 15 17&20,Fleet st
7..Temple bar, 235 Fleet st
6..Temple lane, 5 Lombard st, Fleet st
17..Temple pl, 17 Blackfriars road
17..Temple st, 3 Prospect pl, Newingtn
37..Temple st, 7 Water lane, Fleet st
29..Tenbury place, 56 Commercial road
9..Tenby's buildings, Old st
30..Tench st, Bird st, Wapping church
7..Tennis ct, Middle row, Holborn
1..Tenter alley, 24 Moor la, Cripplegt
15..Tenter alley, Tooley st, Borough
13..Tenter ground, Great Prescot st
9..Tenter row, Shepherd's walk, City road
37..Tenterden st, 11 Shepherd street, Oxford street
29..Terling st, Cross st,St.George's E.
32..Terrace, (Fish's) Walworth road
23..Terrace, l, King's rd, Gray's Inn la
35..Terrace, Palace yard, Westminster
35..Terrace, Pimlico
20..Terrace walk, bottom of Buck- ingham street, Strand
12..Tewkesbury ct, Whitechpl, High st
20..Thackman's ct, Vine st, Chandos st
60..Thale st, Poplar
3 & 14..Thames st, (Low)from London Bridge to Tower hill
3 4 & 5..Thames st, [Up] N. side of London bridge to Earlst.Blackfrs
4..Thames st, 31 Bankside, Southwark
30..Thames st, Rotherhithe, north side of Greenland dock
20..Thanet pl, 232 Strand,nrTemple bar
36..Thatched House ct, St. James's st
20..Thatched court, 418 Strand
7..Thavies Inn, 57 Holborn
53..Thayer st, Manchester sq, opposite 4, Hinde street
13..The Circus, Minories
14..The Cloisters, St. Catherines
8..The Cloisters, 19 Giltspur st
8..The Cloisters (Lit) 44 W. Smithfield
35..The Cloisters, Dean's yd, Westmr
22..The Colonade, Grenville street, Brunswick square
16..The Colour yd, Worcester st, Boro
13..The Crescent, 102, Minories
6..The Inner Temple, Temple,Fleet st
31..The King's rd, btm Bermondsey st
16..The Mount, 293 Kent st, Borough
16..The New Way, Maze, Tooley st
7..The Old Bailey, 26 Ludgate hill
32..The Paragon, New Kent road
22..The Pavillion, Brunswick square
20..The Savoy, 107 Waterloo bridge
15..The Tents, Mazepond, Tooley st
23..The Terrace, l, King's road,Gray's Inn lane
32..The Terrace, left side of the Kent road, below the Bricklayer's Arms, Kent road
20..The Terrace, New st,Spring gardens

Ref. to Plan.

20..The Terrace, New Spring gardens
38..The Terrace, 173 Tottenham ct rd
34..The Terrace, Vauxhall walk
35..The Terrace, New Palace yard
32..The Terrace, Walworth
14..Theobald's ct, East Smithfield
22..Theobald's court, Theobald's road
22..Theobald's road, Redlion square, Holboorn
47..Thirza place, Kent road
8..Thomas's ct, Benjamin st
28..Thomas pas, Charles st, Bethnal gr
27..Thomas pas, Gibraltar rw Hackney rd
31..Thomas pas, Parker's row, Dock hd
38..Thomas's pl, Tottenham court rd
27..Thomas's row, 55 Bethnal green rd
60..Thomas's st, nr West India docks
15..Thomas's st, 42 Borough High st
27..Thomas st, Wilmot square, Bethnal green road
11..Thomas st, 120 Brick la, Spitalfields
12..Thomas st, Charles st, Whchpl rd
32..Thomas st, opposite 6 Middle row, New Kent road
13..Thomas st, Church la, Whitechapel
11..Thomas st, 45 Curtain road
60..Thomas st, New road, Isle of Dogs
15..Thomas st, 114 Horselydown
21..Thomas st, Drury lane
32..Thomas st, near Bricklayers Arms, Kent road   [Locksfields
32..Thomas st, east end of Paragon pl,
29..Thomas st, William st, Cannon st rd
44..Thomas st, near Trafalgar square
5..Thomas st, 5 Gibion st, Waterloo rd
2..Thompson's rents, Flying horse yard
21..Thompson's pas 4 Portugal st Lin.Inn
27..Thorold square, Bethnal green road
38..Thornhaugh st, Gower st
21..Thorney st, Plumbtree st, Broad st, Bloomsbury
53..Thornton pl, Upper York st
8..Thornton st, St. John's Clerkenwl
12..Thrawl st, 208 Brick la, Spitalfields
3..Threadneedle st, 52 and 63 Old Broad st, Bank
7..Three Arrow ct, 95 Chancery lane·
20..Three Colt al, Cinnamon st, Old Gravel lane   [Finsbury square
11..Three Colt court, 8 Worship st
11..Three Colt ct, Hare st, Spitalfields
43..Three Colt la, Dog rw, Bethnal grn
60..Three Colt st, Limehouse church
8..Three Compass ct, 65 Cow cross st, West Smithfield
36..Three Crane court, Castle la, St. James's st, Westminster
4..Three Crane la. 75 Up. Thames st
16..Three Crane yard, 65 Boro High st
4..Three Crown ct, Garlick hill
13..Three Crown court, Jewry st
2..Three Crown court, Foster lane
16..Three Crown court, 269 Borough High street   [Lower Shadwell
29..Three Cup al, near Dean street,

Ref. to Plan.

11..Three Cup alley, 209 Shoreditch
22..Three Cup yd, Princess st, Redlion sq
1..Three Dagger court, 110 Fore st, Cripplegate
16..Three Falcon ct, Fishmonger's al, Borough
7..Three Falcon ct, 144 Fleet st
8..Three Fox ct, 25 Long la, Smithfd
15..Three Hammer alley, Broadway, St. Thomas's street, Borough
3..Three Hand ct, Creechurch lane
1..Three Herring court, 58 Redcross st, Cripplegate
8..Three Horse shoe la Peter's la Smthfd
7..Three King ct, 150 Fleet st
3..Three King ct, 33 Lombard st
13..Three King ct, 10 Minories
36..Three King yard, 15 Davies street, Berkeley square
34..Three Mariners ct, Fore st, Lambth
2..Three Nuns ct, Aldermanbury
13..Three Nuns yard, Aldgate
15..Three Oak la, Horselydown, near Freeschool st
1..Three Pigeon ct, Barbican
23..Three Pigeon ct, 43 Ray st
13..Three Tun al, Middlesex st, Whchpl
3..Three Tun ct, Miles's lane
1..Three Tun court, 54 Redcross st, Cripplegate
16..Three Tun ct, White st, Borough
16..Three Tun al, St. Margaret's hill
1..Three Tuns ct, 100 Bunhill row, Chiswell street
4..Three Tuns passage, 124 Upper Thames street
8..Three Tuns pas, Newgate market
8..Throgmorton ct, Charterhouse lane
2..Throgmorton ct, 70 Old Broad st Bnk
2..Throgmorton st, Royal Exchange
27..Thurlow pl, Birdcage walk, Hackney
32..Thurlow pl, East la, Walworth
17..Thurlow st, York st, Blackfriars rd
12..Till st, Bell lane, Spitalfields
3..Timber st, Upper Thames st
3..Timber st passage, 64 Up Thames st
9..Tilney court, 43 Old st
52..Tilney st, South Audley st
19..Tilt yard, Scotland yard, Whitehall
22..Titchborne ct, 280 Holborn
38..Titchborne st, Fitzroy square
36..Titchborne st, op. 224 Piccadilly
37..Titchfield st, Dean st, Sobo
37..Titchfield st, 20 Great Portland st
29..Titlymouse alley, Farmer st
2..Tokenhouse yard, 44 Lothbury
21..Tolin's ct, 11 Broad st, St. Giles's
68..Tomlin's New town, Edgware rd
37..Tom's ct, 5 Duke st, Grosvenor sq
39..Tonbridge place, Somerstown
2..Tongue yard, Fieldgate st
7..Took's court, Cursitor st
15..Tooley's gateway, 63 Tooley st
15..Tooley st, London bridge, High st, Borough

Ref. to Plan.

35..Torment hill, Broadway, Westmnstr
22..Torrington st, Russell square
29..Torrington st, 22 Keppel st
29..Tory st, Commercial road
35..Tothill ct, Tothill st, Westminster
30 .Tothill fields, west side Millbank-
    wall, Westminster
35..Tothill st, near Abbey, Westminster
8..Tothill st, Laystall st
30..Tottenham ct road, from the east
    end of Oxford st, to Hampstead rd
38..Tottenham ct, 145 Tottenham ct rd
37..Tottenham st, Chapel st, Tot ct rd
16..Toulmin's buildings, opposite 1
    Suffolk st, Blackman st
14..Tower, East of Lower Thames st
14..Tower hill, (Gt & Lit) from Lower
    Thames st, to St. Catherine's
14..Tower hill passage, Tower hill
13..Tower mews, Vine st, Minories
3..Tower Royal, 1 Budge rw, Watling st
3..Tower Royal court, east side of
    Tower Royal
21..Tower st, Seven Dials, Bloomsbury
14..Tower st, (Great) Little Tower st,
    to 9 Tower hill
16..Tower st, near Asylum, Lambeth
16..Townsend ct, 27 Queen st, Borough
4..Townsend lane, near Garlick hill
32..Townsend st, near Asylum, Kent rd
32..Trafalgar Paragon, Lock's fields
33..Trafalgar pl, bottom of Gibraltar-
    row, St. George's fields
32..Trafalgar place, Lock's fields
53..Trafalgar pl, corner of Edgware rd
27..Trafalgar place, Hackney road,
    half a mile from Shoreditch
43..Trafalgar row, Bonner's fields
44..Trafalgar sq, Whitehorse la, Stepney
9..Trafalgar st, Peerless pool
27..Trafalgar st, Hackney road
32..Trafalgar st, from Walworth turn-
    pike to South st, Walworth
• 44..Trafalgar terrace, Stepney, near
    Ocean st
38..Trent's bdgs, Tottenham ct rd
32..Trevot terrace, Knightsbridge
4..Trig lane, 29 Upper Thames st
28..Trinity Alms Houses, Mile end rd
4..Trinity ct, Little Trinity lane,
    Brewer st, Cheapside
1..Trinity ct, 175 Aldersgate st
4..Trinity lane, 26 Bread st, Cheapsd
20..Trinity pl, 6 Charing cross
13..Trinity sq, N. side of Gt Tower hill
60..Trinity st, Low. Queen st, Rotherh
29..Trinity yd, Ratcliff
13..Tripe yd, Cox sq, Petticoat lane,
    Whitechapel
17..Trotterbone al, Duke st, Blackfrs rd
29..Trotter's ct, 6 New Gravel la, Shadw
12..Troy New Town, Spitalfields
43..Troyon's pl, Hackney fields
12..Trump ct, 43 Whitechapel road
2..Trump st, King st, Cheapside

Ref. to Plan.

6..Tudor st, Bridge st, Blackfriars
35..Tufton st, nr Dean's yd, Westmr
11..Turk st, continuation of Tyson st,
    Spitalfields
66..Turk's row, from Lower Sloane st
    to Chelsea hospital
1..Turk's Head ct, 120 Golden lane
8..Turk's Head yd, 74 Turnmill st,
    Clerkenwell
7..Turnagain lane, 36 Fleet market
20..Turner ct, 30 Martin's lane
20..Turner's ct, Bedfordbury
13..Turner's ct, Church la, Whchpl ch
5..Turner's rents. Gravel la, Southw
26..Turner's sq, Coffee house walk
13..Turner st, Cartwright st, Rosemy la
29..Turner st, 220 Whitechapel road
8..Turnmill st, from Clerkenwell green
    to Cow cross
3..Turnwheel la, 7 Cannon st
35..Tarpentine la, W. end of Millbank
11..Turvill st, Church st, Shoreditch
20..Tweezer al, Water la, Strand
43..Twig folly, Bonner's fields
10..Twister's alley, 142 Bunhill row
1..Two Brewers ct, 78 Golden la
15..Tyer's gateway, Bermondsey
1..Tyger's ct, Whitecross st, Cripplgt
37..Tyler's ct, King's st, Oxford st
37..Tyler st, 30 Tyler's ct
1..Type ct, Type st, Chiswell st
1..Type st, 24 Chiswell st, Finsbnry sq
27..Tyrrel st, corner of Thorold square,
    Bethnal green
24..Tyson st, Spafields
1..Tyson ct, nr Whitecross st, Beech
    lane, Cripplegate
11..Tyson st, Church st, Shoreditch
26..Tyssen pl, opposite Ironmongers'
    Almshouses, Kingsland road

U

12..Unanimous row, Queen street,
    Whitechapel road
32..Union bds, New Kent road
32..Union bds, Walworth road
29..Union bds, Shadwell
8..Union bds, 68 Leather lane
11..Union bds, Norfolk pl, Curtain road
11..Union bds, Union st, Kingsland rd
15..Union ct, Alexander's gardens,
    Three Oak lane, Horselydown
8..Union ct, Back hill, Leather la, Holbn
12..Union ct, Fashion st, Spitalfields
2..Union ct, 42 Broad st, Royal Exch
35..Union ct, op. Grey Coat School,
    Westminster
30..Union ct, Green Dragon al, Wappg
7..Union ct, 95 Holborn hill
16..Union ct, Kent st, Borough, nea
    St. George's church
11..Union ct, Kingsland rd
44..Union ct, Stepney green
15..Union ct, Maze, nr Tooley st, Boro
13..Union ct, White's yd, Rosemary la

Ref. to Plan.

37..Union ct, Union st, nr Tot ct rd
32..Union crescent, op. the Paragon, New Kent road
11..Union crescent, Union st,Kingsland
11..Union gardens,Union st, Kingsland
13..Union mews, N. of Crescent,Minrs
37..Union mews, 38 Union st, Marylebn
35..Union pl,Paper bds.nr N w Ranelagh
33..Union pl, Cross st, Newington
9..Union place, City road
32..Union place, Walworth road
5..Union pl, Edward st, Blackfriars rd
34..Union pl, nr Church st, Lambeth
66..Union pl, George st, S. E. corner of Sloane square, Chelsea
53..Union pl, op. the workhouse, New road, Marylebone
35..Union pl, Orchard st, Westminster
39..Union pl, Maiden la, Battle bridge
44..Union pl, Stepney green
16..Union pl, 43 Blackman st, Boro
15..Union row, Snowsfields, Borough
9..Union row, City road
26..Union row, Essex st, Kingsland rd
14..Union row, Little Tower hill
34..Union row, Union st, Lambeth
12..Union row, Union st, Whitechapel
27..Union row, Wilmot st, Bethnal grn
32..Union row, third on the right from the Elephant&Castle,Nw Kent rd
17..Union Bridge row, Gt Guildford st
40..Union sq, Chapel st, Pentonville
30..Union st, Swan st, Rotherhithe
16..Union st, 218 High st, Borough
16..Union st, 138 Bermondsey stj
2..Union st, Little Moorfields
11..Union st, 65 Bishopsgate without
39..Union st, Clarendon square
29..Union st,Cornwall st,St George's E
17..Union st, Dover st, Blackfriars rd
40..Union st, Pentonville
32..Union st, East lane, Wallworth
36..Union st, Hill st, Berkeley square
11..Union st, Kingsland road
35..Union st, King st, Westminster
17..Union st, London rd,2d on the right from the Obelisk, St. George's fds
34..Union st, Walcot, Lambeth
37..Union st, near Goodge st
37..Union st, nr top of New Bond st
32..Union st, Newington
6..Union st,36 New Bridge st,Blackfrs
29..Union st, 229 Shadwell High st
60..Union st, nr East India docks
44..Union st, nr Trafalgar square
18..Union st, Westminster bridge road
5..Union st, Friars st, Blackfriars rd
12..Union st, 28 Whitechapel church
30..Union stairs, 326 Wapping
40..Union ter, Commercial rd, Stepney
11..Union walk,Union st, Kingsland rd, first on the left from Shoredh ch
15..Union yd, nr Vine yd, Tooley st
32..Unwyn's place, Kent road
22..Upper Bedford mews,Up.Russell sq

Ref. to Plan.

22..Upper Bedford pl, Russell sq
51..Upper Belgrave pl, Chelsea road
53..Upper Berkley st, 7 Portman sq
37..Upper Brook st, Grosvenor sq
53..Upper Bryanstone st, 19Edgware rd
38..Upper Charlton st, Clipstone st
18..Upper Cheltenham pl, opposite the Asylum, Westminster road
38..Upper Conway st, 12 Fitzroy pl
53..Upper Dorset st, 20 Manchester st, Manchester square
14..Upper East Smithfield, 17 Manor row, Little Tower hill
51..Upper Eaton st, Pimlico, continuation of Lw Eaton st to Grosvenr pl
9..Upper Fountain pl, City road
31..Upper Fort pl, Blue Anchor road, Bermondsey
34..Upper Fore st, Lambeth
53..Upper George st, 44 Edgware rd
53..Upper Gloucester st, Marylebone
38..Upper Gower mews, Francis st, Upper Gower st
38..Upper Gower st, Bedford sq
5..Upper Green st, Friars st
52..Upper Grosvenor mews, Grosvenor pl, Hyde Park corner
36..Upper Grosvenor st, Grosvenor sq
5..Upper Ground st, Albion pl, Blackfriars bridge
22..Upper Guildford st, Russell sq
30..Upper Gun alley, 144 Green bank, Wapping
37..Upper Harley st, 36 Weymouth st, Gt Portland st
53..Upper Humberstone st, Marylebone
37..Upper James st, Golden sq
36..Upper John st, nr 21 Golden sq
38..Upper John st,Tottenham ct rd
33..Upper Kennington la, from Church row, Newington to Vauxhall
33..Upper Kennington pl, Kenningtn la
22..Upper King st, Bloomsbury
18..Upper Lambeth marsh, Westminsr bridge rd, to the palace, Lambeth
68..Upper Lisson st, Lisson green
39..Upper Maidenhead la, Battle bridge
37..Upper Marylebone st, 54 Gt Portland street
21..Upper St. Martin's la, Long Acre
53..Upper Montague st, Montague sq
37..Upper Newman st, 34 Oxford st
23..Upper North pl, nr Sidmouth st
67..Upper North st, a few doors right in Sloane st, Knightsbridge
53..Upper Norton st, Portland st
55..Upper Pratt pl, Camden town
53..Upper Quebec st, New rd,Marylebn
67..Upper Queen's bdgs, left side of Brompton rd, by Knightsbridge, Brompton
37..Upper Rathbone pl, continuation of Rathbone place
51..Upper Ranelagh st,Five fds,Pimlico
37..Upper Rupert st, Princes st, Soho

Ref. to Plan.
15..Upper Russell st, 90 Bermondsey st
53..Upper Seymour st, 40 Portman st
53..Upper Seymour st, (West) Edgware road
25..Upper st, Islington
53..Upper st, Marylebone
53..Upper Spring st, Crawford st
5..Upper Stamford st, 9 Stamford st, Blackfriars road
39..Upper Spencer st, Maiden lane, Battle bridge
4..Upper Thames st, London bridge, to Earl st, Blackfriars bridge
38..Upper Thornaugh st, Bedford sq
53..Upper Titchfield st,20 Gt Portland st
39..Upper Tonbridge pl, op. Judd's pl, Somers town
29..Upper Turning, 54 Shakespeare's walk, Shadwell
39..Upper Union pl, Maiden place
30..Upper Well alley, 110 Wapping
9..Upper Whitecross st, 86 Chiswell st
37..Upper Wimpole mews, near Beaumont street
37..Upper Wimpole st, 14 Weymouth street, Gt Portland st
53..Upper York st, Quebec street, Portman square
30..Uppom pl, Nutkin's corner
15..Upton pl, nr Bermondsey st
14..Usher's ct, Seething la, Tower st
68..Uxbridge rd, Tyburn turnpike

V

17..Valentine pl & row, op. Bennett's row, Blackfriars road
15..Valiant Soldier al, nr Tooley st
15..Vane st, Glean alley, Tooley st
34..Vauxhall, Lambeth, W. end of Upper Kennington lane
34..Vauxhall gardns, Up Kennington la
50..Vauxhall pl, nr Vauxhall turnpike
50..Vauxhall row, nr Vauxhall turnpk, South Lambeth
34..Vauxhall row, nr Vauxhall stairs
34..Vauxhall st, Kennington lane
34..Vauxhall sq, 13 in Vauxhall row
34..Vauxhall terrace, Vauxhall walk
34..Vauxhall walk, Lambeth Butts
68..Venn pl, Harrow road
21..Vere st, Clare market
37..Vere st, 151 Oxford road
18..Vere's crescent, 1 Barnes's place, Lambeth marsh
22..Vernon pl, Bloomsbury sq
23..Verulum bdgs, op. 48 Gray's Inn la
32..Victory pl, opposite 25 Brandons st, Lock's fields
44..Victory row, Trafalgar sq
44..Victory st, Trafalgar sq, Stepney
32..Victory st, New Kent road
61..Victualling Office row, Deptford
36..Vigo lane, top of Sackville st, Picdl
32..Villa pl, Walworth common
36..Viller's ct, St. James's st, Piccadl

Ref. to Plan.
20..Viller's st, 32 Strand
2..Vincent's ct, 2 Silver st, Falcon sq
33..Vincent's pl, Kennington road
35..Vincent sq & st, Tothill fields
11..Vincent st, Church st, Shoreditch
11..Vine ct, Bishopsgate st without
13..Vine ct, Duke st, Aldgate
16..Vine ct, 116 Blackman st
12..Vine ct, Lamb st, Spitalfields
2..Vine ct, Moor la, Forest, Cripplegt
14..Vine ct, Redcross st, E. Smithfield
4..Vine ct, Three Crane lane, Upper Thames street
19..Vine ct, Narrow wall, Lambeth
12..Vine ct, 229 Whitechapel road
11..Vine pl, Little Pearl st, Spitalfields
68..Vine pl, Paddington
11..Vine st, Saffron hill
13..Vine st. America sq, Minories
23..Vine st, Bedford st, Liquorpond st
21..Vine st, Broad st, Bloomsbury
20..Vine st, Chandos st, Covent garden
68..Vine st,nr Devonshire pl, Edgware rd
35..Vine st, Millbank, Westminster
19..Vine st, Narrow wall, Lambeth
11..Vine st, Lamb's st, Spitalfields
12..Vine st, Spitalfields market
36..Vine yd, Vine st, Piccadilly
15..Vine yd, Tooley st, Borough
23..Vine yd, 27 Coppice row, Clerkenw
1..Vine yd, 96 Aldersgate st
45..Vine yd, 3 Brook st, Ratcliff
23..Vinegar gardens, Coppice row
15..Vinegar yd, 240 Bermondsey st
16..Vinegar yd, George yd, Gt Suffolk st
21..Vinegar yd, nr Belton st, Long Acre
16..Vinegar yd, 116 Blackman st, Boro
23..Vinegar walk, Coppice row
4..Vintner's alley, 184 Up Thames st
11..Virginia st, 51 Ratcliff highway
14..Virginia st, Austin st, Shoredh ch
39..Vittoria pl, Duke's rd, Somers tn

W

60..Wade st, Poplar
4..Wagstaff's bdgs, Maid la, Borough
1..Wakefield pl, 77 Bunhill row
3..Wallbrook, 24 Bucklersbury, to Dowgate hill
9..Wallbrook pl, Chatham gdns,City rd
17..Wallbrook pl, Asylum, Lambeth
26..Wallbrook pl, Hoxton
26..Wallbrook buildings, Hoxton
34..Walcot pl, Westminster bridge rd, near the Asylum
37..Walker's ct, Berwick st, Soho
16..Walker's ct, Newcastle st, Borough
29..Wall st, Chapman st,St.George's E
29..Wallbridge st, nr Cannon st turnpk
18..Waller's pl&row,nr Asylum,Lambh
16..Wallis's al, Mint st, Borough
35..Wallis's bds, Queen's row, Pimlico
11..Wallis's yd, Worship st, Shoreditch
34..Walnut tree walk,Walcot pl,Lambh
11..Walpole alley, 38 Norton Falgate

Ref. to Plan.

18..Walsingham pl,nr Asylum,Lambeth
13..Walton's ct, Cartwright st, Rosemary lane
45..Walton's rents,103 Brook st,Ratcliff
32..Walworth, from Elephant & Castle, Newington,to Camberwell turnpk
32..Walworth common, bottom of Trafalgar st, Walworth
32..Walworth pl, Walworth High st
30..Wapping, from Hermitage dock to the end of New Gravel lane
29..Wapping wall, from the end of New Gravel lane to Fox's lane
30..Wapping dock street stairs, from 230 Wapping
30..Wapping old stairs, 290 Wapping st
30..Wapping new stairs, 261 Wapping st
24..Warden's ct, Clerkenwell close
37..Wardour st, 382 Oxford st
5..Wardrobe terrace, 45 St. Andrew's hill, Blackfriars
1..Ward's ct, 43 Goswell st
35..Ward's row, Stafford row, Pimlico
27..Ward's row, Bethnal green rd
23..Warner st, (Gt. & Lit.)Clerkenwell
14..Warner's yd, Mincing la, Tower st
2..Warnford ct, 29 Throgmorton st
38..Warren mews, 34 Warren street, Fitzroy square
30..Warren's sq, Wapping
38..Warren's st, 7 upper Conway st
22..Warwick ct, 40 High Holborn
8..Warwick ct, Warwick lane
8..Warwick lane, Newgate st
22..Warwick pl, Bedfordrw, Redlion sq
51..Warwick pl, Brewer st, Pimlico
17..Warwick row, nr Friar st
51..Warwick row, Brewer st, Pimlico
8..Warwick sq, Warwick la, Newgt st
37..Warwick st, 371 Oxford st
20..Warwick st, 20 Cockspur street, Charing cross
36..Warwick st, 2 Golden sq
31..Water la, Dockhead, Horselydown
6..Water la, 1 Earl st, Blackfriars
7..Water la, 8 Fleet st
14..Water la, 61 Lower Thames st, Gt Tower street
20..Water st, Arundel st, Strand
15..Water's ct, Stoney la, Boro market
6..Water st, Tudor st, Bridge st, Blkfrs
20..Waterloo bridge, 9 Wellington st, Strand
19..Waterloo bridge rd, Surry side of Waterloo bridge
9..Waterloo ct, Radnor st
36..Waterloo pl, Pall Mall, op. Carlton palace
29..Waterloo pl, Commerl. rd, Whchpl
23..Waterloo pl, Clerkenwell
31..Waterloo pl, Star corner
18..Waterloo pl, op. Cobourg Theatre, Lambeth marsh
17..Waterloo st, Newington causeway
45..Waterloo st, Commercl.rd, Whchpl

Ref. to Plan.

59..Waterworks,(East London) nr Clay hall, Middlesex
24..Waterworks, (New River) New River Head, Islington
68..Waterworks (Grd Junction) Paddtn
51..Waterworks (Chelsea) Turpentine lane, Millbank and Pimlico
59..Waterworks, (West Ham) Mile End road
66..Waterworks, (West Middlesex) Hammersmith
70..Waterworks, (Hampstead) Hampstead ponds
20..Waterworks (York bdgs) Strand
33..Waterworks (South London) Kennington lane, Lambeth
3..Watling st, from north east corner of St Paul's church yard, to Tower Royal Easterly
28..Watson's bdgs, Ducking pond row
17..Watton pl, 119 Blackfriars road, near the Obelisk
15..Weaver's la, west side of Tooley st
11..Weaver's st, Fleet st, Spitalfields
11..Webb's bdgs, 87 Hare st, Spitalfds
11..Webb sq, 49 High st, Shoreditch
31..Webb st, 218 Bermondsey st
15..Webb st, Bermondsey New road, near Star corner
32..Webb's county ter, New Kent rd
18..Webber row, Webber st
18..Webber st,nr Asylum, Lambeth
17..Webber st, first on the left from the Obelisk, Blackfriars road
83..Webster's bdgs, 17 Kennington grn
37..Welbeck mews, north side Little Welbeck street
37..Welbeck st, Cavendish sq
15..Well al, nr Joiner's st, Tooley st
13..Well al, 23 Minories
30..Well al, (Upper) 84 Lower East Smithfield, Wapping church
3..Well ct, 9 Queen st, Cheapside
13..Well ct, Wellclose square
3..Well ct, 48 Bow lane, Cheapside
27..Well's ct, Hackney road
..Well's ct,63 Well's st, Oxford st
37..Well's mews, Well st, Oxford st
60..Well st, nr East India docks
1..Well st, 21 Jewin st, Cripplegate
12..Well st, Montague st, Whitechapel
36..Well's st, Jermyn st, Piccadilly
37..Well st, 63 Oxford st
13..Well st, Wellclose sq
1..Well yd, Little Britain
13..Well yd, 33 Rosemary lane
9..Well and Bucket row, 31 Old st
29..Wellclose sq, 25 Cable st, Ratcliffe highway
13..Wellclose sq, New rd, St. George's in the East
39..Weller's pl, nr Smallpox hospital
38..Wellesley st, Euston sq
..Welling's farm, Regent's park
27..Wellington pl, Bethnal green

Ref. to Plan.
16..Wellington pl, Long la, Borough
32..Wellington pl, East la, Wallworth
34..Wellington pl, Vauxhall walk
29..Wellington pl, Commercial road, Whitechapel
27..Wellington row, Birdcage walk, Hackney road
23..Wellington sq, Gray's Inn lane
21..Wellington st, 134 Strand
20..Wellington st, Waterloo bridge
17..Wellington st, Newington causeway
40..Wellington st, Pentonville
24..Wellington st, 92 Goswell st rd
17..Wellington st, 1 Regency pl, Gt Surry street
9..Wenlock st, Helmet row, Old st
12..Wentworth ct, Wentworth street, Petticoat lane, Whitechapel
44..Wentworth row, nr Stepney green
12..Wentworth st, Whitechapel
27..West's corner, Bethnal green rd
29..West's gardens, 3 upper Shadwell
30..West's lane, 22 Nelson st, Long la, Bermondsey
17..West pl, Prospect pl, Newingtn butts
9..West pl, Ratcliff row, City road
40..West pl, Chapel st, Pentonville
17..West sq, Prospect pl, Lambeth
8..West Smithfield, from the south end of Smithfield bars, to Giltspur st
16..West st, 18 West's pl, Long lane, Bermondsey
21..West st, Seven Dials
40..West st, Somers town
12..West st, 10 Crispin st, Spitalfields
8..West st, 87 West Smithfield
43..West st, Bonner's fields
17..West st, West sq, Lambeth
44..West st, Globe lane, Mile end
51..Westbourn pl, nr Bloody bridge
7..West Harding st, 20 Fetter lane
35..Westminster abbey, west side of Old Palace yd, Wes'minstr bridge
19..Westminster bridge, north side the Abbey, Lambeth
18..Westminster rd, Obelisk, Gt Surry st
1..Westmoreland bds, 159 Aldersgt st
68..Westmoreland bds, Philpot terrace
1..Westmoreland ct, Foster lane
9..Westmoreland la, nr Shepherd and Shepherdess, City road
32..Westmoreland row, Walworth comn
37..Westmoreland mews, 10 Great Marylebone street
15..Weston ct, Weston st, Snowsfields
39..Weston pl, Pancras, opposite the Smallpox hospital
40..Weston st, Clarence pl, Pentonville
15..Weston st, Snowsfields
39..Weston st, 40 Gray's Inn la, Holbn
44..Westover st, nr Trafalgar square
31..Weymond's bds, Grange road
37..Weymouth mews, 42 Weymouth st, Great Portland st
37..Weymouth pl, Hackney road

Ref. to Plan.
22..Weymouth st, op. 15 Rockingham row, New Kent road
37..Weymouth st, 68 Portland place
27..Weymouth ter, Hackney rd, near Shoreditch
2..Whalebone ct, 39 Throgmorton st
3..Whalebone ct, Bow lane, Cheapsd
17..Wharton pl, 146 Holborn
4..Wheatsheaf alley. 109 Up. Thames st
7..Wheatsheaf ct, 22 Fleet market
11..Wheeler st, White Lion st, N Falgt
35..Wheeler st, Tothill fields
21..Whetstone park, Gate st, Lincoln's Inn fields
1..Whip yd, Boro, nr St. Thomas's hospital
3..Whistler's ct, 82 Salter's hall ct, Cannon st
20..Whitcomb st, 18 Panton st, Leicester square
37..Whitcomb's ct, 65 Princes st, Hmkt
7..White's alley, Bream's buildings
7..White's alley, 34 Chancery lane
2..White's al, 60 Coleman st, Old Jewry
13..White's bds, Rosemary lane, near White Lion court
32..White's bds, Knightsbridge
27..White's ct, 72 Bethnal green road
20..White's ct, Oxendon st
3..White's ct, Leadenhall st
2..White's ct. Ropemaker's st
27..White's grounds, 95 Bethnal grn rd
15..White's grounds, Crucifix lane
35..White's rents, Wood st, Millbank
12..White's row, Bakers row, 94 Whitechapel road
14..White's row, 99 Low. E. Smithfield
27..White st, Wilmot square
12..White st, Cutler st, Houndsditch
2..White st, Ropemaker's al, Moorfds
16..White st, from the east corner of St. George's ch, to Long la, Boro
12..White st, Spitalfields
13..White's yd, 57 Rosemary lane
8..White's yd, 23 Saffron hill
1..White's yd, 156 Whitecross street, Cripplegate
13..White Bear al, 18 Aldgate
11..White Bear ct, 183 High st, Shordh
7..White Bear ct, Bear al, Fleet mkt
16..White Bear ct, 264 Kent st, Boro
16..White Bear gdns, Kent st, Boro
13..Whitechapel, continuation of Aldgate to the Church
2..Whitecross alley, 22 Wilson's st, Moorfields
1..Whitecross st, 116 Fore st, Cripplegate to op. St. Luke's church
16..Whitecross st, 96 Queen st, Boro
7..Whitefriars, Water la, Fleet st
7..Whitefriars dock, end of Waterla Fleet street
20..Whitehall, nr Charing cross
20..Whitehall pl, op. the Admiralty
2..Whitehart ct, 199 Bishopsgate st

Ref. to Plan.

15..Whitehart ct, 242 Bermondsey st
20..Whitehart ct,31Castle st,Leicestr sq
3..Whitehart ct, 28 & 40 Gracechurch st, Lombard street
32..Whitehart ct, Weymouth st, New Kent road
32..Whitehart ct, Crown st, Walworth, first from Elephant & Castle
26..Whitehart ct, nr Huntingdon st
8..Whitehart ct,16 Long la, W. Smithfd
8..Whitehart ct, Charterhouse la
2..Whitehart yd, London wall, or 31 Wood street
33..Whitehart pl, 37 Kennington cross
39..Whitehart row, Battle bridge
5..Whitehart rw, op. 29George st,Bkfrs
33..Whitehart row, 17 Kennington la
8..Whitehart st, Newgate market
21..Whitehart yd, 82 Drury lane
66..Whitehead's green, Chelsea com
4..Whitehind al, Maid la, Southwark
11..Whitehind ct, 162 Bishopsgt st wht
8..Whitehorse al, Cowcross st
8..Whitehorse al, 35 Turnmill street, Clerkenwell
13..Whitehorse ct, 174 Rosemary lane
15..Whitehorse ct, nr Bermondsey ch
11..Whitehorse ct, Wheeler st, Spitlfds
1..Whitehorse ct, 125 Golden lane, St. Luke's
15..Whitehorse ct, 9 High st, Borough
44..Whitehorse la, Stepney church
34..Whitehorse la, Lambeth
44..Whitehorse st, Commrl. rd, Stepney
36..Whitehorse st, 67 Piccadilly
15..Whitehorse st, nr Tooley st
2..Whitehorse yd, 16 Coleman street, Old Jewry
21..Whitehorse yd, 109 Drury lane
10..Whitehorse yd, 122 White st, Boro
3..Whitehorse yd, 29 Friday st
1..Whitekey al, Grub st, Cripplegate
15..Whitelion ct, 234 Bermondsey st
8..Whitelion ct, 6 Charterhouse lane
11..Whitelion ct, 13 Norton Falgate
3..Whitelion ct, 21 Birchin la,Cornhill
2..Whitelion ct, Little Bell alley
2..Whitelion ct,20 Throgmorton st
40..Whitelion ct, Whitelion st, Pentonv
5..Whitelion ct, Willow st, Bankside, Southwark
3..Whitelion ct, 64 Cornhill
7..Whitelion ct, 76 Fleet street
14..Whitelion ct, 41 Gt. Tower st
6..Whitelion pl, 16 Wych st
40..Whitelion pl, Pentonville
66..Whitelion st, Jew's row, Chelsea
11..Whitelion st, Spitalfields
40..Whitelion st, Pentonville
13..Whitelion st, Cable st, Rosemary la
4..Whitelion wharf, Up. Thames st
37..Whitelion yd,Castle st, Oxford mkt
34..Whitelion yd, nr Vauxhall stairs
1..Whitelion yd, 172 Whitecross st, Cripplegate

Ref. to Plan.

1..Whiterose al, 58 Whitecross alley, Cripplegate
2..Whiterose ct,31 Coleman st,Lothby
66..White styles, leading from the King's road to Chelsea hospital
10..Whitfields st. Leonard st, Paul st
15..Whiting yd, Dog & Bear yard
35..Whister's ground, Gt. Peter st, Westminster
9..Whitley's ct, 73 Brick la,St.Luke's
16..Wicomb pl, Kent st, Borough
12..Widegate st, 51 Bishopsgate st
8..Widnall's pl, Vine st, Hatton wall
9..Wigley ct, 74 Brick lane
37..Wigmore pl, Cavendish square
37..Wigmore st, Cavendish square
21..Wild ct, Gt Wild st, Drury lane
21..Wild passage, 139 Drury lane
16..Wild's rents, opposite Long lane
20..Wilderness la,Dorset st,Salisbury sq
66..Wilderness row, Jew's row
8..Wilderness row, 35 Goswell st
16..Wilderness st, Baalzephon st
12..Wilkes st, 101 High st, Shoreditch
53..Wilkinson's bdgs, 76 Edgware rd
15..William's bdgs, Three Hammer al
67..William's bds, Yeoman's row
4..William's ct, Maid lane, Southwk
37..William's mews, Devonshire st, near Portland place
10..William ct, William st, Paul st
6..William st, Bridge la, Blackfrs rd
20..William st, Durham st, Strand
5..William st, George st, Blackfrs rd
35..William st, nr Buckingham gate
53..William st, nr Bulstrode st
29..William st, 136 High st, Shoreditch
32..William st, Pitt st, Kent road
32..William st, 7 Middle row, New Kent road
38..William st, Hampstead road
68..William st, Lisson grove
34..William st, Union st, Walcot pl
26..William st, Hoxton
45..William st. Blue Anchor fds, Stepn
35..William st, Pimlico
53..William st, 49 Marylebone lane
53..William st, 30 Thayer st, Manchester square
36..William st, 30 St. James's street, Westminster
15..Willis's rents, 101 Bermondsey st
9..Willow row, 49 Goswell st
5..Willow st, Bankside, Borough
10..Willow st, end of Paul st, Finsbury
35..Willow st, Tothill fields
10..Willow walk, Leonard st, Paul st
35..Willow walk, Tothill fields
39..Wilstead ct, 23 New rd, Tot ct rd
39..Wilstead st, Somers town
24..Wilmington sq, Spafields
16..Wilmot's bdgs, White st, Boro, near St. George's church
27..Wilmot's grove, Wilmot square
27..Wilmot sq, nr 65 Shoreditch

Ref. to Plan.
27..Wilmot st, Bethnal green road
22..Wilmot st, Brunswick sq
5..Wilson ct, 29 Kent st, Borough
16..Wilson ct, 87 Kent st, Borough
20..Wilson pl, 7 Charing cross
60..Wilson st, St. Ann's pl, Limehouse
2..Wilson st, north side of Moorfields
52..Wilton st, 43 Grosvenor pl,Hyde pk
53..Wimpole mews, 38 Weymouth st,
     Portland place
37..Wimpole st, 33 Weymouth st, Gt.
     Portland st
39..Winchester ct, Winchester st,Pentvl
39..Winchester pl, Pentonville
62..Winchester row, 81 Edgware road
2..Winchester st, 53 Broad st, Royal
     Exchange
1..Winchester st, 5 Monkwell st
15..Winchester st, Stoney la, Boro mkt
36..Wincle's ct, west end of Pall mall
53..Windham pl, Crawford st
53..Windham st,Crawford st,
8..Windmill ct, 12 Giltspur st, West
     Smithfield
8..Windmill ct, 1 Providence row,
     Finsbury square
5..Windmill pl, Blackfriars
10..Windmill st, Finsbury square
36..Windmill st, op. 228 Piccadilly
37..Windmill st, 45 Tottenham ct rd
9..Windsor cottages, Canal, City rd
20..Windsor ct, nr 325 Strand
5..Windsor ct, Lit. Knightrider st
1..Windsor ct, Monkwell st
9..Windsor pl, City road, near the
     Shepherd and Shepherdess
12..Windsor st, Widegate st, Bishops-
     gate st without
9..Windsor terrace, near Anderson's
     buildings, City road
11..Wine ct, Lamb st, Spitalfields
7..Wine office ct, 146 Fleet st
24..Wingrove pl, 5 Corporation row
2..Winkworth bds, Austin frs, Broad st
9..Winkworth's bds, nr 46 City road
16..Winter's ct, Long lane, Borough
34..Winter's pl, Lambeth walk
34..Winter's pl,Kennington ln,Vauxhall
37..Winsley st, 68 Oxford st
1..Wither's ct,73 Whitecross st,Old st
21..Woburn ct, Duke st, Bloomsbury
22..Woburn mews, Russell square
22..Woburn pl, 29 Tavistock square
20..Woburn st, Brydges st, Covent gdn
21..Woburn st,Gt. Russell st,Bloomsby
28..Wood's bdgs, 126 Whitechapel rd
32..Wood's bdgs, East la, Walworth
11..Wood's bdgs, New Inn yd,Shoredh
11..Wood's close, Hare st, Spitalfields
37..Wood's close, 81 Oxford st
11..Wood's ct, Norton Falgate
53..Wood's mews, Park st, Grosvnr sq
23..Wood's pl, 45 Coppice row, Clkwl
11..Wood st, 28 Church st, Spitalfds
24..Wood st, Brayne's row

Ref. to Plan.
2..Wood st, 123 Cheapside, and 1
     London wall
23..Wood st,Lucas st,nr Foundling hspt
35..Wood st,64 Millbank, Westminster
10..Wood st, Old st road
12..Wood st, nr Prince's st, Spitalfields
16..Wood's yd, 74 Redcross st, Borough
24..Woodbridge st, 109 St. John's st,
     Clerkenwell   [Oxford st
37..Woodstock ct, Woodstock street,
37..Woodstock mews, opposite 6 Little
     Woodstock street
37..Woodstock st, 303 Oxford st
12..Woolpack alley, Houndsditch
15..Woolpack alley, 242 Bermondsey st
16..Woolpack alley, 54 Kent st, Boro
16..Woolpack yd, 22 Gravel la, Boro
4..Worcester pl, 67 Up Thames st
16..Worcester st, Union st, Borough
29..Worcester st, Old Gravel lane
26..Workhouse lane, Hoxton
44..World's End, north east corner of
     Stepney Church yard
13..Worley's ct, 79 Minories
2..Wormwood's st, 202 Bishopsgate
     street without
11..Worship ct, Worship st
11..Worship sq, Worship st
11..Worship st, Finsbury square
12..Wrestler's ct, Camomile street,
     249 High st, Shoreditch
31..Wright's bdgs, Grange road, Ber-
     mondsey New road
8..Wright's bdgs, Chick lane
60..Wright's pl, East India rd, Poplar
20..Wright's row,Pell st,Ratcliff highw
37..Wright's yd, 40 New Bond st
21..Wych st, 93 Drury lane
16..Wycombe pl, Kent st, Borough
53..Wyndham st, Bryanstone square
24..Wynyatt st, Northampton square,
     Goswell st road

Y

24..Yardley st, op. Spafields chapel
11..Yates's ct, Long alley, Moorfields
16..Yaxley pl, Little Lant st, Borough
21..Yeates's ct, 23Carey st, Chancery la
67..Yeoman's row, Brompton
28..Yokeley's bdgs, Mile End green,
     near the turnpike
20..York bdgs, Buckingham st, Strand
31..York bdgs, Bermondsey New road
32..York bdgs, Locksfields
35..York bdgs, Grub st, Millbank
53..York bdgs, op. 35 Paddington st
39..York bdgs, York st, Pentonville
53..York ct, East st, Manchester sq
10..York ct, 14 Paul st, Finsbury
53..York mews, (N.) David st, York pl
53..York mews, (S.) 32 Paddington st
32..York pl, Walworth
35..York pl, Palmer's village
40..York pl, Islington
18..York pl, Asylum, Westminster rd

M

Ref. to Plan.
53..York pl, Baker's st, Portman sq
10..York pl, 22 Banner st, Bunhill row
66..York pl, Battersea fields
17..York pl, Borough road
9..York pl, Castle st, City rd, nearly opposite Sidney st
44..York pl, Cow lane, Stepney
33..York pl, Francis st, Newington
44..York pl, Trafalgar sq, Stepney
27..York pl, Middlesex pl, Hackney rd
35..York pl, York st, Westminster
66..York pl, nr York hospital, Chelsea
33..York row, Kennington road
51..York row, nr Chelsea bridge
17..York st, op. 7 London road
18..York st, Bridge road, Lambeth
39..York st, Pentonville
32..York st, 1 Bermondsey New road
5..York st, 52 Blackfriars road
16..York st, 276 Borough High st
35..York st, Broadway, Westminster
28..York st, Castle st, Gt. Saffron hill
11..York st, Church st, Shoreditch
46..York st, Clarence st, Rotherhithe
20..York st, Covent garden, second on the left, nr Catherine st

Ref. to Plan.
61..York st, Greenland dock, Rotherh
67..York st, Han's pl, Sloane st
16..York st, Pitt st, Kent road
37..York st, Queen Ann street, east, Portland street
36..York st, St. James's square
32..York st, end of John st, East lane, Walworth
29..York st, Commercl. rd, Whitechpl
26..York st, Kingsland road
53..York st, York pl, Portman square
27..York st, 185 Church st, Bethnal grn
9..York terrace, City road
32..York terrace, Kent road
16..Yorkshire Grey yd, 107 Blackman street, Borough
32..Youl pl, Kent road
9..Youngs bdgs, 23 Horse Shoe alley, Moorfields
16..Young's bdgs, Marshalsea, Boro
9..Young's bdgs, 23 Old street, near Whitecross street

Z

5..Zoar st, Gravel lane, Southwark

PUBLIC BUILDINGS, OFFICES, &c.

Ref. to Plan.
7..Accomptant General's Office, Chancery lane
5..Admiralty Court, Doctors Commons
20..Admiralty Office, 37 Charing cross
35..Adjutant General's Office, Crown st, Westminster
7..Affidavit Office, 10 Symond's Inn, Chancery lane
13..African Company, 60 Mark lane
3..African Company's Office, at Mr. Goslings, Lawrence Pountney la
2..African Office, and Ship Owners' Society, 33 New Broad st
37..Agricultural Museum, George st, Hanover square
36..Albany Chambers, Piccadilly
35..Alien Office, Crown ct, Westminster
6..Alienation Office, 7 King's Bench walk, Temple
20..Allowance Office for Spoiled Stamps, Somerset place, Strand
7..Allowance Transcript Error Office, at Chief Justice's Chambers
37..Ambassador's French Office for Passports, 10 New Cavendish st
3..American Agency Office, for Sale of American Lands, 6 Ingram court, Fenchurch street

Ref. to Plan.
20..American Loyalist Pay Office, Whitehall
2..American Office for Sales, Old Broad street
7..Amicable Assurance Office, 13 Serjeants Inn, Fleet st
20..Antiquarian Society, Somerset pl, Strand
5..Appeals for Prizes of War, Doctors Commons
5..Archdeacon of London's Court, Doctors Commons
5..Archdeacon of Rochester's Court, Bennett's hill, Doctors Commons
20..Armorial Bearing Licence Office, (principal) Somerset pl, Strand
3..Armorial Bearing Licence Office for the City of London, 50 Lombard st
36..Army Barrack Office, 83 Pall Mall
36..Army Medical Board Office, Berkeley st, Piccadilly
20..Army Pay Office, Whitehall
1..Assay Office, Carey la, Foster la
2..Auction Mart, Bartholomew la, City
20..Auditor of Imprest's Office, Somerset House
20..Audit Office, 5 Whitehall place
20..Barrack Office Spring gardens

Ref. to Plan.

36..Basingstoke Canal Office,10 Charles street, St. James's square
29..Ballast Office, Narrow st, Ratcliff cr
13..Ballast Of. Coopers rw,Crutched frs
3..Bank of England, Threadneedle st
22..Bank for Savings,Southampton rw, Bloomsbury
2..Bankrupts Of. 82 Basinghall st
7..Bankrupts Of. Bell yd, Temple bar
7..Bill of Middlesex Of.16 Clifford's Inn
5..Bishop of London's House, 68 St. Paul's Church yard
5..Bishop of London's Of. Knightrider street, Doctors Commons
2..Blackwell Hall, King st, Cheapside
36..Board of Agriculture, Sackville st, Piccadilly
35..Board of Commissioners for the Af fairs of India, Cannon row, Westm
35..Board of Controul for East India Affairs, Cannon row, Westminster
20..Board of Trade Treasury, Whitehall
20..Board of Works, Little Scotland yd, Westminster
16..Borough Court, St. Margaret's hill
2..Bridge Masters Of. Guildhall
19..British Claims on France,(Of. for) 44 Parliament st, Westminster
6..British Loan Establishment, 38 New Bridge st, Blackfriars
3..Bitish Mineralogical Society, Poultry
68..British National Endeavour Society, Paddington green
36..Buckingham House, St. James' park
36..Burlington Arcade, Piccadilly
3..Canal Of. Change al, Lombard st
13..Cape of Good Hope Of. 5Jeffery's sq
36..Carlton Palace, Pall Mall
20..Cart Of. Essex st, Strand
3..Chamber of Commerce, Cornhill
21..Chancery Court, Lincoln's Inn hall
35..Chancery Court, Westminster hall
7..Chancery Of. Southampton bdgs
1..Chapter House,St. Paul's Church yd
8..Charter House, Charterhouse st
35..Chelsea Water Works Of. Abingdon street, Westminster
6..Chirographers Of. Middle Temple
35..Church Commission and Commis sioners on Charities Of. Great George st, Westminster
19..Church and Corporation Land Tax Of. 7 Parliament st
7..Church Missionary House, 14 Salis bury square
4..City Canal Masters Of. Coal harbor
2..City Chambers, Bishopsgate st
14..City Corn Of. 20 Harp la, Tower st
14..City Gaugers Of. 12 Water lane, Tower street
5..City Land Coal Meter's Of. 8 Little Knightrider street
23..City Light Horse Volunteers Riding School, Gray's Inn Lane
2..City of London Auxiliary Bible So-

Ref. to Plan.

ciety's Of. Salvador house, Bi shopsgate street
2..City Solicitors Of. Guildhall
6..Clerk of the Doquets Of. King's Bench Of.
6..Clerk of the Essoigns Of. Elm ct, Temple
20..Clerk of Estreats Of.Somerset house
7..Clerk of the Juries and Habeas Corpus Of. Chancery lane
6..Clerk of the Outlawries Of. 1 Pump court, Middle Temple
18..Clerk of the Peace for Surry, North street, Lambeth
7..Clerk of the Rules of King's Bench Of. Symond's Inn
6..Clerk of the Common Pleas Of. Tanfield ct, Inner Temple
16..Clink Liberty Court of Southwark
14..Coal Exchange, 43 Lw.Thames st
14..Coal Meters Of. Coal Exchange
20..Coal Meters Of. for Westminster, 7 Northumberland st, Strand
8..College of Physicians, Warwick la, Newgate street
35..Colonial Audit Of. 20 St. James's street, Buckingham gate
35..Colonial DepartmentOf. Downing st
20..Commander in Chief's Of. Horse Guards, Whitehall
3..Commercial Dock Of. 106 Fen church street
3..Commercial Road Of. 5 Nicholas passage, Lombard st
15..Commissary Of. and Military Depot, Tooley st, Borough
35..Commissary General's Of. George st, Westminster
35..Commissariat Of.7 James's st, Wstm
5..Commission of Survey's Of. God liman street
20..Commissioners of Assessed Taxes Of. Buckingham st, Strand
21..Commissioners of Sewers Of. 1 Greek st, Soho
8..Commissioners of Sewers Of. 7 Hatton garden
20..Committee of Counsel for Foreign Trade and Plantations, Whitehall
6..Common Pleas Of. 2 Tanfield ct, Temple
20..Comptroller of Army Accounts Of. Horse Guards
2..Comptroller City Of. Guildhall
3..Copper Company's Of. Bush lane and Watling street
13..Corn Exchange, Mark lane
14..Corn Meter Of. Gt Tower st
22..Coroner's of Middlesex Of. 48 Bedford row
20..Council Of. Cock pit, Whitehall
6..Corporation Of. 13 Paper buildings, Inner Temple
7 & 35..Courts of Chancery, Lincoln's Inn and Westminster hall

Ref. to Plan.

2..Court of Requests for the City of London, 15 Aldermanbury

35 & 2..Court of King's Bench, Common Pleas and Exchequer are held in Westminster hall and Guildhall

16..Court of Requests for Southwark, 11 Crosby row, Bermondsey

36..Court of Requests, Vine st, Piccadl

21..Court of Requests, Castle street, Long Acre

22..Court of Requests, Kingsgate st, Hbn

12..Court of Requests, Osborn street, Whitechapel

6..Crown Of. 2 King's Bench Walk, Temple

6..Crown Of. Middle row, Mid. Temple

7..Crown Of. Roll's yd, Chancery la

6..Custos Brevium Of. 4 Elm ct, Temple

14..Custom House, Lower Thames st

7..Cursitor's Of. Roll's yd, Chancery la

6..Deputy Remembrancer's Of. King's Bench walk, Temple

6..Dispensation Of. 4 Elm ct, Temple

2..Domingo (St.) Claim Of. O Broad st

5..Doctors Commons, St. Pauls

20..Duchy of Cornwall Of. Somerset h

20..Duchy of Lancaster Of. Somerset h

2..Dutch Commissioners Of. 28 Great Winchester street

2..Dutch Prize Of. 55 Old Broad st

3..East County Dock Of. 18 Change alley, Cornhill

19..East India Company's Of. Whitehall

12..East India Company's Gun Barrel View Warehouse, Church la, Whpl

12..East India Company's Gun Makers Proof Warehouse, Church la, Whpl

13..East India Company's Indigo Warehouses, Seething la, and Coopers row, Crutched friars

19..East India Military Of. Whitehall

3..East India Packing Of. 4 Abchurch la

45..East India Company's Saltpetre Warehouses, Broad st, Ratcliff

13..East India Company's Spice Warehouses, Haydon square, and 148 Leadenhall street

13..East India Company's Tea Warehouses, Fenchrch st, & Crutched frs

12..East India Dock Company, 11 St. Helen's pl, Bishopsgate

2..East India Cloth Warehouse, Great St. Helens

3..East India House, Leadenhall st

2..East India Stationary Warehouse, Great St. Helen's

..Eastland Company's Of. Stephen la, Wood street

2..East London Waterworks Of. 16 St. Helen's pl, Bishopsgate

36..Egyptian Hall & Exhibition Rooms, Piccadilly

6..Engine House, Earl st, Blackfriars

3..English Copper Company's Of. 27 Upper Thames st

Ref. to Plan.

36..Engineers' Of. 84 Pall Mall

66..Entomological Society, Lit. Chelsea

6..Equity Exchequer Of. King's Bench walk, Inner Temple

22..Error Of. Gray's Inn square

22..Error Of. Southampton buildings

7..Error Of. King's Bench, Chancery la

36..Estate & Mortgage Of. 56 Pall Mail

7..Examiners Of. Roll's yd, Chancery la

3..Exchange Auction Rooms, Sweeting's rents

6..Exchequer Chamber Of. Garden ct, Temple

6..Exchequer Of. King's Bench walk

3..Exchequer Bill Loan Of. Thrdndl st

20..Exchequer Offices, Somerset house, and 9 Lincoln's Inn New sq

14..Excise Distillery, Lower E. Smithfd

14..Excise Export Of. Tower hill

2..Excise Of. Old Broad st, City

13..Excise Permit Of. Sun ct, Aldgate

20..Exeter Change, Strand

14..Export Of. 49 Gt. Tower st

3 & 36..Express Of. for General Post, Lombard st, and Haymarket

5..Faculty Of. Godliman st, Doc. Com.

6..Fenn Of. 3 Tanfield ct, Temple

13..Fenchurch Chambers, 63 Fenchrch st

6..Filazers Of. in the Common Pleas. E. m ct, Temple

6..Filazers Exigenters Of. Pump ct, Temple

6..Foreign Apposers Of. Inner Temple

6..First Fruits Of. 10 Farrar bds, Temple

19..Foreign Of. Downing st

2..Foreign Stock Exchange, Capel ct, Bartholomew lane

2..Founders Weight Of. Founders Hall court, Lothbury

21..Freemasons Hall, Queen st, Lincoln's Inn fields

37..French Passport Of. 8 Weymouth st, Portland place

15..Fruit Meters Of. 1 Dean st, Tooley st

20..Game Licence Of. Somerset place

35..Gazette Of. Parliament st

20..General Accountant Of. of New Duties, Somerset place

1..General Benefit Society, 129 Aldersgate street

20..Grand Junction Canal Of. 21 Surrey street, Strand

68..Grand Junction Waterworks, Paddgn

30 & 3..Grand Surry Dock and Canal Of. Rotherhithe & 1 St. Michael's alley, Cornhill

22..Gray's Inn Chambers, Gray's Inn la

22..Gray's Inn Hall and Chapel, Gray's Inn square

2..Guildhall, King st, Cheapside

20..Hackney Coach Of. 23 Essex st, Strd

20, 3 & 37..Hair Powder Of. Somerset pl, New st, Spring gardens, 50 Lombard st, Cornhill, and Vere street, Oxford street

Ref. to Plan.
20..Half-pay Of. Whitehall
38..Hamstead Water Works Of. 24 Frederick pl, Hamstead road
20..Hanaper Of. Somerset place
20..Hawkers & Pedlars Of. 23 Essex st, Strand
5..Heralds College, Bennett's hill, Doctors Commons
53..Horse Bazaar, 5 King st,Portman sq
20..Horse Duty Of. Somerset pl
20..Horse Guards, Whitehall
21..Horticultural Society, Gerrard st, S ho
35..House of Commons, Old Palace yd
35..House of Lords, Old Palace yd
3..Hudson's BayCompany,Fenchurch st
67..Humane Society Relieving House, Hyde park
3..India House, Leadenhall st
2..Inland Navigation Of. Token house yard
7..Inrolment Of. Chancery lane
6..Inrolment Fines and Receiver's Of. Inner Temple
20..Insolvent Debtors Court,Appraiser's Of. 2 Lyons Inn
3 & 20..Inspector General of Customs Of. Custom house and Whitehall
20..Invalid Of. 19 Craven st, Strand
35..Irish Of. 18 Gt. George st, Westmsr
7..Irish Stamp Of. Lincoln's Inn Old buildings
35..Jerusalem Chamher, Westmr. abbey
14..Jewel Of. Tower
7..Judges Chambers, Sergeant's Inn, Chancery lane
20..King's Barge Houses,Somerset hous
6..King's Bench Of. King's Bench walk, Temple
6..King's Printing Of. Printing st
6..King's Silver Of. Elm ct, Mid.Temp
35..King's StationeryOf. New Palace yd
34..Lambeth Palace, end of Bishop's wk
34..Lambeth Savings Bank,Lambeth grn
6..Lambeth Waterworks Of. 3 Temple place, Blackfriars
2..Land Tax Of. for London, Guildhall yard
20..Land Tax Register Of. Somerset pl
20..Land Revenue Of. Whitehall
3..Lead Company,Martin'sla,Cannon st
3..Levant or Turkey Company, South Sea House, Threadneedle st
7..Lincoln's Inn Hall, opposite the entrance of Lincoln's Inn
20..Linnean Society, Panton square
29..London Dock Excise and Custom House Of. Pennington st, Ratcliffe highway
3..London Dock Company, Princes st, Bank
2..London Dock Company, 33 Winchester st, Westminster
3..London Maratime |Institution, Of. Royal Exchange

M 2

Ref. to Plan.
5..London Register Of. 16 Gt Knightrider street
36..Lord Chamberlain's Of. Stable yd, St. James's
3..Lord Mayor's Court Of. Royal Exch
3..Lord Mayor's Of. Coal Exchange
20..Lord Treasurer's Of. Somerset hous
1..Lord Steward's Of. St. Ann's lane
20..Lottery Of. Somerset house
3..Mansion House, Poultry
2..Margate and Ramsgate Harbour Of. 22 Austin friars
2..Marine Society's Of. 54 Bishopsgt st
12..Marine Society's House, Camomile street
7..Master in Chancery's Of. 25 Southampton buildings, Holborn
20..Master of the Horse Of. 19 Lower King's mews
7..Master of the Roll's Of.Chancery la
7..Medical Society of London, Bolt ct, Fleet street
20..Medicine Licence and Stamp Of. Somerset place
22..Mendicity Society's Of. Red Lion sq
2..Mercantile Agency Company, Cateaton street
3..Merchant Seamen's Of. south side of Royal Exchange
45..Merchant Seamen's Registry Of. Commercial road, Stepney
20..Messengers Officer Insolvent Debtrs Court,6 Lyon's Inn, Newcastle st, Strand
35..Military Account Of. Duke street, Westminster
20..Military Board Of. 24 Spring grdns
3..Million Bank, Nag's Head court, Gracechurch st
3..Mines Royal Company's Of. Budge row, Watling st
13..Mint, Tower hill
3..Monument, Fish st bill
2..Mortgage & Annuity Of. 2 Bartholomew's lane
20..Muster Master General's Of.Whitbll
3..National Benefit Institution,Thread needle street
3..National Debt and Government Life Annuity Of. Old Jewry
3..National Mutual Insurance Benefit Institution Of. 51 Threadneedle st
20..Navy and Navy Pay Of. Somerset h
20..Netherland Embassy, 14 Buckingham street, Strand
13..New Mint, Tower hill
6..New River Company, Dorset street, Salisbury square
24..New River Waterworks Of. New River Head, Islington
3..New South Sea House,Threadndl st
35..New Transport Of. Cannon row, Westminster
7..Newsman's Hall, Blackhorse alley, Fleet street

Ref. to Plan.

36..Nisi Prius Of. Portugal st
11. Norfolk Waggon Of. 32 Sun street, Bishopsgate
20..Office for Investigating West Indian and South American Accounts, 10 Spring gardens
20..Office for Landed Property,5Craigs ct
20..Of.for Military Orders,21Spring gdns
21..Of. for Post Horse Duty, 16 Hyde st
21..Of. for the Promoting the Enlargement of Churches and Chapels, Lincoln's Inn fields
20..Of. for Woods, Forests, and Land Revenue, Whitehall pl, Westmr
2..Old South Sea House, Old Broad st
14..Ordinance Of. (Civil) Tower
36..Ordinance Of. (Military)86Pall Mall
37..Ordinance (Board of) Margaret st, Cavendish square
6..Outlawry Of. Pump ct, Temple
3..Pacific Shipping Assurance Of. 26 Change alley, Cornhill
7..Palace Court Of. 39 Chancery lane
35..Parliament Of. 28 Abingdon street, Westminster
7..Patent Of. 4 Lincoln's Inn Old sq
2..Patriotic Fund Of. 45 Lothbury
20..Pawnbroker's Licence Of. Somerset place
20..Pay Of. (Army) Horse Guards, Whitehall
20..Pay Of. (Navy) Somerset place
35..Pell Of. Westminster Hall
20..Perfumery Licence Of. Somerset pl
7..Petty Bag Of. Roll's yd, Chancery la
17..Philanthropic Society's Manufactory, London road
36..Philological Society,Maryst,Fitzr sq
20..Pipe and Comptroller of the Pipe Of. Somerset house
20..Plantation Of. Whitehall
5..Plate Glass Company, Surry side of Blackfriars bridge
13..Port of London Society's Commercial Sale Rooms, Mincing lane
21..Post Horse Tax Of. Tooke's court, Serle street
3..Post Of. (General) Lombard st
5..Prerogative Of. 6 Gt. Knightrider st, Doctors Commons
6..Presentation Of. 2 Hare ct, Temple
35..Preventive Fire Guard Of. 18 Fludyer st, Westminster
20..Privy Council Of. Treasury
20..Privy Seal Of. Somerset place
6..Prothonotaries Of.Tanfield ct,Templ
20..Provident Institution, Leicester pl
20..Public Accounts Of. Somerset pl
7..Public Of. in Chancery for Affidavits Southampton buildings
35..Public Record Of. Westminsr abbey
20..Quartermaster General's Of. Horse Guards
2..Queen Anne's Bounty Of.680Broad st
36..Queen's Palace, St.James's park

Ref. to Plan.

36..Receiver of Corn Returns Of. 8 Regent st, Piccadilly
20..Receiver General's Of. for Stamps, Somerset place
14..Receiver's Of. for Greenwich Hospital, Tower hill
14..Record Of. Tower
3..Reduction of the National Debt and Life Annuity Of. Bank st, Cornhill
21..Regent's Canal Of. 108 Gt. Russell street, Bloomsbury
5..Register Of. for Wills, (Royal and Peculiar) Doctors Commons
22..Register Of. of Bankruptcies, 34 Red Lion square
2..Register Of. for Shipping,50Broad st
36..Registry of Colonial Slaves, 13 James st, Buckingham gate
7..Registry of Deeds Of. for the County of Middlesex, 23 Bell yd,Tmpl bar
3..Registry Shipping Of. 4 Castle ct, Birchin lane
2..Remembrancer's Of. Guildhall yd
7..Report Of. New bdgs, Chancery la
3..River Dee Of. 6 Royal Exch gallery
7..Rolls Of. Chancery lane
20..Royal Academy of Arts, Somerset pl
36..Royal Baths, Cork st, Bond st
3..Royal Exchange, Cornhill
20..Royal Marine Pay Of. 14 Buckingham st, Strand
66..Royal Military Asylum, Chelsea
..Royal Military Academy, Woolwich
20..Royal Society, Somerset place
3..Russia Company, over Royal Exch
36..St. James's Palace, W. end of Park
53..St. Marylebone Burial Ground, Paddington street
37..St. Marylebone Court House, 157 Oxford street
20..Salt Of. Somerset house
7..Scottish Corporation Of. Crane ct, Fleet street
3..Sea Policy Stamp Of.50 Lombard st
20..Seal Of. Somerset pl, Strand
6..Secondaries Of. King's Bench walk, Temple
2..Secondaries Of. to the Sheriffs of London, 28 Coleman st, Cheapside
7..Secretary of Bankrupts Of. Quality court, Chancery lane
20..Secretary of State's Of. Whitehall
2..Sewers&Commissioners Of Guildhl
29..Shadwell Water Works, Pope's hill, from 75 High street
2..Sheriffs of London Of. Coleman st, Cheapside
22..Sheriffs of Middlesex Of. 24 Red Lion square
20..Sheriffs of Surrey Of. 8 New Inn
2..Ship Owners Society, Nw Broad st
35..Sick & Wounded Officers Transport Of. Dorset sq, Cannon rw,Westm
20..Sick and Hurt Seamen's Of. Somerset house

Ref. to Plan.
3..Sierra Leone Company, Birchin la
20..Signet Of. Somerset pl, Somerset h
2..Sion College, London wall
7..Six Clerks Of. op. 61 Chancery lane
14..Sixpenny Receiver's Hall, Tower hl
13..Sixpenny Duty Of. for Greenwich Hospital, Trinity square
7..Sixpenny Writ Of. Bell yd, Fleet st
17..Skin market, Gt. Suffolk st, Boro
7..Society for Promoting Christian Knowledge, Bartlett's bds, Holbn
2..Society of British North American Merchants, 35 Gt Winchester st
2..Society for Promoting Religious Knowledge among the Poor, Foundershall, Lothbury
6..Society of Guardians for the Protection of Trade against Swindlers and Sharpers, 36 Essex st, Strand
20..Society for the Encouragement of Arts, Manufactures, &c. Adelphi, Strand
7..Society for Prosecuting Felons and for Defraying the Expence of Advertisements, &c. 11 Gray's Inn
20..Society for the Improvement of Medical Knowledge, St. Martin's la
2..Society of Ship Owners, Of. 33 New Broad street
20..Solicitor's Of. to the Commissioners of Stamps, Somerset place
20..Somerset house, Strand
18..South London Gas Works, 2d station, 22 Caroline st, Blackfriars
49..South London Water Works, near Vauxhall
2..South Sea House, Old Broad st
3..South Sea Chambers, 41 Threadndl st
2..Southwark Bridge Company, Maiden lane, Cheapside
4..Southwark Water Works, Park st, Borough
20..Stage Coach Duty Of. Somerset h
20..Stamp Of. Somerset house
20..State Paper Of. Whitehall
35..Stationary Of. James's st, Buckingham gate
7..Stationers' Hall, near Ludgate st
22..Stewards Of. for Gray's Inn, Gray's Inn square
2..Stock Exchange, Capel ct, Bartholomew lane
7..Subpoena Of. Roll's yd, Chancery la
20..Surveyor of Crown Lands Of. Somerset house
20..Tax Of. Somerset House
15..Tax Of. 230 Bermondsey st
6..Tenths Of. Garden ct, Temple
13..Tower Hamlet Sewer Of. Gt Alie st
14..Tower, end of Minories
2..Town Clerk's Of. of City, Guildhall
35..Transport Of. Cannon rw, Westmr
7..Treasurer for the County of Middlesex Of. 12 Staple Inn
20..Treasury Of. Whitehall

Ref. to Plan.
14..Trinity house, Gt Tower hill
3..Turkey Company, Salter's hall, Cannon street
5..Vicar General's Of. 1 Bell yard, Doctors Commons
20..Victualling Of. Somerset house
20..War Of. Horse Guards, Whitehall
6..Warrant of Attorney's Of Pump ct, Middle Temple
20..Waterloo Bridge Of. 8 Beaufort buildings, Strand
2..Waterloo Subscription, Winchester House, Broad st, City
20..West India Commissioners' Of. Spring gardens
2..West India Committee Rooms, 23 New City Chambers
13..West India Dock Compny, Billiter sq
36..Western Exchange, 10 Old Bond st
37..West Middlesex Water Works, 51 Berner st, Oxford st
20..Westminster Coal Meters Of. 15 Northumberland st, Strand
35..Westminster Hall, New Palace yd
20..Westminster Library, Panton sq
20..Whitehall, Charing cross
20..Wine Licence Of. Somerset house
3..Wittington College, College hill
20..York Buildings Water Works, Villiers street, Strand

CHARITABLE INSTITUTIONS, ASYLUMS, &c.

20..African and Asiatic Society for the Relief and Instruction of Poor (late the African Society) 4 Spur st
9..Aged Pilgrim's Friend, 19 Peartree street, Goswell st
33..Aged and Infirm Protestant Dissenting Ministers Society (for the Relief of) 14 Penton st, Walworth
18..Asylum, Westminster bridge road
17..Blind Asylum, London rd, opposite the Obelisk
32..Deaf & Dumb Asylum, Old Kent rd
22..Foundling Hospitl, Lambs Conduit st
29..Guardian Society's Asylum, New rd, St. George's East
40..London Female Penitentiary, Pentonville
12..London Orphan Asylum, 10 St. Mary Axe
17..Magdalen Asylum, Blackfriars road
34..Millbank Penitentiary, Vauxhall brdg
..Naval Asylum, Greenwich
17..New Bethlem, St. George's fields
27..Refuge for Destitute Females, Hackney road
10..Refuge for Destitute Men, Hoxton
9..St. Luke's Lunatic Asylum, Old st

HOSPITALS, DISPENSARIES, INFIRMARIES, &c.

39..Asylum for the Recovery of Health, Tonbridge pl, New rd, St. Pancras

Ref. to Plan.

20..Benevolent Institution, Castle ct, Strand
34..Bethlehem Hospital, Lambeth
21..Bloomsbury Dispensary, 62 Great Russsell st
6..Bridewell Hospital, New Bridge st
21..British Lying-in Hospital, 34 Brown-low st, Long Acre
21..Central Lying-in Charity & Dispensary, Gt Queen st, Lincoln's Inn fds
2..Charitable Fund and Dispensary, 87 London wall
2..Charitable Fund and Dispensary, Lilliput lane, London wall
8..Christ's Hospital, 108 Newgate st
9..City of London Lying-in Hospital, City road
8 & 3..City of London Truss Society, 87 Hatton garden, and Grocers Hall ct, Poultry
3..City Dispensary, Grocers hall, Poulty
8..Corporation of the Caledonian Asylum, for the Support and Education of the Children of Soldiers & Sailors, 16 Cross st, Hatton gdn
2..Dispensary for Diseases in the Eye, Moorfields
2..Dispensary for Relieving sick Poor. at their own Habitations, Aldermanbury
13..Eastern Medical Dispensary, Great Alie street
35..Emanuel Hospital, James st, Westm
37..Endeavour and Benevolent Lying-in Society, Oxford st
24..Finsbury Dispensary, St John st, Clerkenwell
8..Finsbury New Central Dispensary, West Smithfield
22..Foundling Hospital, Guildford st, Gray's Inn lane
9..French Hospital, Pesthouse row, Old st, near St. Luke's
36..General Dispensary, 14 Old Burlington street
1..General Dispensary, Aldersgate st
18. General Lying-in Hospital, Bridge road, Lambeth
15..Guy's Hospital, St. Thomas st, Boro
10..Haberdashers' Hospital, Haberdashers' walk
9..Hospital for French Protestants, Old st, St. Luke's
38..Infirmary, Marybn, nr York pl, New rd
21..Infirmary, (Royal Metropolitan) for Sick Children, Soho
21..Infirmary for Diseases of the Spine and Joints, Upper St. Martin's la
3..Infirmary, (Royal Sea Bathing) 33 Walbrook
11..Infirmary for Asthmas and Consumptions, Union st, Bishopsgate
32..Institution for the Cure of Cancers, Kent road nr Elephant & Castle

Bef. to Plan.

39..Institution for the Cure and Prevention of Contagious Fevers near the Metropolis, St. Pancras
28..Jews' Hospital, (Dutch) Mile End
28..Jews' Hospital, (Portuguese) nearly opposite the last, Mile End
52..Lock Hospital, Grosvenor place, Hyde park corner
12..London Dispensary, Artillery street, Bishopsgate
9..London Electrical Dispnsary, City rd
28..London Hospital, Whitechapel rd
8..London Infirmary for the Eye, Charterhouse square
2..London Opthalmic Infirmry, Moorfds
39..London Smallpox and Fever Hospital, St. Pancras
14..London Vaccine Institution, Burr st, East Smithfield
5..Lying-in Charity, 17 Lit. Knightridr st
10..Lying-in Hospital, south corner of Old st road, City road
37..Middlesex Hospital, Charles street, Goodge st, Tottenham court rd
37..National Vaccine Establishment, 18 Percy st, Rathbone place
5..National Vaccine Establishment, Gt Surry st, Blackfriars road
53..Northern Dispensary, South row, New road
54..Opthalmic Hospital, Regent's park
29..Provident Female Society, for the Relief of Married Lying-in Women 2 Lower Chapman st, Cannon st rd
7..Public Dispensary, Bishop's court, Chancery lane
2..Public Dispensary, Carey st, Foster la
53..Queen Charlotte's Lying-in Hospital, Homer place, New rd
68..Queen's Lying-in Hospital, Manor house, Lisson green
29..Raine's Hospital, St. George's East, op. end of Charles st, Old Gravel la
22..Royal Dispensary for Diseases of the Ear, Dean st, Soho
67..Royal Humane Society, for Recovering Persons apparently Drowned, Hyde park
36..Royal Infirmary, for Diseases of the Eye, Cork st, Bond st
14..Royal Jennerian Society, Burr st, East Smithfield
5..Royal Universal Dispensary for Children, 5 St. Andrew's hill
21..Royal Westminster Infirmary for Diseases of the Eye, Nassau st, Gerrard street
36..Royal Westminster Infirmary, for. Diseases of the Eye, Marylebone st.
8..St. Bartholomew's Hospital, West Smithfield
36..St. George's and St James's Dispensary, 14 Old Burlington street, Bond street
52..St. George's Hospital, Hyde park cor

Ref. to Plan.

37..St James's Infirmary, Poland st
10..St. Luke's Hospital, north side Old street, near the City road
37..St. Marylebone General Dispensary, 77 Wellbeck st
15..St. Thomas's Hospital, High st, Boro
52..Samaritan Society, Office in the London Hospital
17..South London Dispensary, 1 Lmbh rd
16..Surrey Dispensary, Union st, Boro
29..Universal Medical Dispensary, O.d Gravel lane, Ratcliffe
14..Universal Medical Institution, Tower hamlets
15..Vaccine Establishment for the Cow Pock, Park st, Horselydown
37..Vaccine Pock Institution, 42 Broad st, Golden square
20..Western Dispensary, 33 Charles st, Covent garden
37..Western Dispensary and Lying-in hospital, 24 Gt Marlborough st
20..West London Infirmary and Lying-in Institution, Charing cross
21..Westminster General Dispensary, 32 Gerrard street, Soho
35..Westminster Hospital, James st, Westminster
35..Westminster Infirmary, James st, Westminster
18..Westminster Lying-in Hospital, Westminster bridge road
51..York Hospital, Ebury st, Pimlico

WORKHOUSES, ALMS-HOUSES, &c.

1..Aldersgate Workhouse, 129 Aldergt st
12..Aldgate Workhouse, 138 Houndsditch
11..Allen's or Allan's Almshouses, Lamb alley, nr 144 Bishopsgate st witht
9..Alleyn's Almshouses, Bath st, City rd
35..Alley's Almshouses, Gt St. Anne's st, Westminster
12..Almshouse for Six Poor Men, 37 Great St. Helen's
9..Amias Almshouses, George yd, Old st
2..Armourers & Braziers' Almshouses, Bottle Alley, Bishopsgate
15..Bermondsey Workhouse, Russell st, Borough
11..Bethnal Green Workhouse, east end of Hare st, Brick lane
12..Bishopsgate Poorhouse, Rose alley, near 31 Bishopsgate st
11..Bishopsgate Workhouse, Dunning's alley, near 151 Bishopsgate
35..Black Coat Almshouses, Westminsr, west side St. Margaret's church
50..Blake's Almshouses, Vauxhall, near the turnpike
5..Christ Church Almshouses, Green walk, Blackfriars
5..Christ Church Workhouse, Windmill place, Blackfriars rd
36..City Workhouse, Hoxton

Bef. to Plan.

23..Clerkenwell Workhouse, Coppice rw
40..Clothworkers' Almshouses, Islington
28..Cooke's (Capt) Almshouses, Mile end
29..Cooke's Almshouses, south side Church yd, Spring st, Shadwell
45..Cooper's Almshouses, School lane, Brook st, Ratcliffe   [land st
36..Covent Garden Workhouse, Cleve-
2..Cripplegate Workhouse, New Union street, Moorfields
15..Cure's Hospital, Deadman's place
35..Dacre's Almshouses, Lit. Chapel st
26 & 17..Diaper's Almshouses, Kingsland road and Hill st, Wellington street, Blackfriars
10..Dulwich Almshouses, north west corner of St. Luke's Hospital
11..Dulwich Almshouses, Lamb's alley, Bishopsgate street
11..Dutch Almshouses, Crown st, Finsby
5..Edward's Almshouses, Church st, Blackfriars
35..Emery Hill's Almshouses, middle of Rochester row, Westminster
33..Fishmongers' Almshouses, Newington Butts, op. Elephant & Castle
26..Frame Knitters' Almshouses, Kingsland road
28..Fullers' Almshouses, Mile End rd
11..Garrett's Almshouses, Elder street, Whitelion st, Spitalfields
9..Girdler's Almshouses, Bath st, City rd
9..Girdler's Almshouses, for Almsmen's widows, Richmond st, St. Luke's
27..Goldsmith's Almshouses, Hackny rd
10..Haberdashers' Almshouses, Hoxtn fd
7..Haberdashers' Almshouses, 62 Snowhill, Skinner street
60..Haw's Almshouses, Bow la, Poplar
18..Hedge's Almshouses, 20 Webber rw, Blackfriars road
17..Hill's (Rev. R.) Almshouses, Hill st, Wellington st, Blackfriars
11..Hillier's Almshouses, Curtain rd
1..Hinton's Almshouses, Plough alley, Barbican
5..Hopton's Almshouses, Green walk, Blackfriars
9..Hospital for Poor French Protestants, Bath st, City road
2..Hospital for Ten Poor Men and Women, Philip lane, London wall
26..Ironmongers' Almshouses, Kingsland road
25..Islington Workhouse, 20 Lower st, Islington
12..Judd's Almshouses, Gt St. Helen's, Bishopsgate
2..Leathersellers' Almshouses, Clark's court, Bishopsgate
45..Limehouse Workhouse, Narrow st
9..Lumbley's Almshouses, City rd, north side Shepherd & Shepherdess
12..Megg's Almshouses, 228 Whchpl rd
45..Mercer's Almshouses, Stepney

Ref. to Plan.

35..Merchant Tailors' Almshouses, Princes st, Westminster

28..Mile End Poorhouse, near the Old Globe, Mile End

4..Overman's Almshouses, Montague close, St. Saviour's Church, Boro

24..Owen's (Lady) Almshouses, Goswell street road

1..Quaker's Poorhouse, Goswell st

44..Ratcliff Workhouse, Whitehorse st, Stepney

35..Red Lion Almshouses, York street, Westminster

1..Roger's Almshouses, Hart street, Monkwell street

7..Roll's Workhouse, north end of Acorn st, Roll's buildings

46..Rotherhithe Workhouse, Lower rd, Deptford

7..St. Andrew's Workhouse,41 Shoe la

24..St. Andrew's Workhouse, Clerkwll

22..St. Andrew's Workhouse, Holborn, and St. George the Martyr

21..St. Anne'sWorkhouse,1 Rose st,Soho

21..St. Clement's Poorhouse, Portugal street, Lincoln's Inn fields

14..St. Dunstan's Workhouse, St. Dunstan's hill

52..St. George's Hanover square Workhouse, Mount st, Grosvenor sq

21..St. Giles's New, 185 High Holborn

21..St. Giles's Workhouse, 55 Broad st, Bloomsbury

15..St. John's and St. Olave's Workhouse, Parish st, Horselydown

30..St. John's Workhouse, Bird st, Wppg

9..St. Luke's Workhouse, west side Shepherd and Shepherdess,City rd

35..St. Margaret's Workhouse, Orchard street, Westminster

37..St. Martin's Almshouses, Crown st, Soho

20..St. Martin's Workhouse, Hemming's row

53..St. Marylebone Workhouse, Northumberland street

12..St. Saviour's Almshouses, opposite 16 Gravel lane

8..St. Sepulchre's Workhouse, West Smithfield

29..Shadwell Workhouse, north side of Union st, Shadwell High st

1..Sir Ambrose Nicholas' Almshouses, Monkwell st, Cripplegate

1..Sir Thomas Gresham's Almshouses, City green yard, Whitecross st

1..Sir Wm. Staines's Almshouses, Paul's alley, Jewin st

28..Skinners' Almshouses, near Mile End turnpike

27..Spitalfields Workhouse, Thomas's street, Mile End

23. Stafford's Almshouses,Gray's Inn la

9..Tabernacle Almshouses, west side the Tabernacle, City road

Ref. to Plan.

28..TrinityAlmshouses,nr Mile End trpk

5..Upton's Almshouses, 4 Green walk, Blackfriars road

44..Vintners' Almshouses, half a mile below Mile End turnpike

10..Walter's Almshouses, Old st road, near Shoreditch

48..Walworth Workhouse, near the Montpellier Tea Gardens

11..Weavers' Almshouses, St. John st, Spitalfields

10..Westby's Almshouses, north end of Gloucester terrace, Hoxton

13..Whitechapel Workhouse, a little below the Church

2..White's Almshouses, White's alley, Coleman street

23..White's Almshouses, Gray's Inn la

35..Woolstaplers' Almshouses, Great St. Anne's st, Westminster

COMPANY'S HALLS.

6..Apothecaries, Water la, Blackfriars

2..Armourers, Coleman st, Old Jewry

14..Bakers, Harp lane, Tower st

1..Barber Surgeons, Monkwell st

28..Bonner's Hall, Bethnal green

2..Brewers, Addle st, Cheapside

3..Bricklayers, Leadenhall st

3..Butchers,Pudding la, Lit Eastcheap

2..Carpenters, 75 London wall

13..Clothworkers, Mincing lane

1..Coach and Coach Harness makers, Noble st, Falcon square

3..Commercial Dock Company, 106 Fenchurch street

14..Coopers, Basinghall street

4..Copper Company, 12 Up. Thames st

3..Cordwainers, 14 Gt Distaff lane

2..Curriers, 5 London wall

3..Cutlers, 5 Cloak lane

2..Distillers, Drapers'Hall;Thrgmtn st

2..Drapers, 27 Throgmorton st

3..Dyers, Elbow lane, Dowgate hill

2..Embroiderers' Hall, 36 Gutter la, Cheapside

3..Fellowship Porters' Hall, St. Mary at hill

3..Felt Makers, at Pewterers' Hall

3..Fishmongers, Up. Thames st, near London bridge

3..Founders, Lothbury

2..Girdlers, 44 Basinghall street

3..Goldsmiths, 16 Foster lane, Cheapsd

3..Grocers, Grocers Hall ct,36 Poultry

2..Haberdashers, 8 Maiden la,Wood st

3..Hatband Makers, Cutler's Hall, Cloak lane

3..Innholders, Lit.Elbow la,Dowgthill

3..Ironmongers, Fenchurch st

4..Joiners, Upper Thames st

2..Leather Sellers, St. Helen's place, Bishopsgate

2..Masons, Masons' al, Basinghall st

3..Mercers, Ironmonger la, Cheapside

Ref. to Plan.
3..Merchant Tailors, Threadneedle st
3..Painter Stainers, Lit. Trinity lane
2..Parish Clerks, Wood st, Cheapside
3..Pewterers, 17 Lime st, Leadenhall st
2..Pin Makers, Pinnor ct, Broad st
2..Plasterers, Addle st, Cheapside
3..Plumbers, Chequer yd, Dowgt hill
2..Saddlers, Cheapside
3..Salters Hall, St. Swithin's lane
3..Skinners, Dowgate hill
3..Starch Makers, incorporated with
  the Grocers Company
7..Stationers, Stationers hall,Ludgt st
3..Tallow Chandlers, Dowgate hill
4..Vintners, Upper Thames st
4..Upholders, Crane ct, St. Peters hill
3..Watermens, St. Mary at hill
2..Wax Chandlers, Maiden la,Wood st
2..Weavers, Basinghall st

COURTS OF JUSTICE.

35..Common Pleas, New Palace yard,
  Westminster
5..Court of Arches, or Ecclesiastical
  Court, Doctors Commons
35..Exchequer, New Palace yd,Westmr
5..High Court of Admiralty Doc Com
21..Insolvent Debtors, 5 Portugal st,
  Lincoln's Inn fields
35..King's Bench, Westminster
21..Lord Chancellors, Lincoln's Inn
3..Lord Mayors, Royal Exchange
35..Palace Court, Scotland yard
7..Rolls, Chancery lane
24..Sessions House, Clerkenwell green
7..Sessions House, Old Bailey
33..Sessions House for Surrey,Newngtn
21..Vice Chancellors, Lincoln's Inn

INNS OF COURT.

7..Bernard's, Holborn
20..Clements, 3 Pickett st, Strand
7..Clifford's, 187 Fleet st
7..Furnival's, op. Middle row, Holbn
22..Gray's, 134 High Holborn
7..Lincoln's, 40 Chancery lane
20..Lyon's, Newcastle st, Strand
20..New Inn, Wych st, Strand
7..Serjeant's, 4 Chancery lane
7..Serjeant's, Fleet street
7..Staple's, Holborn
7..Symond's, Chancery lane
6..Temple, Fleet street s
7..Thavie's, Holborn

PLACES OF AMUSEMENT.

36..Almack's Rooms,King st,St,James's
37..Argyle Rooms, Argyle st,Oxford st
20..Baker's Panorama, Leicester sq,
  and Strand
20..Exeter Change Menagerie, Strand
37..Hanover Music Rooms, Hanover sq
20..Miss Linwood's Exhibition of Needle
  Work, Leicester square
20..Royal Wax Work, 67 Strand

Ref. to Plan.
34..Vauxhall gardens, Lambeth
36..Waterloo Exhibition Rooms, 94
  Pall Mall
36..Willis's Rooms,King st, St. James's

THEATRES.

20..Adelphi, (late Sanspareil) Strand
18..Cobourg, end of the Waterloo rd,
  Great Charlotte street
21..Covent Garden, Bow st, Covent gdn
19..Davis's (late Astley's)Amphitheatre
  Westminster bridge
21..Drury lane,Brydges st, Covent gdn
20..English Opera House, Strand
36..Haymarket,Haymarket,Cockspur st
36..King's or Italian Opera House,
  Haymarket
20..Lyceum or English Opera House,
  Strand
20..Olympic, Wych st, Strand
13..Royalty or East London, Wellclose sq
24..Saddler's Wells, Spafields
17..Surrey, end of Blackfriars rd
37..West London,Tottenham st,Tot ct rd

PLACES OF WORSHIP.

CHURCHES AND CHAPELS OF EASE.

3..All Hallows, 48 Lombard st
2..All Hallows, London wall
3..All Hallows, Bread street
4..All Hallows, 88 Upper Thames st
14..All Hallows, Barking,54Gt Tower st
13..All Hallows, Staining Church,
  Mark lane
60..All Saints, Poplar
21..Bedford Chapel,Charlotte st,Blmsby
53..Brunswick Chapel of Ease to St.
  Mary le Bone, 13 Upper Berkley st
  Portman square
33..Carlisle Chapel, Kennington lane
37..Chapel of Ease,60King st,Golden sq
20..Chapel of Ease to St. Martin's in the
  Fields, Spring gardens
53..Chapel of Ease to St. George's
  Hanover sq, Lower Connaught
  terrace, Bayswater
37..Chapel of Ease, Langham place,
  Portland place
22..Chapel of Ease to St. Pancras, Tavistock st, Russell square
36..Chapel of Ease to St. James's,
  Westminster, 173 Regent st
35..Chapel of Ease, Broadway, Westm
36..Chapel Royal, St. James's
12..Christ's Church, Spitalfields, 69
  Bishopsgate st
5..Christ's, Gt Surrey st, Blackfriars
8..Christ's, Newgate st
37..Episcopal Chapel, Gt Portland st
37..Episcopal Chapel, Vere st,Oxford st
37..Episcopal Margaret st,Cavendish sq
53..Episcopal, Welbeck chapel, Marybn
53..Episcopal, Baker st, Portman sq

Ref. to Plan.

38..Fitzroy Chapel, London st,Tot ct rd
13..Holy Trinity, Minories
34..Lambeth, Church st, Lambeth
53 .Marylebone Chapel of Ease, High st
53..New Church, Wyndham place, Bryanstone square
19..New Church,Waterloo bridge road
36..New Church, Regent st
37..New Church,Langham pl,Marybone
36..New Church, Stafford st, Marybone
63..New Church,Addington sq,Cambrwl
27..New Church, Hackney
34..New Church, Norwood, Lambeth
50..New Church, Brixton, Lambeth
33..New Church, Kennington
32..New Church, Beckford rw,Nwingtn
9..New Church, Old st, St. Luke's
38..New Church, Somerstown
53..Paddington Chapel of Ease,Homer pl
37..Percy Chapel, of Esse, Charlotte st,
   Rathbone place
2..St. Alban's, Wood st, Cheapside
9..St. Alphage, London wall
7..St. Andrew's, 64 Holborn hill
3..St. Andrew's Undershaft, Leadenhall street
5..St. Andrew's Wardrobe, St. Andrew's hill, Doctors Commons
1..St. Anne and St, Agnes, St. Anne's
   lane, Foster lane
37..St. Anne's, Dean st, Soho
60..St. Anne's, Commrl, rd,Limehouse
1..St. Anne's, Aldersgate st
3..St. Antholin, Budge row, Cannon st
3..St. Augustine's, Watling st
2..St. Bartholomew, Bartholomew la
8..St. Bartholomew the Great,WSmhfd
8..St. Bartholomew the Less,W Smthfd
5..St. Benedict, Bennett's hill
3..St. Bennet Fink,Threadneedle st
3..St. Bennett's, Gracechurch st
2..St. Botolph's, 165 Bishopsgate st
13..St. Botolph's, Aldgate
1..St. Botolph's, Aldersgate st
7..St. Bride's, Bride lane, Fleet st
3..St. Catherine's Coleman,Fenchrh st
3..St. Catherine's Cree,.Leadenhall st
14..St. Catherine's, Little Tower hill
3..St. Clement's,Clement's lane, Lombard street
20..St. Clement's Dane, Strand
3..St Clement's, Eastcheap
3..St. Dionis Back Church, Lime st
45..St. Dunstan's, Stepney
14..St. Dunstan's in the East, St. Dunstan's hil , Lower Thames st
7..St. Dunstan's in the West,Fleet st
3..St. Edmund the King, Lombard st
11..St. Ethelburga, Bishopsgate within
3..St. George's, Botolph lane
36..St. George's,Albemarle st,Piccadlly
37..St. George's, George st, Hanover sq
22..St. George the Martyr, Queen sq,
   Bloomsbury
16..St. George the Martyr, 1Blackman st

Ref. to Plan.

29..St. George's in the E. Ratcliff highw
17..St George's Chapel, London road
21. St. George's, Hart st, Bloomsbury
21..St. Giles's in the Fields, Broad st,
   Bloomsbury
1..St. Giles's without,Fore st,Cripplegt
1..St. Gile's, Redcross st, Cripplegate
12..St. Helen's, Great St. Helen's,
   Bishopsgate street
36..St. James's, Jermyn st, St. James's
38..St. James's Chapel, Hampstead rd
13..St. James's, Duke's st, Aldgate
3..St. James's, Garlick hill, Upper
   Thames street
24..St. James's, Clerkenwell
36..St. James's Westminster, York st,
   Pall Mall
24..St. John's, Clerkenwell
37..St. John's, Marylebone
20..St. John's the Baptist, Savoy
15..St. John's the Evangelist,Horselyda
35..St. John's the Evangelist, Millbank
69..St. John's Chapel, north west side
   of Regent's Park
29..St. John's, High st. Wapping
23..St. John's Chapel, Millman st
2..St. Lawrence's,north end King's st,
   Cheapside
11..St. Leonard's, Shoreditch
63..St. Luke's, Chelsea
10..St. Luke's, N. side Old st,St.Luke's
29..St. Luke's Chapel of Ease, near
   Ratcliff highway
3..St. Magnus, near London bridge
2..St. Margaret's, Lothbury
35..St. Margaret's, nr Westminsr abbey
3..St. Margaret Pattens, Rood lane,
   Fenchurch street
3..St. Mary Abchurch, Abchurch lane
3..St Mary Aldermary, Bow lane
53..St. Mary at Bourn,High st,Marylebn
2..St. Mary Colechurch, Old Jewry
2..St. Mary le Bow, Cheapside
53..St. Mary le Bone, Newrd,Paddingtn
20..St. Mary le Strand, or New Church,
   Strand
15..St. Mary Magdalen, Bermondsey st
4..St. Mary Magdalen, Old Fish st hill
3..St Mary Woolnorth, Lombard st
3..St. Mary at Hill, Lower Thames st,
34..St. Mary's, Lambeth
2..St. Mary's, Love lane, Aldermanby
12..St. Mary's, St. Mary Axe
12..St. Mary's, High st, Whitechapel
4..St. Mary's Somer Hythe, Upper
   Thames street
25..St. Mary's, Islington
33..St. Mary's, Newington Butts
68..St. Mary's, Paddington
20..St. Martin's in the Fields, St. Mar
   tin's lane
7..St. Martin's, Ludgate hill
21..St. Martin's in the Fields Chapel of
   of Ease, Broad ct, Long Acre
3..St. Martin's Outwich Threadneedl st

Ref. to Plan.
3..St. Matthew's, Friday st, Cheapsd
11..St. Matthews, Hare st, Spitalfields
27..St. Matthews, Bethnal green
3..St. Michael's, Cornhill
2..St. Michael's, Wood st, Cheapsd
3..St. Michaels, Crooked la, Cannon st
3..St. Michael's, Royal, College hill
2..St. Michael'sBassishaw,Basinghl st
3..St. Michael's, Queenhithe, Little
 Trinity lane
3..St. Mildred's, Poultry
3..St. Mildred's, Bread st
4..St. Nicholas Cole Abbey,Old Fish st
4..St. Nicholas Olave, Bread st hill
3..St. Olaves, Old Jewry
1..St. Olaves, Silver st, Wood st
15..St. Olave's, Tooley st, Borough
13..St. Olave's, Hart st, Crutched friars
38..St. Pancras(new)New rd,St Pancrs
39..St. Pancras (old) St. Pancras
7..St. PAUL'S CATHEDRAL, top
 of Ludgate hill
20..St. Paul's, Covent garden
29..St. Paul's, Shadwell
14..St. Peter ad Vincula, Tower
3..St. Peter's, Cornhill
2..St. Peter le Poor, Broad st, City
36..St. Phillips' Chapel, Regent street,
 Piccadilly
4..St. Saviour's, Church st, Borough
6..St. Sepulchre's,Skinner st,Snowhill
2..St. Stephen's, Coleman st
3..St. Stephen's Wallbrook, Back of
 Mansion House
3..St. Swithin's, London Stone,
 Cannon street
2..St. Vedast's, Foster la, Cheapside
20..Savoy Precinct, Savoy, Strand
6..Temple Church, Inner Temple lane
36..Trinity Chapel, Conduit st, Bond st
13..Trinity, Little Minories
35..WESTMINSTER ABBEY, or Col
 legiate Church of St. Peter, Parliament street
20..Whitehall Chapel, Whitehall

FOREIGN PROTESTANT CHURCHES AND CHAPELS.

12..Armenian, Prince's row, Spitalfields
36..Bavarian, Warwick st, Golden sq
13..Danish, centre of Wellclose sq
2..Dutch, Austin friars
36..Dutch, St. James's palace
21..French, Crown st, Soho
3..French, Threadneedle st
2..French, Austin friars
3..French, Cannon street
12..French, Parliament ct, Artillery st,
 Bishopsgate
27..French, St. John's ct,Bethnal green
12..French, Brick lane, Spitalfields
36..German, St. James's palace
20..German Lutheran, Savoy, Strand

Ref. to Plan.
7..German, Ludgate hill
3..German, Little Trinity lane
2..German, Austin friars
13..German, Little Alie street
12..German, Brown's lane, Spitalfields
21..Helvetic. Moor st, Seven Dials
29..Swedes, Prince's sq,Ratcliffe highw
21..Swiss, Moor st, Seven Dials

DISSENTERS' CHAPELS.

ARIANS.

1..Jewin st, Aldersgate street

BAPTISTS.

32..Alfred pl. Kent-road
15..Blackfields, Horselydown
53..Blanford st, Manchester square
31..Bermondsey, King John's court
15..Carter lane, Tooley street
39..Chapel path, Somerstown
66..Paradise Chapel, Chelsea
5..Church st, Blackfriars
7..Clement's lane, Strand
15..Crosby row, Snowsfields
15..Dean st, Tooley st
12..Devonshire sq, Bishopsgate st
21..Dudley st, Soho
5..Duke st, Stamford st, Blackfriars
22..Eagle st, Red Lion square
37..Edward st, Soho.
17..Ewer st, Borough
7..Elim ct, Fetter lane
21..Grafton st, Soho
30..Jamaica row, Rotherhithe
16..Kent st, Southwark
22..Keppel st, Russel square
35..Lewisham st, Westminster
15..Maze pond, Southwark
15..Meeting House Walk, Snowsfields
9..Mitchel st, Old st
34..Paradise row, Lambeth
13..Prescott st, Goodman's fields
16..Queen st, Southwark
1..Redcross st, Cripplegate
53..Shouldham st, Edgware road
24..Spencer pl, Goswell st road
12..Still alley, Houndsditch
16..Gt. Suffolk st, Borough
10..Tabernacle walk, Finsbury
15..Unicorn yd, Tooley street
32..Walworth
21..Wild st, (Lit.) Lincoln's Inn fields
2..Wood st, London wall
36..York st, St. James's

BAPTIST AND UNITARIAN.

11..Worship st, Finsbury

BEERSHEBA.

17..Prospect pl, St. George's fields

CAMBRIAN UNION SOCIETY.

15..Fair st, Horselydown

N

CALVINISTS.

Including Independents.

Ref. to Plan.
2..Albion chapel, Moorfields [Scotch]
2..Aldermanbury postern
1..Aldersgate st, Glasshouse yard
12..Artillery st, Bishopsgate st
13..Alie st, Goodman's fields
15..Back st, Horselydown
7..Baker's court, Holborn
1..Barbican
28..Bethnal green
12..Boar's Head court, Petticoat lane
16..Borough Chapel, Upper Chapel ct,
    124 Borough High st
12..Brick la, Spitalfields
2..Broad st, [New] Bishopsgate
44..Bull lane, Stepney
38..Burton Crescent
13..Bury st, St. Mary Axe
13..Cable street
12..Camomile st, Bishopsgate
37..Chapel st, Soho
28..Church st, Mile end
9..City road, at the Orphan school
16..Collier's rents, Long lane, Southwk
40..Claremont Chapel, Angel terrace,
    near the Angel, Islington
8..Cross st, Hatton garden (Scotch)
21..Crown ct, Little Russell st
11..Cumberland st, Curtain road
7..Fetter lane
2..Founders' hall, Lothbury
21..Gate st, Lincoln's Inn fields
27..Gibraltar Chapel, Gibraltar row
5..Green walk, Blackfriars road
1..Grub street
63..Hanover Chapel, Peckham
1..Hare ct, Aldersgate street
12..Hope st, Spitalfields
26..Hoxton Academy
31..Jamaica row, Rotherhithe
1..Jewin street
13..Jewry st, Aldgate
30..Johnson's st, Old Gravel lane
29..Leading st, Shadwell
7..Leather lane, Holborn
3..Little Eastcheap
32..Lock's fields
17..London road
2..London wall [Scotch]
13..Mark lane
37..Market st, May fair
1..Middlesex ct, Bartho'omew close
3..Miles lane, Cannon st [Scotch]
21..New Court, Carey street
33..Newington Butts
39..New road, Claremont Chapel, Pen-
    tonville
68..New road, Paddington
39..New road, Somers town
29..New road, St. George's in the East
14..Nightingale lane, East Smithfield
3..Oxford court, Cannon st
35..Palace st, Pimlico

Ref. to Plan.
2..Pavement, Moorfields
13..Pell st, Ratcliffe highway
37..Peter's st, Soho [Scotch]
3..Poultry
29..Rose lane, Ratcliffe
15..Salisbury st, Bermondsey
3..Salter's hall court, Oxford court
13..Shakespeare's walk, Shadwell
7..Shoe lane, Fleet street
2..Silver st, Falcon square
2..Staining lane, Cheapside
4..Three Crane lane, Thames street
7..Trinity Chapel, Leather lane
16..Union st, Borough
30..Wapping
32..West lane, Walworth
37..Well's st, Oxford st [Scotch]
68..Wharf road, Paddington
12..White's row, Spitalfields
30..Floating Chapel, Old Wapping stairs

LADY HUNTINGDON'S.

20..Adelphi, Strand
20..Orange st, Leicester square
31..Grange road
7..Gray's Inn lane
39..John's st, Somerstown

METHODISTS (WESLEYAN).

63..Camberwell
34..China terrace, Lambeth
34..Church st, Lambeth
9..City road
5..Duke st, Stamford st, Blackfriars
12..Eagle st, Spitalfields
37..Fitzroy Chapel, London st, Tot-
    tenham court road
29..Free Chapel, 2 Lower Chapman st,
21..Great Queen st, Lincoln's Inn fds
14..Gainsford st, Borough
11..Hackney road
53..Hind st, Manchester square
11..Holywell mount, Shoreditch
45..Horseferry road
26..Hoxton
18..Lambeth Chapel, Canterbury place
7..Leather lane, Holborn
45..Limehouse
2..Little St. Helen's
16..Long lane, Borough
32..Walworth
8..Wilderness row, Goswell st

METHODISTS (WHITFIELD).

5..Blackfriars road
11..Cumberland st, Curtain road
24..Spafields Chapel
10..Tabernacle walk, Finsbury
30..Tottenham court road

MORAVIANS (UNITED BRE-THREN.)

7..Fetter lane

PHILADELPHIA UNIVER-SALISTS.

10..Windmill st, Finsbury

PHILANTHROPIC.
Ref. to Plan.
17..St. George's road

PRESBYTERIANS.
2..[Albion] Moorfields
8..[Caledonian] Hatton garden
21..Crown st, Covent garden
2..[Scotch Church] London wall
36..Swallow st, Piccadilly
3..Miles lane, Cannon street
20..Oxendon st, Haymarket
37..Well st, Oxford street

SANDEMONIANS.
1..Paul's alley, Redcross st, Cripplegt

SWEDENBORGIANS.
21..Hanover st, Long Acre
5..Ireland yard, Blackfriars
20..Lisle st, Leicester square
19..Waterloo bridge road
36..York street, St James's

UNITARIANS
5..Carter lane, Doctors Commons
6..Essex street, Strand
12..Parliament ct, Artillery la, Bishopsgt
19..Waterloo bridge road
16..Whitehorse yd, nr Borough High st
33..Newington green

WELCH CHAPELS.
12..St. Mary Axe
1..Crescent, Jewin st, Aldersgate st
16..Little Guildford st, Borough
38..Whites field's, Grafton st, Tot ct rd

JEWS SYNAGOGUES.
20..Back alley, Denmark ct, Strand
3..Bakers gardens, Leadenhall st
3..Church row, Fenchurch st
13..German, Duke st, Aldgate
12..Portuguese, Duke st, Houndsditch
12..Portuguese, Hennage la, Bevis marks
36..Queen st, Curzon st, May fair

QUAKERS MEETING HOUSES.
11..Devonshire House, Bishopsgate
    street without
45..Schoolhouse lane, Ratcliffe highway
16..Redcross st, Union st, Borough
8..St. John's st, West Smithfield
20..St. Peter's ct, St. Martin's lane
3..White Hart ct, Lombard st

ROMAN CATHOLIC CHAPELS.
39..Clarendon square
21..Denmark ct, Crown st, Soho
21..Duke st, Lincoln's Inn fields
31..East lane, Bermondsey
45..Horseferry road
17..London road, Surry
2..Moorfields, nr the London Institution
17..Prospect pl, St. George's fields
52..South st, May fair
53..Spanish pl, Manchester square
21..Sutton st, Soho

Ref. to Plan.
29..Virginia st, Ratcliffe highway
36..Warwick st, Golden square
2..White st, Moorfields

POLICE OFFICES AND COURTS OF REQUESTS.
21..Bow street, Covent garden
16..No. 9 Crosby row, Snowsfields
37..Great Marlborough street
2..Guildhall, King st, Cheapside
7..Hatton garden, Holborn
29..High street, Shadwell
13..Lambeth st, Whitechapel
3..Mansion House, Poultry
53..Marylebone, 57 Paddington st
53..Marylebone, 86 High st, Marylebone
35..Queen square, Westminster
16..Union Hall, Borough
30..Thames Police, High st, Wapping
16..Town Hall, High st, Borough
11..Worship st, Shoreditch
12..Whitechapel Court, Whitechapel

PRISONS.
15..Borough Compter, Mill la, Tooley st
6..City Bridewell, Bridge st, Blackfriars
7..Fleet Prison, Fleet market
8..Giltspur st Compter, Giltspur st
23..House of Correction, Coldbath fields
17..King's Bench, St. George's fields
16..Marshalsea, 150 High st, Borough
23..Middlesex House of Correction,
    Coldbath fields
16..New County Gaol and House of
    Correction, Horsemonger la, Boro
1..New Debtors Prison, Whitecross st,
    Cripplegate
7..Newgate, Old Bailey
24..New Prison, Clerkenwell
30..Tothill fields Bridewell, Westminstr

RELIGIOUS, LITERARY, SCIENTIFIC AND MEDICAL INSTITUTIONS
35..African Institution, 3 Fludyer st
36..Alfred Society, Albemarle st
7..Amicable Society, Serjeants Inn
5..Benevolent Society of St. Patrick,
    Stamford st, Blackfriars
36..Board of Agriculture, Burlington gdns
6..British and Foreign Bible Society,
    10 Earl st, Blackfriars
17..British and Foreign School Society,
    nearly opposite Pearl row, Blackfrs
36..British Institution, 52 Pall Mall
21..British Museum, Great Russell st,
    Bloomsbury
36..Burlington House, 52 Piccadilly
20..Cambrian Institution, 41 Lisle st,
    Leicester square   [lane
3..Candlewick Ward Chamber, Crooked
7..Church Missionary Society, Salis-
    bury square
3..Clergyman's Society for the Relief
    of the Poor, 22 Finch la, Cornhil

Ref. to Plan.

6..City Philosophical Society, Dorset st, Salisbury square

8..College of Physicians, Warwick la

21..College [Royal] of Surgeons, or Surgeons' Hall, 41 Lincolns Inn fds

2..Commercial Travellers' Society, Cateaton street

8..Corporation of the Caledonian Asylum, Cross st, Hatton garden

22..Corporation of the Sons of the Clergy, Bloomsbury place

3..Corporation for Working Mines in Scotland, Sun Fire Office, Cornhill

35..Cottonian Library and MSS. behind the Painters' Chamber, House of Lords

1..Dr. Williams' Library for the Use of Dissenting Ministers, Redcross street, Cripplegate

8..Dr. Bray's Institution Office, 52 Hatton garden

36..Gallery of the Society of Painters in Water Colours, Pall Mall

24..General Philanthropic Society, Clerkenwell

20..Geological Society, Bedford st, Strnd

3..Gresham College, Royal Exchange

2..Home Missionary Society, 18 Aldermanbury

36..Horticultural Society, 23 Regent st, Piccadilly

2..Hunterian Society, 18 Aldermanbury

21..Hunter's Museum, Portugal street, Lincoln's Inn fields

20..Institution of Civil Engineers, 15 Buckingham st, Strand

3..Irish Evangelical Society, 16 Old Jewry

37..Ismene Gallery, corner of Welbeck street, Cavendish square

7..Jennerian Society, Central House, 15 Salisbury square, Fleet st

20..Leicester square Gallery, Leicestr sq

21..Linean Society, 32 Soho square

21..Literary Fund Office, 4 Lincoln's Inn fields

2..London Hibernian Society, 18 Aldermanbury

2..London Institution, Moorfields

2..London Literary Society, 18 Aldermanbury

12..London Orphan Society, 10 St. Mary Axe

10..London Electric Institution, 16 Bushell row, and 25 Tabernacle row, City road

12..Mathematical Society, Crispin st, Spitalfields

21..Medical and Chirurgical Society, 55 Lincoln's Inn fields

7..Medical Society of London, 3 Bolt ct, Fleet street

26..Medical Theatre, 42 Gt Windmill st

30..Medico Botanical Society of London, 30 Spring gardens

Ref. to Plan.

22..Mendicity Society Office, 13 Red Lion square

2..Merchant Seamen's Bible Society, Pinners Hall, Broad st

6..Metropolitan Literary Institution, 11 Bridge st, Blackfriars

3..Missionary Society, and Museum, Old Jewry

21..National Benevolent Institution, Gt. Russell st, Bloomsbury

36..Naval and Military Bible Society, 113 Jermyn st, Haymarket

36..Naval Institution, 28 Albemarle st

36..New Picture Gallery, 53 Pall Mall

28..Philanthropic Society, Mile End

7..Prayer Book and Homily Society, 134 Salisbury court, Fleet st

8..Religious Tract Society, 56 Paternoster row

1..Redcross st Library, Cripplegate

20..Royal Academy, Somerset House

36..Royal Harmonic Institution, Argyll-rooms, Regent st

6..Royal Humane Society, 29 New Bridge st, Blackfriars

36..Royal Institution, 21 Albemarle st

20..Royal Society, Somerset house

20..Royal Society of Musicians, 12 Lisle st, Leicester square

22..Russell Institution, Great Coram st, Russell square

2..St. Paul's College, 2 St. Paul's Church yard

7..Scotch Corporation Charity, Crane court, Fleet street

8..Society for the Encouragement of Servants, Hatton garden, Holborn

36..Society for the Encouragement of Servants, 10 Pall Mall

20..Society of Antiquaries, Somerset Ho

6..Society of Apothecaries of London, Water lane, Blackfriars

20..Society of Arts, 18 John st, Adelphi

3..Society for Promoting Christian Knowledge among the Poor, Bank Coffee house, Cornhill

36..Society for Propagating the Gospel in Foreign Parts, Regent st, Pall Mall

5..Society for Promoting Christianity amongst the Jews, 10 Wardrobe pl, Doctors Commons

36..Society for Bettering the Conditions of the Poor, 192 Piccadilly

7..Society for Promoting Christian Knowledge, Bartlett's bdgs, Holbn

7..Society for Promoting Christian Knowledge Depository, 21 Fleet st

20..Society for the Relief of Persons Imprisoned for Small Debts, Craven street, Strand

7..Society for the Relief of Widows and Orphans of Medical Men, Gray's Inn Coffee House

2..Society for the Improvement of Prison Discipline, 18 Aldermanbry

Ref. to Plan.
37..Theatre of Anatomy, Blenheim st
15..Theatre of Anatomy, Webb street,
Bermondsey
7..Tract Society, 21 Fleet st
36..Travellers Society, Waterloo place,
Pall Mall
39..Veterinary College, St. Pancras,
(Patron the King)
7..Wesleyan Missionary House, Hatton garden

SCHOOLS.

1..Aldersgate School, 77 Little Britain
21..Bedford (Free) Museum st, Bloomsby
5..Benevolent Society of St. Patrick's,
Stamford st, Blackfriars
15..Bermondsey National Free School
for Girls
3..Billingsgate School, St. Mary at hill
36..Blue Coat, St. James's st, Westmstr
6..Boys' Sunday, Church st, Blackfriars
4..Bridge Candlewick & Dowgate Ward
Upper Thames street
4..Bridge yard School, Old Swan lane
29..British Union (Free) on the Lancasterian Plan, Shakespeare-walk,
Shadwell
2..Broad street Ward, London wall
36..Burlington Free School, Boyle st
8..Charter House, Charter House st
5..Christchurch School, Windmill pl
20..Christian Benevolence School, back
of 20 Bedfordbury
2..City of London Central National,
White st, Little Moorfields
4..City of London National, Fish st
7..City of London National, Harp al,
Shoe lane
2..City of London National School
Swan alley, Coleman st
13..City of London, for Instruction and
Industry, Mitre st, Aldgate
3..Cordwainers' School, Old Change
2..Cripplegate Ward, London wall
1..Cripplegate Without, Redcross st
10..Dissenters, (for Orphans) Old st rd
13..East London (Irish Free) Goodman's yard, Minories
1..Farringdon Within Charity School,
Bull and Mouth st
21..Free Grammar School, Camberwell
18..Freemason's, (for Female Children)
Westminster Bridge road
20..German, near 124 Strand
13..German and English School, 26
Little Ayliffe st, Goodman's fields
38..Gowers, Chenies st, Bedford square
15..Green School, Unicorn yd, Tooley-
street, Borough
35..Grey Coat School, Westminster
11..Jews Free School, Bell ct, Spitalfds
23..Kentish & Camden National School,
North end of Gray's Inn road
8..Ladies' Charity, 37 King st, West
Smithfield

Ref. to Plan.
34..Lambeth School, George st, Lambth
12..Lancasterian, King's Arms ct, Whcpl
3..Langbourn School, Lime st, Fenchurch street
27..London Orphan Asylum Schools,
Hackney road
2..London Society's Protestant School,
5 Ropemaker's st, Moorfields
10..Methodist Sch, Providence rw, Finsb
3..Mercers Grammar School, College hil
3..Merchant Tailors School, Suffolk la,
Upper Thames street
29..Middlesex Society School, 18 Cannon street road
45..Mile End Old Town Sch, Stepney gr
33..Millford House School, 30 Canterbury row, Newington Butts
33..National and Sunday School, 1
Queen's Head row, Newington
8..National Society's Central School,
Baldwin's Gardens, Holborn
15..Newcomen's Charity School, Bowling alley, Snowsfields
13..Orphan School, 10 Bevis marks
9..Orphan Working School, City road
68..Paddington Free School, Harrow rd
38..Pancras Female Charity School, S.
side the Chapel, Hampstead rd
34..Parochial School, Lambeth green
17..Philanthropic Society School, St.
George's fields
53..Philological Society's School, King-
street West, Bryanstone sq
29..Protestant Dissenters Sch. for Boys,
Shakespeare's walk, Shadwell
8..Protestant Dissenters Charity School
Ball ct, Giltspur street
15..Protestant Dissenters School, Maze
pond, Tooley street, Borough
1..Protestant Dissenters School, 44
Bartholomew close
12..Protestant Free School, Gower's
walk, Church lane, Whitechapel
4..Queenhithe Charity School, 5 near
the Church, Old Fish st
30..Rotherhithe Charity School, south
side Rotherhithe
9..Royal Lancasterian or British Institution, North st, City road
37..St. Anne's Sch, nr Dean st, Soho
1..St. Anne's Society School, Aldrsgt st
2..St. Anne's School, St. Anne's lane,
Foster lane
8..St. Andrew's Charity, 43 W Smithfd
13..St. George's German and English
School, Lit. Alie st, Goodmn's fds
22..St George the Martyr's, Queen sq,
Holborn
21..St. Giles's in the Fields, and St.
George's Bloomsbury School,
Museum st, Bloomsbury
30..St. John's School, Bird st, Wapping
26..St. Leonard's Charity School, first
house on the right pailed in Kingsland road

Ref. to Plan.
1..St. Luke's School, 90 Golden lane, Barbican
35..St. Margaret's School, Westminster
53..St. Marylebone School, 110 High st
15..St. Olaves Free School, Tooley st, Borough
38..St. Pancras School, Hampstead rd
36..St. Pancras Female School, St. James's pl, Hampstead r ad
1..St. Paul's School, 2 St. Paul's Ch yd
16..St. Saviour's College and National School, Park st, Borough market
16..St. Saviour's National Free School for Girls, Union st, Borough
68..School for Female Orphans of the Clergy, Chapel st, Lisson green
2..Sion College, London wall
13..Sir John Casse's School, Aldgate
11..Spitalfields National School, Quaker st
45..Stepney Meeting School, Garden st
14..Tower Ward School, 91 Gt Tower st
33..United Parochial National Schools of St. Mary Newington, Newington Butts
4..Vintry Ward School, Up Thames st
30..Wapping Charity School, south side of Wapping Church
23..Welsh Charity School, St. Andrew's, Gray's Inn road
35..Westminster (New Charity) Dacre st

SUBSCRIPTION HOUSES.

36..Albion Club, 85 St. James st
36..Alfred Club, Albemarle st
36..Arthur's Club, 69 St. James st
36..Austin's Club, St. James st
35..Boodle's Club, 31 St. James st
36..Brookes's Club, 60 St. James st
36..Cocoa-tree Club, St. James st
36..Colonial Club, 60 St. James st
36..Fielder's Club, Bennet st, St. James st
36..Graham's Club, 87 St. James st
36..Guard's Club, 49 St. James st
36..Mile's Club, St. James st
36..Military Club, (New) Waterloo pl, Pall Mall
36..New Jerusalem Club, 10 York st, St. James's
36..St. James's Coffee House & Club, St James st
37..Stratford Club, (Davidson's) 1 Stratford place
36..Travellers' Club, 12 Waterloo pl
21..Verulam Club, Lincoln's Inn fields
36..White's Club, 43 St. James st
36..Watier's Club, 79 Piccadilly

FIRE, LIFE, &c.
INSURANCE COMPANIES.

7..Albion Fire and Life Insurance, New Bridge st, Blackfriars

Ref. to Plan.
7..Amicable Society for a Perpetual Assurance, Office Sergeant's Inn, Fleet street
2..Atlas Fire and Life Assurance, Cheapside
6..Beacon Fire Insurance, Chatham pl, Blackfriars
3..British Commercial, Cornhill
3 & 20..British Fire and Westminster Life Office, 21 Cornhill & 429, Strnd
36..County Fire and Provident Life Office, for insurance of lives grant and purchase of annuities and endowment of children, Regent street
3 & 36..Eagle Fire and Life Insurance, Cornhill and Regent street
6..Equitable Assurance Office on Lives and Survivorships, Bridge st, Blkfrs
6..European Insurance for Lives and Annuities, 10 Chatham pl, Black frs
3..Guardian Fire and Life Assurance, 11 Lombard street
3 & 36..Globe Fire and Life Insurance Pall Mall and Cornhill
6..Hand in Hand Fire Office, Bridge street, Blackfriars
6..Hope Insurance, Bridge st, Blackfrs
3 & 36..Imperial Insurance, Sun court, Cornhill, and 5 St. James's st
4..London Annuity Society for the benefit of Widows, 25 Old Fish st
3..London Marine Fire and Life Assurance, 19 Birchin lane
29..London Life Association, 35 Cannon street
36..Norwich Union Fire and Life Insurance Society, Waterloo place, Pall Mall
3 & 20..Pelican Life Insurance Office, Lombard st, and Spring gardens
3 & 20..Phœnix Fire Office, Lombard street and Charing cross, for property from fire at home & abroad
6..Rock Life Assurance Office, on Lives and Survivorships, 14 New Bridge street, Blackfriars
3 & 36..Royal Exchange Assurance Office, Royal Exchange and Pall Mall, for assuring buildings, goods and ships from fire; also for assuring lives and granting annuities
3 & 20..Sun Fire Office, Cornhill and Craig's court, Charing cross
3 & 53..Union Fire and Life Assurance Office, Cornhill and 70 Baker st
6..West of England Fire and Life, 90 New Bridge st, Black friars
20..Westminster Fire Office, Bedford-street, Covent garden

LONDON BANKERS.

Ref. to Plan.
- 2..BANK OF ENGLAND, Threadneedle-street
- 3..Barclay, Tritton, Bevan and Co. 54, Lombard-street
- 3..Barnard, Dimsdale and Dimsdale, 50, Cornhill
- 3..Bond, Sons and Pattishal, 2, Exchange-alley
- 3..Bosanquet, Pitt, Anderson and Franks, 73, Lombard-street
- 20..Bouverie and Antrobus, 35, Craven-street
- 7..Brooks and Dixon, 25, Chancery-lane
- 3..Brown, Janson and Co. 32, Abchurch-lane
- 2..Bruce, Simpson and Co. 9, Austin-friars, Throgmorton-street
- 37..Chambers and Son, 160, New Bond-street
- 7..Child and Co. 1, Fleet-street, next to Temple-bar
- 20..Cocks, Cocks, Ridge and Biddulph, 43, Charing-cross
- 20..Coutts and Company, 59, Strand
- 3..Cunliffes, Brookes, Cunliffe and Co. 24, Bucklersbury
- 3..Curries, Raikes and Co. 29, Cornhill
- 3..Curtis (Sir Wm. Bart.) Robarts and Curtis, 15, Lombard street
- 3..Dennison Joseph and Co. 106, Fenchurch street
- 3..Dorrien, Magens, Dorrien and Mello, 22, Finch-lane
- 2..Drewett and Fowler, 60, Old Broad-street
- 20..Drummonds and Co. 49, Charing-cross
- 3..Esdaile (Sir James) Esdailes, Hammetts and Co. 21, Lombard-street
- 3..Everett, Walker, Maltby, Ellis and Co. 9, Mansion-house-street
- 3..Frys and Chapman, 4, Mildred's-court, Poultry
- 3..Fuller (Richard and George) and Co. 84, Cornhill
- 3..Glynn (Sir Rd. Carr) Mills, Halifax, Glynn, Mills and Co. 12, Birchin-lane
- 3..Gill T. and Co. 42, Lombard-street
- 7..Gosling (Francis and Wm.) and Sharp, 19, Fleet-street
- 3..Grote, Prescott and Grote, 62, Threadneedle-street
- 36..Hammersleys, Greenwood and Brooksbank, 69, Pall Mall
- 3..Hanburys, Taylor and Lloyds, 60, Lombard-street
- 3..Hankeys and Co. 7, Fenchurch-street
- 36..Herries, Farquhar, Hallidays and Chapman, 16, St. James's-street
- 7..Hoare Henry, Henry Hugh, Charles, Wm. Henry, & Henry Merrik, 37, Fleet-st
- 3..Hoare, Barnetts, Hoare and Co. 62, Lombard-street
- 20..Hodsoll & Stirling, (Sir Walter, Bart.) 345, near Catherine-street, Strand
- 36..Hopkinsons George Cæsar, Charles & Edmund, Regent-street, St. James's
- 2..Jones, Loyd and Co. 43, Lothbury
- 8..Jones John, 41, West Smithfield
- 2..Kinloch and Sons, 1, New Broad-street
- 3..Ladbrokes, Watson and Gillman, Bank-buildings
- 3..Lees, Brassey, Farr and Lee, 71, Lombard-street
- 3..Lubbock (Sir J. W. Bart.) Forster, Clarke and Co. 11, Mansion-house-street
- 3..Marryatt, Kay, Price and Coleman, 1, Mansion-house-street
- 37..Marsh, Stracey, Fauntleroy and Graham, 6, Berner-street
- 36..Marten, Call and Arnold, 25, Old Bond-street
- 3..Martin, Stone and Martin, 68, Lombard-street
- 3..Masterman, Peters, Mildred, Masterman & Co. 35, Nicholas-lane, Lombard-st
- 36..Morlands Auriol and Co. 50, Pall Mall
- 6..Pares and Heygate, 25, New Bridge-street, Blackfriars
- 2..Paxtons, Cockerell, Trail and Co. 8, Austin-friars
- 3..Perring (Sir John) Shaw, Barber and Co. 72, Cornhill
- 16..Pinhorn (Sir John, Knt.) Weston and Son, 37, Borough High-street
- 2..Pole (Sir Peter, Bart.) Thornton, Free, Down & Sott, 1, Bartholomew-lane
- 7..Praeds, Mackworth, Newcombe and Fame, 189, Fleet-street
- 8..Puget, Bainbridge and Co. College, Warwick-lane
- 36..Ransom and Company, 1, Pall Mall, East
- 3..Remington and Co. 69, Lombard street
- 7..Rogers, Towgood, Rogers, Olding and Boycott, 29, Clement's-lane
- 3..Sansom, Postlethwaite and Sansom, 65, Lombard-street
- 8..Sharp Wm. and Sons, 8, West Smithfield
- 3..Sykes, Snaith and Co. 5, Mansion-house-street

Ref. to Plan.
3..Smith, Payne and Smiths, Mansion-house-place
20..Snow, Paul and Co. 217. Strand
3..Spooner, Attwoods and Spooner, 27, Gracechurch-street
3..Stevenson and Salt, 20, Lombard street
3..Veres, Ward and Co. 77, Lombard-street
3..Wentworth, Chaloner and Rishworth, 25, Threadneedle-street
3..Whitmore, Wells and Whitmore, 24, Lombard-street
3..Williams, Williams, Burgess and Williams, 20, Birchin-lane
3..Willis, Percival and Co. 76. Lombard-street
20..Wright Thomas and Co. 5, Henrietta-street, Covent-garden

HACKNEY COACH, CHARIOT AND CABRIOLET FARES.

Fares according to Distance.

Not exceeding	s.	d.	Not exceeding	s.	d.
one mile	1	0	six miles and a half	8	0
one mile and a half	1	6	seven miles	8	6
two miles	2	0	seven miles and a half	9	0
two miles and a half	3	0	eight miles	9	6
three miles	3	6	eight miles and a half	10	6
three miles and a half	4	0	nine miles	11	0
four miles	4	6	nine miles and a half	11	6
four miles and a half	5	6	ten miles	12	0
five miles	6	0	ten miles and a half	13	0
five miles and half	6	6	eleven miles	13	6
six miles	7	0	twelve miles	15	0

And so on, at the rate of 6d. for every half mile, and an additional 6d. for every two miles completed.

Fares according to Time.

Not exceeding	s.	d.	Not exceeding	s.	d.
thirty minutes	1	0	two hours and 20 minutes	6	0
forty-five minutes	1	6	two hours and 40 minutes	7	0
one hour	2	0	three hours	8	0
one hour and 20 minutes	3	0	three hours and 20 minutes	9	0
one hour and 40 minutes	4	0	three hours and 40 minutes	10	6
two hours	5	6	four hours	11	0

And so on at the rate of 6d. for any fifteen minutes further time.

CABRIOLET FARES are one-third less than the Hackney Coach Fares.

The fares are to be taken by the hour or mile only, and not by the day.
Coaches discharged after sun-set hours (viz after 8 between Lady Day and Michaelmas, and after 5 between Michaelmas and Lady Day,) between the carriage-way pavement, or if hired at a stand beyond the same, may demand the full fare back to such extremity or standing. For coaches hired to go into the country in the day time, and there discharged, additional fares are to be taken for their return to the pavement or next stand where hired, as follows: for 10 miles, 5s.; 8 miles, 4s.; 6 miles, 3s.; and 4 miles, 2s. If under 4 Miles, nothing.
Coachmen are not compellable to take more than four adult persons inside, and a servant out: but if they agree to take more, then 1s. in addition to the fare must be paid for each extra person; and if the coach be hired for the country, and to return, 1s. for each extra person going, and 1s. for his returning.
Hackney Coach License Act.—The following clause was added as a rider to the act:—" And be it further enacted, that it shall be lawful for any person to require any hackney coachman to drive for a stated sum of money a distance in the discretion of such hackney coachman, and in case such coachman shall exceed the distance to which such person was entitled to be driven for such stated sum of money, the coachman shall not be entitled to demand more than the sum for which he was so engaged to drive.

RATES OF WATERMEN.

FROM LONDON BRIDGE.

WESTWARD.	Oars.	Scull	EASTWARD,	Oars.	Scull
To Windsor	21s.		To Gravesend	15s.	
Staines	18 0		Greenhithe..........	12 0	
Hampton.............	12 0		Woolwich..........	5 0	
Twickenham	9 0		Blackwall	3 6	
Richmond	8 0		Greenwich.........	2 6	1 3
Brentford	7 0		Deptford	2 0	1 0
Hammersmith	5 0		Duke Shore Stairs		
Putney	4 0		Radcliff Cross,		
Chelsea Bridge	2 6	1 3	Great Stone Stairs		
Vauxhall	2 0	1 0	and King & Queen		
Lambeth	1 6	0 9	Stairs	1 6	0 9
Any place between			Shadwell Dock, New		
Westminster Bridge			Crane Church, ex-		
and Arundel-street			ecution Dock, and		
inclusive	1 0	0 6	Wapping New and		
Blackfriars Bridge....	0 8	0 4	Old Stairs	1 0	0 6

Over the Water directly to the opposite Shore between Windsor and Greenwich with a Sculler, two-pence, or a penny for each person.

The Watermen may demand payment at the rate of 3d. [sculler], and 6d. (oars) for every half hour, *in lieu* of the above fares, when detained by his passengers on his way to the place at which they choose ultimately to be set down. For detention after having set down his company, he is to be paid 3d. (sculler,) and 6d, (oars) or every half hour, after the first, in addition to the above fares.

Note.—Oars in all cases are double the Sculler's fare.

Wilkinson, Printer.

CPSIA information can be obtained
at www.ICGtesting.com
Printed in the USA
BVHW092253061021
618394BV00011B/255